BLACKBOOK PRICE GUIDE OF UNITED STATES POSTAGE STAMPS

ELEVENTH EDITION

BY MARC HUDGEONS, N.L.G.

HOUSE OF COLLECTIBLES
NEW YORK, NEW YORK 10022

Stamps appearing on cover photo courtesy of Jacques C. Schiff, Jr., Incorporated.

©1988 Random House, Inc.

All rights reserved under International and Pan-American Copyright Conventions.

Published by: The House of Collectibles
201 East 50th Street
New York, New York 10022

Distributed by Ballantine Books, a division of Random House, Inc., New York and simultaneously in Canada by Random House of Canada Limited, Toronto.

Manufactured in the United States of America

Library of Congress Catalog Card Number: 80-644087

ISBN: 0-876-37098-9

10 9 8 7 6 5 4 3 2 1

TABLE OF CONTENTS

The publisher also wishes to express special thanks to Mr. Armin R. Crowe at the Collectors Institute, Ltd., Omaha, Nebraska 68144, the United States Postal System for photographs and illustrations, and for the special help provided by *Linn's Stamp News*.

MARKET REVIEW

The stamp collecting market is still trying to gain ground. The market is stronger than last year, and some strong gains are being reported on certain rare issues. It appears that collectors are looking for, and finding, many bargains. Stamp auctions have been playing an important part in stimulating collecting interest, as they activate a steady flow of exceptional material that usually never reaches the collector. These sales appear to be reaching the new collectors that, in general, do not seek the type of material offered by auction houses. If you carefully study auction catalogs, you will find a lot of material listed that is rarely offered in normal channels of sale. These rare and unusual items create a great deal of excitement and buying activity. All of this helps move the market. It's a great idea to investigate the stamp auction market and request a catalog. If nothing more, it will keep you in touch with the movement of a vast amount of fine material and, ultimately, the prices and sale of the issues involved.

A great deal more high-grade material has been sold this past year than in previous years. Without question, this has resulted in many of the increases experienced on these issues. If the trend continues, the market will continue on its upward move. While many gains on scarce material are being experienced, it must be noted that many issues are still very flat with little or no increase over the last couple of years. It really is difficult to understand, because it does not follow any special trend. The market must be studied and looked at very carefully before purchasing. One thing is certain; if you look carefully, bargains are still available and should be snapped up, as the market appears to be gaining strength. The bright spot in the market is the purchases of very select material, which is causing the investor to return to the marketplace. Due to the unsteady and unpredictable financial markets, a lot of investors have been discouraged and, because of this, they are looking elsewhere. They are looking to new areas of investment that are more stable, less volatile, and that produce positive profits over a longer period of time. The philatelic market is that kind of investment. For many years it has been a haven for those looking to enjoy the collecting of interesting relics of the past while still enjoying a profit; that is, if one chooses to sell. While the serious collector is still the mainstay of the market, it is the investor that generates the excitement and supports the advancing prices that are important to stamp collectors.

Still important, and often forgotten, are the new collectors. Young people becoming interested should be educated and encouraged by all of us interested in collecting stamps. Remember, these are the collectors of tomorrow; if we want the hobby to remain strong, helping the new collector should be incorporated into our participation as a collector. Collectors will certainly be encouraged by all of the publicity generated by recent patriotic and historic events, such as the Statue of Liberty celebration and the anniversary of the signing of the Constitution. Such important events spark a great deal of public interest. The release of both philatelic and numismatic issues of particular items commemorating these events are being promoted by everyone in the field. These events always create a lot of publicity which, in turn, brings many new collectors into the hobby. All of this points toward the stimulation of interest in stamp collecting.

The ever-popular Zepplin, still one of our most famous issues, has gained ever so slightly. A complete set of Zepplin singles cost $4.55 in 1930. Now it sells for between $2,200 and $2,400, while the unused plate block is selling for between

$13,700 and $14,000. Recalling that this block could have been purchased at the post office in 1930 for $14.50, it is very exciting to think about.

Confederate stamp issues remain very popular, and its activity in the market has been above normal. Prices have moved upward only slightly, and many bargains still remain. This is a series to look to for movement.

Duck stamps still rate high in popularity. There has been a great deal of activity, but with only slight gains being recorded. This beautiful series has a broad selection and often appeals to the new collector. Prices are reasonable, and a nice collection can be accumulated for very little.

Mint sheets, still popular, have posted increases overall. This series seems to be attracting the investor, and market activity indicates that this is a series to watch.

Plate blocks have posted some gains on relatively moderate trading. Investors appear to be buying the many bargains that still exist in this series.

While the market has shown increased activity, it still has a way to go before it can be considered strong. Hopefully, the coming year will reflect the many interesting things happening in the hobby.

THE STORY OF U.S. STAMPS

The world's first postage stamps were issued by Great Britain in 1840 and pictured its new queen, Victoria, then 21 years old. It was not until 1847 that the U.S. released postage stamps, but prior to that time some city postmasters issued stamps of their own. These very valuable stamps, known as "postmaster provisionals," were used in St. Louis, New York, Annapolis and a number of other cities.

The first federally released postage stamps comprised a 5¢ denomination picturing Benjamin Franklin and a 10¢ showing George Washington. Their size was very similar to that of modern non-commemoratives and they had gummed backs, just like our stamps. The chief difference was that they carried no little holes or perforations between each specimen on a sheet, to aid in separation. Instead they had to be cut apart with scissors or creased and torn by hand. These stamps are called "imperforates," or "without perforations." All stamps in those days, including Europe's, were made in this way. The U.S. did not start perforating its stamps until 1857, ten years later.

Imperforates rank today as the hobby's aristocrats, its elder statesmen and foremost classics. They have long been dear to the hearts of collectors, and not merely on grounds of their antiquity. Some specialists maintain that these issues, every one of them bearing a statesman's portrait, are more elegantly engraved than any of their descendants. In addition, they can be found (with luck and the necessary cash) in super specimens that put ordinary perforated stamps to shame. When a stamp is perforated, every one on the sheet is of identical size. Some sheets may be better centered than others, depending on how the paper is fed, but no specimens will be physically larger than any others. With imperforates, it's quite another matter. The cutting was never done very evenly. Some specimens were cropped or cut into by scissor wielders and left with margins so immense that portions of all the surrounding stamps are visible. These are called jumbo margin copies and the prices collectors will give for them is often astronomic, provided the condition is otherwise good. It is not at all unusual for one of these oversized beauties to command three or four times the normal sum. Collectors must take care though, because in philately as in most other things, all that sparkles is not necessarily diamonds. Larcenous persons have been known to take very ordinary average stamps and add fake margins.

Not all imperforates are equally easy (or hard) to get with four full margins. This is all a matter of how closely together they were printed on the sheet. The cutter is less apt to make a mistake if the stamps are further apart on the sheet. Scott's #11, the 3¢ 1851, is by far the most difficult to find with full margins. It also happens to be the least expensive imperforate, thanks to the enormous quantities printed. While the usual specimen will fetch only $4–$6 used, a jumbo margin #11 has no trouble selling for $20, $30 or more.

The second series of imperforates, issued from 1851 to 1856, comprised values from 1¢ to 12¢. There were five stamps, with Washington appearing on three of them; the other two used portraits of Franklin and Jefferson. In 1857 the same group of stamps was released again, this time with perforations and three high values: a 24¢ and 90¢ pictured Washington, and a 30¢ portrayed Franklin. The 90¢ stamp was not exceeded in face value until the Columbian Exposition series in 1893. Because very little mail required the paying of so much postage, most specimens of the 90¢ 1857–1861 that went to private hands never got on letters. Consequently this stamp is much more difficult to find used than unused, a rare circumstance for a U.S. issue. Needless to say, counterfeit cancels exist.

There was no question that by this time postage stamps had scored a big success. Any doubts or complaints that some users may have had about them at the beginning had long since vanished. So fond did certain persons become of stamps that they began saving them, used as well as unused, and thus the hobby of philately was born. For the government, stamps brought greater economy to the postal service than anticipated. They also allowed mail to travel faster. There was just one problem: some people were abusing the system. During the Civil War, and shortly thereafter, it became apparent that many stamps were going through the mails twice or more. People were cleaning off the cancels and using them again. This may have been done by individuals but, more likely, it was a large scale operation in which used stamps were cleaned in wholesale quantities and sold to business houses and other volume mailers at a discount. The government was being bilked out of thousands of dollars but there seemed no solution until a plan was devised to use "grills" on the faces of stamps in 1867. These were networks of tiny embossed dots which weakened the paper and would, presumably, cause it to break apart if any attempt was made at erasing the cancel. After just two years the grill was dropped but had appeared on enough stamps in that short time to provide philatelists with an intriguing subspecialty. Not all the grills were alike. They differed in size and style and collecting them is quite a sport.

The year 1869 marked the first year of U.S. pictorial stamps that portrayed things or events rather than portraits. They cannot really be termed commemoratives in the modern sense but they were extremely pictorial. Subjects included a pony express rider, a rail locomotive, panoramas of the landing of Columbus, the signing of the Declaration of Independence, and others. This series also presented the first stamps to be printed in more than one color. Multicolor printing was no small operation in those days. It required two separate plates: one consisting of frames to be printed in one color, and the other central designs to be printed in a different color. The sheets were fed through one press, allowed to dry, then fed into the next to receive the final printing. As the feeding was done by hand, human error occasionally occurred. A few sheets were fed upside down the second time around, resulting in the first, but not the most famous, U.S. inverts, or stamps with upside down centers. These are very valuable and seldom offered on the market. The king of all United States inverts is a twentieth century stamp, the 24¢ airmail of 1918. This small stamp has a central design of a Curtiss Jenny single engine plane. It was printed 100 to a sheet. On the day it was issued, a Washington, D.C. collector, William T. Robey, took a few minutes from his lunch hour to go into the local post office and buy a sheet. He had no intention of using the stamps but merely wanted them for his collection. After putting down his $24 he received what appeared to be a normal sheet, but after looking closer, Mr. Robey found that on every stamp the airplane was upside down. This incident stirred a furor of considerable proportion. The government was embarrassed since it had claimed that the old 1869 inverts could not happen again with its new machinery and rigid controls. It tried, without success, to buy the sheet back from Robey. Meanwhile it notified postmasters around the country to check their stocks for further error sheets. No more were found, and when it became evident that Robey's sheet was the only one in existence he began receiving substantial offers from collectors and dealers. The offers seemed tempting and he finally sold his treasure for $15,000 to Eugene Klein of Philadelphia, a prominent dealer. Klein immediately resold the sheet to Col. Edward H. R. Green of New York, the legendary collector who also owned the only five known specimens of the 1913 Liberty nickel. It is believed Green paid at least $17,500 for this philatelic morsel, a huge sum in those days but only about one third as much as each of the 100 stamps are now individually worth. Green broke up the sheet into blocks, selling most of them and recovering his entire cost. Several single specimens were subsequently lost, one supposed to have disappeared into a vacuum cleaner while Green's housekeeper was tidying up.

FACTORS BEHIND STAMP PRICES

The collector value (or "market value") of any stamp rests with a variety of factors. Philately becomes a bit less mysterious when one understands the forces at work in the stamp marketplace.

A beginner will normally presume that expensive stamps are expensive because of rarity. Certainly there is a great deal of talk about stamp rarities within the hobby, and so it is natural enough to ascribe high prices to the phenomenon of rarity. In fact rarity is only one of several factors that influence stamp prices, and the influence it carries is not particularly clear-cut.

In this book you will note some stamps (mostly among the early regular issues) with values of $1,000, $2,000, and even higher. Obviously these stamps are rarer than those selling for $10 or $15. But once having said that, we have virtually summed up our useful knowledge of rarity and its effect on prices. A comparison of prices, between stamps in roughly similar ranges of value, does not indicate which is the rarer. A stamp selling for $1,000 is not necessarily rarer than one selling for $500. A $10,000 stamp may actually be more abundant than one which commands $5,000. This hard-to-comprehend fact of philatelic life prevails because of the other factors involved in determining a stamp's price. If rarity were the only factor, one could, of course, easily see which stamps are the rarest by the prices they fetch.

The word "rare" is an elixir to many collectors, not only of stamps but other collector's items. Sellers are well aware of this, and seldom fail to sprinkle the word liberally in their sales literature. There is no law against calling a stamp rare, as this represents a personal opinion more than anything else and opinions are allowable in advertising. Unfortunately there is no standard definition for rarity. Does "rare" mean just a handful of specimens in existence, with one reaching the sales portals once in five years? Does it mean 100 in existence, or 1,000, or some other number? Since stamps are—today, at any rate—printed in the multimillions, a thousand surviving specimens might seem a very tiny total to some people. Further complicating this situation is the fact that the specific rarity of most stamps cannot be determined, or even estimated with any hope of accuracy. The quantities printed are recorded for most of our stamps, going back even into the nineteenth century, but the quantity *surviving* of any particular stamp is anyone's guess. It is obvious that a stamp that goes through the auction rooms once a year is fairly rare, but this provides no sound basis for guessing the number of specimens in existence. That could only be accomplished if some sort of grand census could be taken, and all specimens tallied. This of course is nothing but a pipe dream. Some collectors would not participate in such a census; some might be unaware that it was being conducted. Then, too, there are many scarce or rare stamps in hands other than those of collectors, such as dealers and museums. Additionally, there could be (and probably are) existing specimens of rare stamps yet to be discovered, as fresh discoveries are made periodically in the hobby through attic cleaning and the like.

In terms of influence on price, rarity is outdistanced somewhat by *popularity*. Some stamps, for one reason or other, are simply more popular than others. They have a sort of innate appeal for hobbyists, either through reputation, exquisite designing, circumstances of issue, oddity, or various other potential reasons. These stamps sell out rapidly from the stocks of dealers, while some stamps that are supposedly scarcer will linger in stock albums for ages and ages waiting to tempt a customer. It is no wonder, then, that the prices of popular stamps rise more quickly than those that are scarce but not in brisk demand. The Columbian series typifies the effect of popularity on stamp values. If stamp prices were fixed by scarcity alone, none of the Columbians would be selling for nearly as much. Much of their value derives from their overwhelming popularity with collectors of U.S. stamps. It would be safe to say, in fact, that *all* of the Columbians, from the lowest face value to the $5, are more plentiful than other U.S. stamps selling for precisely the same sums. Every dealer has Columbians in stock, and quite a few dealers have the high values of the set, too. They are not "hard to get." But they *are* very costly.

Popularity, of course, does not remain constant forever. There are shifts in philatelic popularity, usually slight but occasionally extreme. The popularity of commemoratives as a whole versus regular issues as a whole can change from time to time. Then, too, there are swings of popularity for airmails, first day covers, blocks, coil pairs, mint sheets, and all other philatelic material. A climb or decline in the price of any philatelic item is often an indication of the forces of popularity at work. Then there are activities of investors to consider, whose buying habits seldom reflect those of the pure collector. A great deal of buying by investors in any short period of time (such as occurred during 1979 and 1980, and to less extent in 1981) can make prices seem well out of balance.

Also on the subject of prices, it is important for the beginner to realize that arithmetic is usually futile when dealing with stamp values. You cannot determine the price of one philatelic item by knowing the value of a similar one. This can best be shown by the relative values of singles and blocks of four. A block of four is, as one would expect, worth *more* than four times as much as single specimens of that stamp. It is not just four specimens of the stamp, but four of them *attached*, which lends added scarcity and appeal. The difficulty lies in trying to use mathematics to determine a block's value. Some blocks are worth five times as much as the single stamp; some six times; some ten times or even more. Almost all blocks—except very common ones—will vary somewhat in value, in relation to the value of the individual stamp. There is no satisfactory explanation for this, other than the presumption that some blocks are scarcer than others or just in greater demand than others.

In the case of common philatelic items, the value hinges greatly on the method of sale. If you want to buy one specimen of a common cover, you may have to pay $1.50. But if you were willing to buy a hundred common first day covers *of the dealer's choice,* you could very likely get them for $75 or 75¢ each. Buying in quantity, and allowing the dealer to make the selections, can save a great deal of money. Of course one may then ask: What is the real value of those covers? Is it $1.50 or 75¢? The only answer is that it depends on how you buy!

If this article has seemed to raise a great many questions without supplying many answers, it will, hopefully, serve to show that stamp collecting is not bound to rigid formulas. What happens in the stamp market is largely beyond prediction, or precise explanation. This, indeed, is one of the exciting aspects of the hobby.

STAMP COLLECTORS' TERMINOLOGY

Adhesives—A term given to stamps that have gummed backs and are intended to be pasted on articles and items that are to be mailed.

Aerophilately—The collecting of airmail or any form of stamps related to mail carried by air.

Airmail—Any mail carried by air.

Albino—An uncolored embossed impression of a stamp generally found on envelopes.

Approvals—Stamps sent to collectors. They are examined by the collector, who selects stamps to purchase and returns balance with payment for the stamps he retained.

Arrow Block—An arrow-like mark found on blocks of stamps in the selvage. This mark is used as a guide for cutting or perforating stamps.

As-Is—A term used when selling a stamp. It means no representation is given as to its condition or authenticity. Buyers should beware.

Backprint—Any printing that may appear on reverse of stamp.

Backstamp—The postmark on the back of a letter indicating what time or date the letter arrived at the post office.

Bantams—A miniature stamp given to a war economy issue of stamps from South Africa.

Batonne—Watermarked paper used in printing stamps.

Bicolored—A two-color printed stamp.

Bisect—A stamp that could be used by cutting in half and at half the face value.

Block—A term used for a series of four or more stamps attached at least two high and two across.

Bourse—A meeting or convention of stamp collectors and dealers where stamps are bought, sold and traded.

Cachet—A design printed on the face of an envelope generally celebrating the commemoration of a new postage stamp issue. Generally called a first day cover.

Cancelled to Order—A stamp cancelled by the government without being used. Generally remainder stamps or special issues. Common practice of Soviet nations.

Cancellation—A marking placed on the face of a stamp to show that it has been used.

Centering—The manner in which the design of a stamp is printed and centered upon the stamp blank. A perfectly centered stamp would have equal margins on all sides.

Classic—A popular, unique, highly desired or very artistic stamp. Not necessarily a rare stamp, but one sought after by the collector. Generally used only of nineteenth-century issues.

Coils—Stamps sold in rolls for use in vending machines.

Commemorative—A stamp issued to commemorate or celebrate a special event.

Crease—A fold or wrinkle in a stamp.

Cut square—An embossed staple removed from the envelope by cutting.

Dead Country—A country no longer issuing stamps.

Demonetized—A stamp no longer valid for use.

Error—A stamp printed or produced with a major design or color defect.

Essay—Preliminary design for a postage stamp.

Face Value—The value of a stamp indicated on the face or surface of the stamp.

Frank—A marking on the face of an envelope indicating the free and legal use of postage. Generally for government use.

Fugitive Inks—A special ink used to print stamps, which can be rubbed or washed off easily, to eliminate erasures and forgeries.

General Collector—One who collects all kinds of issues and all types of stamps from different countries.

Granite Paper—A type of paper containing colored fibers to prevent forgery.

Gum—The adhesive coating on the back of a stamp.

Handstamped—A stamp that has been handcancelled.

Hinge—A specially gummed piece of glassine paper used to attach a stamp to the album page.

Imperforate—A stamp without perforations.

Inverted—Where one portion of a stamp's design is inverted or upside down from the remainder of the design.

Local Stamps—Stamps that are only valid in a limited area.

Margin—The unprinted area around a stamp.

Miniature Sheet—A smaller than usual sheet of stamps.

Mint Condition—A stamp in original condition as it left the postal printing office.

Mirror Print—A stamp error printed in reverse as though looking at a regular stamp reflected in a mirror.

Multicolored—A stamp printed in three or more colors.

Never Hinged—A stamp in original mint condition never hinged in an album.

Off Paper—A used stamp that has been removed from the envelope to which it was attached.

On Paper—A used stamp still attached to the envelope.

Original Gum—A stamp with the same or original adhesive that was applied in the manufacturing process.

Pair—Two stamps unseparated.

Pen Cancellation—A stamp cancelled by pen or pencil.

Perforation Gauge—A printed chart containing various sizes of perforation holes used in determining the type or size of perforation of a stamp.

Perforations—Holes punched along stamp designs allowing stamps to be easily separated.

Philatelist—One who collects stamps.

Pictorial Stamps—Stamps that bear large pictures of animals, birds, flowers, etc.

Plate Block Number—The printing plate number used to identify a block of four or more stamps taken from a sheet of stamps.

Postally Used—A stamp that has been properly used and cancelled.

Precancels—A stamp that has been cancelled in advance. Generally used on bulk mail.

Reissue—A new printing of an old stamp that has been out of circulation.

Revenue Stamp—A label or stamp affixed to an item as evidence of tax payment.

Se-tenant—Two or more stamps joined together each having a different design or value.

Seals—An adhesive label that looks like a stamp, used for various fund raising campaigns.

Sheet—A page of stamps as they are printed usually separated before distribution to post offices.

Soaking—Removing used stamps from paper to which they are attached by soaking in water. *(NOTE: Colored cancels may cause staining to other stamps.)*

Souvenir Sheet—One or more specially designed stamps printed by the government in celebration of a special stamp.

Splice—The splice made between rolls of paper in the printing operation. Stamps printed on this splice are generally discarded.

Tete-Bechs—A pair of stamps printed together so that the images point in opposite vertical directions.

Transit Mark—A mark made by an intermediate post office between the originating and final destination post office.

Typeset Stamp—A stamp printed with regular printer's type, as opposed to engraved, lithographed, etc.

Ungummed—Stamps printed without an adhesive back.

Unperforated—A stamp produced without perforations.

Unhinged—A stamp that has never been mounted with the use of a hinge.

Vignette—The central design portion of a stamp.

Want List—A list of stamps a collector needs to fill gaps in his collection.

Watermark—A mark put into paper by the manufacturer, not readily seen by the naked eye.

Wrapper—A strip of paper with adhesive on one end, used for wrapping bundles of mail. Especially in Britain, it refers to any bit of paper to which a used stamp is still attached.

HOW TO GRADE STAMPS

A person need not be an expert to judge the quality or grade of a stamp. All he needs is a discerning eye, possibly a small linear measuring device, and the grading instructions listed below.

The major catalogs traditionally list stamps simply as "Unused" or "Used." Auction houses, however, will describe the stamps for sale in a more informative manner. The greater the value of the stamp, the more thoroughly it is described.

There is no officially accepted system of grading stamps. What we have done in this book is essentially to set up a system of grading stamps using the suggestions and practices of stamp dealers from all over the country. Total agreement was made to the following categories and grades of stamps that are most frequently traded.

CATEGORIES

Mint—The perfect stamp with superb centering, no faults and usually with original gum (if issued with gum).

Unused—Although unused this stamp may have a hinge mark or may have suffered some change in its gum since it was issued.

Used—Basically this will be the normal stamp that passed through the government postal system and will bear an appropriate cancellation.

Cancelled to Order—These are stamps that have not passed through the postal system but have been carefully cancelled by the government usually for a commemoration. These are generally considered undesirable by collectors.

GRADE—STAMP CENTERING

Average—The perforations cut slightly into the design.

Fine—The perforations do not touch the design at all, but the design will be off center by 50% or more of a superb centered stamp.

Very Fine—The design will be off center by less than 50% of a superb stamp. The off centered design will be visibly noticeable.

Extra Fine—The design will be almost perfectly centered. The margin will be off by less than 25% of a superb stamp.

Superb—This design will be perfectly centered with all four margins exactly the same. On early imperforate issues, superb specimens will have four clear margins that do not touch the design at any point.

Average
Centering

Fine
Centering

Very Fine
Centering

Extra Fine
Centering

Superb
Centering

GRADE—STAMP GUM

Original Gum—This stamp will have the same gum on it that it had the day it was issued.

Regummed—This stamp will have new gum applied to it as compared to an original gummed stamp. Regummed stamps are worth no more than those with gum missing.

No Gum—This stamp will have had its gum removed or it may have not been issued with gum.

Never Hinged—This stamp has never been hinged so the gum should not have been disturbed in any way.

Lightly Hinged—This stamp has had a hinge applied. A lightly wetted or peelable hinge would do very little damage to the gum when removed.

Heavily Hinged—This stamp has had a hinge applied in such a manner as to secure it to the stamp extremely well. Removal of this hinge usually proves to be disastrous, in most cases, since either part of the hinge remains on the stamp or part of the stamp comes off on the hinge, causing thin spots on the stamp.

GRADE—STAMP FAULTS

Any fault in a stamp such as thin paper, bad perforations, creases, tears, stains, ink marks, pin holes, etc., and depending upon the seriousness of the fault, usually results in grading the stamp to a lower condition.

OTHER STAMP CONSIDERATIONS

CANCELLATIONS

Light Cancel—This stamp has been postally cancelled but the wording and lines are very light and almost unreadable.

Normal Cancel—This stamp has been postally cancelled with just the right amount of pressure. Usually the wording and lines are not distorted and can be made out.

Heavy Cancel—This stamp has been postally cancelled. In the process excessive pressure was used, and the wording and lines are extremely dark and sometimes smeared and in most cases unreadable.

PERFORATIONS

Not to be overlooked in the appearance of a stamp are its perforations. The philatelist might examine these "tear apart" holes with a magnifying glass or microscope to determine the cleanliness of the separations. One must also consider that the different types of paper, upon which the stamp was printed, will sometimes make a difference in the cleanliness of the separations. The term "pulled perf" is used to denote a badly separated stamp in which the perforations are torn or ragged.

COLOR

Other important factors such as color affect the appearance and value of stamps. An expert will have a chart of stamp colors. Chemical changes often occur in inks. Modern printing sometimes uses metallic inks. These "printings" will oxidize upon contact with the natural secretions from animal skin.

The color of certain stamps has been deliberately altered by chemicals to produce a rare shade. Overprints can be eliminated. Postmarks may be eradicated. Replacing gum is a simple process. Some stamps have been found to bear forged watermarks. The back of the paper was cut away and then the stamps rebacked with appropriately watermarked paper.

There are stamp experts who earn a living in the business of stamp repairing. They are craftsmen of the first order. A thin spot on a stamp can be repaired by gluing it on a new layer of paper. Missing perforations can be added. Torn stamps can be put back together. Pieces of stamps may be joined.

In some countries it is accepted practice for an expert, upon examination of a stamp, to certify the authenticity by affixing his signature to the back of the stamp. If the stamp is not genuine, it is his right and duty to so designate on the stamp; but these signatures can also be faked.

REPAIRS, FAKES, AND OTHER UNDESIRABLES

Philately, like most hobbies, is not without its pitfalls. The collector who buys from reputable dealers runs very little risk, as today's stamp pros have high principles and are hard to fool. Buying from auction sales and small dealers, who may not have expert knowledge, is another matter. Here the collector must call into play his own expertise and learn to distinguish the bad from the good.

In the early years of philately, stamps provided a playground for fakers and swindlers. They took advantage of the public's gullibility and the general lack of published information about stamps. Copies were printed of rare stamps, as well as of stamps that never existed in the first place. Cancels were bleached from used specimens to make them appear unused. Fake margins were added to imperforates, to allow ordinary copies to be sold as "superb with jumbo margins." Perforated stamps were reperforated to make them better centered. Thin spots in the paper were filled in, tears closed, missing portions of paper replaced. Stamps were doctored and manipulated in more ways than could be imagined, all in the hope of fooling collectors and making anywhere from a few extra cents to thousands of dollars on each. One of the favorite tricks of fakers was to apply bogus overprints or surcharges. By merely using a rubber handstamp and a pad of ink, they could stamp out a hundred or more "rarities" in a few minutes, turning ordinary British or other issues into varieties not found in any catalogue. It was all a great game and proved very profitable, until collectors and the philatelic public at large became wary of such practices. Even though most of these fakes from the hobby's pioneer years have disappeared out of circulation, a few still turn up and must be guarded against.

United States stamps have not been faked nearly so extensively as those of many other nations, notably South America and Japan. Still the collector should learn to watch for fakes and also repaired specimens.

Total Fake. The counterfeit stamp always varies somewhat from a genuine specimen, though the difference may be very slight. Detection can usually be made if the suspect stamp is examined alongside one known to be genuine. By using a magnifier, the lines of engraving and paper quality can be compared. The ink on a fake is likely to have a fresher appearance and will lie on the surface as a result of being printed at a later date and on less sophisticated equipment; however, this is not always the case. Experts say that when a stamp appears to be a fake, or a reprint, the odds are very good that it is. Some experience is necessary before anyone can get a first glance reaction to a stamp. The presence or absence of a cancel has no bearing on the likelihood of a stamp being a fake, as cancels can be faked too.

Faked Cancel. Faked cancels are very rare on U.S. stamps as nearly all are worth more unused than used. One notable exception is the 90¢ 1857–1861. These are applied either with a fake handstamp or simply drawn with pen and ink. Skillfully drawn faked cancels can be very deceptive. Faked cancels are *much more numerous* on covers than loose stamps.

Removed Cancels. So-called cleaned copies of used stamps, sold as unused, were once very plentiful and are still encountered from time to time. The faker of course chooses lightly canceled specimens from which the obliteration can be removed without leaving telltale evidence. In the case of imperforates he may trim down the margins to remove part of the cancel. Rarely will he attempt to clean a stamp whose cancel falls across the face or any important portion of the stamp. Holding the stamp to a strong light may reveal the cancel lines. X-ray examination provides positive proof.

Added Margin(s). When margins have been added to an imperforate stamp, the paper fibers are woven together (after moistening) along the back and at the front where the margin extends beyond the stamp's design. They can usually be detected by looking closely for a seam or joint at the point where the design ends and the margin begins. A magnifying glass will be necessary for this. When held against a light, the reverse side will probably show evidence of the weaving operation. Sometimes the added margins are of a slightly different grade of paper.

Reperforated. A stamp that has been reperforated to improve its centering will usually be slightly smaller than a normal specimen, and this can be revealed by placing it atop an untampered copy.

Filled In Thin Spots. If held to a light and examined with a good magnifier, filled in thin spots will normally appear darker than the remainder of the stamp. Such spots are often mistaken for discoloration by beginners. Thin spots are filled in by making a paste of paper pulp and glue and applying it gradually to the injured area. After drying, the stamp is placed in a vise so that no telltale hills or valleys are left. This is not really considered forgery but honest repair work; it becomes forgery only if done with the intent of selling the stamp as undamaged.

Closed Tears. These are almost visible against a light with a magnifier, even if small. A routine examination of any rare stamp should include a check of its margins for possible closed or open tears.

HOW TO USE THIS BOOK

The main section of this book lists all U.S. stamps with the exception of special issues such as airmail, revenues, etc. Special issues are grouped separately in sections of their own. Please refer to the Table of Contents.

Before pricing your stamps, be sure they are correctly identified. Use the photo section as an aid. In some cases, two or more stamp issues are very similar in appearance and can be distinguished only by minor details. These are always noted in the text. Sometimes the evidence is obvious. If a stamp has perforations, it cannot be earlier than 1857.

Prices are given in columns for used and unused specimens, usually in two grades of condition. You need only refer to the column that applies to your stamp and its condition grade.

Prices shown in this book are actual selling prices, so one should not necessarily expect to receive a discount when buying from dealers.

When a dash (—) appears in place of a price, this indicates that the item is either unavailable in that condition grade or is so seldom available that its price is open to question. It should not be assumed, however, that such items are invariably more valuable than those for which prices are shown.

Prices are given for hinged stamps that have been in collections. In today's stamp market a premium value is placed on stamps that have never been hinged. To determine the premium on any stamp, refer to the premium percentages shown on every page.

The stated values are general guides only and cannot reflect the price of occasional superb specimens, such as imperforates with four wide margins, which may sell considerably higher.

A small box has been provided to the left of each listing for keeping a record of the stamps in your collection.

IMPORTANT

Because of the space limitation on each page we have not been able to include very fine, extra fine, never hinged, or lightly hinged pricing on each stamp. To determine these prices please use the following procedure.

Very Fine Pricing—Prior to 1941: *Double the average price quoted.*

Very Fine Pricing—After 1941: *Add 25% to the fine price.*

Extra Fine Pricing—Prior to 1941: *Triple the average price quoted.*

Never Hinged Pricing—Prior to 1941: *Add the percentage indicated at the right of the issue to any price listed. Example: (N-H add 5%).*

Never Hinged Pricing—After 1941: *Add 15% to any price listed.*

Lightly Hinged Pricing—Add one half of the N-H percentage indicated for each issue to any price listed.

DEALER BUYING PRICES

Buying prices will vary greatly depending upon condition, rarity, and existing dealers' stock of a particular stamp. With these facts in mind, a dealer can be expected to buy stamps between 40 percent and 50 percent of their quoted prices; but this will depend upon supply and demand.

EQUIPMENT

To collect stamps properly a collector will need some "tools of the trade." These need not be expensive and need not all be bought at the very outset. That might in fact be the worst thing to do. Many a beginning collector has spent his budget on equipment, only to have little or nothing left for stamps and then loses interest in the hobby.

It may be economical in the long run to buy the finest quality accessories but few collectors, just starting out, have a clear idea of what they will and will not be needing. It is just as easy to make impulse purchases of accessories as of stamps and just as unwise. Equipment must be purchased on the basis of what sort of collection is being built *now,* rather than on what the collection may be in the future. There is no shame in working up from an elementary album.

Starter Kits. Starter or beginner outfits are sold in just about every variety shop, drugstore, etc. These come in attractive boxes and contain a juvenile or beginner's album, some stamps, which may be on paper and in need of removal, a packet of gummed hinges, tongs, a pocket stockbook or file; and often other items such as a perforation gauge, booklet on stamp collecting, magnifier, and watermark detector. These kits are specially suited to young collectors and can provide a good philatelic education.

Albums. When the hobby began, more than a century ago, collectors mounted their stamps in whatever albums were at hand. Scrapbooks, school exercise tablets and diaries all were used, as well as homemade albums. Today a number of firms specialize in printing albums of all kinds for philatelists, ranging from softbounds for the cautious type to huge multi-volume sets that cost hundreds of dollars. There are general worldwide albums, country albums, U.N. albums, and albums for mint sheets, covers, and every other conceivable variety of philatelic material. Choose your album according to the specialty you intend to pursue. It is not necessary, however, to buy a printed album at all. Many collectors feel there is not enough room for creativity in a printed album and prefer to use a binder with unprinted sheets. This allows items to be arranged at will on the page, rather than following the publisher's format, and for a personal write-up to be added. Rod-type binders will prove more durable and satisfactory than ring binders for heavy collections. The pages of an album should not be too thin, unless only one side is used. The presence of tiny crisscrossing lines (quadrilled sheets) is intended as an aid to correct alignment. Once items have been mounted and written up, these lines are scarcely visible and do not interfere with the attractiveness of the page.

Hinges. These are small rectangular pieces of lightweight paper, usually clear or semiopaque, gummed and folded. One side is moistened and affixed to the back of the stamp and the other to the album page. Hinges are sold in packets of 1,000 and are very inexpensive. Though by far the most popular device for mounting stamps, the hobbyist has his choice of a number of other products if hinges are not satisfactory to him. These include cello mounts which encase the stamp in clear sheeting and have a black background to provide a kind of frame. These are self-sticking. Their cost is much higher than hinges. The chief advantage of cello mounts is that they prevent injuries to the stamp and eliminate the moistening necessary in using hinges; however, they add considerably to the weight of each page, making flipping through an album less convenient, and become detached from the page more readily than hinges.

Glassine Interleaving. These are sheets made of thin semitransparent glassine paper, the same used to make envelopes in which stamps are stored. They come punched to fit albums of standard size and are designed to be placed between each set of sheets, to prevent stamps on one page from becoming entangled with those on the facing page. Glassine interleaving is not necessary if cello mounts are used, but any collection mounted with conventional hinges should be interleaved. The cost is small. Glassine interleaving is sold in packets of 100 sheets.

Magnifier. A magnifier is a necessary tool for *most* stamp collectors, excepting those who specialize in first day covers or other items that would not likely require study by magnification. There are numerous types and grades on the market, ranging in price from about $1 to more than $20. The quality of magnifier to buy should be governed by the extent to which it is likely to be used, and the collector's dependence upon it for identification and study. A collector of plate varieties ought to have the best magnifier he can afford, and carry it whenever visiting dealers, shows or anywhere that he may wish to examine specimens. A good magnifier is also necessary for a specialist in grilled stamps and for collectors of Civil War and other nineteenth-century covers. Those with built-in illumination are best in these circumstances.

Tongs. Beginners have a habit of picking up stamps with their fingers, which can cause injuries, smudges and grease stains. Efficient handling of tongs is not difficult to learn, and the sooner the better. Do not resort to ordinary tweezers, but get a pair of philatelic tongs which are specially shaped and of sufficiently large size to be easily manipulated.

Perforation Gauge. A very necessary inexpensive article, as the identification of many stamps depends upon a correct measuring of their perforations.

TIPS ON STAMP BUYING

There are many ways to buy stamps: packets, poundage mixtures, approvals, new issue services, auctions and a number of others. To buy wisely a collector must get to know the language of philately and the techniques used by dealers and auctioneers in selling stamps.

Packets of all different worldwide stamps are sold in graduated sizes from 1,000 up to 50,000. True to their word, they contain no duplicates. The stamps come from all parts of the world and date from the 1800s to the present. Both mint and used are included. When you buy larger quantities of most things, a discount is offered; with stamp packets, it works in reverse. The larger the packet, the higher its price per stamp. This is because the smaller packets are filled almost exclusively with low grade material.

Packets are suitable only as a collection base. A collector should never count on them to build his entire collection. The contents of one worldwide packet are much like that of another. Country packets are sold in smaller sizes, but there are certain drawbacks with packets.

1. Most packets contain some canceled-to-order stamps, which are not very desirable for a collection. These are stamps released with postmarks already on them, and are classified as used but have never gone through the mail. Eastern Europe and Russia are responsible for many C.T.O.'s.

2. The advertised value of packets bears little relation to the actual value. Packet makers call attention to the catalog values of their stamps, based on prices listed in standard reference works. The lowest sum at which a stamp can be listed in these books is 2¢, therefore, a packet of 1,000 automatically has a minimum catalog value of $20. If the retail price is $3 this seems like a terrific buy when in fact most of those thousand stamps are so common they are almost worthless.

Poundage mixtures are very different than packets. Here the stamps are all postally used (no C.T.O.'s) and still attached to small fragments of envelopes or parcel wrappings. Rather than sold by count, poundage mixtures are priced by the pound or ounce and quite often by kilos. Price varies depending on the grade, and the grade depends on where the mixture was assembled. Bank mixtures are considered the best as banks receive a steady flow of foreign registered mail. Mission mixtures are also highly rated. Of course the mixture should be sealed and unpicked. Unless a mixture is advertised as unpicked the high values have been removed. The best poundage mixtures are sold only by mail. Those available in shops are of medium or low quality. Whatever the grade, poundage mixtures can be counted on to contain duplicates.

If you want to collect the stamps of a certain country you can leave a standing order for its new releases with a new issue service. Whenever that government puts out stamps, they will be sent to the collector along with a bill. Usually the service will supply only mint copies. The price charged is not the face value, but the face value with a surcharge added to meet the costs of importing, handling and the like. New issue services are satisfactory only if the collector is positive he wants all the country's stamps, no matter what. Remember that its issues could include semipostals, long and maybe expensive sets, and extra high values.

By far the most popular way to buy stamps is via approvals. There is nothing new about approvals, as they go back to the Victorian era. Not all services are alike, though. Some offer sets, while others sell penny approvals. Then there are remainder approvals, advanced approvals, and seconds on approval. Penny approvals are really a thing of the past, though the term is still used. Before inflation, dealers would send a stockbook containing several thousand stamps, all priced at a penny each. If all the stamps were kept, the collector got a discount plus the book! Today the same sort of service can be found but instead of 1¢ per stamp, the price is anywhere from 3¢ to 10¢. Remainder approvals are made up from collection remainders. Rather than dismount and sort stamps from incoming collections, the approval merchant saves himself time by sending them out right on the album pages. The collector receives leaves from someone else's collection with stamps mounted just as he arranged them. Seconds on approval are slightly defective specimens of scarce stamps, which would cost more if perfect. Advanced approvals are designed for specialized collectors who know exactly what they want and have a fairly substantial stamp budget.

In choosing an approval service you should know the ground rules of approval buying and not be unduly influenced by promotional offers. Most approval merchants allow the selections to be kept for ten days to two weeks. The unbought stamps are then returned along with payment for those kept. As soon as the selection is received back, another is mailed. This will go on, regardless of how much or how little is bought, until the company is notified to refrain from sending further selections. The reputable services will always stop when told.

Approval ads range from splashy full pagers in the stamp publications to small three line classified announcements in magazines and newspapers. Most firms catering to beginners offer loss leaders, or stamps on which they take a loss for the sake of getting new customers. If an approval dealer offers 100 pictorials for a dime, it is obvious he is losing money on that transaction, as 10¢ will not even pay the postage. It is very tempting to order these premiums. Remember that when ordering approvals. What sort of service is it? Will it offer the kind of stamps desired? Will prices be high to pay for the loss leaders? Be careful of confusing advertisements. Sometimes the premium offers seem to promise more than they actually do. A rare, early stamp may be pictured. Of course you do not receive the stamp, but merely a modern commemorative picturing it.

Auction Sales. Stamp auctions are held all over the country and account for millions of dollars in sales annually. Buying at auction is exciting and can be economical. Many sleepers turn up—stamps that can be bought at less than their actual value. To be a good auction buyer, the philatelist must know stamps and their prices pretty well, and know the ropes of auctions. An obvious drawback of auctions is that purchases are not returnable. A dealer will take back a stamp that proves not to be a collector's liking, but an auctioneer will not. Also, auctioneers require immediate payment while a dealer may extend credit.

Stamps sold at auction come from private collections and the stocks of dealers; not necessarily defunct dealers, but those who want to get shelf space. Because they were brought together from a variety of sources, the nature and condition will vary. In catalog descriptions the full book value will be given for each stamp, but of course defective stamps will sell for much less than these figures. A bidder must calculate how much less. Other lots which can be difficult for the bidder to evaluate are those containing more than one stamp. Sometimes a superb specimen will be lotted along with a defective one. Then there are bulk lots which contain odds and ends from collections and such. It is usual in auctioning a collection for the better stamps to be removed and sold separately. The remainder is then offered in a single lot, which may consist of thousands or even tens of thousands of stamps. By all means examine lots before bidding. A period of inspection is always allowed before each sale, usually for several days. There may or may not be an inspection on sale day. If the bidder is not able to make a personal examination but must bid on strength of the catalog description, he should scale his bids for bulk lots much lower than for single stamp lots. He might bid $50 on a single stamp lot with a catalog value of $100, if the condition is listed as top notch, but to bid one-half catalog value on a bulk lot would not be very wise. These lots are not scrutinized very carefully by the auctioneers and some stamps are bound to be disappointing. There may be some heavily canceled, creased, torn, etc. Also, there will very likely be duplication. A bid of one-fifth the catalog value on a bulk lot is considered high. Often a one-tenth bid is successful.

The mechanics of stamp auctions may strike the beginner as complicated. They are run no differently than other auctions. All material to be sold is lotted by the auctioneer; that is, broken down into lots or units and bidding is by lot. Everything in the lot must be bid on, even if just one of the stamps is desired. The motive of bulk lotting is to save time and give each lot a fair sales value.

Before the sale a catalog is published listing all the lots, describing the contents and sometimes picturing the better items. Catalogs are in the mail about 30 days before the sale date. If a bid is to be mailed, it must be sent early. Bids that arrive after the sale are disqualified, even if they would have been successful.

When the bid is received it is entered into a bidbook, along with the bidder's name and address. On sale day each lot opens on the floor at one level above the second highest mail bid. Say the two highest mail bids are $30 and $20. The floor bidding would begin at $25. If the two highest bids are $100 and $500, the opening bid would probably be $150. The larger the amounts involved, the bigger will be the advances. The auctioneer will not accept an advance of $5 on a $500 lot; but on low value lots one dollar advances are sometimes made. Then it becomes a contest of floor versus book. The auctioneer acts as an agent, bidding for the absentee until his limit is reached. If the floor tops him, he has lost. If the floor does not get as high as his bid, he wins the lot at one advance over the highest floor bid.

When a collector buys stamps by mail from a dealer, he should choose one who belongs to the American Stamp Dealers' Association or A.S.D.A. The emblem is carried in their ads.

SELLING YOUR STAMPS

Almost every collector becomes a stamp seller sooner or later. Duplicates are inevitably accumulated, no matter how careful one may be in avoiding them. Then there are the G and VG stamps that have been replaced with F and VF specimens, and have become duplicates by intent. In addition to duplicates, a more advanced collector is likely also to have stamps that are not duplicates but for which he has no further use. These will be odds and ends, sometimes quite valuable ones, that once suited the nature of his collection but are now out of place. Collectors' tastes change. The result is a stockpile of stamps that can be converted back to cash.

The alternative to selling the stamps you no longer need or want is trading them with a collector who does want them, and taking his unwanted stamps in return. All stamp clubs hold trading sessions. Larger national stamp societies operate trade-by-mail services for their members. The APS (American Philatelic Society) keeps $8,000,000 worth of stamps constantly circulating in its trading books or "circuit" books. Trading can be an excellent way of disposing of surplus stamps. In most cases it takes a bit longer than selling. Another potential drawback, especially if you are not a club member, is finding the right person with the right stamps.

The nature and value of the material involved may help in deciding whether to sell outright or trade. Also, there are your own personal considerations. If you're not going to continue in the stamp hobby, or need cash for some purpose other than stamp buying, trading is hardly suitable. Likewise, if you have developed an interest in some very exotic group of stamps or other philatelic items it may be impossible to find someone to trade with.

Once you have decided to sell, if indeed you do make that decision, the matter revolves upon: how? To a stamp shop? To another collector? Through an auction house? Possibly by running your own advertisements and issuing price lists, if you have enough stamps and spare time to make this worthwhile?

While some individuals have an absolute horror at the prospect of selling anything, stamp collectors tend to enjoy selling. It is difficult to say why. Some enjoy it so much they keep right on selling stamps, as a business, long after their original objective is achieved. Nearly all professional stamp dealers were collectors before entering the trade.

Selling your stamps outright to a dealer, especially a local dealer whom you can personally visit, is not necessarily the most financially rewarding but it is quick and very problem-free. Of course it helps if the dealer knows you and it's even better if he knows some of your stamps. Dealers have no objection to repurchasing stamps they've sold to you. You will find that the dealers encourage their customers to sell to them just as much as they encourage them to buy. The dealers are really anxious to get your stamps if you have good salable material from popular countries. In fact most dealers would prefer buying from the public rather than any other source.

The collector selling stamps to a dealer has to be reasonable in his expectations. A dealer may not be able to use all the stamps you have. It is simply not smart business for a dealer to invest money in something he may not be able to sell. So, if you have esoteric or highly specialized items for sale, it might be necessary to find a specialist who deals in those particular areas rather than selling to a neighborhood stamp shop.

The local stamp shop will almost certainly want to buy anything you can offer in the way of medium to better grade United States stamps of all kinds, including the so-called "back of the book" items. He may not want plate blocks or full sheets of commemoratives issued within the past 20 years. Most dealers are well supplied with material of this nature and have opportunities to buy more of it every day. The same is true of first day covers, with a few exceptions, issued from the 1960s to the present. The dealers either have these items abundantly or can get them from a wholesaler at rock-bottom prices. They would rather buy stamps that are a bit harder to get from the wholesalers, or for which the wholesalers charge higher prices. On the whole you will meet with a favorable reception when offering U.S. stamps to a local dealer. With foreign stamps it becomes another matter: what do you have and how flexible are you in price? Nearly all the stamp shops in this country do stock foreign stamps to one extent or another. They do not, as a rule, attempt to carry comprehensive or specialized stocks of them. In the average shop you will discover that the selection of general foreign consists of a combination of modern mint sets, topicals, souvenir sheets, packets, which come from the wholesaler, and a small sprinkling of older material, usually pre-1900. The price range of this older material will be $5 to $50. Non-specialist collectors of foreign stamps buy this type of item and that is essentially who the local shop caters to. When a local dealer buys rare foreign stamps or a large foreign collection, it is not for himself. He buys with the intent of passing them along to another dealer who has the right customers lined up. He acts only as a middleman or go-between. Therefore the price you receive for better grade foreign stamps tends to be lower than for better grade U.S., which the dealer buys for his own use.

What is a fair price to get for your stamps? This is always difficult to say, as many variable factors are involved. Consider their condition. Think in terms of what the dealer could reasonably hope to charge for them at retail and stand a good chance of selling them. Some of your stamps may have to be discounted because of no gum, poor centering, bent perfs, hinge remnants, repairs, or other problems. But even if your stamps are primarily F or VF, a dealer cannot pay book values for them. If you check his selling prices on his specimens of those same stamps, you can usually count on receiving from 40 to 50 percent of those prices. Considering the discount made from book values by the dealer in pricing his stock, your payment may work out to about 25 percent of book values. For rare United States stamps in top condition you can do better than 25 percent, but on most stamps sold to a dealer this is considered a fair offer. Keep in mind that the difference between a dealer's buying and selling prices is not just "profit margin." Most of the markup goes toward operating costs, for without this markup, there would be no stamp dealers.

IMPORTANT NOTICE: On stamps issued before 1890, prices of unused specimens are for ones without original gum. Specimens with original gum can be expected to command a premium of as much as 50 percent. Beware of regummed specimens

Scott No.		Fine Unused Each	Ave. Unused Each	Fine Used Each	Ave. Used Each
GENERAL ISSUES					
1847. FIRST ISSUE					
☐ 1	5¢ Red Brown	—	3100.00	800.00	550.00
☐ 2	10¢ Black	—	13600.00	2800.00	1700.00
1875. REPRODUCTIONS OF 1847 ISSUE					
☐ 3	5¢ Red Brown	1700.00	1200.00	—	—
☐ 4	10¢ Black	2000.00	1300.00	—	—
1851–1856. REGULAR ISSUE—IMPERFORATE					
☐ 5A	1¢ Blue (1b)	—	—	4100.00	2700.00
☐ 6	1¢ Blue (1a)	—	—	4600.00	3000.00
☐ 7	1¢ Blue (II)	550.00	320.00	150.00	90.00
☐ 8	1¢ Blue (III)	—	1600.00	950.00
☐ 8A	1¢ Blue (IIIa)	—	1650.00	650.00	450.00
☐ 9	1¢ Blue (IV)	350.00	250.00	150.00	70.00
☐ 10	3¢ Orange Brown (I)	—	950.00	75.00	45.00
☐ 11	3¢ Dull Red (I)	160.00	90.00	15.00	9.00
☐ 12	5¢ Red Brown (I)	—	1400.00	850.00
☐ 13	10¢ Green (I)	—	750.00	450.00
☐ 14	10¢ Green (II)	—	910.00	320.00	200.00
☐ 15	10¢ Green (III)	—	1100.00	320.00	200.00
☐ 16	10¢ Green (IV)	—	1400.00	910.00
☐ 17	12¢ Black	—	1150.00	300.00	190.00
1857–1861. SAME DESIGNS AS 1851–1856 ISSUE—PERF. 15					
☐ 18	1¢ Blue (I)	800.00	420.00	375.00	230.00
☐ 19	1¢ Blue (Ia)	—	—	2100.00	1600.00
☐ 20	1¢ Blue (II)	600.00	310.00	150.00	90.00
☐ 21	1¢ Blue (III)	—	2200.00	1150.00	650.00
☐ 22	1¢ Blue (IIIa)	650.00	360.00	230.00	140.00
☐ 23	1¢ Blue (IV)	—	1200.00	270.00	180.00
☐ 24	1¢ Blue (V)	190.00	85.00	40.00	22.00
☐ 25	3¢ Rose (I)	—	410.00	42.00	22.00
☐ 26	3¢ Dull Red (II)	64.00	38.00	6.00	2.90
☐ 26A	3¢ Dull Red (IIa)	140.00	85.00	23.00	16.00
☐ 27	5¢ Brick Red (I)	—	4100.00	920.00	630.00
☐ 28	5¢ Red Brown (I)	—	900.00	310.00	200.00
☐ 28A	5¢ Indian Red (I)	—	—	1225.00	710.00
☐ 29	5¢ Brown (I)	710.00	440.00	210.00	130.00
☐ 30	5¢ Orange Brown (II)	760.00	460.00	900.00	550.00
☐ 30A	5¢ Brown (II)	475.00	260.00	210.00	120.00
☐ 31	10¢ Green (I)	—	2600.00	500.00	310.00
☐ 32	10¢ Green (II)	1600.00	900.00	170.00	120.00

Scott No.			Fine Unused Each	Ave. Unused Each	Fine Used Each	Ave. Used Each
☐ 33	10¢	Green (III)	1550.00	860.00	180.00	110.00
☐ 34	10¢	Green (IV)	—	—	1460.00	850.00
☐ 35	10¢	Green (V)	200.00	120.00	90.00	60.00
☐ 36	12¢	Black (I)	320.00	185.00	110.00	60.00
☐ 36b	12¢	Black (II)	260.00	150.00	120.00	65.00
☐ 37	24¢	Gray Lilac	660.00	410.00	230.00	165.00
☐ 38	30¢	Orange	820.00	470.00	320.00	175.00
☐ 39	90¢	Blue	1620.00	860.00	—	—

1875. REPRINTS OF 1857–1861 ISSUE

☐ 40	1¢	Bright Blue	510.00	350.00	—	—
☐ 41	3¢	Scarlet	2300.00	1700.00	—	—
☐ 42	5¢	Orange Brown	860.00	620.00	—	—
☐ 43	10¢	Blue Green	2100.00	1450.00	—	—
☐ 44	12¢	Greenish Black	2100.00	1550.00	—	—
☐ 45	24¢	Blackish Violet	2350.00	1570.00	—	—
☐ 46	30¢	Yellow Orange	2350.00	1725.00	—	—
☐ 47	90¢	Deep Blue	3650.00	2550.00	—	—

1861. FIRST DESIGNS—PERF. 12

☐ 56	3¢	Brown Red	730.00	490.00	—	—
☐ 62B	10¢	Dark Green	—	—	560.00	330.00

1861–1862. SECOND DESIGNS

☐ 63	1¢	Blue	130.00	75.00	25.00	14.00
☐ 63b	1¢	Dark Blue	135.00	95.00	27.00	19.00
☐ 64	3¢	Pink	—	1920.00	290.00	175.00
☐ 64b	3¢	Rose Pink	275.00	180.00	53.00	31.00
☐ 65	3¢	Rose	60.00	37.00	2.75	1.30
☐ 66	3¢	Lake	—	1050.00	—	—
☐ 67	5¢	Buff	—	2600.00	410.00	240.00
☐ 68	10¢	Yellow Green	270.00	160.00	26.00	17.00
☐ 69	12¢	Black	450.00	315.00	55.00	34.00
☐ 70	24¢	Red Lilac	515.00	330.00	82.00	45.00
☐ 70b	24¢	Steel Blue	—	—	285.00	170.00
☐ 70c	24¢	Violet	—	1675.00	540.00	320.00
☐ 71	30¢	Orange	470.00	280.00	75.00	44.00
☐ 72	90¢	Blue	1150.00	640.00	240.00	155.00

1861–1866. NEW VALUES OR NEW COLORS

☐ 73	2¢	Black	160.00	85.00	33.00	18.00
☐ 74	3¢	Scarlet	3450.00	2250.00	1500.00	1000.00
☐ 75	5¢	Red Brown	1275.00	760.00	210.00	130.00
☐ 76	5¢	Brown	280.00	210.00	56.00	40.00
☐ 77	15¢	Black	510.00	275.00	92.00	60.00
☐ 78	24¢	Lilac	250.00	142.00	52.00	37.00

Scott No.		Fine Unused Each	Ave. Unused Each	Fine Used Each	Ave. Used Each

1867. SAME DESIGNS AS 1861-1866 ISSUE
GRILL WITH POINTS UP
A. GRILL COVERING ENTIRE STAMP

| ☐ 79 | 3¢ Rose | 1710.00 | 1100.00 | 460.00 | 255.00 |

C. GRILL ABOUT 13 x 16 MM.

| ☐ 83 | 3¢ Rose | 1470.00 | 910.00 | 380.00 | 220.00 |

GRILL WITH POINTS DOWN
D. GRILL ABOUT 12 x 14 MM.

| ☐ 84 | 2¢ Black | 1800.00 | 1365.00 | 810.00 | 415.00 |
| ☐ 85 | 3¢ Rose | 1100.00 | 660.00 | 335.00 | 190.00 |

Z. GRILL ABOUT 11 x 14 MM.

☐ 85B	2¢ Black	960.00	570.00	310.00	180.00
☐ 85C	3¢ Rose	2250.00	1600.00	770.00	430.00
☐ 85E	12¢ Black	1450.00	870.00	500.00	290.00

E. GRILL ABOUT 11 x 13 MM.

☐ 86	1¢ Blue	610.00	350.00	200.00	130.00
☐ 87	2¢ Black	310.00	180.00	75.00	45.00
☐ 88	3¢ Rose	220.00	130.00	10.00	7.00
☐ 89	10¢ Green	1050.00	610.00	160.00	90.00
☐ 90	12¢ Black	1220.00	710.00	180.00	97.00
☐ 91	15¢ Black	2350.00	1400.00	360.00	230.00

F. GRILL ABOUT 9 x 13 MM.

☐ 92	1¢ Blue	245.00	140.00	90.00	53.00
☐ 93	2¢ Black	160.00	83.00	33.00	18.00
☐ 94	3¢ Red	90.00	54.00	430.00	2.75
☐ 95	5¢ Brown	760.00	435.00	210.00	116.00
☐ 96	10¢ Yellow Green	550.00	330.00	90.00	60.00
☐ 97	12¢ Black	600.00	330.00	92.00	60.00
☐ 98	15¢ Black	600.00	350.00	100.00	65.00
☐ 99	24¢ Gray Lilac	1200.00	650.00	500.00	240.00
☐ 100	30¢ Orange	1250.00	760.00	350.00	200.00
☐ 101	90¢ Blue	3100.00	1800.00	900.00	600.00

1875. RE-ISSUE OF 1861-1866 ISSUES

☐ 102	1¢ Blue	—	350.00	—	460.00
☐ 103	2¢ Black	—	1750.00	—	2100.00
☐ 104	3¢ Brown Red	—	2100.00	—	2600.00
☐ 105	5¢ Light Brown	—	1600.00	—	1180.00
☐ 106	10¢ Green	—	1610.00	—	2350.00
☐ 107	12¢ Black	—	3300.00	—	2700.00
☐ 108	15¢ Black	—	2400.00	—	2750.00
☐ 109	24¢ Deep Violet	—	2350.00	—	3300.00
☐ 110	30¢ Brownish Orange	—	2925.00	—	4300.00
☐ 111	90¢ Blue	—	3850.00	—	6100.00

Scott No.		Fine Unused Each	Ave. Unused Each	Fine Used Each	Ave. Used Each

1869. PICTORIAL ISSUES
GRILL ABOUT 9½ x 9½ MM.

☐ 112	1¢ Buff	240.00	170.00	75.00	50.00
☐ 113	2¢ Brown	170.00	118.00	30.00	17.00
☐ 114	3¢ Ultramarine	145.00	90.00	9.00	6.00
☐ 115	6¢ Ultramarine	720.00	420.00	95.00	65.00
☐ 116	10¢ Yellow	820.00	470.00	100.00	67.00
☐ 117	12¢ Green	690.00	400.00	120.00	72.00
☐ 118	15¢ Brown & Blue (I)	1710.00	1050.00	250.00	165.00
☐ 119	15¢ Brown & Blue (II)	830.00	530.00	135.00	80.00
☐ 120	24¢ Green & Violet	2450.00	1550.00	490.00	320.00
☐ 121	30¢ Blue & Carmine	2100.00	1300.00	320.00	190.00
☐ 122	90¢ Carmine & Black	7300.00	4750.00	1275.00	760.00

1875. RE-ISSUE OF 1869 ISSUE. HARD WHITE PAPER—
WITHOUT GRILL

☐ 123	1¢ Buff	340.00	220.00	240.00	140.00
☐ 124	2¢ Brown	430.00	260.00	330.00	200.00
☐ 125	3¢ Blue	2450.00	1650.00	1250.00	900.00
☐ 126	6¢ Blue	—	670.00	—	360.00
☐ 127	10¢ Yellow	—	1100.00	—	730.00
☐ 128	12¢ Green	—	1175.00	—	85.00
☐ 129	15¢ Brown & Blue (III)	—	1050.00	—	410.00
☐ 130	24¢ Green & Violet	—	980.00	—	370.00
☐ 131	30¢ Blue & Carmine	—	1275.00	—	740.00
☐ 132	90¢ Carmine & Black	—	3700.00	—	5950.00

1880. SAME AS ABOVE—SOFT POROUS PAPER

☐ 133	1¢ Buff	240.00	150.00	160.00	95.00

1870-1871. PRINTED BY NATIONAL BANK NOTE CO.—GRILLED

☐ 134	1¢ Ultramarine	460.00	270.00	63.00	40.00
☐ 135	2¢ Red Brown	310.00	180.00	35.00	25.00
☐ 136	3¢ Green	230.00	140.00	11.00	7.00
☐ 137	6¢ Carmine	1375.00	770.00	250.00	150.00
☐ 138	7¢ Vermilion	1050.00	620.00	225.00	140.00
☐ 139	10¢ Brown	1310.00	860.00	370.00	260.00
☐ 140	12¢ Light Violet	—	—	2200.00	1350.00
☐ 141	15¢ Orange	1410.00	900.00	630.00	420.00
☐ 142	24¢ Purple	—	—	—	7000.00
☐ 143	30¢ Black	—	2600.00	800.00	540.00
☐ 144	90¢ Carmine	—	3100.00	660.00	450.00

1870-1871. SAME AS ABOVE—WITHOUT GRILL

☐ 145	1¢ Ultramarine	145.00	95.00	9.00	550.00
☐ 146	2¢ Red Brown	65.00	40.00	6.00	4.00
☐ 147	3¢ Green	110.00	62.00	1.00	.75
☐ 148	6¢ Carmine	220.00	130.00	13.00	8.00
☐ 149	7¢ Vermilion	310.00	175.00	55.00	29.50
☐ 150	10¢ Brown	220.00	120.00	14.00	9.00

Scott No.		Fine Unused Each	Ave. Unused Each	Fine Used Each	Ave. Used Each
☐ 151	12¢ Dull Violet	480.00	290.00	55.00	34.00
☐ 152	15¢ Bright Orange	430.00	250.00	57.00	34.00
☐ 153	24¢ Purple	560.00	320.00	80.00	45.00
☐ 154	30¢ Black	910.00	530.00	99.00	67.00
☐ 155	90¢ Carmine	1150.00	660.00	145.00	92.00

1873. SAME DESIGNS AS 1870–1871 ISSUE—WITH SECRET MARKS
PRINTED BY THE CONTINENTAL BANK NOTE CO.
THIN HARD GRAYISH WHITE PAPER

☐ 156	1¢ Ultramarine	55.00	35.00	2.90	1.75
☐ 157	2¢ Brown	130.00	87.00	8.75	5.50
☐ 158	3¢ Green	43.00	26.00	.30	.20
☐ 159	6¢ Dull Pink	175.00	110.00	10.00	6.00
☐ 160	7¢ Orange Vermilion	365.00	215.00	57.00	38.00
☐ 161	10¢ Brown	175.00	110.00	12.00	8.00
☐ 162	12¢ Black Violet	515.00	340.00	72.00	47.00
☐ 163	15¢ Yellow Orange	485.00	265.00	53.00	37.00
☐ 165	30¢ Gray Black	450.00	242.00	54.00	35.00
☐ 166	90¢ Rose Carmine	1100.00	610.00	165.00	99.00

1875. REGULAR ISSUE

☐ 178	2¢ Vermilion	147.00	92.00	490.00	3.20
☐ 179	5¢ Blue	150.00	95.00	10.00	5.75

DESIGNS
1879. SAME AS 1870–1875 ISSUES
PRINTED BY THE AMERICAN BANK NOTE CO.
SOFT POROUS YELLOWISH WHITE PAPER

☐ 182	1¢ Dark Ultramarine	96.00	57.00	1.75	1.00
☐ 183	2¢ Vermilion	55.00	36.00	1.60	.90
☐ 184	3¢ Green	48.00	31.00	.21	.15
☐ 185	5¢ Blue	185.00	106.00	10.00	5.80
☐ 186	6¢ Pink	430.00	275.00	12.00	7.50
☐ 187	10¢ Brown (no secret mark)	630.00	425.00	15.00	9.00
☐ 188	10¢ Brown (secret mark)	400.00	225.00	19.00	11.00
☐ 188b	10¢ Black Brown	575.00	350.00	65.00	43.00
☐ 189	15¢ Red Orange	160.00	87.00	23.00	14.00
☐ 190	30¢ Full Black	435.00	265.00	29.00	15.00
☐ 191	90¢ Carmine	990.00	645.00	145.00	105.00

1882. REGULAR ISSUE

☐ 205	5¢ Yellow Brown	89.00	54.00	5.50	3.10

1881–1882. DESIGNS OF 1873 ISSUE RE-ENGRAVED (N-H ADD 95%)

☐ 206	1¢ Gray Blue	34.00	21.00	.90	.50
☐ 207	3¢ Blue Green	43.00	28.00	.40	.20
☐ 208	6¢ Rose	235.00	117.00	53.00	29.75
☐ 208a	6¢ Brown Red	210.00	108.00	64.00	41.50

Scott No.		Fine Unused Each	Ave. Unused Each	Fine Used Each	Ave. Used Each
☐ 209	10¢ Brown	85.00	56.00	2.90	1.60
☐ 209b	10¢ Black Brown	105.00	60.00	9.50	5.60

1883. REGULAR ISSUE
☐ 210	2¢ Red Brown	28.00	17.00	.20	.12
☐ 211	4¢ Blue Green	137.00	94.00	8.50	5.75

1887. REGULAR ISSUE
☐ 212	1¢ Ultramarine	56.00	38.00	.90	.60
☐ 213	2¢ Green	32.00	23.00	.16	.12
☐ 214	3¢ Vermilion	49.00	39.00	35.00	23.00

1888. SAME DESIGNS AS 1870–1883 ISSUES
☐ 215	4¢ Carmine	130.00	78.00	12.00	7.50
☐ 216	5¢ Indigo	135.00	82.00	8.00	4.50
☐ 217	30¢ Orange Brown	360.00	216.00	81.00	53.00
☐ 218	90¢ Purple	723.00	475.00	140.00	89.00

IMPORTANT NOTICE: From this point onward, values of unused stamps and blocks are for specimens with original gum. Prices given for **blocks** are for blocks of 4, **without** plate number.

Scott No.		Fine Unused Block	Ave. Unused Block	Fine Unused Each	Ave. Unused Each	Fine Used Each	Ave. Used Each
1890–1893. SMALL DESIGN (N-H ADD 95%)							
☐ 219	1¢ Dull Blue	213.00	133.00	25.00	13.00	.16	.10
☐ 219D	2¢ Lake	885.00	655.00	140.00	84.00	.57	.36
☐ 220	2¢ Carmine	143.00	108.00	16.00	12.00	.15	.10
☐ 220a	2¢ Carmine (Cap on left 2)	375.00	250.00	45.00	30.00	1.25	.80
☐ 220c	2¢ Carmine (Cap both 2's)	965.00	690.00	122.00	78.00	7.75	4.50
☐ 221	3¢ Purple	495.00	360.00	60.00	38.00	5.75	3.50
☐ 222	4¢ Dark Brown	630.00	462.00	60.00	38.00	2.20	1.25
☐ 223	5¢ Chocolate	630.00	460.00	58.00	39.00	1.95	1.10
☐ 224	6¢ Brown Red	620.00	435.00	62.00	38.00	16.00	11.00
☐ 225	8¢ Lilac	360.00	275.00	39.00	25.00	11.00	6.75
☐ 226	10¢ Green	740.00	575.00	120.00	75.00	2.50	1.70
☐ 227	15¢ Indigo	1110.00	870.00	148.00	92.00	19.00	13.50
☐ 228	30¢ Black	1610.00	1320.00	240.00	140.00	22.00	13.50
☐ 229	90¢ Orange	3600.00	2675.00	400.00	205.00	99.00	53.00
1893. COLUMBIAN ISSUE (N-H ADD 95%)							
☐ 230	1¢ Blue	187.00	134.00	26.00	16.50	.50	.30
☐ 231	2¢ Violet	175.00	126.00	23.00	13.50	.16	.10
☐ 231c	2¢ "Broken Hat"	412.00	312.00	75.00	48.00	.62	.40
☐ 232	3¢ Green	335.00	252.00	53.00	35.00	17.00	11.00
☐ 233	4¢ Ultramarine	613.00	475.00	81.00	54.00	7.75	5.50
☐ 234	5¢ Chocolate	675.00	545.00	84.00	57.00	8.25	5.75
☐ 235	6¢ Purple	665.00	525.00	82.00	51.00	24.00	17.00
☐ 236	8¢ Magenta	610.00	470.00	53.00	34.00	9.00	6.75
☐ 237	10¢ Black Brown	915.00	690.00	122.00	81.00	7.80	5.75
☐ 238	15¢ Dark Green	1970.00	1435.00	235.00	143.00	72.00	43.00

Scott No.		Fine Unused Block	Ave. Unused Block	Fine Unused Each	Ave. Unused Each	Fine Used Each	Ave. Used Each
☐ 239	30¢ Orange Brown	2850.00	2200.00	342.00	215.00	112.00	64.00
☐ 240	50¢ Slate Blue	3195.00	2410.00	405.00	243.00	170.00	107.00
☐ 241	$1 Salmon	—	—	1031.00	716.00	565.00	375.00
☐ 242	$2 Brown Red	—	—	1320.00	870.00	510.00	312.00
☐ 243	$3 Yellow Green	—	—	2575.00	1420.00	935.00	522.00
☐ 244	$4 Crimson Lake	—	—	3410.00	1725.00	1290.00	715.00
☐ 245	$5 Black	—	—	3920.00	2410.00	1460.00	895.00

1894. UNWATERMARKED (N-H ADD 95%)

Scott No.		Fine Unused Block	Ave. Unused Block	Fine Unused Each	Ave. Unused Each	Fine Used Each	Ave. Used Each
☐ 246	1¢ Ultramarine	172.00	138.00	23.00	13.00	3.60	1.95
☐ 247	1¢ Blue	395.00	290.00	55.00	32.00	1.80	1.15
☐ 248	2¢ Pink, Type I	110.00	69.00	19.00	12.00	2.50	1.50
☐ 249	2¢ Carmine Lake, Type I	730.00	565.00	117.00	74.00	1.35	.90
☐ 250	2¢ Carmine, Type I	187.00	140.00	22.00	13.00	.30	.16
☐ 251	2¢ Carmine, Type II	1430.00	1225.00	162.00	112.00	3.50	2.20
☐ 252	2¢ Carmine, Type III	563.00	392.00	83.00	49.00	3.75	2.50
☐ 253	3¢ Purple	540.00	355.00	79.00	42.00	8.00	5.35
☐ 254	4¢ Dark Brown	590.00	420.00	92.00	53.00	3.25	1.95
☐ 255	5¢ Chocolate	514.00	372.00	66.00	42.00	4.50	2.75
☐ 256	6¢ Dull Brown	1035.00	795.00	133.00	72.00	17.00	10.00
☐ 257	8¢ Violet Brown	850.00	620.00	100.00	62.00	11.00	7.50
☐ 258	10¢ Dark Green	1560.00	1140.00	183.00	117.00	8.00	4.25
☐ 259	15¢ Dark Blue	2170.00	1670.00	270.00	143.00	45.00	28.00
☐ 260	50¢ Orange	2650.00	1970.00	362.00	210.00	81.00	45.00
☐ 261	$1 Black (I)	6210.00	4875.00	912.00	561.00	229.00	115.00
☐ 261A	$1 Black (II)	—	—	1840.00	1035.00	465.00	305.00
☐ 262	$2 Blue	—	—	2315.00	1310.00	535.00	337.00
☐ 263	$5 Dark Green	—	—	3600.00	1950.00	1070.00	590.00

1895. DOUBLE LINE WATERMARKED "U.S.P.S."
PERF. 12 (N-H ADD 95%)

Scott No.		Fine Unused Block	Ave. Unused Block	Fine Unused Each	Ave. Unused Each	Fine Used Each	Ave. Used Each
☐ 264	1¢ Blue	45.00	33.00	6.50	4.50	.16	.10
☐ 265	2¢ Carmine, Type I	232.00	162.00	26.00	13.00	.90	.60
☐ 266	2¢ Carmine, Type II	282.00	207.00	27.00	15.00	3.50	2.00
☐ 267	2¢ Carmine, Type III	45.00	32.00	5.00	3.50	.13	.10
☐ 268	3¢ Purple	275.00	182.00	35.00	18.50	1.50	.70
☐ 269	4¢ Dark Brown	292.00	212.00	37.00	21.00	1.50	.75
☐ 270	5¢ Chocolate	275.00	187.00	33.00	18.00	2.00	1.30
☐ 271	6¢ Dull Brown	412.00	310.00	74.00	47.00	4.10	2.30
☐ 272	8¢ Violet Brown	232.00	145.00	32.00	17.00	1.50	.76
☐ 273	10¢ Dark Green	350.00	252.00	57.00	34.00	1.60	.80
☐ 274	15¢ Dark Blue	815.00	635.00	175.00	103.00	9.75	6.10
☐ 275	50¢ Dull Orange	1390.00	1065.00	285.00	145.00	22.00	14.00
☐ 276	$1 Black (I)	2910.00	2000.00	610.00	385.00	75.00	48.00
☐ 276A	$1 Black (II)	—	—	1270.00	820.00	125.00	80.00
☐ 277	$2 Blue	—	—	940.00	610.00	260.00	137.00
☐ 278	$5 Dark Green	—	—	1910.00	1140.00	400.00	228.00

Scott No.		Fine Unused Block	Ave. Unused Block	Fine Unused Each	Ave. Unused Each	Fine Used Each	Ave. Used Each

1898. REGULAR ISSUE PERF. (N-H ADD 95%)

Scott No.		Fine Unused Block	Ave. Unused Block	Fine Unused Each	Ave. Unused Each	Fine Used Each	Ave. Used Each
☐ 279	1¢ Deep Green	68.00	43.00	11.00	6.70	.16	.10
☐ 279B	2¢ Red	70.00	44.00	10.00	6.90	.17	.10
☐ 279C	2¢ Rose Carmine	770.00	605.00	152.00	90.00	33.00	19.00
☐ 279D	2¢ Orange Red	67.00	4200.00	11.50	7.50	.30	.17
☐ 280	4¢ Rose Brown	194.00	127.00	32.00	17.00	1.50	.70
☐ 281	5¢ Dark Blue	212.00	144.00	37.00	19.00	1.50	.70
☐ 282	6¢ Lake	347.00	238.00	47.00	27.00	2.60	1.25
☐ 282a	6¢ Purplish Lake	463.00	348.00	58.00	32.00	3.00	1.40
☐ 282C	10¢ Brown (I)	835.00	640.00	153.00	92.00	2.90	1.30
☐ 283	10¢ Orange Brown (II)	721.00	526.00	108.00	64.00	2.20	1.15
☐ 284	15¢ Olive Green	810.00	575.00	127.00	76.00	7.60	4.50

1898. TRANS-MISSISSIPPI EXPOSITION ISSUE (N-H ADD 90%)

Scott No.		Fine Unused Block	Ave. Unused Block	Fine Unused Each	Ave. Unused Each	Fine Used Each	Ave. Used Each
☐ 285	1¢ Yellow Green	233.00	142.00	33.00	15.00	6.70	4.10
☐ 286	2¢ Copper Red	225.00	126.00	31.00	15.00	2.00	1.00
☐ 287	4¢ Orange	1036.00	742.00	148.00	98.00	272.00	17.00
☐ 288	5¢ Dull Blue	1000.00	740.00	127.00	74.00	23.00	13.75
☐ 289	8¢ Violet Brown	1255.00	970.00	173.00	112.00	45.00	27.00
☐ 290	10¢ Gray Violet	1675.00	1221.00	216.00	128.00	24.00	15.00
☐ 291	50¢ Sage Green	—	—	745.00	480.00	173.00	114.00
☐ 292	$1 Black	—	—	1930.00	1190.00	615.00	414.00
☐ 293	$2 Orange Brown	—	—	3060.00	1710.00	862.00	531.00

1901. PAN-AMERICAN ISSUE (N-H ADD 75%)

Scott No.		Fine Unused Block	Ave. Unused Block	Fine Unused Each	Ave. Unused Each	Fine Used Each	Ave. Used Each
☐ 294	1¢ Green & Black	167.00	123.00	25.00	14.00	6.00	3.75
☐ 295	2¢ Carmine & Black	159.00	102.00	22.00	14.00	1.30	.76
☐ 296	4¢ Chocolate & Black	765.00	580.00	103.00	61.00	21.00	13.50
☐ 297	5¢ Ultramarine & Black	812.00	615.00	117.00	68.00	22.00	14.00
☐ 298	8¢ Brown Violet Black	1087.00	795.00	152.00	93.00	75.00	48.00
☐ 299	10¢ Yellow Brown Black	1450.00	1130.00	215.00	127.00	37.00	21.00

1902–1903. PERF. 12 (N-H ADD 80%)

Scott No.		Fine Unused Block	Ave. Unused Block	Fine Unused Each	Ave. Unused Each	Fine Used Each	Ave. Used Each
☐ 300	1¢ Blue Green	69.00	48.00	11.00	5.75	.15	.10
☐ 301	2¢ Carmine	94.00	62.00	13.00	7.75	.16	.12
☐ 302	3¢ Violet	441.00	312.00	54.00	33.00	3.75	2.00
☐ 303	4¢ Brown	490.00	340.00	57.00	35.00	1.51	.70
☐ 304	5¢ Blue	590.00	420.00	60.00	37.00	1.50	.70
☐ 305	6¢ Claret	645.00	452.00	65.00	41.00	2.80	1.65
☐ 306	8¢ Violet Black	340.00	250.00	40.00	24.00	2.70	1.40
☐ 307	10¢ Red Brown	735.00	620.00	69.00	44.00	1.75	.98
☐ 308	13¢ Purple Black	305.00	185.00	41.00	25.00	9.75	6.00
☐ 309	15¢ Olive Green	1205.00	825.00	162.00	107.00	6.15	4.50
☐ 310	50¢ Orange	4010.00	2820.00	560.00	325.00	33.00	19.00
☐ 311	$1 Black	5950.00	4740.00	890.00	515.00	65.00	43.00
☐ 312	$2 Dark Blue	—	—	1210.00	730.00	195.00	120.00
☐ 313	$5 Dark Green	—	—	2820.00	1445.00	630.00	342.00

Scott No.		Fine Unused Block	Ave. Unused Block	Fine Unused Each	Ave. Unused Each	Fine Used Each	Ave. Used Each
1906–1908. IMPERFORATED (N-H ADD 70%)							
☐ 314	1¢ Blue Green	185.00	120.00	34.00	25.00	22.00	19.00
☐ 315	5¢ Blue	4625.00	3475.00	621.00	500.00	345.00	245.00
1903. PERF. 12 (N-H ADD 50%)							
☐ 319	2¢ Carmine	63.00	44.00	8.00	5.50	.15	.10
☐ 319a	2¢ Lake	92.00	60.00	10.00	6.50	.21	.14
1906. IMPERFORATED (N-H ADD 70%)							
☐ 320	2¢ Carmine	197.00	122.00	33.00	18.00	24.00	15.00
☐ 320a	2¢ Lake	450.00	305.00	71.00	42.00	33.00	19.25
1904. LOUISIANA PURCHASE ISSUE PERF. 12 (N-H ADD 75%)							
☐ 323	1¢ Green	213.00	142.00	30.00	17.00	6.00	4.00
☐ 324	2¢ Carmine	212.00	140.00	27.00	15.00	2.00	1.50
☐ 325	3¢ Violet	585.00	415.00	87.00	48.00	32.00	20.00
☐ 326	5¢ Dark Blue	805.00	600.00	117.00	72.00	22.00	14.00
☐ 327	10¢ Red Brown	1695.00	1190.00	213.00	128.00	34.00	23.50
1907. JAMESTOWN EXPOSITION ISSUE (N-H ADD 75%)							
☐ 328	1¢ Green	246.00	170.00	24.00	14.00	5.00	2.50
☐ 329	2¢ Carmine	240.00	160.00	30.00	16.00	4.00	2.10
☐ 330	5¢ Blue	1300.00	850.00	139.00	81.00	29.00	16.50
1908–1909. DOUBLE LINE WATERMARKED "U.S.P.S." PERF. 12 (N-H ADD 50%)							
☐ 331	1¢ Green	43.00	29.00	9.00	6.00	.12	.10
☐ 332	2¢ Carmine	42.00	29.00	9.00	5.90	.12	.10
☐ 333	3¢ Violet	290.00	197.00	31.00	18.00	3.75	2.10
☐ 334	4¢ Orange Brown	270.00	173.00	32.00	18.00	1.20	.75
☐ 335	5¢ Blue	360.00	245.00	43.00	25.00	2.50	1.60
☐ 336	6¢ Red Orange	420.00	300.00	57.00	32.00	5.75	4.50
☐ 337	8¢ Olive Green	280.00	170.00	33.00	18.00	3.50	1.80
☐ 338	10¢ Yellow	465.00	345.00	69.00	42.00	1.90	1.50
☐ 339	13¢ Blue Green	390.00	245.00	40.00	24.00	32.00	22.00
☐ 340	15¢ Pale Ultramarine ..	424.00	306.00	69.00	42.00	8.00	4.50
☐ 341	50¢ Violet	1630.00	1200.00	315.00	162.00	19.00	12.00
☐ 342	$1 Violet Black	2550.00	1750.00	530.00	345.00	89.00	56.00
IMPERFORATE (N-H ADD 65%)							
☐ 343	1¢ Green	64.00	42.00	8.50	5.75	4.80	2.90
☐ 344	2¢ Carmine	106.00	72.00	12.00	6.75	4.60	2.40
☐ 345	3¢ Deep Violet	195.00	115.00	24.00	13.75	14.75	8.75
☐ 346	4¢ Orange Brown	405.00	261.00	43.00	26.00	22.00	12.75
☐ 347	5¢ Blue	476.00	332.00	63.00	39.75	35.00	22.00

Scott No.		Fine Unused Line Pair	Ave. Unused Line Pair	Fine Unused Each	Ave. Unused Each	Fine Used Each	Ave. Used Each
1908–1910 COIL STAMPS							
PERF. 12 HORIZONTALLY (N-H ADD 70%)							
☐ 348	1¢ Green	177.00	121.00	24.00	13.00	15.00	9.50
☐ 349	2¢ Carmine	200.00	142.00	53.00	33.00	8.00	5.10
☐ 350	4¢ Orange Brown	6.75	460.00	122.00	80.00	77.00	43.75
☐ 351	5¢ Blue	745.00	565.00	147.00	91.00	85.00	50.00
PERF. 12 VERTICALLY (N-H ADD 70%)							
☐ 352	1¢ Green	270.00	175.00	57.00	32.00	21.00	12.50
☐ 353	2¢ Carmine	245.00	142.00	48.00	28.00	8.50	6.00
☐ 354	4¢ Orange Brown	685.00	510.00	136.00	78.00	51.00	33.00
☐ 355	5¢ Blue	795.00	575.00	142.00	84.00	72.00	42.00
☐ 356	10¢ Yellow	—	—	1235.00	740.00	429.00	268.00

Scott No.		Fine Unused Block	Ave. Unused Block	Fine Unused Each	Ave. Unused Each	Fine Used Each	Ave. Used Each
1909. BLUISH GRAY PAPER							
PERF. 12 (N-H ADD 70%)							
☐ 357	1¢ Green	720.00	517.00	121.00	71.00	107.00	62.50
☐ 358	2¢ Carmine	705.00	490.00	116.00	64.00	82.00	51.00
☐ 359	3¢ Violet	—	—	1385.00	845.00	—	—
☐ 360	4¢ Orange Brown	—	—	9290.00	6410.00	—	—
☐ 361	5¢ Blue	—	—	3210.00	1795.00	—	—
☐ 362	6¢ Orange	—	—	960.00	610.00	—	—
☐ 363	8¢ Olive Green	—	—	1110.00	7210.00	—	—
☐ 364	10¢ Yellow	—	—	1160.00	665.00	—	—
☐ 365	13¢ Blue Green	—	—	2210.00	1235.00	—	—
☐ 366	15¢ Pale Ultramarine	—	—	980.00	610.00	—	—
1909. LINCOLN MEMORIAL ISSUE (N-H ADD 75%)							
☐ 367	2¢ Carmine	58.00	41.00	8.50	5.50	3.50	2.00
☐ 368	2¢ Carmine, Impf.	306.00	222.00	49.00	28.00	32.00	18.50
☐ 369	2¢ Carmine (On B.G. Paper)	1540.00	1235.00	285.00	176.00	198.00	117.00
1909. ALASKA-YUKON ISSUE (N-H ADD 70%)							
☐ 370	2¢ Carmine	121.00	86.00	13.00	8.00	3.00	1.50
☐ 371	2¢ Carmine. Impf.	314.00	211.00	55.00	37.00	41.00	27.50
1909. HUDSON-FULTON ISSUE (N-H ADD 70%)							
☐ 372	2¢ Carmine	106.00	73.00	15.00	9.00	5.75	3.50
☐ 373	2¢ Carmine, Impf.	422.00	286.00	61.00	41.00	36.00	21.00
1910–1911. SINGLE LINE WATERMARKED "U.S.P.S."							
PERF. 12 (N-H ADD 75%)							
☐ 374	1¢ Green	71.00	47.00	9.00	6.50	.16	.11
☐ 375	2¢ Carmine	49.00	37.00	8.00	5.60	.14	.11
☐ 376	3¢ Deep Violet	127.00	101.00	17.00	12.00	2.00	1.30
☐ 377	4¢ Brown	177.00	137.00	27.00	15.00	.65	.42

Scott No.		Fine Unused Block	Ave. Unused Block	Fine Unused Each	Ave. Unused Each	Fine Used Each	Ave. Used Each
☐ 378	5¢ Blue	212.00	155.00	29.00	16.00	.62	.43
☐ 379	6¢ Red Orange	321.00	216.00	37.00	22.00	.95	.60
☐ 380	8¢ Olive Green	692.00	517.00	117.00	72.00	14.00	9.75
☐ 381	10¢ Yellow	643.00	495.00	112.00	67.00	5.00	3.25
☐ 382	15¢ Ultramarine	1502.00	1160.00	260.00	150.00	15.00	11.00

IMPERFORATE (N-H ADD 70%)

☐ 383	1¢ Green	30.00	19.00	5.00	2.75	3.75	2.10
☐ 384	2¢ Carmine	53.00	38.00	7.50	4.50	2.00	1.50

Scott No.		Fine Unused Line Pair	Ave. Unused Line Pair	Fine Unused Each	Ave. Unused Each	Fine Used Each	Ave. Used Each

1910–1913. COIL STAMPS
PERF. 12 HORIZONTALLY (N-H ADD 70%)

☐ 385	1¢ Green	180.00	104.00	25.00	14.50	15.00	9.50
☐ 386	2¢ Carmine	272.00	161.00	35.00	20.00	13.00	8.50

PERF. 12 VERTICALLY (N-H ADD 70%)

☐ 387	1¢ Green	310.00	172.00	76.00	43.00	24.00	14.00
☐ 388	2¢ Carmine	3060.00	2250.00	550.00	370.00	106.00	60.00

PERF. 8½ HORIZONTALLY (N-H ADD 70%)

☐ 390	1¢ Green	30.00	20.00	6.00	3.75	4.50	2.70
☐ 391	2¢ Carmine	214.00	137.00	36.00	20.00	9.20	6.25

PERF. 8½ VERTICALLY (N-H ADD 70%)

☐ 392	1¢ Green	104.00	67.00	21.00	14.00	17.00	12.50
☐ 393	2¢ Carmine	197.00	128.00	46.00	34.00	32.00	18.00
☐ 394	3¢ Violet	340.00	216.00	51.00	34.00	32.00	18.00
☐ 395	4¢ Brown	335.00	216.00	51.00	34.00	32.00	18.00
☐ 396	5¢ Blue	375.00	242.00	56.00	36.00	33.00	18.00

Scott No.		Fine Unused Block	Ave. Unused Block	Fine Unused Each	Ave. Unused Each	Fine Used Each	Ave. Used Each

1913–1915. PANAMA-PACIFIC ISSUE
PERF. 12 (N-H ADD 80%)

☐ 397	1¢ Green	123.00	82.00	21.00	14.00	2.00	1.20
☐ 398	2¢ Carmine	176.00	117.00	23.00	16.00	81.00	.60
☐ 399	5¢ Blue	640.00	460.00	87.00	60.00	12.00	7.75
☐ 400	10¢ Orange Yellow	985.00	730.00	152.00	97.00	29.00	17.50
☐ 400A	10¢ Orange	1610.00	1190.00	247.00	147.00	20.00	12.50

PERF. 10 (N-H ADD 80%)

☐ 401	1¢ Green	221.00	160.00	32.00	20.00	8.00	4.80
☐ 402	2¢ Carmine	535.00	370.00	92.00	53.00	2.10	1.25
☐ 403	5¢ Blue	1810.00	1340.00	226.00	132.00	21.00	12.20
☐ 404	10¢ Orange	7010.00	4775.00	1360.00	860.00	83.00	51.00

Scott No.		Fine Unused Block	Ave. Unused Block	Fine Unused Each	Ave. Unused Each	Fine Used Each	Ave. Used Each

1912–1914. REGULAR ISSUE
PERF. 12 (N-H ADD 70%)

☐ 405	1¢ Green	55.00	42.00	8.00	5.60	.17	.09
☐ 406	2¢ Carmine	84.00	60.00	7.20	4.90	.17	.10
☐ 407	7¢ Black	512.00	386.00	100.00	65.00	7.90	5.60

IMPERFORATE (N-H ADD 70%)

| ☐ 408 | 1¢ Green . . . . | 14.00 | 11.00 | 2.00 | 1.25 | .75 | .55 |
| ☐ 409 | 2¢ Carmine . . . . | 17.00 | 13.00 | 2.10 | 1.30 | .84 | .60 |

Scott No.		Fine Unused Line Pair	Ave. Unused Line Pair	Fine Unused Each	Ave. Unused Each	Fine Used Each	Ave. Used Each

1912. COIL STAMPS
PERF. 8½ HORIZONTALLY (N-H ADD 70%)

| ☐ 410 | 1¢ Green . . . . | 66.00 | 44.00 | 7.50 | 5.75 | 4.00 | 2.60 |
| ☐ 411 | 2¢ Carmine . . . . | 73.00 | 51.00 | 9.50 | 7.00 | 4.00 | 2.75 |

PERF. 8½ VERTICALLY (N-H ADD 80%)

| ☐ 412 | 1¢ Green . . . . | 111.00 | 75.00 | 22.00 | 13.50 | 6.10 | 4.20 |
| ☐ 413 | 2¢ Carmine . . . . | 174.00 | 126.00 | 34.00 | 20.00 | .90 | .60 |

Scott No.		Fine Unused Block	Ave. Unused Block	Fine Unused Each	Ave. Unused Each	Fine Used Each	Ave. Used Each

1912–1914. SINGLE LINE WATERMARKED "U.S.P.S."
PERRF. 12 (N-H ADD 75%)

☐ 414	8¢ Olive Green	226.00	153.00	37.00	24.00	1.90	1.20
☐ 415	9¢ Salmon Red	295.00	196.00	49.00	32.00	14.00	9.10
☐ 416	10¢ Orange Yellow	280.00	187.00	38.00	24.00	41.00	.27
☐ 417							
☐ 12¢	Claret Brown	320.00	216.00	39.00	25.00	4.21	3.10
☐ 418	15¢ Gray	540.00	4.00	76.00	51.00	3.80	3.00
☐ 419	20¢ Ultramarine	1210.00	830.00	166.00	111.00	15.00	8.60
☐ 420	30¢ Orange Red	950.00	730.00	116.00	72.00	16.00	8.70
☐ 421	50¢ Violet	2910.00	2050.00	542.00	330.00	15.00	8.70

1912. DOUBLE LINE WATERMARKED "U.S.P.S."
(N-H ADD 75%)

| ☐ 422 | 50¢ Violet . . . . | 1840.00 | 1400.00 | 272.00 | 152.00 | 16.00 | 11.00 |
| ☐ 423 | $1 Violet Black . . . . | 3410.00 | 2455.00 | 575.00 | 360.00 | 77.00 | 48.00 |

1914–1915. SINGLE LINE WATERMARKED "U.S.P.S."
PERF. 10 (N-H ADD 55%)

☐ 424	1¢ Green	39.00	29.00	4.00	2.10	.16	.11
☐ 425	2¢ Carmine	25.00	16.00	4.00	2.00	.17	.12
☐ 426	3¢ Deep Violet	1.50	65.00	12.50	9.00	1.90	1.25
☐ 427	4¢ Brown	217.00	142.00	34.00	19.00	.65	.40
☐ 428	5¢ Blue	211.00	127.00	30.00	16.00	.62	.42
☐ 429	6¢ Orange	271.00	172.00	43.00	24.00	1.55	.93

Scott No.		Fine Unused Block	Ave. Unused Block	Fine Unused Each	Ave. Unused Each	Fine Used Each	Ave. Used Each
☐ 430	7¢ Black	481.00	336.00	92.00	57.00	5.60	4.00
☐ 431	8¢ Olive Green	267.00	177.00	37.00	21.00	2.00	1.20
☐ 432	9¢ Salmon Red	447.00	316.00	47.00	25.00	11.00	6.50
☐ 433	12¢ Orange Yellow	337.00	226.00	45.00	25.00	.40	.25
☐ 434	11¢ Dark Green	168.00	112.00	22.00	12.00	6.50	4.10
☐ 435	12¢ Claret Brown	190.00	137.00	25.00	13.00	4.50	2.30
☐ 435a	12¢ Copper Red	221.00	151.00	29.00	15.00	5.00	3.00
☐ 437	15¢ Gray	830.00	611.00	117.00	62.00	7.00	4.20
☐ 438	20¢ Ultramarine	1200.00	910.00	212.00	119.00	4.50	2.50
☐ 439	30¢ Orange Red	1330.00	1000.00	270.00	142.00	14.00	8.50
☐ 440	50¢ Violet	4050.00	2940.00	730.00	480.00	19.00	11.50

Scott No.		Fine Unused Line Pair	Ave. Unused Line Pair	Fine Unused Each	Ave. Unused Each	Fine Used Each	Ave. Used Each
1914. COIL STAMPS							
PERF. 10 HORIZONTALLY (N-H ADD 75%)							
☐ 441	1¢ Green	8.50	6.00	1.20	.75	1.20	.67
☐ 442	2¢ Carmine	48.00	33.00	12.00	8.00	9.00	6.20
PERF. 10 VERTICALLY (N-H ADD 70%)							
☐ 443	1¢ Green	98.00	64.00	25.00	14.00	6.10	3.75
☐ 444	2¢ Carmine	154.00	111.00	37.00	21.00	1.60	1.10
☐ 445	3¢ Violet	1360.00	1100.00	241.00	123.00	122.00	80.50
☐ 446	4¢ Brown	585.00	415.00	162.00	94.00	40.00	26.00
☐ 447	5¢ Blue	217.00	128.00	43.00	28.00	26.00	16.00
1914–1916. ROTARY PRESS COIL STAMPS							
PERF. 10 HORIZONTALLY (N-H ADD 70%)							
☐ 448	1¢ Green	47.00	31.00	8.00	5.00	3.50	2.30
☐ 449	2¢ Red (I)	—	—	1495.00	1065.00	142.00	94.00
☐ 450	2¢ Carmine (III)	82.00	53.00	14.00	9.00	3.40	2.40
PERF. 10 VERTICALLY (N-H ADD 70%)							
☐ 452	1¢ Green	80.00	53.00	9.75	6.50	2.00	1.50
☐ 453	2¢ Red (I)	705.00	516.00	132.00	82.00	4.50	3.00
☐ 454	2¢ Carmine (II)	745.00	561.00	137.00	84.00	15.00	9.00
☐ 455	2¢ Carmine (III)	92.00	62.00	14.00	8.00	1.50	.75
☐ 456	3¢ Violet	1111.00	831.00	260.00	136.00	108.00	69.00
☐ 457	4¢ Brown	128.00	94.00	35.00	23.00	18.00	12.00
☐ 458	5¢ Blue	132.00	98.00	37.00	24.00	18.50	13.00
IMPERFORATE (N-H ADD 60%)							
☐ 459	2¢ Carmine	2196.00	1480.00	480.00	320.00	—	—

Scott No.		Fine Unused Block	Ave. Unused Block	Fine Unused Each	Ave. Unused Each	Fine Used Each	Ave. Used Each

1915. DOUBLE LINE WATERMARKED "U.S.P.S." PERF. 10 (N-H ADD 60%)

| ☐ 460 | $1 Violet Black .... | 4210.00 | 4000.00 | 870.00 | 605.00 | 92.00 | 60.00 |

1915. SINGLE LINE WATERMARKED "U.S. P.S." PERF. 11 (N.H. ADD 60%)

| ☐ 461 | 2¢ Pale Carmine Rose ... | 341.00 | 95.00 | 63.00 | 84.00 | 53.00 | — |

1916–1917. UNWATERMARKED PERF. 10 (N-H ADD 70%)

☐ 462	1¢ Green	89.00	55.00	7.60	5.75	.40	.24
☐ 463	2¢ Carmine	39.00	27.00	5.00	3.10	.20	.15
☐ 464	3¢ Violet	452.00	311.00	86.00	58.00	17.00	11.00
☐ 465	4¢ Orange Brown	380.00	265.00	54.00	34.00	2.50	1.30
☐ 466	5¢ Blue	440.00	300.00	81.00	50.00	2.20	1.30
☐ 467	5¢ Carmine (error)	—	785.00	541.00	560.00	—	—
☐ 468	6¢ Red Orange	500.00	360.00	90.00	60.00	7.60	5.50
☐ 469	7¢ Black	615.00	485.00	121.00	69.00	15.50	9.00
☐ 470	.58¢ Olive Green	385.00	295.00	54.00	34.00	5.80	3.60
☐ 471	9¢ Salmon Red	355.00	245.00	57.00	35.00	14.90	9.60
☐ 472	12¢ Orange Yellow	625.00	465.00	111.00	72.00	1.30	.67
☐ 473	11¢ Dark Green	205.00	140.00	32.00	20.00	16.10	11.50
☐ 474	12¢ Claret Brown	360.00	230.00	51.00	31.00	6.60	4.60
☐ 475	15¢ Gray	1115.00	851.00	177.00	121.00	12.75	8.10
☐ 476	20¢ Ultramarine	2410.00	1810.00	310.00	176.00	12.80	8.70
☐ 477	50¢ Light Violet	6310.00	4700.00	1360.00	973.00	82.00	51.00
☐ 478	$1 Violet Black	4305.00	2905.00	840.00	642.00	19.00	12.50

1916–1917. DESIGN OF 1902–03 PERF. 10 (N-H ADD 70%)

| ☐ 479 | $2 Dark Blue .... | 2610.00 | 1852.00 | 550.00 | 331.00 | 45.00 | 28.00 |
| ☐ 480 | $5 Light Green .... | 2311.00 | 1710.00 | 435.00 | 251.00 | 51.00 | 32.00 |

IMPERFORATE (N-H ADD 70%)

☐ 481	1¢ Green	11.50	7.50	1.30	.94	1.50	.82
☐ 482	2¢ Carmine	21.00	16.00	2.00	1.15	1.95	1.15
☐ 483	3¢ Violet (I)	121.00	124.00	21.00	14.00	9.50	6.28
☐ 484	3¢ Violet (II)	78.00	53.00	15.00	9.10	4.80	3.12

Scott No.		Fine Unused Line Pair	Ave. Unused Line Pair	Fine Unused Each	Ave. Unused Each	Fine Used Each	Ave. Used Each

1916–1922. ROTARY PRESS COIL STAMPS PERF. 10 HORIZONTALLY (N-H ADD 60%)

☐ 486	1¢ Green	5.30	4.10	1.15	.65	.24	.16
☐ 487	2¢ Carmine (II)	154.00	117.00	22.00	13.00	3.75	2.60
☐ 488	2¢ Carmine (III)	27.50	19.00	4.30	2.85	1.90	1.10
☐ 489	3¢ Violet	34.00	19.00	5.60	3.50	136.00	.87

Scott No.		Fine Unused Line Pair	Ave. Unused Line Pair	Fine Unused Each	Ave. Unused Each	Fine Used Each	Ave. Used Each
PERF. 10 VERTICALLY (N-H ADD 60%)							
☐ 490	1¢ Green	6.60	4.50	.78	.50	.24	.15
☐ 491	2¢ Carmine (II)	—	—	1150.00	880.00	189.00	124.00
☐ 492	2¢ Carmine (III)	63.00	42.00	12.00	7.00	.25	.17
☐ 493	3¢ Violet (I)	125.00	80.00	25.00	17.00	3.00	1.65
☐ 494	3¢ Violet (II)	94.00	60.00	15.00	9.00	.90	.55
☐ 495	4¢ Orange Brown	99.00	63.00	13.00	8.00	3.90	2.25
☐ 496	5¢ Blue	35.00	23.00	5.00	2.75	1.00	.55
☐ 497	10¢ Orange Yellow	161.00	111.00	26.00	17.00	13.00	7.60

Scott No.		Fine Unused Block	Ave. Unused Block	Fine Unused Each	Ave. Unused Each	Fine Used Each	Ave. Used Each
1917–1919. FLAT PLATE PRINTING							
PERF. 11 (N-H ADD 60%)							
☐ 498	1¢ Green	7.80	6.50	.55	.40	.17	.11
☐ 499	2¢ Rose (I)	8.50	6.75	.60	.40	.16	.11
☐ 500	2¢ Deep Rose (Ia)	1710.00	1200.00	285.00	155.00	121.00	71.00
☐ 501	3¢ Violet (I)	125.00	83.00	15.00	10.00	.17	.16
☐ 502	3¢ Violet (II)	133.00	99.00	20.00	13.00	.40	.24
☐ 503	4¢ Brown	114.00	73.00	15.00	9.00	.27	.20
☐ 504	5¢ Blue	84.00	58.00	11.00	7.00	.21	.15
☐ 505	5¢ Rose (error)	—	—	525.00	310.00	—	—
☐ 506	6¢ Red Orange	126.00	88.00	16.00	9.10	.40	.24
☐ 507	7¢ Black	206.00	137.00	35.00	20.00	1.50	.95
☐ 508	8¢ Olive Bistre	121.00	86.00	14.00	8.20	.95	.62
☐ 509	9¢ Salmon Red	151.00	97.00	17.00	11.00	2.70	1.45
☐ 510	10¢ Orange Yellow	172.00	112.00	20.00	11.00	.18	.12
☐ 511	11¢ Light Green	86.00	60.00	12.00	7.50	3.80	2.25
☐ 512	12¢ Claret Brown	79.00	53.00	13.00	8.00	.67	.40
☐ 513	13¢ Apple Green	87.00	61.00	14.00	8.00	7.20	5.15
☐ 514	15¢ Gray	391.00	261.00	50.00	30.00	1.25	.75
☐ 515	20¢ Ultramarine	521.00	382.00	62.00	36.40	.35	.22
☐ 516	30¢ Orange Red	411.00	311.00	55.00	33.00	1.25	.76
☐ 517	50¢ Red Violet	631.00	451.00	114.00	62.00	.95	.62
☐ 518	$1 Violet Brown	826.00	611.00	97.00	57.00	1.90	1.03
☐ 518b	$1 Deep Brown	3060.00	2410.00	633.00	421.00	191.00	121.00
1917. DOUBLE LINE WATERMARKED "U.S.P.S."							
DESIGN OF 1908–1909							
PERF. 11 (N-H ADD 60%)							
☐ 519	2¢ Carmine	1405.00	1136.00	242.00	151.00	237.00	145.00
1918. UNWATERMARKED							
PERF. 11 (N-H ADD 55%)							
☐ 523	$2 Orange Red & Black	8105.00	6010.00	1190.00	1120.00	205.00	112.00
☐ 524	$5 Deep Green & Black	3115.00	2221.00	451.00	362.00	28.00	17.00

Scott No.		Fine Unused Block	Ave. Unused Block	Fine Unused Each	Ave. Unused Each	Fine Used Each	Ave. Used Each

1918–1920. OFFSET PRINTING
PERF. 11 (N-H ADD 60%)

		Fine Unused Block	Ave. Unused Block	Fine Unused Each	Ave. Unused Each	Fine Used Each	Ave. Used Each
☐ 525	1¢ Gray Green	22.00	12.00	2.60	1.75	.80	.50
☐ 526	2¢ Carmine (IV)	214.00	152.00	32.00	22.00	4.60	2.85
☐ 527	2¢ Carmine (V)	135.00	106.00	19.00	12.00	1.11	.62
☐ 528	2¢ Carmine (Va)	55.00	39.00	10.00	5.75	.24	.17
☐ 528A	2¢ Carmine (VI)	280.00	210.00	50.00	28.00	1.17	.72
☐ 528B	2¢ Carmine (VII)	151.00	111.00	22.00	13.00	.17	.13
☐ 529	3¢ Violet (III)	32.00	23.00	2.90	1.72	.22	.17
☐ 530	3¢ Purple (IV)	12.00	6.60	1.25	.73	.15	.10

IMPERFORATE (N-H ADD 60%)

☐ 531	1¢ Gray Green	76.00	55.00	13.00	8.00	11.00	8.00
☐ 532	2¢ Carmine (IV)	283.00	192.00	52.00	34.00	33.00	21.00
☐ 533	2¢ Carmine (V)	1510.00	1110.00	260.00	161.00	76.00	52.00
☐ 534	2¢ Carmine (Va)	112.00	71.00	19.00	13.00	12.00	8.00
☐ 534A	2¢ Carmine (VI)	242.00	172.00	44.00	28.00	32.00	19.00
☐ 534B	2¢ Carmine (VII)	—	—	1710.00	1035.00	410.00	272.00
☐ 535	3¢ Violet	69.00	50.00	13.00	9.00	8.00	6.00

PERF. 12½ (N-H ADD 65%)

☐ 536	1¢ Gray Green	121.00	89.00	17.00	11.00	15.00	8.50

IMPORTANT NOTICE: Beginning here, prices of **blocks** are for blocks of 4 with **plate number attached.** Ordinary blocks of 4 bring lower prices. Plate blocks consisting of more than 4 stamps would sell higher than these sums. Always check the **headings** of price columns to accurately value your stamps.

Scott No.		Fine Unused Plate Blk	Ave. Unused Plate Blk	Fine Unused Each	Ave. Unused Each	Fine Used Each	Ave. Used Each

1919. VICTORY ISSUE (N-H ADD 45%)

☐ 537	3¢ Violet	221.00	142.00	12.00	8.00	5.00	2.75

1919–1921. REGULAR ISSUE
ROTARY PRESS PRINTING
PERF. 11 x 10 (N-H ADD 70%)

☐ 538	1¢ Green	107.00	76.00	11.00	7.00	9.75	6.75
☐ 538a	Same Impf. Horiz. Pair	—	—	60.00	37.00	—	—
☐ 539	2¢ Carmine Rose (II)	—	—	2210.00	1295.00	690.00	415.00
☐ 540	2¢ Carmine Rose (III)	105.00	72.00	12.00	7.75	9.50	6.75
☐ 540a	Same Impf. Horiz. Pair	—	—	64.00	40.00	—	—
☐ 541	3¢ Violet	392.00	273.00	45.00	29.00	40.00	25.00

PERF. 10 x 11 (N-H ADD 70%)

☐ 542	1¢ Green	116.00	78.00	7.00	6.00	1.20	.86

PERF. 10 x 10 (N-H ADD 70%)

☐ 543	1¢ Green	17.75	12.00	.80	.67	.17	.12

Scott No.		Fine Unused Plate Blk	Ave. Unused Plate Blk	Fine Unused Each	Ave. Unused Each	Fine Used Each	Ave. Used Each
PERF. 11 x 11 (N-H ADD 70%)							
☐544	1¢ Green	—	—	—	—	1580.00	1036.00
☐545	1¢ Green	910.00	710.00	162.00	118.00	97.00	62.00
☐546	2¢ Carmine Rose	560.00	425.00	94.00	75.00	66.00	43.00
FLAT PLATE PRINTING							
PERF. 11 (N-H ADD 60%)							
☐547	$2 Carmine & Black	—	—	405.00	242.00	38.00	25.00
1920. PILGRIM ISSUE (N-H ADD 55%)							
☐548	1¢ Green	60.00	45.00	7.00	4.50	3.50	1.95
☐549	2¢ Carmine Rose	89.00	67.00	11.00	7.00	2.60	1.60
☐550	5¢ Deep Blue	772.00	545.00	55.00	36.00	22.00	12.75
1922–1925 PERF. FLAT PLATE PRINTING							
PERF. 11 (N-H ADD 55%)							
☐551	½¢ Olive Brown	12.00	8.60	17.10	11.50	15.00	.10
☐552	1¢ Deep Green	34.00	21.00	3.00	1.60	.15	.10
☐553	1½¢ Yellow Brown	49.00	34.00	4.75	3.10	.35	.20
☐554	2¢ Carmine	47.00	32.00	1.90	1.10	.12	.08
☐555	3¢ Violet	27.00	184.00	24.00	15.00	1.34	.83
☐556	4¢ Yellow Brown	276.00	197.00	25.00	15.00	.25	.16
☐557	5¢ Dark Blue	296.00	211.00	23.00	14.00	.18	.13
☐558	6¢ Red Orange	565.00	411.00	41.00	25.00	.98	.63
☐559	7¢ Black	110.00	80.00	11.00	6.50	.95	.57
☐560	8¢ Olive Green	8.90	700.00	47.00	31.00	1.00	.63
☐561	9¢ Rose	216.00	151.00	18.00	12.00	1.50	.80
☐562	10¢ Orange	392.00	281.00	24.00	15.00	.20	.14
☐563	11¢ Blue	47.50	32.00	2.50	1.40	.40	.25
☐564	12¢ Brown Violet	116.00	84.00	9.00	6.00	.19	.15
☐565	14¢ Dark Blue	88.00	70.00	7.00	4.50	1.00	.64
☐566	15¢ Gray	316.00	221.00	25.00	14.00	.17	.13
☐567	20¢ Carmine Rose	316.00	221.00	30.00	17.00	.14	.09
☐568	25¢ Green	312.00	221.00	30.00	16.00	.66	.41
☐569	30¢ Olive Brown	532.00	391.00	42.00	24.00	.50	.32
☐570	50¢ Lilac	10.75	791.00	72.00	51.00	.25	.17
☐571	$1 Violet Black	611.00	421.00	59.00	39.00	.47	.30
☐572	$2 Deep Blue	1610.00	1210.00	161.00	97.00	11.20	7.95
☐573	$5 Carmine & Blue	9245.00	6015.00	367.00	226.00	19.40	12.50
IMPERFORATE (N-H ADD 45%)							
☐575	1¢ Green	154.00	121.00	12.00	7.20	5.20	3.25
☐576	1½¢ Yellow Brown	33.00	22.00	2.75	1.50	2.00	1.25
☐577	2¢ Carmine	36.00	24.00	2.75	1.60	2.00	1.50
1923–1926. ROTARY PRESS PRINTING							
PERF. 11 x 10 (N-H ADD 55%)							
☐578	1¢ Green	785.00	610.00	78.00	53.00	73.00	45.00
☐579	2¢ Carmine	440.00	310.00	54.00	36.00	45.00	29.00

Scott No.		Fine Unused Plate Blk	Ave. Unused Plate Blk	Fine Unused Each	Ave. Unused Each	Fine Used Each	Ave. Used Each
PERF. 10 (N-H ADD 55%)							
☐ 581	1¢ Green	122.00	84.00	8.00	4.50	1.20	.70
☐ 582	1½¢ Brown	56.00	33.00	4.75	3.00	.95	.63
☐ 583	2¢ Carmine	32.00	20.00	2.50	1.60	.16	.09
☐ 584	3¢ Violet	305.00	215.00	30.00	18.00	2.40	1.20
☐ 585	4¢ Yellow Brown	223.00	142.00	16.00	9.75	.60	.33
☐ 586	5¢ Blue	187.00	122.00	14.10	8.60	.35	.24
☐ 587	6¢ Red Orange	84.00	62.00	9.10	6.00	.65	.42
☐ 588	7¢ Black	107.00	73.00	12.00	7.50	6.10	4.10
☐ 589	8¢ Olive Green	305.00	211.00	32.00	18.75	3.85	2.20
☐ 590	9¢ Rose	60.00	39.00	6.00	4.10	2.85	1.45
☐ 591	10¢ Orange	755.00	521.00	69.00	44.00	.17	.11
PERF. 11							
☐ 595	2¢ Carmine	1630.00	1200.00	185.00	120.00	165.00	110.00

Scott No.		Fine Unused Line Pair	Ave. Unused Line Pair	Fine Unused Each	Ave. Unused Each	Fine Used Each	Ave. Used Each
1923–1929. ROTARY PRESS COIL STAMPS							
PERF. 10 VERTICALLY (N-H ADD 55%)							
☐ 597	1¢ Green	3.70	2.60	.50	.26	.13	.11
☐ 598	1½¢ Deep Brown	7.60	5.30	.73	.45	.20	.15
☐ 599	2¢ Carmine (I)	2.60	1.70	.40	.24	.13	.09
☐ 599A	2¢ Carmine (II)	722.00	531.00	136.00	81.00	13.00	7.60
☐ 600	3¢ Deep Violet	56.00	37.00	8.70	5.50	.15	.13
☐ 601	4¢ Yellow Brown	58.00	38.00	6.00	3.00	.61	.42
☐ 602	5¢ Dark Blue	15.00	11.00	1.70	.96	.23	.15
☐ 603	10¢ Orange	29.00	19.00	4.30	2.70	.17	.12
PERF. 10 HORIZONTALLY (N-H ADD 55%)							
☐ 604	1¢ Green	5.15	3.50	.28	.17	.14	.10
☐ 605	1½¢ Yellow Brown	3.75	2.40	.29	.17	.20	.14
☐ 606	2¢ Carmine	2.75	1.85	.31	.20	.15	.11

Scott No.		Fine Unused Plate Blk	Ave. Unused Plate Blk	Fine Unused Each	Ave. Unused Each	Fine Used Each	Ave. Used Each
1923. HARDING MEMORIAL ISSUE (N-H ADD 45%)							
☐ 610	2¢ Black, pf. 11	37.00	25.00	1.20	.65	.16	.10
☐ 611	2¢ Black, imperf.	184.00	132.00	13.00	9.00	6.20	4.25
☐ 612	2¢ Black, pf. 10 rotary ...	492.00	376.00	23.00	14.00	2.70	1.30
1924. HUGUENOT-WALLOON ISSUE (N-H ADD 45%)							
☐ 614	1¢ Green	84.00	62.00	6.00	3.30	4.50	2.78
☐ 615	2¢ Carmine Rose	112.00	78.00	8.00	6.00	3.20	1.84
☐ 616	5¢ Dark Blue	515.00	371.00	47.00	28.00	22.00	13.65

Scott No.		Fine Unused Plate Blk	Ave. Unused Plate Blk	Fine Unused Each	Ave. Unused Each	Fine Used Each	Ave. Used Each

1925. LEXINGTON-CONCORD SESQUICENTENNIAL (N-H ADD 45%)

☐ 617	1¢ Green	82.00	55.00	5.75	3.50	4.70	3.20
☐ 618	2¢ Carmine Rose	141.00	98.00	9.10	6.60	6.10	4.10
☐ 619	5¢ Dark Blue	527.00	386.00	45.00	30.00	22.00	13.75

1925. NORSE-AMERICAN ISSUE (N-H ADD 40%)

| ☐ 620 | 2¢ Carmine & Black | 182.00 | 117.00 | 7.50 | 4.70 | 5.00 | 3.25 |
| ☐ 621 | 5¢ Dark Blue & Black | 831.00 | 650.00 | 23.00 | 14.00 | 22.00 | 12.50 |

1925–1926

| ☐ 622 | 13¢ Green | 205.00 | 126.00 | 19.00 | 12.00 | .82 | .55 |
| ☐ 623 | 17¢ Black | 227.00 | 163.00 | 22.00 | 14.00 | .42 | .27 |

1926–1927. COMMEMORATIVES

1926. SESQUICENTENNIAL EXPOSITION (N-H ADD 50%)

| ☐ 627 | 2¢ Carmine Rose | 64.00 | 42.00 | 4.40 | 2.90 | .75 | .50 |

1926. ERICSSON MEMORIAL ISSUE (N-H ADD 50%)

| ☐ 628 | 5¢ Gray Lilac | 134.00 | 100.00 | 12.00 | 7.20 | 5.00 | 2.90 |

1926. BATTLE OF WHITE PLAINS (N-H ADD 45%)

| ☐ 629 | 2¢ Carmine Rose | — | 62.00 | 3.50 | 2.10 | 2.30 | 1.40 |
| ☐ 630 | 2¢ Souv. Sheet of 25 | — | 462.00 | 360.00 | — | — | |

1926–1928. DESIGNS OF 1922–1925
ROTARY PRESS PRINTING IMPERFORATE (N-H ADD 40%)

| ☐ 631 | 1½¢ Brown | 94.00 | 64.00 | 2.90 | 2.00 | 2.30 | 1.50 |

PERF. 11 x 10½ (N-H ADD 50%)

☐ 632	1¢ Green	3.40	2.12	.18	.13	.14	.09
☐ 633	1½¢ Yellow Brown	120.00	83.00	3.40	1.96	.16	.10
☐ 634	2¢ Carmine (I)	2.30	1.50	.18	.11	.12	.08
☐ 634A	2¢ Carmine (II)	—	—	371.00	271.00	17.00	11.00
☐ 635	3¢ Violet	7.00	5.00	.63	.41	.12	.09
☐ 636	4¢ Yellow Brown	122.00	87.00	4.00	2.40	.18	.13
☐ 637	5¢ Dark Blue	29.00	18.00	3.40	2.40	.12	.09
☐ 638	6¢ Red Orange	32.00	20.00	4.50	2.40	.12	.09
☐ 639	7¢ Black	29.00	18.00	3.70	2.40	.14	.09
☐ 640	8¢ Olive Green	30.00	19.00	4.00	2.40	.11	.08
☐ 641	9¢ Orange Red	32.00	22.00	3.70	2.40	.12	.08
☐ 642	10¢ Orange	54.00	35.00	7.00	3.70	.12	.08

1927. VERMONT SESQUICENTENNIAL (N.H ADD 45%)

| ☐ 643 | 2¢ Carmine Rose | 69.00 | 49.00 | 2.15 | 1.50 | 1.40 | 1.10 |

1927. BURGOYNE CAMPAIGN ISSUE (N.H ADD 45%)

| ☐ 644 | 2¢ Carmine | 73.00 | 52.00 | 5.00 | 3.20 | 3.80 | 2.70 |

1928. VALLEY FORGE ISSUE (N.H ADD 45%)

| ☐ 645 | 2¢ Carmine | 62.00 | 44.00 | 1.30 | .90 | .68 | .43 |

1928. BATTLE OF MONMOUTH (N.H ADD 45%)

| ☐ 646 | 2¢ Carmine | 71.00 | 51.00 | 1.60 | 1.10 | 1.34 | .92 |

Scott No.	Fine Unused Plate Blk	Ave. Unused Plate Blk	Fine Unused Each	Ave. Unused Each	Fine Used Each	Ave. Used Each
1928. DISCOVERY OF HAWAII (N.H ADD 45%)						
☐ 647　2¢ Carmine Rose	230.00	142.00	6.10	4.10	5.00	3.30
☐ 648　5¢ Blue	530.00	390.00	20.00	12.00	20.00	14.00
1928. AERONAUTICS CONFERENCE (N.H ADD 40%)						
☐ 649　2¢ Carmine	25.00	16.00	1.50	.92	1.30	1.00
☐ 650　5¢ Blue	102.00	65.00	7.10	5.00	4.80	3.30
1929. GEORGE ROGERS CLARK (N.H ADD 40%)						
☐ 651　2¢ Carmine & Black	17.00	12.00	.89	.63	.84	.63
1929. DESIGNS OF 1922–1925						
ROTARY PRESS PRINTING—PERF. 11 x 10½ (N.H ADD 40%)						
☐ 653　½¢ Olive Brown	2.30	1.40	.13	.10	.13	.10
1929. EDISON COMMEMORATIVE						
FLAT PLATE PRINTING—PERF. 11 (N.H ADD 40%)						
☐ 654　2¢ Carmine Rose	49.00	32.00	.96	.65	1.25	.90
ROTARY PRESS PRINTING—PERF. 11 x 10½ (N.H ADD 40%)						
☐ 655　2¢ Carmine Rose	90.00	54.00	.93	.70	.40	.27

Scott No.	Fine Unused Line Pair	Ave. Unused Line Pair	Fine Unused Each	Ave. Unused Each	Fine Used Each	Ave. Used Each
ROTARY PRESS COIL STAMPS—PERF. 10 VERTICALLY (N-H ADD 40%)						
☐ 656　2¢ Carmine Rose	92.00	60.00	16.00	10.00	2.60	1.70

Scott No.	Fine Unused Plate Blk	Ave. Unused Plate Blk	Fine Unused Each	Ave. Unused Each	Fine Used Each	Ave. Used Each
1929. SULLIVAN EXPEDITION (N-H ADD 40%)						
☐ 657　2¢ Carmine Rose	32.00	19.00	1.10	.72	.90	.70
1929. 632–42 OVERPRINTED (KANS.) (N-H ADD 45%)						
☐ 658　1¢ Green	41.00	23.00	2.50	1.70	2.20	1.40
☐ 659　1½¢ Brown	49.00	30.00	4.00	2.60	4.20	3.10
☐ 660　2¢ Carmine	58.00	40.00	3.70	2.40	.90	.60
☐ 661　3¢ Violet	202.00	131.00	21.00	13.00	14.00	8.70
☐ 662　4¢ Yellow Brown	217.00	160.00	24.00	17.00	8.60	6.10
☐ 663　5¢ Deep Blue	174.00	116.00	15.00	11.00	12.00	7.60
☐ 664　6¢ Red Orange	467.00	331.00	28.00	17.00	18.00	12.00
☐ 665　7¢ Black	463.00	326.00	31.00	19.00	25.00	16.00
☐ 666　8¢ Olive Green	812.00	611.00	90.00	61.00	69.50	45.00
☐ 667　9¢ Light Rose	221.00	160.00	15.50	12.00	12.00	9.10
☐ 668　10¢ Orange Yellow	362.00	255.00	24.00	17.00	11.00	7.30
1929. 632–42 OVERPRINTED (NEBR.) (N-H ADD 45%)						
☐ 669　1¢ Green	37.00	24.00	2.50	1.70	2.30	1.50
☐ 670　1½¢ Brown	60.00	37.00	3.30	2.20	2.80	1.80

Scott No.		Fine Unused Plate Blk	Ave. Unused Plate Blk	Fine Unused Each	Ave. Unused Each	Fine Used Each	Ave. Used Each
☐ 671	2¢ Carmine	43.00	29.00	2.30	1.60	.95	.70
☐ 672	3¢ Violet	211.00	133.00	13.00	8.60	9.50	6.50
☐ 673	4¢ Brown	242.00	171.00	20.00	12.10	11.10	7.75
☐ 674	5¢ Blue	256.00	176.00	18.00	11.50	12.10	7.75
☐ 675	6¢ Orange	542.00	401.00	38.00	24.50	26.00	15.50
☐ 676	7¢ Black	277.00	189.00	23.00	12.10	16.10	11.00
☐ 677	8¢ Olive Green	312.00	206.00	29.00	16.00	23.50	15.00
☐ 678	9¢ Rose	423.00	236.00	40.00	23.00	32.00	21.00
☐ 679	10¢ Orange Yellow	852.00	641.00	107.00	70.00	20.00	12.50

1929. BATTLE OF FALLEN TIMBERS (N-H ADD 35%)
| ☐ 680 | 2¢ Carmine Rose .... | 44.00 | 32.00 | 1.20 | .72 | 1.01 | .64 |

1929. OHIO RIVER CANALIZATION (N-H ADD 30%)
| ☐ 681 | 2¢ Carmine Rose .... | 36.00 | 22.00 | .87 | .57 | .82 | .52 |

1930–1931. COMMEMORATIVES

1930. MASSACHUSETTS BAY COLONY (N-H ADD 35%)
| ☐ 682 | 2¢ Carmine Rose .... | 45.00 | 29.00 | .73 | .52 | .66 | .43 |

1930. CAROLINA-CHARLESTON ISSUE (N-H ADD 35%)
| ☐ 683 | 2¢ Carmine Rose .... | 77.00 | 51.00 | 1.65 | 1.10 | 1.70 | 1.15 |

1930. REGULAR ISSUE
ROTARY PRESS PRINTING—PERF. 11 x 10½ (N-H ADD 35%)
| ☐ 684 | 1½¢ Brown............... | 4.30 | 3.00 | .47 | .32 | .13 | .11 |
| ☐ 685 | 4¢ Brown............... | 12.00 | 9.00 | .95 | .63 | .14 | .12 |

Scott No.		Fine Unused Line Pair	Ave. Unused Line Pair	Fine Unused Each	Ave. Unused Each	Fine Used Each	Ave. Used Each

ROTARY PRESS COIL STAMPS
PERF. 10 VERTICALLY (N-H ADD 40%)
| ☐ 686 | 1½¢ Brown............... | 12.50 | 9.20 | 2.00 | 1.30 | .13 | .09 |
| ☐ 687 | 4¢ Brown............... | 17.00 | 12.00 | 3.50 | 2.15 | .60 | .42 |

Scott No.		Fine Unused Plate Blk	Ave. Unused Plate Blk	Fine Unused Each	Ave. Unused Each	Fine Used Each	Ave. Used Each

1930. BATTLE OF BRADDOCK'S FIELD (N-H ADD 40%)
| ☐ 688 | 2¢ Carmine Rose .... | 63.00 | 41.00 | 1.25 | .87 | 1.60 | 1.12 |

1930. VON STEUBEN ISSUE (N-H ADD 40%)
| ☐ 689 | 2¢ Carmine Rose .... | 38.00 | 24.00 | .67 | .45 | .75 | .53 |

1931. PULASKI ISSUE (N-H ADD 40%)
| ☐ 690 | 2¢ Carmine Rose .... | 28.00 | 21.00 | .32 | .21 | .23 | .15 |

1931. DESIGNS OF 1922–1926
ROTARY PRESS PRINTING—PERF. 11 x 10½ (N-H ADD 40%)
| ☐ 692 | 11¢ Light Blue .... | 33.00 | 21.00 | 3.70 | 2.50 | .18 | .12 |
| ☐ 693 | 12¢ Brown Violet .... | 48.00 | 33.00 | 6.40 | 5.10 | .12 | .10 |

Scott No.		Fine Unused Plate Blk	Ave. Unused Plate Blk	Fine Unused Each	Ave. Unused Each	Fine Used Each	Ave. Used Each
☐ 694	13¢ Yellow Green	28.00	20.00	2.90	1.90	.26	.18
☐ 695	14¢ Dark Blue	42.00	29.00	5.00	3.10	.63	.43
☐ 696	15¢ Gray	82.00	52.00	12.00	9.00	.13	.11

PERF. 10½ x 11 (N-H ADD 40%)

☐ 697	17¢ Black	47.00	32.00	6.90	5.00	.40	.24
☐ 698	20¢ Carmine Rose	104.00	73.00	13.50	8.50	.13	.09
☐ 699	25¢ Blue Green	91.00	65.00	12.10	7.50	.15	.12
☐ 700	30¢ Brown	136.00	100.00	19.10	11.00	.14	.09
☐ 701	50¢ Lilac	368.00	241.00	60.00	37.00	.14	.11

1931. RED CROSS ISSUE (N-H ADD 40%)

☐ 702	2¢ Black & Red	3.60	2.20	.19	.14	.22	.17

1931. SURRENDER OF YORKTOWN (N-H ADD 40%)

☐ 703	2¢ Carmine Rose & Black	4.50	3.60	.55	.42	.56	.44

1932. WASHINGTON BICENTENNIAL (N-H ADD 40%)

☐ 704	½¢ Olive Brown	6.38	4.76	.13	.09	.14	.10
☐ 705	1¢ Green	7.10	5.60	.21	.15	.13	.10
☐ 706	1½¢ Brown	32.00	21.00	.57	.38	.18	.12
☐ 707	2¢ Carmine	3.40	2.60	.13	.10	.14	.12
☐ 708	3¢ Purple	29.50	18.00	.86	.63	.15	.12
☐ 709	4¢ Light Brown	9.80	6.75	.37	.27	.16	.12
☐ 710	5¢ Blue	25.00	13.50	2.30	1.35	.19	.15
☐ 711	6¢ Orange	96.00	65.00	6.10	4.30	.17	.12
☐ 712	7¢ Black	12.00	8.00	.60	.45	.24	.17
☐ 713	8¢ Olive Bistre	106.00	72.10	6.60	5.10	.98	.66
☐ 714	9¢ Pale Red	74.00	49.00	4.10	2.40	.31	.21
☐ 715	10¢ Orange Yellow	213.00	141.00	18.00	10.60	.17	.13

1932. COMMEMORATIVES

1932. OLYMPIC WINTER GAMES (N-H ADD 30%)

☐ 716	2¢ Carmine Rose	17.00	13.00	.63	.45	.32	.22

1932. ARBOR DAY ISSUE (N-H ADD 30%)

☐ 717	2¢ Carmine Rose	12.50	8.90	.20	.15	.17	.14

1932. OLYMPIC SUMMER GAMES (N-H ADD 30%)

☐ 718	3¢ Purple	26.00	18.00	2.40	2.60	.17	.13
☐ 719	5¢ Blue	41.00	26.00	4.00	3.40	.35	.24

Scott No.		Fine Unused Line Pair	Ave. Unused Line Pair	Fine Unused Each	Ave. Unused Each	Fine Used Each	Ave. Used Each

1932. ROTARY PRESS COIL STAMPS

☐ 720	3¢ Deep Violet	2.50	1.80	.25	.17	.11	.07

PERF. 10 VERTICALLY (N-H ADD 30%)

☐ 721	3¢ Deep Violet	11.00	6.50	3.40	2.60	.13	.12

Scott No.	Fine Unused Line Pair	Ave. Unused Line Pair	Fine Unused Each	Ave. Unused Each	Fine Used Each	Ave. Used Each
PERF. 10 HORIZONTALLY (N-H ADD 30%)						
☐ 722 3¢ Deep Violet	5.80	4.10	2.00	1.20	.90	.60
DESIGN OF 1922–1925—PERF. 10 VERTICALLY (N-H ADD 30%)						
☐ 723 6¢ Deep Orange	72.00	49.00	16.70	9.80	.30	.21

Scott No.	Fine Unused Plate Blk	Ave. Unused Plate Blk	Fine Unused Each	Ave. Unused Each	Fine Used Each	Ave. Used Each
1932. WILLIAM PENN ISSUE (N-H ADD 30%)						
☐ 724 3¢ Violet	20.00	12.00	.50	.32	.27	.21
1932. DANIEL WEBSTER ISSUE (N-H ADD 30%)						
☐ 725 3¢ Violet	38.00	24.00	.68	.50	.42	.30
1933. COMMEMORATIVES						
1933. GEORGIA BICENTENNIAL (N-H ADD 30%)						
☐ 726 3¢ Violet	24.00	16.00	.42	.30	.26	.19
1933. PEACE SESQUICENTENNIAL (N-H ADD 30%)						
☐ 727 3¢ Violet	8.00	5.00	.16	.14	.13	.10
1933. CENTURY OF PROGRESS EXPOSITION (N-H ADD 30%)						
☐ 728 1¢ Yellow Green	3.90	2.50	.16	.10	.11	.08
☐ 729 3¢ Purple	6.90	3.60	.20	.11	.12	.08
1933. A.P.S. CONVENTION AND EXHIBITION AT CHICAGO IMPERFORATE—UNGUMMED (N-H ADD 30%)						
☐ 730 1¢ Yellow Green, Sheet of 25	—	—	50.00	36.00	—	—
☐ 730a 1¢ Yellow Green, sgl.	—	—	.92	.68	.77	.60
☐ 731 3¢ Violet Sheet of 25	—	—	43.00	—	38.00	—
☐ 731a 3¢ Violet, single	—	—	.87	.65	.60	.40
1933. N.R.A. ISSUE (N-H ADD 25%)						
☐ 732 3¢ Violet	3.85	2.40	.16	.13	.10	.08
1933. BYRD ANTARCTIC EXPEDITION (N-H ADD 30%)						
☐ 733 3¢ Dark Blue	32.00	21.00	.93	.65	1.06	.75
1933. KOSCIUSZKO ISSUE (N-H ADD 30%)						
☐ 734 5¢ Blue	70.00	46.00	.85	.62	.41	.26
1934. NATIONAL PHILATELIC EXHIBITION IMPERFORATE—UNGUMMED (N-H ADD 30%)						
☐ 735 3¢ Dark Blue Sheet of 6	—	—	26.00	—	22.00	15.00
☐ 735a 3¢ Dark Blue, sgl.	—	—	4.00	2.40	2.90	1.98
1934. COMMEMORATIVES						
1934. MARYLAND TERCENTENARY (N-H ADD 30%)						
☐ 736 3¢ Rose	18.00	12.00	.21	.14	.19	.14

Scott No.		Fine Unused Plate Blk	Ave. Unused Plate Blk	Fine Unused Each	Ave. Unused Each	Fine Used Each	Ave. Used Each
1934. MOTHER'S DAY ISSUE							
ROTARY PRESS PRINTING—PERF. 11 x 10½ (N-H ADD 30%)							
□ 737	3¢ Deep Violet	2.40	1.80	.19	.14	.12	.08
FLAT PRESS PRINTING-PERF. 11 (N-H ADD 30%)							
□ 738	3¢ Deep Violet	8.75	6.70	.28	.18	.35	.22
1934. WISCONSIN TERCENTENARY (N-H ADD 30%)							
□ 739	3¢ Deep Violet	7.70	5.40	.25	.17	.19	.13
1934. NATIONAL PARKS ISSUE (N-H ADD 25%)							
□ 740	1¢ Green	2.40	1.70	.16	.10	.15	.11
□ 741	2¢ Red	2.30	1.50	.21	.14	.15	.12
□ 742	3¢ Purple	4.60	3.40	.25	.17	.16	.12
□ 743	4¢ Brown	18.00	11.00	.61	.43	.62	.44
□ 744	5¢ Blue	20.00	13.00	1.20	.85	.92	.67
□ 745	6¢ Indigo	36.00	22.00	1.45	.96	1.35	.97
□ 746	7¢ Black	20.00	13.00	1.25	.87	1.25	.77
□ 747	8¢ Green	36.00	22.00	3.60	2.40	2.80	1.70
□ 748	9¢ Salmon	35.00	22.00	3.40	2.20	.80	.55
□ 749	10¢ Gray Black	59.00	41.00	5.00	3.50	1.50	.96
1934. A.P.S. CONVENTION AND EXHIBITION AT ATLANTIC CITY							
IMPERFORATE SOUVENIR SHEET (N-H ADD 25%)							
□ 750	3¢ Purple, sheet of 6	—	—	43.00	—	47.00	38.00
□ 750a	3¢ Purple, single	—	—	6.00	4.00	5.00	2.90
1934. TRANS-MISSISSIPPI PHILATELIC EXPOSITION AND							
CONVENTION AT OMAHA							
IMPERFORATE SOUVENIR SHEET (N-H ADD 25%)							
□ 751	1¢ Green, sheet of 6	—	—	20.00	—	20.00	13.50
□ 751a	1¢ Green, single	—	—	2.70	2.00	1.70	1.30

Scott No.		Plate Block	Block Plain	Mint Each	Used Each
1935. "FARLEY SPECIAL PRINTINGS"					
DESIGNS OF 1933–1934					
PERF. 10½ x 11—UNGUMMED (N-H ADD 25%)					
□ 752	3¢ Violet	18.00	1.25	.17	.15
PERF. 11—GUMMED (N-H ADD 25%)					
□ 753	3¢ Dark Blue	25.00	5.00	.57	.62
IMPERFORATE—UNGUMMED (N-H ADD 25%)					
□ 754	3¢ Deep Violet	26.00	5.00	.83	.86
□ 755	3¢ Deep Violet	26.00	6.00	.89	.97
NATIONAL PARKS					
IMPERFORATE—UNGUMMED (N-H ADD 25%)					
□ 756	1¢ Green	10.00	1.20	.22	.34
□ 757	2¢ Red	11.00	1.75	.36	.31

Scott No.		Plate Block	Block Plain	Mint Each	Used Each
☐ 758	3¢ Deep Violet	25.00	3.10	.70	.70
☐ 759	4¢ Brown	32.00	9.00	1.34	1.30
☐ 760	5¢ Blue	37.00	14.00	2.34	2.10
☐ 761	6¢ Dark Blue	60.00	16.50	4.10	3.10
☐ 762	7¢ Black	54.00	13.00	2.30	1.90
☐ 763	8¢ Sage Green	66.00	14.50	2.80	2.20
☐ 764	9¢ Red Orange	70.00	15.50	2.80	2.50
☐ 765	10¢ Gray Black	80.00	28.50	4.60	4.10

IMPERFORATE—UNGUMMED (N-H ADD 25%)

☐ 766a	1¢ Yellow Green	—	14.00	.98	.73
☐ 767a	3¢ Violet	—	14.00	1.00	.72
☐ 768a	3¢ Dark Blue	—	20.00	4.20	3.00
☐ 769a	1¢ Green	—	12.00	1.75	1.40
☐ 770a	3¢ Deep Violet	—	22.00	3.60	3.80

DESIGN OF CE 1 (N-H ADD 30%)

☐ 771	16¢ Dark Blue	120.00	21.00	3.50	3.40

1935–1936. COMMEMORATIVES

Scott No.		Fine Unused Plate Blk	Ave. Unused Plate Blk	Mint Each	Used Each

1935. CONNECTICUT TERCENTENARY (N-H ADD 25%)

☐ 772	3¢ Red Violet	2.40	1.75	.17	.11

1935. CALIFORNIA PACIFIC EXPOSITION (N-H ADD 25%)

☐ 773	3¢ Purple	2.40	1.50	.16	.14

1935. BOULDER DAM ISSUE (N-H ADD 25%)

☐ 774	3¢ Purple	2.20	1.60	.15	.13

1935. MICHIGAN CENTENARY (N-H ADD 25%)

☐ 775	3¢ Purple	2.60	1.34	.15	.12

1936. TEXAS CENTENNIAL (N-H ADD 25%)

☐ 776	3¢ Purple	2.20	1.60	.22	.14

1936. RHODE ISLAND TERCENTENARY (N-H ADD 25%)

☐ 777	3¢ Purple	2.50	1.50	.23	.15

1936. THIRD INTL. PHILATELIC EXHIBITION "TIPEX" IMPERFORATE SOUVENIR SHEET DESIGNS OF 772, 773, 775, 776 (N-H ADD 25%)

☐ 778	3¢ Red Violet, sheet of 4	—	—	4.10	3.45
☐ 778a	3¢ Red Violet, single	—	—	.98	1.12
☐ 778b	3¢ Red Violet, single	—	—	.98	1.12
☐ 778c	3¢ Red Violet, single	—	—	.98	1.12
☐ 778d	3¢ Red Violet, single	—	—	.98	1.12

1936. ARKANSAS CENTENNIAL (N-H ADD 25%)

☐ 782	3¢ Purple	2.12	1.40	.14	.12

Scott No.		Fine Unused Plate Blk	Ave. Unused Plate Blk	Fine Unused Each	Ave. Unused Each	Fine Used Each	Ave. Used Each
1936. OREGON TERRITORY CENTENNIAL (N-H ADD 25%)							
☐ 783	3¢ Purple	1.45	1.10	.15	.12	.10	.08
1936. SUFFRAGE FOR WOMEN ISSUE (N-H ADD 25%)							
☐ 784	3¢ Dark Violet	1.20	.92	.13	.12	.10	.08
1936–1937. ARMY AND NAVY ISSUE							
ARMY COMMEMORATIVES (N-H ADD 20%)							
☐ 785	1¢ Green	1.60	.98	.12	.09	.10	.06
☐ 786	2¢ Carmine	1.34	1.10	.17	.12	.10	.07
☐ 787	3¢ Purple	1.95	1.50	.25	.20	.14	.11
☐ 788	4¢ Gray	19.00	15.00	.83	.60	.25	.18
☐ 789	5¢ Ultramarine	20.00	15.00	.92	.68	.26	.19
NAVY COMMEMORATIVES (N-H ADD 25%)							
☐ 790	1¢ Green	—	1.10	.16	.15	.10	.08
☐ 791	2¢ Carmine	1.50	1.20	.21	.15	.10	.07
☐ 792	3¢ Purple	1.70	1.25	.24	.18	.14	.11
☐ 793	4¢ Gray	21.00	16.00	.72	.52	.23	.16
☐ 794	5¢ Ultramarine	23.00	16.00	.93	.68	.23	.17
1937. COMMEMORATIVES							
1937. NORTHWEST ORDINANCE ISSUE (N-H ADD 25%)							
☐ 795	3¢ Violet	2.10	1.60	.20	.12	.10	.08
1937. VIRGINIA DARE ISSUE (N-H ADD 20%)							
☐ 796	5¢ Gray Blue	12.00	10.00	.50	.25	.25	.18
1937. S.P.A. CONVENTION ISSUE (N-H ADD 25%)							
DESIGN OF 749 IMPERFORATE SOUVENIR SHEET							
☐ 797	10¢ Blue Green	—	1.42	—		.86	.65
1937. CONSTITUTIONAL SESQUICENTENNIAL (N-H ADD 25%)							
☐ 798	3¢ Red Violet	1.45	1.10	.19	.14	.11	.09
1937. TERRITORIAL PUBLICITY ISSUE (N-H ADD 25%)							
☐ 799	3¢ Violet	3.10	2.10	.20	.15	.12	.08
☐ 800	3¢ Violet	3.10	2.10	.20	.15	.12	.08
☐ 801	3¢ Bright Violet	3.10	2.10	.20	.15	.12	.08
☐ 802	3¢ Light Violet	3.10	2.10	.20	.15	.12	.08
1938. PRESIDENTIAL SERIES							
ROTARY PRESS PRINTING—PERF. 11 x 10½ (N-H ADD 25%)							
☐ 803	½¢ Red Orange	.81	.62	.11	.07	.10	.07
☐ 804	1¢ Green	.49	.36	.13	.08	.09	.06
☐ 805	1½¢ Bistre Brown	.51	.38	.13	.10	.09	.06
☐ 806	2¢ Rose Carmine	.73	.53	.17	.13	.10	.07
☐ 807	3¢ Deep Violet	.62	.47	.15	.10	.10	.07
☐ 808	4¢ Red Violet	2.65	1.92	.44	.28	.10	.07
☐ 809	4½¢ Dark Gray	2.40	1.83	.24	.17	.13	.10

Scott No.		Fine Unused Plate Blk	Ave. Unused Plate Blk	Fine Unused Each	Ave. Unused Each	Fine Used Each	Ave. Used Each
☐810	5¢ Bright Blue	2.27	1.75	.30	.21	.13	.10
☐811	6¢ Red Orange	2.60	1.80	.47	.30	.12	.09
☐812	7¢ Sepia	2.65	1.85	.42	.25	.12	.08
☐813	8¢ Olive Green	3.45	2.60	.65	.40	.12	.08
☐814	9¢ Rose Pink	3.60	2.70	.77	.46	.12	.09
☐815	10¢ Brown Red	2.70	1.90	.60	.32	.10	.09
☐816	11¢ Ultramarine	6.10	4.30	.90	.50	.15	.11
☐817	12¢ Bright Violet	12.00	8.10	1.27	.76	.14	.11
☐818	13¢ Blue Green	12.90	8.60	1.51	.81	.16	.12
☐819	14¢ Blue	8.60	6.80	1.32	.76	.16	.13
☐820	15¢ Blue Gray	4.20	3.20	.92	.55	.12	.08
☐821	16¢ Black	11.70	8.10	1.21	.61	.66	.41
☐822	17¢ Rose Red	10.50	7.60	1.31	.72	.15	.12
☐823	18¢ Brown Carmine	16.50	13.00	2.95	1.81	.14	.11
☐824	19¢ Bright Violet	13.25	8.70	1.55	.92	.83	.62
☐825	20¢ Bright Blue Green	8.50	6.00	1.20	.62	.10	.08
☐826	21¢ Dull Blue	15.00	11.10	2.85	2.10	.26	.21
☐827	22¢ Vermilion	18.00	13.75	1.30	.76	.77	.55
☐828	24¢ Gray Black	37.50	28.00	5.30	4.10	.29	.22
☐829	25¢ Deep Red Lilac	9.20	7.00	1.21	.66	.12	.08
☐830	30¢ Deep Ultramarine	44.10	33.00	7.60	5.20	.11	.08
☐831	50¢ Light Red Violet	61.00	41.00	12.00	7.60	.11	.09

FLAT PLATE PRINTING—PERF. 11 (N-H ADD 20%)

☐832	$1 Purple & Black	59.00	42.00	12.00	8.00	.14	.11
☐832b	$1 Watermarked	—	—	250.00	186.00	77.00	55.00
☐832c	$1 Dry Printing, Thick Paper (1954)	50.00	40.00	10.00	7.75	.18	.13
☐833	$2 Green & Black	211.00	171.00	35.00	21.00	7.60	6.00
☐834	$5 Carmine & Black	782.00	596.00	141.00	99.00	7.20	5.50

1938–1939. COMMEMORATIVES

1938. CONSTITUTION RATIFICATION (N-H ADD 25%)

☐835	3¢ Deep Violet	6.00	4.50	.23	.17	.15	.11

1938. SWEDISH-FINNISH TERCENTENARY (N-H ADD 25%)

☐836	3¢ Red Violet	6.00	4.10	.22	.15	.17	.12

1938. NORTHWEST COLONIZATION (N-H ADD 25%)

☐837	3¢ Bright Violet	15.00	11.00	.29	.21	.15	.10

1938. IOWA TERRITORY CENTENNIAL (N-H ADD 25%)

☐838	3¢ Violet	11.00	8.00	.29	.20	.16	.12

Scott No.		Fine Unused Line Pair	Ave. Unused Line Pair	Fine Unused Each	Ave. Unused Each	Fine Used Each	Ave. Used Each

1939. ROTARY PRESS COIL STAMPS
PERF. 10 VERTICALLY (N-H ADD 25%)

		Line Pair	Line Pair	Each	Each	Each	Each
☐ 839	1¢ Green	1.65	1.40	.46	.31	.12	.09
☐ 840	1½¢ Bistre Brown	2.20	1.75	.52	.43	.12	.09
☐ 841	2¢ Rose Carmine	2.60	1.85	.66	.52	.10	.09
☐ 812	3¢ Deep Violet	2.70	2.10	.60	.40	.11	.08
☐ 843	4¢ Red Violet	35.00	28.00	10.00	8.00	.55	.38
☐ 844	4½¢ Dark Gray	8.00	5.50	.95	.66	.72	.53
☐ 845	5¢ Bright Blue	33.00	24.00	7.50	5.60	.45	.28
☐ 846	6¢ Red Orange	12.00	9.00	1.50	.82	.20	.12
☐ 847	10¢ Brown Red	64.00	47.00	18.00	14.00	.08	.45

PERF. 10 HORIZONTALLY (N-H ADD 25%)

☐ 848	1¢ Green	3.60	2.40	.90	.70	.16	.14
☐ 849	1½¢ Bistre Brown	4.30	3.50	1.60	1.10	.55	.40
☐ 850	2¢ Rose Carmine	7.50	6.00	2.70	2.00	.70	.43
☐ 851	3¢ Deep Violet	8.10	6.00	2.70	2.10	.65	.43

Scott No.		Fine Unused Plate Blk	Ave. Unused Plate Blk	Fine Unused Each	Ave. Unused Each	Fine Used Each	Ave. Used Each

1939. GOLDEN GATE INTERNATIONAL EXPOSITION (N-H ADD 25%)

☐ 852	3¢ Bright Purple	2.20	1.50	.22	.17	.12	.10

1939. NEW YORK WORLD'S FAIR (N-H ADD 20%)

☐ 853	3¢ Deep Purple	2.50	1.75	.22	.16	.12	.11

1939. WASHINGTON INAUGURATION SESQUICENTENNIAL (N-H ADD 20%)

☐ 854	3¢ Bright Red Violet	4.80	3.30	.33	.22	.16	.12

1939. BASEBALL CENTENNIAL (N-H ADD 20%)

☐ 855	3¢ Violet	4.10	2.89	.56	.42	.12	.10

1939. 25TH ANNIVERSARY PANAMA CANAL (N-H ADD 20%)

☐ 856	3¢ Deep Red Violet	5.00	3.50	.30	.20	.13	.12

1939. COLONIAL PRINTING TERCENTENARY (N-H ADD 20%)

☐ 857	3¢ Rose Violet	1.90	1.60	.18	.14	.11	.12

1939. 50TH ANNIVERSARY OF STATEHOOD (N-H ADD 20%)

☐ 858	3¢ Rose Violet	2.60	1.80	.19	.15	.13	.10

1940. FAMOUS AMERICANS SERIES
AMERICAN AUTHORS (N-H ADD 20%)

☐ 859	1¢ Bright Blue Green	1.85	1.30	.13	.09	.13	.08
☐ 860	2¢ Rose Carmine	2.12	1.40	.19	.14	.15	.11
☐ 861	3¢ Bright Red Violet	2.60	1.70	.20	.15	.12	.09
☐ 862	5¢ Ultramarine	20.00	16.00	.42	.30	.40	.28
☐ 863	10¢ Dark Brown	73.00	56.00	2.30	2.10	1.95	1.65

Scott No.		Fine Unused Plate Blk	Ave. Unused Plate Blk	Fine Unused Each	Ave. Unused Each	Fine Used Each	Ave. Used Each
AMERICAN POETS (N-H ADD 20%)							
☐ 864	1¢ Bright Blue Green	3.20	2.20	.16	.13	.17	.13
☐ 865	2¢ Rose Carmine	3.40	2.60	.16	.12	.12	.09
☐ 866	3¢ Bright Red Violet	5.10	3.10	.24	.18	.11	.08
☐ 867	5¢ Ultramarine	19.00	14.00	.83	.62	.36	.24
☐ 868	10¢ Dark Brown	65.00	51.00	2.60	1.85	2.50	1.85
AMERICAN EDUCATORS (N-H ADD 20%)							
☐ 869	1¢ Bright Blue Green	316.00	2.10	.15	.09	.14	.09
☐ 870	2¢ Rose Carmine	290.00	2.60	.15	.10	.14	.09
☐ 871	3¢ Bright Red Violet	5.00	4.10	.34	.21	.12	.09
☐ 872	5¢ Ultramarine	19.00	14.10	.72	.56	.43	.33
☐ 873	10¢ Dark Brown	54.00	39.00	2.60	1.34	2.20	1.50
AMERICAN SCIENTISTS (N-H ADD 20%)							
☐ 874	1¢ Bright Blue Green	2.30	1.85	.13	.09	.12	.08
☐ 875	2¢ Rose Carmine	2.10	1.95	.15	.12	.13	.09
☐ 876	3¢ Bright Red Violet	2.20	1.75	.20	.13	.13	.08
☐ 877	5¢ Ultramarine	17.50	14.00	.38	.30	.34	.24
☐ 878	10¢ Dark Brown	51.00	39.00	2.25	1.45	2.20	1.45
AMERICAN COMPOSERS (N-H ADD 20%)							
☐ 879	1¢ Bright Blue Green	1.70	1.35	.12	.09	.12	.08
☐ 880	2¢ Rose Carmine	1.75	1.25	.21	.12	.12	.09
☐ 881	3¢ Bright Red Violet	2.30	1.55	.20	.13	.15	.12
☐ 882	5¢ Ultramarine	23.00	15.00	.82	.62	.40	.27
☐ 883	10¢ Dark Brown	62.00	47.00	5.75	4.20	2.20	1.60
AMERICAN ARTISTS (N-H ADD 20%)							
☐ 884	1¢ Bright Blue Green	1.70	1.20	.12	.09	.12	.09
☐ 885	2¢ Rose Carmine	1.70	1.20	.15	.12	.13	.09
☐ 886	3¢ Bright Red Violet	1.70	1.50	.27	.21	.12	.09
☐ 887	5¢ Ultramarine	22.00	14.00	.72	.52	.44	.32
☐ 888	10¢ Dark Brown	54.00	43.00	2.45	1.70	2.40	1.70
AMERICAN INVENTORS (N-H ADD 20%)							
☐ 889	1¢ Bright Blue Green	3.90	2.85	.16	.12	.14	.10
☐ 890	2¢ Rose Carmine	1.85	1.20	.16	.13	.12	.09
☐ 891	3¢ Bright Red Violet	3.30	2.20	.30	.23	.10	.09
☐ 892	5¢ Ultramarine	32.00	23.00	1.30	.93	.60	.42
☐ 893	10¢ Dark Brown	155.00	130.00	18.00	12.00	3.60	2.60

1940. COMMEMORATIVES

1940. 80TH ANNIVERSARY OF PONY EXPRESS (N-H ADD 20%)

☐ 894	3¢ Henna Brown	6.10	4.80	.55	.40	.25	.20

1940. 50TH ANNIVERSARY OF PAN-AMERICAN UNION (N-H ADD 20%)

☐ 895	3¢ Light Violet	6.10	4.50	.56	.40	.19	.16

Scott No.		Fine Unused Plate Blk	Ave. Unused Plate Blk	Fine Unused Each	Ave. Unused Each	Fine Used Each	Ave. Used Each

1940. 50TH ANNIVERSARY OF IDAHO (N-H ADD 20%)

| ☐ 896 | 3¢ Bright Violet .... | 4.30 | 3.10 | .25 | .16 | .16 | .10 |

1940. 50TH ANNIVERSARY OF WYOMING (N-H ADD 20%)

| ☐ 897 | 3¢ Brown Violet .... | 3.30 | 2.50 | .22 | .18 | .15 | .11 |

1940. 400TH ANNIVERSARY OF COLORADO EXPEDITION (N-H ADD 20%)

| ☐ 898 | 3¢ Violet .... | 3.20 | 2.70 | .25 | .20 | .16 | .13 |

1940. NATIONAL DEFENSE ISSUE (N-H ADD 20%)

☐ 899	1¢ Bright Blue Green	1.12	.80	.17	.13	.10	.08
☐ 900	2¢ Rose Carmine	1.12	.80	.20	.13	.09	.08
☐ 901	3¢ Bright Violet	1.12	.80	.20	.13	.09	.08

1940. 75TH ANNIVERSARY EMANCIPATION AMENDMENT (N-H ADD 20%)

| ☐ 902 | 3¢ Deep Violet .... | 6.80 | 6.10 | .33 | .24 | .20 | .15 |

IMPORTANT NOTICE: Values for mint sheets are provided for the following listings. To command the stated prices, sheets must be complete as issued with the plate number (or numbers) intact.

Scott No.		Mint Sheet	Plate Block	Fine Unused Each	Fine Used Each

1941–1943. COMMEMORATIVES

1941. VERMONT STATEHOOD

| ☐ 903 | 3¢ Light Violet .... | 12.75 | 4.00 | .24 | .16 |

1942. KENTUCKY SESQUICENTENNIAL ISSUE

| ☐ 904 | 3¢ Violet .... | 11.00 | 2.25 | .30 | .16 |

1942. WIN THE WAR ISSUE

| ☐ 905 | 3¢ Violet .... | 12.00 | .85 | .17 | .09 |

1942. CHINA ISSUE

| ☐ 906 | 5¢ Bright Blue .... | 35.00 | 24.00 | .60 | .33 |

1943. ALLIED NATIONS ISSUE

| ☐ 907 | 2¢ Rose Carmine .... | 7.10 | .76 | .17 | .11 |

1943. FOUR FREEDOMS ISSUE

| ☐ 908 | 1¢ Green .... | 6.10 | 1.10 | .14 | .09 |

1943–1944. OVERRUN COUNTRIES SERIES

☐ 909	5¢ (Poland)	24.00	15.00	.30	.25
☐ 910	5¢ (Czechoslovakia)	19.00	6.00	.31	.22
☐ 911	5¢ (Norway)	9.30	2.70	.22	.18
☐ 912	5¢ (Luxembourg)	9.30	2.70	.22	.18
☐ 913	5¢ (Netherlands)	9.30	2.70	.22	.18
☐ 914	5¢ (Belgium)	9.30	2.70	.22	.18
☐ 915	5¢ (France)	9.30	2.70	.22	.18
☐ 916	5¢ (Greece)	46.00	26.00	.75	.69

*No hinge pricing from 1941 to date is figured at (N-H ADD 15%)

Scott No.		Mint Sheet	Plate Block	Fine Unused Each	Fine Used Each
☐ 917	5¢ (Yugoslavia)	34.00	11.00	.51	.41
☐ 918	5¢ (Albania)	29.00	12.00	.46	.45
☐ 919	5¢ (Austria)	22.00	10.00	.30	.32
☐ 920	5¢ (Denmark)	29.00	11.00	.38	.41
☐ 921	5¢ (Korea)	19.00	10.00	.27	.24

1944. COMMEMORATIVES

1944. RAILROAD ISSUE

☐ 922	3¢ Violet	17.00	2.60	.27	.16

1944. STEAMSHIP ISSUE

☐ 923	3¢ Violet	9.75	2.40	.21	.13

1944. TELEGRAPH ISSUE

☐ 924	3¢ Bright Red Violet	7.75	1.70	.19	.13

1944. CORREGIDOR ISSUE

☐ 925	3¢ Deep Violet	8.90	2.40	.20	.15

1944. MOTION PICTURE ISSUE

☐ 926	3¢ Deep Violet	7.95	1.65	.15	.15

1945. COMMEMORATIVES

1945. FLORIDA ISSUE

☐ 927	3¢ Bright Red Violet	6.20	1.30	.15	.11

1945. PEACE CONFERENCE ISSUE

☐ 928	5¢ Ultramarine	7.95	.90	.20	.12

1945. IWO JIMA ISSUE

☐ 929	3¢ Yellow Green	7.00	.62	.14	.12

1945–1946. ROOSEVELT MEMORIAL ISSUE

☐ 930	1¢ Blue Green	3.00	.26	.10	.07
☐ 931	2¢ Carmine Rose	4.50	.46	.12	.09
☐ 932	3¢ Purple	6.10	.63	.16	.12
☐ 933	5¢ Bright Blue	8.50	.93	.20	.11

1945. ARMY ISSUE

☐ 934	3¢ Olive Gray	6.50	.57	.14	.08

1945. NAVY ISSUE

☐ 935	3¢ Blue	5.50	.62	.13	.09

1945. COAST GUARD ISSUE

☐ 936	3¢ Bright Blue Green	5.50	.62	.13	.09

1945. ALFRED SMITH ISSUE

☐ 937	3¢ Purple	9.75	.54	.14	.10

1945. TEXAS CENTENNIAL ISSUE

☐ 938	3¢ Blue	5.50	.54	.14	.09

*No hinge pricing from 1941 to date is figured at (N-H ADD 15%)

Scott No.		Mint Sheet	Plate Block	Fine Unused Each	Fine Used Each
1946–1947. COMMEMORATIVES					
1946. MERCHANT MARINE ISSUE					
☐ 939	3¢ Blue Green	5.30	.53	.13	.08
1946. HONORABLE DISCHARGE EMBLEM ISSUE					
☐ 940	3¢ Dark Violet	9.60	.54	.13	.08
1946. TENNESSEE ISSUE					
☐ 941	3¢ Dark Violet	5.50	.55	.13	.08
1946. IOWA STATEHOOD ISSUE					
☐ 942	3¢ Deep Blue	5.20	.53	.13	.08
1946. SMITHSONIAN INSTITUTION ISSUE					
☐ 943	3¢ Violet Brown	5.20	.54	.13	.08
1946. NEW MEXICO ISSUE					
☐ 944	3¢ Brown Violet	5.25	.53	.13	.08
1947. EDISON ISSUE					
☐ 945	3¢ Bright Red Violet	6.95	.54	.13	.08
1947. PULITZER PRIZE					
☐ 946	3¢ Purple	5.70	.53	.13	.08
1947. U.S. POSTAGE STAMP CENTENARY					
☐ 947	3¢ Deep Blue	5.20	.53	.13	.08
1947. "CIPEX" SOUVENIR SHEET					
☐ 948	5¢ & 10 Sheet of 2	—	—	1.41	1.42
☐ 948a	5¢ Blue, sgl. stp.	—	—	.53	.42
☐ 948b	10¢ Brown Orange, sgl. stp.	—	—	.83	.53
1947. DOCTORS ISSUE					
☐ 949	3¢ Brown Violet	5.25	.53	.12	.09
1947. UTAH ISSUE					
☐ 950	3¢ Dark Violet	5.25	.53	.12	.09
1947. U.S.F. CONSTITUTION ISSUE					
☐ 951	3¢ Blue Green	5.40	.54	.12	.08
1947. EVERGLADES ISSUE					
☐ 952	3¢ Bright Green	5.20	.53	.13	.08
1948. COMMEMORATIVES					
1948. CARVER ISSUE					
☐ 953	3¢ Red Violet	6.95	.53	.13	.08
1948. GOLD RUSH ISSUE					
☐ 954	3¢ Dark Violet	5.20	.53	.13	.08
1948. MISSISSIPPI TERRITORY ISSUE					
☐ 955	3¢ Brown Violet	5.35	.53	.13	.08

*No hinge pricing from 1941 to date is figured at (N-H ADD 15%)

Scott No.	Mint Sheet	Plate Block	Fine Unused Each	Fine Used Each
1948. FOUR CHAPLAINS ISSUE				
☐ 956 3¢ Gray Black	5.25	.53	.13	.08
1948. WISCONSIN CENTENNIAL ISSUE				
☐ 957 3¢ Dark Violet	5.60	.53	.13	.08
1948. SWEDISH PIONEER ISSUE				
☐ 958 5¢ Deep Blue	7.60	1.00	.16	.13
1948. 100 YEARS PROGRESS OF WOMEN				
☐ 959 3¢ Dark Violet	5.60	.58	.13	.08
1948. WILLIAM ALLEN WHITE ISSUE				
☐ 960 3¢ Red Violet	6.10	.93	.13	.08
1948. U.S.-CANADA FRIENDSHIP				
☐ 961 3¢ Blue	5.20	.53	.13	.08
1948. FRANCIS SCOTT KEY ISSUE				
☐ 962 3¢ Rose Pink	5.20	.53	.13	.08
1948. SALUTE TO YOUTH ISSUE				
☐ 963 3¢ Deep Blue	5.35	.53	.13	.08
1948. OREGON TERRITORY ISSUE				
☐ 964 3¢ Brown Red	5.60	.75	.16	.12
1948. HARLAN FISKE STONE				
☐ 965 3¢ Bright Red Violet	8.40	1.90	.22	.13
1948. MT. PALOMAR OBSERVATORY				
☐ 966 3¢ Blue	11.00	2.50	.24	.13
1948. CLARA BARTON ISSUE				
☐ 967 3¢ Rose Pink	5.20	.53	.13	.08
1948. POULTRY ISSUE				
☐ 968 3¢ Sepia	5.50	.57	.13	.08
1948. GOLD STAR MOTHERS				
☐ 969 3¢ Orange Yellow	5.60	.55	.13	.08
1948. FORT KEARNY ISSUE				
☐ 970 3¢ Violet	5.60	.54	.13	.10
1948. VOLUNTEER FIREMEN				
☐ 971 3¢ Bright Rose Carmine	5.50	.56	.13	.10
1948. INDIAN CENTENNIAL				
☐ 972 3¢ Dark Brown	5.70	.56	.13	.10
1948. ROUGH RIDERS				
☐ 973 3¢ Violet Brown	6.10	.63	.14	.10
1948. JULIETTE LOW				
☐ 974 3¢ Blue Green	5.75	.63	.13	.10

*No hinge pricing from 1941 to date is figured at (N-H ADD 15%)

Scott No.		Mint Sheet	Plate Block	Fine Unused Each	Fine Used Each
1948. WILL ROGERS					
☐ 975	3¢ Bright Red Violet	6.10	.65	.16	.10
1948. FORT BLISS					
☐ 976	3¢ Henna Brown	9.90	2.90	.19	.15
1948. MOINA MICHAEL					
☐ 977	3¢ Rose Pink	5.85	.55	.14	.12
1948. GETTYSBURG ADDRESS					
☐ 978	3¢ Bright Blue	5.50	.54	.14	.12
1948. AMERICAN TURNERS					
☐ 979	3¢ Carmine	5.50	.54	.14	.12
1948. JOEL CHANDLER HARRIS					
☐ 980	3¢ Bright Red Violet	7.60	.90	.14	.12
1949-1950. COMMEMORATIVES					
1949. MINNESOTA CENTENNIAL					
☐ 981	3¢ Blue Green	5.65	.56	.14	.10
1949. WASHINGTON & LEE UNIVERSITY					
☐ 982	3¢ Ultramarine	5.15	.55	.13	.10
1949. PUERTO RICO ISSUE					
☐ 983	3¢ Green	5.20	.54	.12	.11
1949. ANNAPOLIS TERCENTENARY					
☐ 984	3¢ Aquamarine	5.10	.54	.12	.10
1949. G.A.R. ISSUE					
☐ 985	3¢ Bright Rose Carmine	5.60	.54	.12	.11
1950. EDGAR ALLAN POE					
☐ 986	3¢ Bright Red Violet	6.80	.54	.14	.10
1950. BANKERS ASSOCIATION					
☐ 987	3¢ Yellow Green	5.20	.54	.14	.10
1950. SAMUEL GOMPERS					
☐ 988	3¢ Bright Red Violet	6.70	.60	.15	.10
1950. WASHINGTON SESQUICENTENNIAL					
☐ 989	3¢ Bright Blue	5.60	.60	.15	.10
☐ 990	3¢ Deep Green	5.75	.62	.15	.10
☐ 991	3¢ Light Violet	5.75	.55	.15	.10
☐ 991	3¢ Rose Violet	5.75	.55	.15	.10
1950. RAILROAD ENGINEERS					
☐ 993	3¢ Violet Brown	5.20	.56	.14	.10
1950. KANSAS CITY CENTENARY					
☐ 994	3¢ Violet	5.20	.56	.14	.10

*No hinge pricing from 1941 to date is figured at (N-H ADD 15%)

Scott No.		Mint Sheet	Plate Block	Fine Unused Each	Fine Used Each
1950. BOY SCOUTS ISSUE					
☐ 995	3¢ Sepia	5.65	.58	.15	.10
1950. INDIANA SESQUICENTENNIAL					
☐ 996	3¢ Bright Blue	5.25	.55	.14	.10
1950. CALIFORNIA STATEHOOD					
☐ 997	3¢ Yellow Orange	5.25	.55	.14	.10
1951-1952 COMMEMORATIVES					
1951. UNITED CONFEDERATE VETERANS					
☐ 998	3¢ Gray	5.60	.60	.15	.11
1951. NEVADA SETTLEMENT					
☐ 999	3¢ Light Olive Green	5.25	.55	.14	.11
1951. LANDING OF CADILLAC					
☐ 1000	3¢ Bright Blue	5.25	.55	.15	.11
1951. COLORADO STATEHOOD					
☐ 1001	3¢ Violet Blue	5.25	.56	.14	.11
1951. AMERICAN CHEMICAL SOCIETY					
☐ 1002	3¢ Violet Brown	5.60	.57	.15	.10
1951. BATTLE OF BROOKLYN ISSUE					
☐ 1003	3¢ Violet	5.20	.55	.15	.10
1952. BETSY ROSS ISSUE					
☐ 1004	3¢ Carmine Rose	5.85	.57	.15	.11
1952. 4-H CLUB ISSUE					
☐ 1005	3¢ Blue Green	5.60	.55	.14	.11
1952. BALTIMORE & OHIO RAILROAD					
☐ 1006	3¢ Bright Blue	7.70	.60	.16	.10
1952. AMERICAN AUTOMOBILE ASSOCIATION (AAA)					
☐ 1007	3¢ Deep Blue	5.60	.55	.15	.10
1952. NORTH ATLANTIC TREATY ORGANIZATION					
☐ 1008	3¢ Deep Violet	9.50	.55	.14	.10
1952. GRAND COULEE DAM ISSUE					
☐ 1009	3¢ Blue Green	5.40	.55	.14	.10
1952. ARRIVAL OF LAFAYETTE					
☐ 1010	3¢ Ultramarine	5.50	.55	.15	.10
1952. MOUNT RUSHMORE					
☐ 1011	3¢ Blue Green	5.10	.56	.14	.10
1952. SOCIETY OF CIVIL ENGINEERS					
☐ 1012	3¢ Violet Blue	5.10	.56	.14	.10

*No hinge pricing from 1941 to date is figured at (N-H ADD 15%)

Scott No.		Mint Sheet	Plate Block	Fine Unused Each	Fine Used Each
1952. WOMEN IN ARMED FORCES					
☐ 1013	3¢ Deep Blue	5.10	.55	.15	.10
1952. GUTENBERG PRINTING					
☐ 1014	3¢ Violet	5.25	.56	.16	.09
1952. NEWSPAPERBOYS					
☐ 1015	3¢ Violet	5.10	.55	.15	.09
1952. INTERNATIONAL RED CROSS					
☐ 1016	3¢ Deep Blue & Carmine	5.20	.55	.14	.09
1953-1954. COMMEMORATIVES					
1953. NATIONAL GUARD					
☐ 1017	3¢ Bright Blue	5.10	.54	.15	.09
1953. OHIO STATEHOOD					
☐ 1018	3¢ Chocolate	8.10	.66	.15	.10
1953. WASHINGTON TERRITORY					
☐ 1019	3¢ Green	5.20	.54	.15	.09
1953. LOUISIANA PURCHASE					
☐ 1020	3¢ Violet Brown	5.20	.54	.14	.09
1953. OPENING OF JAPAN					
☐ 1021	3¢ Green	9.50	1.60	.19	.10
1953. AMERICAN BAR ASSOCIATION					
☐ 1022	3¢ Rose Violet	5.10	.55	.15	.10
1953. SAGAMORE HILL					
☐ 1023	3¢ Yellow Green	5.10	.55	.14	.10
1953. FUTURE FARMERS					
☐ 1024	3¢ Deep Blue	5.10	.54	.15	.10
1953. TRUCKING INDUSTRY					
☐ 1025	3¢ Violet	5.25	.54	.14	.10
1953. GENERAL PATTON					
☐ 1026	3¢ Blue Violet	8.50	.92	.15	.10
1953. NEW YORK CITY					
☐ 1027	3¢ Bright Red Violet	6.00	.55	.15	.09
1953. GADSDEN PURCHASE					
☐ 1028	3¢ Copper Brown	5.10	.55	.14	.08
1954. COLUMBIA UNIVERSITY					
☐ 1029	3¢ Blue	5.10	.56	.14	.08
1954-1961. LIBERTY SERIES					
☐ 1030	½¢ Red Orange	4.50	.56	.14	.08
☐ 1031	1¢ Dark Green	5.10	.32	.09	.08
☐ 1031A	1¼¢ Turquoise	5.40	1.05	.11	.09

*No hinge pricing from 1941 to date is figured at (N-H ADD 15%)

Scott No.		Mint Sheet	Plate Block	Fine Unused Each	Fine Used Each
☐ 1032	1½¢ Brown	10.50	4.50	.12	.09
☐ 1033	2¢ Rose Carmine	7.10	.50	.11	.08
☐ 1034	2½¢ Dark Blue	8.95	.95	.10	.09
☐ 1035	3¢ Deep Violet	8.50	.45	.10	.08
☐ 1036	4¢ Red Violet	10.75	.55	.14	.08
☐ 1037	4½¢ Green	13.25	1.22	.29	.10
☐ 1038	5¢ Deep Blue	16.50	.92	.24	.09
☐ 1039	6¢ Orange Red	62.00	2.52	.52	.10
☐ 1040	7¢ Deep Carmine	26.00	2.45	.40	.10
☐ 1041	8¢ Dark Violet Blue, Carmine	26.00	3.35	.19	.08
☐ 1042	8¢ Violet Blue, Carmine (Re-engraved)	30.00	1.55	.49	.10
☐ 1042A	8¢ Brown	30.00	2.10	.38	.09
☐ 1043	9¢ Rose Lilac	28.00	2.60	.38	.08
☐ 1044	10¢ Rose Lake	36.00	1.60	.49	.09
☐ 1044A	11¢ Carmine, Violet Blue	28.00	2.20	.38	.12
☐ 1045	12¢ Red	43.50	2.40	.53	.12
☐ 1046	15¢ Maroon	69.00	3.50	.77	.12
☐ 1047	20¢ Ultramarine	90.00	3.80	.82	.14
☐ 1048	25¢ Green	251.00	12.00	2.20	.14
☐ 1049	30¢ Black	163.00	8.00	1.70	.14
☐ 1050	40¢ Brown Carmine	336.00	16.00	3.20	.14
☐ 1051	50¢ Bright Violet	321.00	15.00	2.80	.14
☐ 1052	$1 Deep Violet	1472.00	54.00	12.00	.14
☐ 1053	$5 Black	13400.00	486.00	107.00	9.10

1954-1965. ROTARY PRESS COIL STAMPS PERF. 10 VERTICALLY OR HORIZONTALLY

Scott No.		Fine Unused Line Pair	Ave. Unused Line Pair	Fine Unused Each	Ave. Unused Each	Fine Used Each	Ave. Used Each
☐ 1054	1¢ Deep Green	1.45	1.15	.32	.25	.11	.09
☐ 1055	2¢ Rose Carmine	.77	.36	.11	.09	.11	.09
☐ 1056	2½¢ Gray Blue	7.25	5.65	.42	.30	.32	.22
☐ 1057	3¢ Deep Violet	1.10	.75	.15	.11	.10	.08
☐ 1058	4¢ Red Violet	1.60	.80	.21	.15	.11	.08
☐ 1059	4½¢ Green	22.00	18.00	2.12	1.65	1.90	1.25
☐ 1059A	25¢ Green	2.80	2.20	.57	.43	.32	.20

Scott No.		Mint Sheet	Plate Block	Fine Unused Each	Fine Used Each

1954. NEBRASKA TERRITORY

☐ 1060	3¢ Violet	5.10	.58	.15	.10

1954. KANSAS TERRITORY

☐ 1061	3¢ Brown Orange	5.10	.58	.15	.10

1954. GEORGE EASTMAN ISSUE

☐ 1062	3¢ Violet Brown	7.00	.62	.15	.10

*No hinge pricing from 1941 to date is figured at (N-H ADD 15%)

Scott No.		Mint Sheet	Plate Block	Fine Unused Each	Fine Used Each
1954. LEWIS & CLARK EXPEDITION					
☐ 1063	3¢ Dark Brown	5.30	.60	.15	.09
1955. COMMEMORATIVES					
1955. PENNSYLVANIA ACADEMY OF FINE ARTS					
☐ 1064	3¢ Rose Brown	5.60	.57	.15	.10
1955. LAND GRANT COLLEGES					
☐ 1065	3¢ Green	5.15	.56	.14	.09
1955. ROTARY INTERNATIONAL ISSUE					
☐ 1066	8¢ Deep Blue	13.50	.15	.27	.12
1955. ARMED FORCES RESERVE					
☐ 1067	3¢ Red Violet	5.60	.58	.16	.10
1955. OLD MAN OF THE MOUNTAINS					
☐ 1068	3¢ Blue Green	5.70	.58	.15	.09
1955. SOO LOCKS CENTENNIAL					
☐ 1069	3¢ Blue	5.60	.58	.15	.09
1955. ATOMS FOR PEACE					
☐ 1070	3¢ Blue	5.40	.62	.16	.09
1955. FORT TICONDEROGA BICENTENNIAL					
☐ 1071	3¢ Sepia	5.90	.57	.15	.09
1955. ANDREW MELLON ISSUE					
☐ 1072	3¢ Deep Carmine	6.80	.56	.15	.08
1956. COMMEMORATIVES					
1956. 250TH ANNIVERSARY FRANKLIN'S BIRTH					
☐ 1073	3¢ Rose Carmine	5.10	.57	.15	.09
1956. BOOKER T. WASHINGTON ISSUE					
☐ 1074	3¢ Deep Blue	4.90	.58	.16	.08
1956. FIFTH INTL. PHILATELIC EXHIBITION DESIGNS OF 1035 & 1041 IN IMPERF. SOUVENIR SHEET					
☐ 1075	3¢ & 8¢ Sheet of 2	—	—	5.10	5.00
1956. FIFTH INTL. PHILATELIC EXHIBITION					
☐ 1076	3¢ Deep Violet	5.40	.65	.17	—
1956. WILDLIFE CONSERVATION ISSUE					
☐ 1077	3¢ Rose Lake	5.80	.72	.16	.11
☐ 1078	3¢ Brown	5.80	.72	.16	.11
☐ 1079	3¢ Green	5.80	.72	.16	.11
1956. PURE FOOD & DRUG ACT					
☐ 1080	3¢ Dark Blue Green	5.20	.57	.15	.08
1956. HOME OF PRESIDENT BUCHANAN					
☐ 1081	3¢ Black Brown	5.20	.57	.15	.08

*No hinge pricing from 1941 to date is figured at (N-H ADD 15%)

Scott No.		Mint Sheet	Plate Block	Fine Unused Each	Fine Used Each
1956. LABOR DAY ISSUE					
☐ 1082	3¢ Deep Blue	5.30	.57	.15	.08
1956. NASSAU HALL—PRINCETON					
☐ 1083	3¢ Black on Orange	5.20	.57	.15	.08
1956. DEVIL'S TOWER					
☐ 1084	3¢ Purple	5.50	.62	.15	.08
1956. CHILDREN'S ISSUE					
☐ 1085	3¢ Dark Blue	5.30	.62	.15	.08
1957. COMMEMORATIVES					
1957. ALEXANDER HAMILTON ISSUE					
☐ 1086	3¢ Rose Red	5.60	.57	.15	.08
1957. POLIO ISSUE					
☐ 1087	3¢ Light Purple	5.15	.57	.15	.08
1957. COAST & GEODETIC SURVEY					
☐ 1088	3¢ Dark Blue	5.15	.57	.15	.08
1957. ARCHITECTS ISSUE					
☐ 1089	3¢ Red Lilac	5.15	.57	.15	.08
1957. STEEL INDUSTRY CENTENNIAL					
☐ 1090	3¢ Bright Ultra	5.15	.57	.15	.08
1957. INTERNATIONAL NAVAL REVIEW					
☐ 1091	3¢ Blue Green	5.15	.57	.15	.08
1957. OKLAHOMA STATEHOOD					
☐ 1092	3¢ Dark Blue	5.40	.63	.15	.08
1957. SCHOOL TEACHERS					
☐ 1093	3¢ Rose Lake	5.20	.57	.13	.08
1957. U.S. FLAG ISSUE					
☐ 1094	4¢ Blue & Red	5.70	.66	.15	.08
1957. 350TH SHIPBUILDING ANNIVERSARY					
☐ 1095	3¢ Purple	6.60	.57	.15	.08
1957. PHILIPPINES—CHAMPION OF LIBERTY					
☐ 1096	8¢ Red, Blue, & Gold	12.00	1.20	.22	.16
1957. BIRTH OF LAFAYETTE					
☐ 1097	3¢ Maroon	5.75	.57	.14	.09
1957. WILDLIFE CONSERVATION ISSUE					
☐ 1098	3¢ Blue, Green & Yellow	5.15	.57	.14	.08
1957. RELIGIOUS FREEDOM					
☐ 1099	3¢ Black	5.15	.57	.14	.08

*No hinge pricing from 1941 to date is figured at (N-H ADD 15%)

Scott No.	Mint Sheet	Plate Block	Fine Unused Each	Fine Used Each
1958. COMMEMORATIVES				
1958. GARDENING & HORTICULTURE				
☐ 1100 3¢ Deep Green	5.30	.57	.14	.08
1958. BRUSSELS EXHIBITION				
☐ 1104 3¢ Deep Claret	5.30	.57	.14	.08
1958. JAMES MONROE BICENTENNIAL				
☐ 1105 3¢ Purple	6.90	.57	.15	.10
1958. MINNESOTA STATEHOOD				
☐ 1106 3¢ Green	5.15	.57	.14	.09
1958. INTERNATIONAL GEOPHYSICAL YEAR				
☐ 1107 3¢ Black & Orange	5.35	.71	.14	.10
1958. GUNSTON HALL BICENTENARY				
☐ 1108 3¢ Light Green	5.30	.58	.14	.09
1958. MACKINAC BRIDGE ISSUE				
☐ 1109 3¢ Bluish Green	5.20	.57	.13	.09
1958. SOUTH AMERICA—CHAMPION OF LIBERTY				
☐ 1110 4¢ Olive Bistre...........................	7.50	.65	.16	.10
☐ 1111 8¢ Red, Blue & Gold	19.00	3.60	.27	.19
1958. ATLANTIC CABLE CENTENNIAL				
☐ 1112 4¢ Reddish Purple	5.40	.65	.13	.09
1958-1959. LINCOLN COMMEMORATIVE ISSUE				
☐ 1113 1¢ Green	2.20	.28	.12	.09
☐ 1114 3¢ Rust Brown	5.00	.65	.16	.09
☐ 1115 4¢ Sepia	6.50	.70	.16	.08
☐ 1116 4¢ Blue	6.50	.70	.16	.08
1958. HUNGARY—CHAMPION OF LIBERTY				
☐ 1117 4¢ Bluish Green	7.60	.66	.15	.09
☐ 1118 8¢ Red, Blue & Gold	20.00	2.90	.25	.15
1958. FREEDOM OF THE PRESS				
☐ 1119 4¢ Black	6.60	.65	.15	.09
1958. OVERLAND MAIL CENTENNIAL				
☐ 1120 4¢ Crimson Rose	6.10	.60	.15	.09
1958. NOAH WEBSTER				
☐ 1121 4¢ Dark Carmine Rose	7.50	.60	.15	.10
1958. FOREST CONSERVATION				
☐ 1122 4¢ Yellow, Brown & Green	6.00	.60	.15	.09
1958. FORT DUQUESNE BICENTENNIAL				
☐ 1123 4¢ Blue	5.60	.60	.15	.11

*No hinge pricing from 1941 to date is figured at (N-H ADD 15%)

Scott No.		Mint Sheet	Plate Block	Fine Unused Each	Fine Used Each
1959. COMMEMORATIVES					
1959. OREGON STATEHOOD					
☐ 1124	4¢ Blue Green	5.60	.60	.15	.09
1959. ARGENTINA & CHILE—CHAMPION OF LIBERTY					
☐ 1125	4¢ Blue	7.50	.62	.15	.09
☐ 1126	8¢ Red, Blue & Gold	17.00	1.65	.27	.16
1959. 10TH ANNIVERSARY N.A.T.O.					
☐ 1127	4¢ Blue	7.60	.54	.15	.09
1959. ARCTIC EXPLORATIONS					
☐ 1128	4¢ Blue	5.40	.86	.15	.09
1959. WORLD PEACE & TRUST					
☐ 1129	8¢ Maroon	11.00	1.90	.25	.16
1959. SILVER DISCOVERY CENTENNIAL					
☐ 1130	4¢ Black	5.50	.57	.15	.10
1959. ST. LAWRENCE SEAWAY ISSUE					
☐ 1131	4¢ Red & Blue	5.50	.57	.15	.10
1959. 49-STAR FLAG ISSUE					
☐ 1132	4¢ Blue, Red & Yellow	5.50	.57	.15	.10
1959. SOIL CONSERVATION					
☐ 1133	4¢ Yellow, Green & Blue	5.60	.63	.15	.10
1959. PETROLEUM INDUSTRY CENTENNIAL					
☐ 1134	4¢ Brown	5.50	.57	.15	.10
1959. DENTAL HEALTH ISSUE					
☐ 1135	4¢ Green	5.50	.57	.15	.09
1959. GERMANY—CHAMPION OF LIBERTY					
☐ 1136	4¢ Gray	7.90	.70	.16	.11
☐ 1137	8¢ Red, Blue & Gold	19.00	2.60	.26	.16
1959. DR. EPHRAIM MCDOWELL					
☐ 1138	4¢ Maroon	7.50	.60	.16	.11
1960–1961. CREDO OF AMERICA SERIES					
☐ 1139	4¢ Dark Violet, Blue & Carmine	6.50	.66	.16	.11
☐ 1140	4¢ Olive Bistre & Green	6.50	.66	.16	.11
☐ 1141	4¢ Gray & Red	6.50	.80	.18	.11
☐ 1142	4¢ Red & Blue	6.50	.80	.18	.11
☐ 1143	4¢ Violet & Green	9.00	1.00	.25	.11
☐ 1144	4¢ Green & Brown	8.50	1.00	.25	.11
1960. COMMEMORATIVES					
1960. BOY SCOUTS GOLDEN JUBILEE					
☐ 1145	4¢ Red, Khaki & Blue	5.65	.72	.16	.11

*No hinge pricing from 1941 to date is figured at (N-H ADD 15%)

Scott No.		Mint Sheet	Plate Block	Fine Unused Each	Fine Used Each
1960. WINTER OLYMPIC GAMES					
☐ 1146	4¢ Blue	7.40	.86	.18	.11
1960. CZECHOSLOVAKIA—CHAMPION OF LIBERTY					
☐ 1147	4¢ Blue	7.70	.58	.16	.10
☐ 1148	8¢ Yellow, Blue & Red	16.90	1.82	.28	.18
1960. WORLD REFUGEE YEAR					
☐ 1149	4¢ Gray Black	5.60	.57	.16	.10
1960. WATER CONSERVATION					
☐ 1150	4¢ Blue, Green & Orange Brown	5.60	.57	.16	.10
1960. SOUTHEAST ASIA TREATY ORGANIZATION					
☐ 1151	4¢ Blue	7.50	.66	.16	.10
1960. HONORING AMERICAN WOMAN					
☐ 1152	4¢ Violet	5.60	.70	.15	.10
1960. 50-STAR FLAG ISSUE					
☐ 1153	4¢ Red & Blue	5.60	.66	.15	.10
1960. PONY EXPRESS CENTENNIAL					
☐ 1154	4¢ Sepia	6.30	.72	.19	.11
1960. EMPLOY THE HANDICAPPED					
☐ 1155	4¢ Blue	5.60	.64	.19	.12
1960. WORLD FORESTRY CONGRESS					
☐ 1156	4¢ Green	6.00	.72	.16	.10
1960. MEXICAN INDEPENDENCE SESQUICENTENNIAL					
☐ 1157	4¢ Red & Green	5.60	.60	.16	.10
1960. UNITED STATES—JAPAN TREATY CENTENNIAL					
☐ 1158	4¢ Blue & Pink	5.60	.60	.17	.11
1960. POLAND—CHAMPION OF LIBERTY					
☐ 1159	4¢ Blue	8.00	.60	.17	.11
☐ 1160	8¢ Red, Blue & Gold	16.00	1.90	.30	.16
1960. ROBERT A. TAFT MEMORIAL ISSUE					
☐ 1161	4¢ Dull Violet	7.50	.60	.17	.11
1960. WHEELS OF FREEDOM					
☐ 1162	4¢ Dark Blue	5.60	.60	.16	.10
1960. BOYS' CLUBS OF AMERICA					
☐ 1163	4¢ Indigo, Slate & Red	5.60	.65	.16	.10
1960. FIRST AUTOMATED POST OFFICE					
☐ 1164	4¢ Dark Blue & Carmine	5.60	.59	.16	.10
1960. FINLAND—CHAMPION OF LIBERTY					
☐ 1165	4¢ Blue	7.60	.60	.17	.11
☐ 1166	8¢ Red, Blue & Gold	17.00	2.00	.29	.16

*No hinge pricing from 1941 to date is figured at (N-H ADD 15%)

Scott No.		Mint Sheet	Plate Block	Fine Unused Each	Fine Used Each
1960. CAMP FIRE GIRLS					
☐ 1167	4¢ Dark Blue & Red	5.50	.60	.16	.11
1960. ITALY—CHAMPION OF LIBERTY					
☐ 1168	4¢ Green	7.40	.60	.16	.09
☐ 1169	8¢ Red, Blue & Gold	16.90	1.60	.30	.16
1960. WALTER F. GEORGE MEMORIAL ISSUE					
☐ 1170	4¢ Dull Violet	7.25	.60	.17	.10
1960. ANDREW CARNEGIE					
☐ 1171	4¢ Deep Claret	8.00	.66	.18	.11
1960. JOHN FOSTER DULLES MEMORIAL ISSUE					
☐ 1172	4¢ Dull Violet	7.40	.60	.17	.09
1960. "ECHO I" SATELLITE					
☐ 1173	4¢ Deep Violet	17.90	2.10	.50	.14
1961. COMMEMORATIVES					
1961. INDIA—CHAMPION OF LIBERTY					
☐ 1174	4¢ Red Orange	7.60	.60	.18	.09
☐ 1175	8¢ Red, Blue & Gold	16.00	2.00	.28	.17
1961. RANGE CONSERVATION					
☐ 1176	4¢ Blue, Slate & Brown Orange	5.50	.65	.17	.10
1961. HORACE GREELEY					
☐ 1177	4¢ Dull Violet	7.20	.65	.17	.10
1961-1965. CIVIL WAR CENTENNIAL SERIES					
1961. FORT SUMTER					
☐ 1178	4¢ Light Green	8.25	.93	.21	.11
1962. BATTLE OF SHILOH					
☐ 1179	4¢ Black on Peach	6.30	.70	.20	.10
1963. BATTLE OF GETTYSBURG					
☐ 1180	5¢ Blue & Gray	7.75	.70	.20	.10
1964. BATTLE OF THE WILDERNESS					
☐ 1181	5¢ Dark Red & Black	7.75	.82	.20	.10
1965. APPOMATTOX					
☐ 1182	5¢ Black & Blue	7.80	1.10	.20	.10
1961. KANSAS STATEHOOD					
☐ 1183	4¢ Brown, Dark Red & Green on Yellow Paper	5.50	.70	.17	.10
1961. GEORGE W. NORRIS BIRTH CENTENARY					
☐ 1184	4¢ Blue Green	5.50	.64	.17	.10
1961. NAVAL AVIATION GOLDEN JUBILEE					
☐ 1185	4¢ Blue	5.50	.64	.17	.11

*No hinge pricing from 1941 to date is figured at (N-H ADD 15%)

Scott No.		Mint Sheet	Plate Block	Fine Unused Each	Fine Used Each
1961. WORKMEN'S COMPENSATION LAW					
☐1186	4¢ Ultramarine	5.60	.62	.17	.12
1961. F. REMINGTON BIRTH CENTENNIAL					
☐1187	4¢ Blue, Red & Yellow	6.12	.80	.17	.10
1961. REPUBLIC OF CHINA ISSUE					
☐1188	4¢ Blue	5.50	.64	.17	.10
1961. DR. J. NAISMITH—BASKETBALL FOUNDER					
☐1189	4¢ Brown	6.00	.80	.17	.10
1961. NURSING PROFESSION					
☐1190	4¢ Blue, Red, Black & Green	5.50	.70	.17	.09
1962. COMMEMORATIVES					
1962. NEW MEXICO STATEHOOD					
☐1191	4¢ Blue, Maroon, Bistre	5.60	.65	.18	.12
1962. ARIZONA STATEHOOD					
☐1192	4¢ Red, Deep Blue, Green	5.60	.72	.18	.12
1962. PROJECT MERCURY					
☐1193	4¢ Dark Blue & Yellow	6.40	.90	.18	.12
1962. MALARIA ERADICATION					
☐1194	4¢ Blue & Bistre	5.50	.67	.15	.10
1962. CHARLES EVANS HUGHES BIRTH CENTENNIAL					
☐1195	4¢ Black on Buff	5.50	.70	.15	.10
1962. SEATTLE WORLD'S FAIR					
☐1196	4¢ Red & Dark Blue	5.50	.70	.15	.10
1962. LOUISIANA STATEHOOD					
☐1197	4¢ Blue, Green, Red	5.50	.70	.16	.10
1962. THE HOMESTEAD ACT					
☐1198	4¢ Slate	5.75	.70	.15	.10
1962. GIRL SCOUTS 50TH ANNIVERSARY					
☐1199	4¢ Red	5.50	.67	.15	.10
1962. BRIEN MCMAHON MEMORIAL ISSUE					
☐1200	4¢ Purple	5.80	.70	.15	.10
1962. NATIONAL APPRENTICESHIP ACT					
☐1201	4¢ Black on Buff	5.50	.66	.15	.10
1962. SAM RAYBURN MEMORIAL ISSUE					
☐1202	4¢ Brown & Blue	5.50	.66	.15	.10
1962. DAG HAMMARSKJOLD MEMORIAL					
☐1203	4¢ Yellow, Brown & Black	5.50	.66	.15	.10
☐1204	4¢ Yellow Color Inverted	12.00	3.60	.20	.19

*No hinge pricing from 1941 to date is figured at (N-H ADD 15%)

Scott No.		Mint Sheet	Plate Block	Fine Unused Each	Fine Used Each
1962. CHRISTMAS TREE					
☐ 1205	4¢ Green & Red	12.90	.70	.15	.08
1962. HIGHER EDUCATION					
☐ 1206	4¢ Green & Black	6.50	.70	.15	.10
1962. WINSLOW HOMER					
☐ 1207	4¢ Brown & Blue	7.40	.75	.20	.10
1963. 50-STAR FLAG					
☐ 1208	5¢ Red & Blue	12.90	.70	.15	.10
1962-1963. REGULAR ISSUE					
☐ 1209	1¢ Green	3.90	.34	.11	.10
☐ 1213	5¢ Dark Blue Gray	13.40	.81	.23	.10

1962-1963. ROTARY PRESS COIL STAMPS PERF. 10 VERTICALLY

Scott No.		Fine Unused Plate Blk	Ave. Unused Plate Blk	Fine Unused Each	Ave. Unused Each	Fine Used Each	Ave. Used Each
☐ 1225	1¢ Green	1.15	.82	.18	.13	.13	.08
☐ 1229	5¢ Dark Blue Gray	4.00	3.20	1.40	1.10	.12	.08

Scott No.		Mint Sheet	Plate Block	Fine Unused Each	Fine Used Each
1963 COMMEMORATIVES—CAROLINA CHARTER TERCENTENARY					
☐ 1230	5¢ Dark Carmine & Brown	6.80	.89	.20	.10
1963. FOOD FOR PEACE—FREEDOM FROM HUNGER					
☐ 1231	5¢ Green, Buff & Red	6.60	.75	.17	.10
1963. WEST VIRGINIA STATEHOOD					
☐ 1232	5¢ Green, Red & Black	6.60	.75	.17	.09
1963. EMANCIPATION PROCLAMATION					
☐ 1233	5¢ Black, Blue & Red	6.60	.75	.17	.09
1963. ALLIANCE FOR PROGRESS					
☐ 1234	5¢ Bright Blue & Green	6.60	.75	.17	.09
1963. CORDELL HULL					
☐ 1235	5¢ Blue Green	6.60	.75	.17	.09
1963. ELEANOR ROOSEVELT					
☐ 1236	5¢ Light Purple	6.60	.75	.17	.09
1963. THE SCIENCES					
☐ 1237	5¢ Blue & Black	6.90	.83	.20	.10
1963. CITY MAIL DELIVERY					
☐ 1238	5¢ Red, Blue & Gray	6.70	.75	.17	.10

*No hinge pricing from 1941 to date is figured at (N-H ADD 15%)

Scott No.		Mint Sheet	Plate Block	Fine Unused Each	Fine Used Each
1963. INTERNATIONAL RED CROSS CENTENARY					
☐ 1239	5¢ Slate & Carmine	6.60	.74	.17	.09
1963. CHRISTMAS ISSUE					
☐ 1240	5¢ Dark Blue, Blue Black & Red	13.40	.80	.17	.09
1963. JOHN JAMES AUDUBON					
☐ 1241	5¢ Blue, Brown, Bistre	6.90	.87	.19	.09
1964. COMMEMORATIVES					
1964. SAM HOUSTON					
☐ 1242	5¢ Black	6.60	.75	.18	.09
1964. CHARLES M. RUSSELL					
☐ 1243	5¢ Indigo, Red Brown & Olive	8.40	.93	.23	.11
1964. NEW YORK WORLD'S FAIR					
☐ 1244	5¢ Green	6.80	.79	.19	.10
1964. JOHN MUIR—CONSERVATIONIST					
☐ 1245	5¢ Brown, Green & Olive	6.60	.75	.17	.10
1964. JOHN F. KENNEDY MEMORIAL					
☐ 1246	5¢ Blue Gray	6.60	.78	.17	.10
1964. NEW JERSEY TERCENTENARY					
☐ 1247	5¢ Ultramarine	8.40	.92	.23	.11
1964. NEVADA STATEHOOD					
☐ 1248	5¢ Red, Yellow & Blue	6.67	.75	.17	.10
1964. REGISTER AND VOTE					
☐ 1249	5¢ Dark Blue & Red	6.67	.75	.17	.10
1964. WILLIAM SHAKESPEARE					
☐ 1250	5¢ Brown on Tan	6.67	.75	.17	.10
1964. DOCTORS MAYO					
☐ 1251	5¢ Green	6.67	.75	.17	.10
1964. AMERICAN MUSIC					
☐ 1252	5¢ Red, Black & Blue	6.67	.75	.17	.10
1964. AMERICAN HOMEMAKERS					
☐ 1253	5¢ Multicolored	6.67	.75	.17	.10
1964. CHRISTMAS ISSUE					
☐ 1254	5¢ Red & Green	—	—	.67	.10
☐ 1255	5¢ Red & Green	—	—	.67	.10
☐ 1256	5¢ Red & Green	—	—	.67	.10
☐ 1257	5¢ Red & Green	—	—	.67	.10
1964. VERRAZANO—NARROWS BRIDGE					
☐ 1258	5¢ Green	6.65	.75	.18	.10

*No hinge pricing from 1941 to date is figured at (N-H ADD 15%)

Scott No.	Mint Sheet	Plate Block	Fine Unused Each	Fine Used Each
1964. STUART DAVIS—MODERN ART				
☐ 1259 5¢ Ultramarine, Black & Red	6.60	.75	.18	.10
1964. RADIO AMATEURS				
☐ 1260 5¢ Red Lilac	6.60	.75	.18	.10
1965. COMMEMORATIVES				
1965. BATTLE OF NEW ORLEANS				
☐ 1261 5¢ Carmine, Blue & Gray	6.30	.75	.18	.10
1965. PHYSICAL FITNESS—SOKOL CENTENNIAL				
☐ 1262 5¢ Maroon & Black	6.30	.75	.18	.10
1965. CRUSADE AGAINST CANCER				
☐ 1263 5¢ Black, Purple, Orange	6.30	.75	.18	.10
1965. SIR WINSTON CHURCHILL MEMORIAL				
☐ 1264 5¢ Black	6.50	.80	.18	.10
1965. MAGNA CARTA 750TH ANNIVERSARY				
☐ 1265 5¢ Black, Ochre, Red Lilac	6.40	.75	.18	.10
1965. INTERNATIONAL COOPERATION YEAR				
☐ 1266 5¢ Dull Blue & Black	6.40	.75	.18	.10
1965. SALVATION ARMY				
☐ 1267 5¢ Red, Black & Blue	6.40	.75	.18	.10
1965. DANTE ALIGHIERI				
☐ 1268 5¢ Maroon on Tan	6.40	.75	.18	.09
1965. HERBERT HOOVER				
☐ 1269 5¢ Red Rose	6.40	.75	.18	.09
1965. ROBERT FULTON BIRTH BICENTENNIAL				
☐ 1270 5¢ Black & Blue	6.40	.75	.18	.09
1965. FLORIDA SETTLEMENT QUADRICENTENNIAL				
☐ 1271 5¢ Red, Yellow & Black	6.40	.80	.18	.09
1965. TRAFFIC SAFETY				
☐ 1272 5¢ Green, Black, Red	6.40	.84	.18	.09
1965. JOHN SINGLETON COPLEY—ARTIST				
☐ 1273 5¢ Black, Brown, Olive	7.60	.88	.18	.11
1965. INTERNATIONAL TELECOMMUNICATION UNION				
☐ 1274 11¢ Black, Carmine, Bistre	37.00	12.00	.60	.29
1965. ADLAI E. STEVENSON MEMORIAL				
☐ 1275 5¢ Light & Dark Blue, Black & Red	6.40	.74	.18	.10
1965. CHRISTMAS ISSUE				
☐ 1276 5¢ Red, Green & Yellow	15.00	.74	.18	.10

*No hinge pricing from 1941 to date is figured at (N-H ADD 15%)

Scott No.		Mint Sheet	Plate Block	Fine Unused Each	Fine Used Each

1965-1968. PROMINENT AMERICANS SERIES

Scott No.		Mint Sheet	Plate Block	Fine Unused Each	Fine Used Each
☐ 1278	1¢ Green	4.00	.34	.10	.07
☐ 1279	1¼¢ Green	40.00	.33	.12	.14
☐ 1280	2¢ Slate Blue	6.30	.40	.10	.08
☐ 1281	3¢ Purple	8.50	.57	.12	.08
☐ 1282	4¢ Black	11.50	.83	.14	.08
☐ 1283	5¢ Blue	13.75	1.14	.23	.10
☐ 1283B	5¢ Blue	13.75	.85	.23	.10
☐ 1284	6¢ Gray Brown	20.00	1.10	.23	.10
☐ 1285	8¢ Violet	22.00	1.45	.29	.10
☐ 1286	10¢ Lilac	25.00	1.60	.31	.10
☐ 1286A	12¢ Black	29.00	2.20	.35	.10
☐ 1287	13¢ Brown	33.00	2.50	.34	.12
☐ 1288	15¢ Rose Claret	44.00	3.00	.40	.11
☐ 1289	20¢ Olive Green	44.00	2.90	.56	.10
☐ 1290	25¢ Rose Lake	53.00	3.30	.57	.10
☐ 1291	30¢ Light Purple	78.00	3.90	.78	.12
☐ 1292	40¢ Dark Blue	86.00	5.10	1.07	.12
☐ 1293	50¢ Maroon	114.50	6.20	1.50	.09
☐ 1294	$1 Purple	257.00	16.00	2.80	.16
☐ 1295	$5 Gray	1340.00	54.00	14.00	4.05

Scott No.		Fine Unused Line Pair	Ave. Unused Line Pair	Fine Unused Each	Ave. Unused Each	Fine Used Each	Ave. Used Each

PERF. 10 HORIZONTALLY

| ☐ 1297 | 3¢ Purple | .75 | .60 | .13 | .09 | .12 | .10 |
| ☐ 1298 | 6¢ Gray Brown | 1.90 | 1.40 | .32 | .23 | .12 | .10 |

PERF. 10 VERTICALLY

☐ 1299	1¢ Green	.32	.23	.10	.07	.11	.10
☐ 1303	4¢ Black	1.00	.80	.19	.13	.11	.11
☐ 1304	5¢ Blue	.70	.50	.19	.14	.10	.11
☐ 1305	6¢ Gray Brown	.99	.70	.30	.21	.10	.11
☐ 1305C	$1 Purple	6.40	4.70	2.15	1.70	.90	.64

Scott No.		Mint Sheet	Plate Block	Fine Unused Each	Fine Used Each

1966. COMMEMORATIVES
1966. MIGRATORY BIRD TREATY

| ☐ 1306 | 5¢ Red, Blue, Black | 7.35 | .82 | .17 | .09 |

1966. HUMANE TREATMENT OF ANIMALS

| ☐ 1307 | 5¢ Orange Brown & Black | 6.90 | .72 | .17 | .09 |

1966. INDIANA STATEHOOD

| ☐ 1308 | 5¢ Ochre, Brown & Violet Blue | 6.90 | .72 | .17 | .09 |

*No hinge pricing from 1941 to date is figured at (N-H ADD 15%)

Scott No.	Mint Sheet	Plate Block	Fine Unused Each	Fine Used Each
1966. AMERICAN CIRCUS				
☐ 1309 5¢ Red, Blue, Pink, Black	7.25	.73	.18	.10
1966. SIXTH INTL. PHILATELIC EXHIBITION "SIPEX"				
☐ 1310 5¢ Multicolored	6.90	.68	.17	.10
IMPERFORATE SOUVENIR SHEET				
☐ 1311 5¢ Multicolored	—	—	.35	.30
1966. BILL OF RIGHTS				
☐ 1312 5¢ Red, Dark & Light Blue	6.80	.67	.18	.09
1966. POLISH MILLENNIUM				
☐ 1313 5¢ Red	7.10	.67	.18	.09
1966. NATIONAL PARK SERVICE				
☐ 1314 5¢ Yellow, Black & Green	6.60	.66	.18	.09
1966. MARINE CORPS RESERVE				
☐ 1315 5¢ Black, Red, Blue, Olive	6.60	.66	.18	.09
1966. GENERAL FEDERATION OF WOMEN'S CLUBS				
☐ 1316 5¢ Blue, Pink, Black	6.60	.66	.18	.09
1966. AMERICAN FOLKLORE—JOHNNY APPLESEED				
☐ 1317 5¢ Red, Black, Green	6.60	.66	.18	.09
1966. BEAUTIFICATION OF AMERICA				
☐ 1318 5¢ Emerald, Pink, Black	7.20	.92	.18	.09
1966. GREAT RIVER ROAD				
☐ 1319 5¢ Yellow, Red, Blue, Green	6.90	.77	.20	.10
1966. SERVICEMEN & SAVINGS BONDS				
☐ 1320 5¢ Red, Light Blue, Dark Blue	6.90	.77	.19	.10
1966. CHRISTMAS ISSUE				
☐ 1321 5¢ Multicolored	14.00	.84	.19	.10
1966. MARY CASSATT—ARTIST				
☐ 1322 5¢ Multicolored	9.60	1.50	.24	.10
1967. COMMEMORATIVES				
1967. NATIONAL GRANGE CENTENARY				
☐ 1323 5¢ Orange, Yellow, Black, Brown & Green ...	7.20	.70	.17	.10
1967. CANADA CENTENNIAL				
☐ 1324 5¢ Green, Light & Dark Blue, Black	7.40	.77	.17	.10
1967. ERIE CANAL SESQUICENTENNIAL				
☐ 1325 5¢ Light & Dark Blue, Red & Black	7.20	.77	.17	.10
1967. SEARCH FOR PEACE—LIONS INTL.				
☐ 1326 5¢ Red, Blue & Black	7.30	.70	.17	.10
1967. HENRY DAVID THOREAU				
☐ 1327 5¢ Black, Red & Green	7.90	.77	.19	.10

*No hinge pricing from 1941 to date is figured at (N-H ADD 15%)

Scott No.		Mint Sheet	Plate Block	Fine Unused Each	Fine Used Each

1967. NEBRASKA STATEHOOD CENTENNIAL

| ☐ 1328 | 5¢ Yellow Green & Brown | 7.35 | .70 | .17 | .10 |

1967. VOICE OF AMERICA

| ☐ 1329 | 5¢ Red, Blue & Black | 7.35 | .70 | .17 | .10 |

1967. AMERICAN FOLKLORE—DAVY CROCKETT

| ☐ 1330 | 5¢ Green & Black | 7.35 | .75 | .17 | .10 |

1967. SPACE ACCOMPLISHMENTS

| ☐ 1331 | 5¢ Light & Dark Blue, Red, Black | — | — | .88 | .30 |
| ☐ 1332 | 5¢ Light & Dark Blue, Red, Black | — | — | .88 | .30 |

1967. URBAN PLANNING

| ☐ 1333 | 5¢ Blue & Black | 8.50 | 1.43 | .18 | .10 |

1967. FINNISH INDEPENDENCE

| ☐ 1334 | 5¢ Blue | 8.50 | 1.43 | .18 | .10 |

1967. THOMAS EAKINS—ARTIST

| ☐ 1335 | 5¢ Gold & Multicolored | 8.80 | 1.43 | .18 | .10 |

1967. CHRISTMAS ISSUE

| ☐ 1336 | 5¢ Multicolored | 7.30 | .82 | .18 | .10 |

1967. MISSISSIPPI STATEHOOD

| ☐ 1337 | 5¢ Multicolored | 8.60 | 1.30 | .20 | .10 |

1968–1971. REGULAR ISSUES

1968. FLAG ISSUE

| ☐ 1338 | 6¢ Red, Blue, Green | 17.65 | .84 | .20 | .10 |

1968. COMMEMORATIVES

1968. ILLINOIS STATEHOOD

| ☐ 1339 | 6¢ Black, Gold, Pink | 8.75 | .90 | .23 | .11 |

1968. HEMISFAIR '68

| ☐ 1340 | 6¢ Indigo, Carmine, White | 8.75 | .90 | .23 | .11 |

1968. AIRLIFT TO SERVICEMEN

| ☐ 1341 | $1 Multicolored | 285.00 | 34.00 | 6.60 | 4.20 |

1968. SUPPORT OUR YOUTH (ELKS)

| ☐ 1342 | 6¢ Red & Blue | 8.90 | .90 | .24 | .11 |

1968. LAW AND ORDER

| ☐ 1343 | 6¢ Blue & Black | 8.90 | .90 | .24 | .11 |

1968. REGISTER & VOTE

| ☐ 1344 | 6¢ Black & Gold | 8.90 | .87 | .24 | .11 |

1968. HISTORIC AMERICAN FLAGS

| ☐ 1345 | 6¢ Dark Blue | — | — | 1.40 | .70 |
| ☐ 1346 | 6¢ Red & Dark Blue | — | — | 1.25 | .70 |

*No hinge pricing from 1941 to date is figured at (N-H ADD 15%)

Scott No.		Mint Sheet	Plate Block	Fine Unused Each	Fine Used Each
☐ 1347	6¢ Dark, Blue, Olive Green	—	—	.60	.47
☐ 1348	6¢ Dark Blue & Red	—	—	.60	.50
☐ 1349	6¢ Black, Yellow, Red	—	—	.60	.49
☐ 1350	6¢ Dark Blue & Red	—	—	.60	.49
☐ 1351	6¢ Blue, Olive Green, Red	—	—	.60	.49
☐ 1352	6¢ Dark Blue & Red	—	—	.60	.49
☐ 1353	6¢ Blue, Yellow, Red	—	—	.60	.50
☐ 1354	6¢ Blue Red, Yellow			.80	.50

1968. WALT DISNEY
☐ 1355	6¢ Multicolored	11.50	2.20	.28	.09

1968. FATHER MARQUETTE—EXPLORATIONS
☐ 1356	6¢ Black, Brown, Green	8.80	.95	.20	.09

1968. AMERICAN FOLKLORE—DANIEL BOONE
☐ 1357	6¢ Brown, Yellow, Black, Red	8.80	.93	.20	.09

1968. ARKANSAS RIVER NAVIGATION
☐ 1358	6¢ Black & Blue	8.80	.93	.21	.09

1968. LEIF ERIKSON
☐ 1359	6¢ Dark Brown on Brown	8.80	.93	.21	.09

1968. CHEROKEE STRIP LAND RUSH
☐ 1360	6¢ Brown	10.80	1.15	.24	.10

1968. JOHN TRUMBULL PAINTING
☐ 1361	6¢ Yellow Red, Black.....................	12.50	1.25	.27	.10

1968. WILDLIFE CONSERVATION—DUCKS
☐ 1362	6¢ Multicolored	12.30	1.60	.34	.10

1968. CHRISTMAS ISSUE
☐ 1363	6¢ Multicolored	8.70	1.30	.25	.10

1968. AMERICAN INDIAN
☐ 1364	6¢ Multicolored	16.80	3.10	.37	.13

1969. COMMEMORATIVES

1969. BEAUTIFICATION OF AMERICA
☐ 1365	6¢ Multicolored	—	—	.90	.16
☐ 1366	6¢ Multicolored	—	—	.90	.16
☐ 1367	6¢ Multicolored	—	—	.90	.16
☐ 1368	6¢ Multicolored	—	—	.90	.16

1969. AMERICAN LEGION
☐ 1369	6¢ Red, Blue, Black	8.90	.85	.23	.10

1969. GRANDMA MOSES PAINTING
☐ 1370	6¢ Multicolored	8.90	.90	.23	.09

1969. APOLLO 8 MOON ORBIT
☐ 1371	6¢ Black, Blue, Ochre	13.40	1.90	.29	.11

*No hinge pricing from 1941 to date is figured at (N-H ADD 15%)

Scott No.		Mint Sheet	Plate Block	Fine Unused Each	Fine Used Each
1969. W. C. HANDY—MUSICIAN					
☐ 1372	6¢ Multicolored	8.30	.80	.22	.09
1969. SETTLEMENT OF CALIFORNIA					
☐ 1373	6¢ Multicolored	8.30	.80	.22	.09
1969. MAJOR JOHN WESLEY POWELL—GEOLOGIST					
☐ 1374	6¢ Multicolored	8.30	.80	.22	.09
1969. ALABAMA STATEHOOD					
☐ 1375	6¢ Red, Yellow, Brown	8.30	.80	.22	.09
1969. XI INTL. BOTANICAL CONGRESS					
☐ 1376	6¢ Multicolored	—	—	1.45	.19
☐ 1377	6¢ Multicolored	—	—	1.45	.19
☐ 1378	6¢ Multicolored	—	—	1.45	.19
☐ 1379	6¢ Multicolored	—	—	1.45	.19
1969. DARTMOUTH COLLEGE CASE					
☐ 1380	6¢ Green	8.50	.80	.21	.10
1969. PROFESSIONAL BASEBALL CENTENARY					
☐ 1381	6¢ Multicolored	23.00	2.30	.56	.12
1969. INTERCOLLEGIATE FOOTBALL CENTENARY					
☐ 1382	6¢ Red & Green	14.00	1.40	.34	.10
1969. DWIGHT D. EISENHOWER MEMORIAL					
☐ 1383	6¢ Blue, Black & Red	6.00	.80	.23	.10
1969. CHRISTMAS ISSUE					
☐ 1384	6¢ Multicolored	8.00	2.14	.23	.10
1969. HOPE FOR THE CRIPPLED					
☐ 1385	6¢ Multicolored	8.20	.80	.22	.10
1969. WILLIAM M. HARNETT PAINTING					
☐ 1386	6¢ Multicolored	5.30	.80	.22	.10
1970. COMMEMORATIVES					
1970. NATURAL HISTORY					
☐ 1387	6¢ Multicolored	—	—	.23	.14
☐ 1388	6¢ Multicolored	—	—	.23	.14
☐ 1389	6¢ Multicolored	—	—	.23	.14
☐ 1390	6¢ Multicolored	—	—	.23	.14
1970. MAINE STATEHOOD SESQUICENTENNIAL					
☐ 1391	6¢ Multicolored	7.90	.85	.23	.11
1970. WILDLIFE CONSERVATION—BUFFALO					
☐ 1392	6¢ Black on Tan	7.90	.85	.23	.11
1970–1974. REGULAR ISSUE					
☐ 1393	6¢ Blue Gray	16.70	1.00	.20	.10
☐ 1393D	7¢ Light Blue	17.60	.96	.20	.10

*No hinge pricing from 1941 to date is figured at (N-H ADD 15%)

Scott No.			Mint Sheet	Plate Block	Fine Unused Each	Fine Used Each
☐ 1394	8¢	Black, Blue, Red	18.00	1.00	.23	.10
☐ 1395	8¢	Rose Violet	—	—	.35	.10
☐ 1396	8¢	Multicolored	20.00	6.60	.23	.10
☐ 1397	14¢	Brown	32.00	1.85	.40	.13
☐ 1398	16¢	Orange Brown	37.00	1.95	.42	.16
☐ 1399	18¢	Purple	42.00	1.98	.47	.16
☐ 1400	21¢	Green	47.00	2.30	.55	.26

Scott No.			Fine Unused Line Pair	Ave. Unused Line Pair	Fine Unused Each	Ave. Unused Each	Fine Used Each	Ave. Used Each
1970–1971. ROTARY PRESS COIL STAMPS—PERF. 10 VERTICALLY								
☐ 1401	6¢	Blue Gray	.72	.60	.22	.17	.13	.10
☐ 1402	8¢	Rose Violet	.72	.60	.22	.17	.13	.10

Scott No.			Mint Sheet	Plate Block	Fine Unused Each	Fine Used Each
1970. EDGAR LEE MASTERS—POET						
☐ 1405	6¢	Black & Olive Bistre	8.00	.93	.21	.11
1970. 50th ANNIVERSARY WOMEN'S SUFFRAGE						
☐ 1406	6¢	Blue	7.90	.93	.21	.11
1970. SOUTH CAROLINA TERCENTENARY						
☐ 1407	6¢	Multicolored	7.90	.93	.21	.11
1970. STONE MOUNTAIN MEMORIAL						
☐ 1408	6¢	Gray Black	7.90	.93	.21	.11
1970. FORT SNELLING						
☐ 1409	6¢	Multicolored	7.90	.93	.21	.11
1970. ANTI-POLLUTION						
☐ 1410	6¢	Multicolored	—	—	.34	.17
☐ 1411	6¢	Multicolored	—	—	.34	.17
☐ 1412	6¢	Multicolored	—	—	.34	.17
☐ 1413	6¢	Multicolored	—	—	.34	.17
1970. CHRISTMAS ISSUE						
☐ 1414	6¢	Multicolored	9.30	2.10	.23	.07
☐ 1415	6¢	Multicolored	—	—	.70	.14
☐ 1416	6¢	Multicolored	—	—	.70	.14
☐ 1417	6¢	Multicolored	—	—	.70	.14
☐ 1418	6¢	Multicolored	—	—	.70	.14
1970. PRECANCELLED CHRISTMAS ISSUE						
☐ 1414a	6¢	Multicolored	10.60	4.10	.25	.13
☐ 1415a	6¢	Multicolored	—	—	1.45	.16
☐ 1416a	6¢	Multicolored	—	—	1.45	.16
☐ 1417a	6¢	Multicolored	—	—	1.45	.16
☐ 1418a	6¢	Multicolored	—	—	1.45	.16

*No hinge pricing from 1941 to date is figured at (N-H ADD 15%)

Scott No.		Mint Sheet	Plate Block	Fine Unused Each	Fine Used Each
1970. UNITED NATIONS 25th ANNIVERSARY					
☐ 1419	6¢ Black, Red, Blue	7.85	.86	.21	.11
1970. PILGRIM LANDING 350th ANNIVERSARY					
☐ 1420	6¢ Multicolored	7.85	.86	.21	.11
1970. DISABLED AMERICAN VETERANS AND SERVICEMEN ISSUE					
☐ 1421	6¢ Blue, Black, Red	—	—	.20	.13
☐ 1422	6¢ Blue, Black, Red	—	—	.20	.13
1971. COMMEMORATIVES					
1971. ADVENT OF SHEEP TO AMERICA					
☐ 1423	6¢ Multicolored	7.85	.83	.19	.10
1971. GENERAL DOUGLAS MacARTHUR					
☐ 1424	6¢ Red, Blue, Black	7.85	.83	.19	.10
1971. BLOOD DONORS PROGRAM					
☐ 1425	6¢ Light Blue, Scarlet, Indigo	7.85	.83	.19	.10
1971. MISSOURI STATEHOOD					
☐ 1426	8¢ Multicolored	10.00	3.40	.25	.12
1971. WILDLIFE CONSERVATION					
☐ 1427	8¢ Multicolored	—	—	.55	.14
☐ 1428	8¢ Multicolored	—	—	.24	.14
☐ 1429	8¢ Multicolored	—	—	.24	.14
☐ 1430	8¢ Multicolored	—	—	.24	.14
1971. ANTARCTIC TREATY					
☐ 1431	8¢ Red & Blue	10.70	1.15	.28	.10
1971. AMERICAN REVOLUTION BICENTENNIAL					
☐ 1432	8¢ Red, Blue, Black	19.00	2.20	1.10	.10
1971. JOHN SLOAN PAINTING					
☐ 1433	8¢ Multicolored	10.00	1.15	.26	.10
1971. DECADE OF SPACE ACHIEVEMENTS					
☐ 1434	8¢ Multicolored	—	—	.24	.11
☐ 1435	8¢ Multicolored	—	—	.24	.11
1971. EMILY DICKINSON—POET					
☐ 1436	8¢ Multicolored	9.40	1.10	.23	.10
1971. SAN JUAN 450th ANNIVERSARY					
☐ 1437	8¢ Brown, Carmine, Blk.	9.40	1.10	.23	.10
1971. DRUG ADDICTION					
☐ 1438	8¢ Blue & Black	9.40	1.10	.23	.10
1971. CARE ANNIVERSARY					
☐ 1439	8¢ Multicolored	9.40	1.10	.25	.11
☐ 1440	8¢ Dark Brown & Ochre	—	—	.27	.13

*No hinge pricing from 1941 to date is figured at (N-H ADD 15%)

Scott No.		Mint Sheet	Plate Block	Fine Unused Each	Fine Used Each
☐ 1441	8¢ Dark Brown & Ochre	—	—	.27	.13
☐ 1442	8¢ Dark Brown & Ochre	—	—	.27	.13
☐ 1443	8¢ Dark Brown & Ochre	—	—	.27	.13

1971. CHRISTMAS

☐ 1444	8¢ Multicolored	9.40	2.70	.26	.10
☐ 1445	8¢ Multicolored	9.40	2.70	.26	.10

1972. COMMEMORATIVES

1972. SIDNEY LANIER—POET

☐ 1446	8¢ Multicolored	9.70	1.00	.24	.10

1972. PEACE CORPS

☐ 1447	8¢ Red & Blue	9.70	1.55	.24	.10

1972. NATIONAL PARKS CENTENNIAL

☐ 1448	2¢ Multicolored	—	—	.10	.10
☐ 1449	2¢ Multicolored	—	—	.13	.12
☐ 1450	2¢ Multicolored	—	—	.13	.12
☐ 1451	2¢ Multicolored	—	—	.13	.12
☐ 1452	6¢ Multicolored	8.00	1.00	.23	.15
☐ 1453	8¢ Multicolored	6.50	1.10	.26	.10
☐ 1454	15¢ Multicolored	19.00	1.90	.41	.43

1972. FAMILY PLANNING

☐ 1455	8¢ Multicolored	9.90	1.10	.25	.11

1972. AMERICAN REVOLUTION BICENTENNIAL—COLONIAL CRAFTMEN

☐ 1456	8¢ Deep Brown, Yellow	—	—	.24	.14
☐ 1457	8¢ Deep Brown, Yellow	—	—	.24	.14
☐ 1458	8¢ Deep Brown, Yellow	—	—	.24	.14
☐ 1459	8¢ Deep Brown, Yellow	—	—	.24	.14

1972. OLYMPIC GAMES

☐ 1460	6¢ Multicolored	11.50	2.70	.30	.16
☐ 1461	8¢ Multicolored	13.50	3.10	.30	.11
☐ 1462	15¢ Multicolored	22.00	5.50	.51	.56

1972. PARENT TEACHER ASSOCIATION

☐ 1463	8¢ Black & Yellow	9.30	1.15	.25	.10
☐ 1463a	8¢ Black & Yellow, Reversed Pl. No.	—	1.17	—	—

1972. WILDLIFE CONSERVATION

☐ 1464	8¢ Multicolored	—	—	.24	.12
☐ 1465	8¢ Multicolored	—	—	.24	.12
☐ 1466	8¢ Multicolored	—	—	.24	.12
☐ 1467	8¢ Multicolored	—	—	.24	.12

1972. MAIL ORDER BUSINESS

☐ 1468	8¢ Multicolored	9.50	2.80	.25	.10

*No hinge pricing from 1941 to date is figured at (N-H ADD 15%)

Scott No.		Mint Sheet	Plate Block	Fine Unused Each	Fine Used Each
1972. OSTEOPATHIC MEDICINE					
☐ 1469	8¢ Yellow Orange, Brown	9.50	1.50	.26	.09
1972. TOM SAWYER—AMERICAN FOLKLORE					
☐ 1470	8¢ Multicolored	9.50	1.20	.26	.09
1972. CHRISTMAS					
☐ 1471	8¢ Multicolored	9.50	2.90	.26	.09
☐ 1472	8¢ Multicolored	9.50	2.90	.26	.09
1972. PHARMACY					
☐ 1473	8¢ Multicolored	9.50	1.20	.26	.09
1972. STAMP COLLECTING					
☐ 1474	8¢ Multicolored	8.50	1.15	.26	.10
1973. COMMEMORATIVES					
1973. LOVE—"FOR SOMEONE SPECIAL"					
☐ 1475	8¢ Red, Green, Blue	9.50	1.40	.22	.08
1973. COLONIAL COMMUNICATIONS					
☐ 1476	8¢ Black, Red, Blue	9.60	1.20	.24	.11
☐ 1477	8¢ Blue, Red, Brown	9.60	1.20	.24	.11
☐ 1478	8¢ Multicolored	9.60	1.20	.24	.11
☐ 1479	8¢ Multicolored	9.60	1.20	.24	.11
1973. BOSTON TEA PARTY					
☐ 1480	8¢ Multicolored	—	—	.24	.14
☐ 1481	8¢ Multicolored	—	—	.24	.14
☐ 1482	8¢ Multicolored	—	—	.24	.14
☐ 1483	8¢ Multicolored	—	—	.24	.14
1973. GEORGE GERSHWIN—COMPOSER					
☐ 1484	8¢ Multicolored	8.30	2.80	.22	.10
1973. ROBINSON JEFFERS—POET					
☐ 1485	8¢ Multicolored	8.30	2.80	.22	.10
1973. HENRY OSSAWA TANNER—ARTIST					
☐ 1486	6¢ Multicolored	8.30	2.80	.22	.10
1973. WILLA CATHER—NOVELIST					
☐ 1487	8¢ Multicolored	8.30	2.80	.22	.10
1973. NICOLAUS COPERNICUS					
☐ 1488	8¢ Black & Orange	10.40	1.10	.23	.11
1973. POSTAL PEOPLE					
☐ 1489	8¢ Multicolored	—	—	.21	.13
☐ 1490	8¢ Multicolored	—	—	.21	.13
☐ 1491	8¢ Multicolored	—	—	.21	.13
☐ 1492	8¢ Multicolored	—	—	.21	.13
☐ 1493	8¢ Multicolored	—	—	.21	.13
☐ 1494	8¢ Multicolored	—	—	.21	.13

*No hinge pricing from 1941 to date is figured at (N-H ADD 15%)

Scott No.		Mint Sheet	Plate Block	Fine Unused Each	Fine Used Each
☐ 1495	8¢ Multicolored	—	—	.21	.13
☐ 1496	8¢ Multicolored	—	—	.21	.13
☐ 1497	8¢ Multicolored	—	—	.21	.13
☐ 1498	8¢ Multicolored	—	—	.21	.13

1973. HARRY S. TRUMAN MEMORIAL
| ☐ 1499 | 8¢ Black, Red, Blue | 7.30 | 1.10 | .25 | .12 |

1973. PROGRESS IN ELECTRONICS
☐ 1500	6¢ Multicolored	8.90	1.20	.21	.21
☐ 1501	8¢ Multicolored	9.80	1.20	.25	.10
☐ 1502	15¢ Multicolored	18.75	2.50	.46	.51

1973. LYNDON B. JOHNSON MEMORIAL
| ☐ 1503 | 8¢ Multicolored | 7.20 | 3.20 | .24 | .12 |

1973. ANGUS CATTLE—RURAL AMERICA
| ☐ 1504 | 8¢ Multicolored | 10.60 | .95 | .25 | .11 |

1974. CHAUTAUQUA—RURAL AMERICA
| ☐ 1505 | 10¢ Multicolored | 12.60 | 1.25 | .26 | .11 |

1974. WINTER WHEAT—RURAL AMERICA
| ☐ 1506 | 10¢ Multicolored | 12.00 | 1.20 | .28 | .11 |

1973. CHRISTMAS
| ☐ 1507 | 8¢ Multicolored | 10.00 | 3.80 | .28 | .10 |
| ☐ 1508 | 8¢ Multicolored | 10.00 | 3.80 | .25 | .10 |

1973–1974. REGULAR ISSUES
☐ 1509	10¢ Red & Blue	22.00	5.00	.28	.09
☐ 1510	10¢ Blue	22.00	1.20	.28	.09
☐ 1511	10¢ Multicolored	22.00	2.10	.28	.09

Scott No.		Fine Unused Line Pair	Ave. Unused Line Pair	Fine Unused Each	Ave. Unused Each	Fine Used Each	Ave. Used Each
1973–1974. COIL STAMPS—PERF. 10 VERTICALLY							
☐ 1518	63¢ Orange	.90	.75	.20	.15	.18	.14
☐ 1519	10¢ Red & Blue	—	—	.31	.23	.15	.11
☐ 1520	10¢ Blue	.90	.70	.33	.23	.15	.11

Scott No.		Mint Sheet	Plate Block	Fine Unused Each	Fine Used Each
1974. COMMEMORATIVES						
1974. VETERANS OF FOREIGN WARS						
☐ 1525	10¢ Carmine & Blue	11.50	1.25	.27	.11

1974. ROBERT FROST—POET
| ☐ 1526 | 10¢ Black | 11.50 | 1.25 | .27 | .11 |

1974. EXPO '74—PRESERVE THE ENVIRONMENT
| ☐ 1527 | 10¢ Multicolored | 9.10 | 3.50 | .27 | .11 |

*No hinge pricing from 1941 to date is figured at (N-H ADD 15%)

Scott No.		Mint Sheet	Plate Block	Fine Unused Each	Fine Used Each
1974. HORSE RACING					
☐ 1528	10¢ Multicolored	11.70	3.40	.27	.11
1974. SKYLAB PROJECT					
☐ 1529	10¢ Multicolored	11.70	1.25	.27	.10
1974. UNIVERSAL POSTAL UNION CENTENARY					
☐ 1530	10¢ Multicolored	—	—	.26	.23
☐ 1531	10¢ Multicolored	—	—	.26	.23
☐ 1532	10¢ Multicolored	—	—	.26	.23
☐ 1533	10¢ Multicolored	—	—	.26	.23
☐ 1534	10¢ Multicolored	—	—	.26	.23
☐ 1535	10¢ Multicolored	—	—	.26	.23
☐ 1536	10¢ Multicolored	—	—	.26	.23
☐ 1537	10¢ Multicolored	—	—	.26	.23
1974. MINERALS HERITAGE ISSUE					
☐ 1538	10¢ Multicolored	—	—	.23	.14
☐ 1539	10¢ Multicolored	—	—	.23	.14
☐ 1540	10¢ Multicolored	—	—	.26	.13
☐ 1541	10¢ Multicolored	—	—	.26	.13
1974. FORT HARROD BICENTENNIAL					
☐ 1542	10¢ Multicolored	1.45	1.20	.29	.10
1974. CONTINENTAL CONGRESS					
☐ 1543	10¢ Red, Blue, Gray	—	—	.27	.12
☐ 1544	10¢ Red, Blue, Gray	—	—	.27	.12
☐ 1545	10¢ Red, Blue, Gray	—	—	.27	.12
☐ 1546	10¢ Red, Blue, Gray	—	—	.27	.12
1974. ENERGY CONSERVATION					
☐ 1547	10¢ Multicolored	11.50	1.15	.27	.11
1974. LEGEND OF SLEEPY HOLLOW					
☐ 1548	10¢ Multicolored	11.50	1.15	.27	.11
1974. RETARDED CHILDREN					
☐ 1549	10¢ Light & Dark Brown	11.50	1.15	.27	.11
1974. CHRISTMAS					
☐ 1550	10¢ Multicolored	11.60	2.60	.32	.10
☐ 1551	10¢ Multicolored	11.60	3.60	.32	.10
☐ 1552	10¢ Multicolored	11.60	5.20	.35	.11
☐ 1552	10¢ Multicolored, Plate Block of 12	—	3.60	—	—
1975. COMMEMORATIVES—AMERICAN ARTS					
1975. BENJAMIN WEST—ARTIST					
☐ 1553	10¢ Multicolored	11.50	3.00	.29	.11
1975. PAUL LAURENCE DUNBAR—POET					
☐ 1554	10¢ Multicolored	11.50	3.00	.29	.11

*No hinge pricing from 1941 to date is figured at (N-H ADD 15%)

Scott No.		Mint Sheet	Plate Block	Fine Unused Each	Fine Used Each

1975. D. W. GRIFFITH—MOTION PICTURES
| ☐ 1555 | 10¢ Multicolored | 11.25 | 1.22 | .29 | .11 |

1975. PIONEER 10 SPACE MISSION
| ☐ 1556 | 10¢ Multicolored | 11.25 | 1.22 | .29 | .11 |

1975. MARINER 10 SPACE MISSION
| ☐ 1557 | 10¢ Multicolored | 11.25 | 1.22 | .29 | .11 |

1975. COLLECTIVE BARGAINING
| ☐ 1558 | 10¢ Blue, Red, Purple | 11.25 | 2.40 | .29 | .11 |

1975. CONTRIBUTORS TO THE CAUSE
☐ 1559	8¢ Multicolored	9.75	2.70	.24	.21
☐ 1560	10¢ Multicolored	11.25	3.00	.29	.11
☐ 1561	10¢ Multicolored	11.25	3.00	.30	.11
☐ 1562	18¢ Multicolored	24.50	5.70	.60	.50

1975. LEXINGTON AND CONCORD BATTLES BICENTENNIAL
| ☐ 1563 | 10¢ Multicolored | 11.00 | 4.00 | .28 | .11 |

1975. BATTLE OF BUNKER HILL
| ☐ 1564 | 10¢ Multicolored | 10.50 | 3.70 | .28 | .11 |

1975. CONTINENTAL MILITARY SERVICE UNIFORMS
☐ 1565	10¢ Multicolored	—	—	.27	.12
☐ 1566	10¢ Multicolored	—	—	.27	.12
☐ 1567	10¢ Multicolored	—	—	.27	.12
☐ 1568	10¢ Multicolored	—	—	.27	.12

1975. U.S.—SOVIET JOINT SPACE MISSION
| ☐ 1569 | 10¢ Multicolored | — | — | .26 | .16 |
| ☐ 1570 | 10¢ Multicolored | — | — | .26 | .16 |

1975. INTERNATIONAL WOMEN'S YEAR
| ☐ 1571 | 10¢ Multicolored | 11.75 | 1.85 | .23 | .08 |

1975. U.S. POSTAL SERVICE BICENTENNIAL
☐ 1572	10¢ Multicolored	—	—	.27	.14
☐ 1573	10¢ Multicolored	—	—	.27	.14
☐ 1574	10¢ Multicolored	—	—	.27	.14
☐ 1575	10¢ Multicolored	—	—	.27	.14

1975. WORLD PEACE THROUGH LAW
| ☐ 1576 | 10¢ Blue, Green, Brown | 11.30 | 1.35 | .26 | .10 |

1975. BANKING AND COMMERCE
| ☐ 1577 | 10¢ Multicolored | — | — | .26 | .09 |
| ☐ 1578 | 10¢ Multicolored | — | — | .26 | .09 |

1975. CHRISTMAS
| ☐ 1579 | 10¢ Multicolored | 11.25 | 3.30 | .27 | .12 |
| ☐ 1580 | 10¢ Multicolored | 11.25 | 3.30 | .27 | .12 |

*No hinge pricing from 1941 to date is figured at (N-H ADD 15%)

1975–1980. AMERICANA SERIES

Scott No.			Mint Sheet	Plate Block	Fine Unused Each	Fine Used Each
☐ 1581	1¢	Blue on Green	4.30	.40	.10	.10
☐ 1582	2¢	Brown on Green	5.30	.44	.10	.10
☐ 1584	3¢	Olive on Green	7.50	.49	.11	.10
☐ 1585	4¢	Maroon on Green	8.90	.60	.11	.10
☐ 1590	9¢	Slate on Green	—	—	.19	.10
☐ 1591	9¢	Green on Gray	16.00	.97	.23	.10
☐ 1592	10¢	Purple	22.50	1.10	.23	.10
☐ 1593	11¢	Orange on Gray	26.75	1.25	.26	.10
☐ 1594	12¢	Maroon	19.25	1.90	.36	.10
☐ 1595	13¢	Brown	—	—	.36	.10
☐ 1596	13¢	Multicolored	26.75	4.70	.36	.10
☐ 1597	15¢	Multicolored	33.50	2.80	.36	.10
☐ 1598	15¢	Multicolored	—	—	.67	.10
☐ 1599	16¢	Blue & Black	35.50	2.30	.52	.10
☐ 1603	24¢	Red on Blue	58.00	3.30	.70	.12
☐ 1604	28¢	Brown & Blue	65.00	3.80	.70	.14
☐ 1605	29¢	Blue & Blue	65.00	4.20	.70	.23
☐ 1606	30¢	Green on Blue	47.50	3.25	.64	.15
☐ 1608	50¢	Black & Orange	75.50	5.50	1.00	.17
☐ 1610	$1	Multicolored	131.00	10.75	1.95	.17
☐ 1611	$2	Multicolored	282.00	20.00	3.70	.65
☐ 1612	$5	Multicolored	805.00	43.00	9.10	3.50

1975–1978. COIL STAMPS

Scott No.			Fine Unused Line Pair	Ave. Unused Line Pair	Fine Unused Each	Ave. Unused Each	Fine Used Each	Ave. Used Each
☐ 1613	3.1¢	Brown on Yellow	1.05	.85	.14	.11	.13	.10
☐ 1614	7.7¢	Gold on Yellow	1.55	1.21	.30	.23	.17	.13
☐ 1615	7.9¢	Red on Yellow	1.65	1.32	.34	.25	.13	.10
☐ 1615C	8.4¢	Blue on White	1.95	1.42	.29	.21	.18	.15
☐ 1616	9¢	Green on Gray	1.25	.92	.23	.19	.13	.10
☐ 1617	10¢	Purple on Gray	1.05	.83	.23	.19	.13	.10
☐ 1618	13¢	Brown	1.15	.88	.33	.26	.17	.13

1975–1977. REGULAR ISSUES

Scott No.			Mint Sheet	Plate Block	Fine Unused Each	Fine Used Each
☐ 1622	13¢	Red, Brown, Blue	29.00	8.00	.34	.10
☐ 1623	13¢	Blue, Red	29.00	8.00	.34	.10
☐ 1623c	13¢	Blue, Red, pf 10	—	—	.34	.10

1975. COIL STAMPS

Scott No.			Fine Unused Each	Ave. Unused Each	Fine Used Each	Ave. Used Each
☐ 1625	13¢	Red, Brown, Blue	.42	.31	.11	.08

*No hinge pricing from 1941 to date is figured at (N-H ADD 15%)

HOW TO FIND YOUR STAMP

This new stamp catalog takes the confusion out of finding and identifying individual stamps. A complete new FULL COLOR FAST FIND—PHOTO INDEX is illustrated on the following pages. All of the stamp photographs are arranged in Scott numerical order and date of issue. Below each stamp picture is the Scott number and the page number the stamp listing appears on.

1, 39, 48a
PG 21

2, 4, 948b
PG 21

5, 9, 18–24, 40
PG 21

10, 11, 25, 26
41–PG 21

12, 27–30A
42–PG 21

13–16, 31–35,
43–PG 21

17, 36, 44
PG 21

37, 45
PG 22

38, 46
PG 22

39, 47
PG 22

56, 63, 85, 86
92, 102–PG 22

64–66, 74, 79, 88
94, 104–PG 22

57–67, 75, 76, 80
95, 195–PG 22

58–62B, 68, 85D,
89, 96, 106–PG 22

59, 69, 85E, 90
97, 107–PG 22

60, 70, 78, 99
109–PG 22

61, 71, 81, 100,
110–PG 22

62, 72, 101,
111–PG 22

73, 84, 85B, 87,
93, 103–PG 22

77, 85F, 91, 98,
108–PG 22

112, 123, 133
PG 24

113, 124
PG 24

114, 125
PG 24

115, 126
PG 24

116, 127
PG 24

117, 128
PG 24

118, 119, 129
PG 24

120, 130
PG 24

121, 131
PG 24

122, 132
PG 24

134, 156, 167
182, 206–PG 24

135, 157, 168
203–PG 24

136, 158, 169,
214–PG 24

137, 148, 159,
195, 208–PG 24

138, 149, 160
171, 196–PG 24

139, 150, 161,
197, 209–PG 24

140–151, 162,
173, 198–PG 24

141, 152, 163,
189, 199–PG 24

142, 153, 164,
175, 200–PG 24

143, 154, 165,
201, 2117–PG 24

144, 155, 166,
202, 218–PG 24

179, 181, 185,
204–PG 25

205, 205C, 216
PG 25

210, 211B, 213,
PG 26

211, 211D, 215
PG 26

212–PG 26

219–PG 26

219D, 220–PG 26

221–PG 26

222–PG 26

223–PG 26   224–PG 26   225–PG 26   226–PG 26   227–PG 26

228–PG 26   229–PG 26   230–PG 26   231–PG 26

232–PG 26   233–PG 26   234–PG 26

235–PG 26   236–PG 26   237–PG 26

238–PG 26   239–PG 27   240–PG 27

241–PG 27

242–PG 27

243–PG 27

244–PG 27

245–PG 27

246, 247, 264,
279–PG 27

248–252, 265–267,
279B–PG 27

253, 268
PG 27

254, 269, 280
PG 27

255, 270, 281
PG 27

256, 271, 282
PG 27

257, 272
PG 27

258, 273, 282C,
283–PG 27

259, 273, 284
PG 27

260, 275
PG 27

261–261A, 276,
276A–PG 27

262, 277
PG 27

263, 278–PG 27

285–PG 28

286–PG 28

287–PG 28

GENERAL ISSUE—SCOTT NO. 288–308 (1898–1902)

288-PG 28

289-PG 28

290-PG 28

291-PG 28

292-PG 28

293-PG 28

294-PG 28

295-PG 28

296-PG 28

297-PG 28

298-PG 28

299-PG 28

300, 314, 316, 318-PG 28

301-PG 28

302-PG 28

303, 314A PG 28

304, 315, 317 PG 28

305-PG 28

306-PG 28

307-PG 28

308-PG 28

309–PG 28   310–PG 28   311–PG 28   312, 479
PG 28   313, 480
PG 28   319–322
PG 29

323–PG 29   324–PG 29   325–PG 29

326–PG 29   327–PG 29   328–PG 29   329–PG 29

330–PG 29   331, 392
PG 29   332–393, 519
PG 29   333–541
PG 29   367, 369
PG 30

370, 371–PG 30   372, 373–PG 30   397, 401–PG 31   398, 402–PG 31

399, 403
PG 31

400, 400A, 404
PG 31

405–545
PG 32

406–546
PG 32

414–518
PG 32

523, 524, 547
PG 35

537–PG 36

548–PG 37

549–PG 37

550–PG 37

551, 653
PG 37

552, 575, 578,
604, 632–PG 37

553, 576, 598,
605, 633–PG 37

583, 599–99A
634–34A–PG 38

555, 584, 600,
635–PG 37

556–585, 601
636–PG 37

557, 586, 602,
637–PG 37

558, 587, 638,
723–PG 37

559, 588, 639
PG 37

560, 589, 640
PG 37

561, 590, 641
PG 37

562, 591, 603,
641–PG 37

563, 692
PG 37

564, 693
PG 37

GENERAL ISSUE—SCOTT NO. 565–623 (1925)

565, 695–PG 37   566, 696–PG 37   567, 698–PG 37   568, 699–PG 37   569, 700–PG 37

570, 701–PG 37   571–PG 37   572–PG 37   573–PG 37   610–613–PG 38

614–PG 38   615–PG 38   616–PG 38

617–PG 39   618–PG 39   619–PG 39

620–PG 39   621–PG 39   622, 694–PG 39   623, 697–PG 39

89

627–PG 39   628–PG 39   629–PG 39   643–PG 39

644–PG 39   645–PG 39   646–PG 39   647–PG 40   648–PG 40

649–PG 40   650–PG 40   651–PG 40

654–656–PG 40   657–PG 40   680–PG 41   681–PG 41   682–PG 41

683–PG 41   684, 686–PG 41   685, 687–PG 41   688–PG 41   689–PG 41

690–PG 41

702–PG 42

703–PG 42

704–PG 42

705–PG 42

706–PG 42

707–PG 42

708–PG 42

709–PG 42

710–PG 42

711–PG 42

712–PG 42

713–PG 42

714–PG 42

715–PG 42

716–PG 42

717–PG 42

718–PG 42

719–PG 42

720–722
PG 42

724–PG 43

725–PG 43

726–PG 43

727, 752
PG 43

728, 730, 766
PG 43

729, 731, 767
PG 43

732–PG 43

733, 735, 753
PG 43

734–PG 43

736–PG 43

737, 738, 754–PG 44

739, 755–PG 44

740, 751, 756,
769–PG 44

741, 757–PG 44

742, 750, 758, 770–PG 44

743, 759–PG 44

744, 760–PG 44

745, 761–PG 44

746, 762–PG 44

747, 763–PG 44

748, 764-PG 44   749, 765, 797-PG 44   772, 778A-PG 45

773, 778B-PG 45   774-PG 45   775, 778C-PG 45   776, 778D-PG 45

777-PG 45   782-PG 45   783-PG 46   784-PG 46

785-PG 46   786-PG 46   787-PG 46

788–PG 46

789–PG 46

790–PG 46

791–PG 46

792–PG 46

793–PG 46

794–PG 46

795–PG 46

796–PG 46

798–PG 46

799–PG 46

800–PG 46

801–PG 46

802–PG 46

GENERAL ISSUE—SCOTT NO. 803-836 (1938)

803–PG 46   804, 848–PG 46   805, 849–PG 46   806–PG 46   807–PG 46   808, 843–PG 46

809, 844–PG 46   810, 845–PG 47   811, 846–PG 47   812–PG 47   813–PG 47   814–PG 47

815, 847–PG 47   816–PG 47   817–PG 47   818–PG 47   819–PG 47   820–PG 47

821–PG 47   822–PG 47   823–PG 47   824–PG 47   825–PG 47   826–PG 47

827–PG 47   828–PG 47   829–PG 47   830–PG 47   831–PG 47   832–PG 47

833–PG 47   834–PG 47   835–PG 47   836–PG 47

837-PG 47   838-PG 47   852-PG 48   853-PG 48

854-PG 48   855-PG 48   856-PG 48   857-PG 48

858-PG 48   859-PG 48   860-PG 48   861-PG 48

862-PG 48   863-PG 48   864-PG 49   865-PG 49   866-PG 49

GENERAL ISSUE—SCOTT NO. 867–891 (1940)

867–PG 49   868–PG 49   869–PG 49   870–PG 49   871–PG 49

872–PG 49   873–PG 49   874–PG 49   875–PG 49   876–PG 49

877–PG 49   878–PG 49   879–PG 49   880–PG 49   881–PG 49

882–PG 49   883–PG 49   884–PG 49   885–PG 49   886–PG 49

887–PG 49   888–PG 49   889–PG 49   890–PG 49   891–PG 49

892–PG 49 893–PG 49 894–PG 49 895–PG 49

896–PG 50 897–PG 50 898–PG 50 899–PG 50

900–PG 50 901–PG 50 902–PG 50 903–PG 50

904–PG 50 905–PG 50 906–PG 50 907–PG 50

GENERAL ISSUE—SCOTT NO. 908–933 (1943–1946)

908–PG 50

909–PG 50

921–PG 51

922–PG 51

923–PG 51

924–PG 51

925–PG 51

926–PG 51

927–PG 51

928–PG 51

929–PG 51

930–PG 51

931–PG 51

932–PG 51

933–PG 51

934-PG 51

935-PG 51

936-PG 51

937-PG 51

938-PG 51

939-PG 52

940-PG 52

941-PG 52

942-PG 52

943-PG 52

944-PG 52

945-PG 52

946-PG 52

947-PG 52

GENERAL ISSUE—SCOTT NO. 948–958 (1947–1948)

948–PG 52

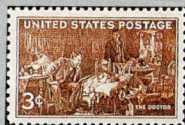

949–PG 52

950–PG 52

951–PG 52

952–PG 52

953–PG 52

954–PG 52

955–PG 52

956–PG 53

957–PG 53

958–PG 53

959–PG 53

960–PG 53

961–PG 53

962–PG 53

963–PG 53

964–PG 53

965–PG 53

966–PG 53

967–PG 53

968–PG 53

969–PG 53

970–PG 53

971–PG 53

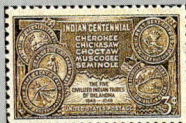

972–PG 53

973–PG 53

974–PG 53

GENERAL ISSUE—SCOTT NO. 975–992 (1948–1950)

 975–PG 54

 976–PG 54

 977–PG 54

 978–PG 54

 979–PG 54

 980–PG 54

 981–PG 54

 982–PG 54

 983–PG 54

 984–PG 54

 985–PG 54

 986–PG 54

 987–PG 54

 988–PG 54

 989–PG 54

 990–PG 54

 991–PG 54

 992–PG 54

993–PG 54

994–PG 54

995–PG 55

996–PG 55

997–PG 55

998–PG 55

999–PG 55

1000–PG 55

1001–PG 55

1002–PG 55

1003–PG 55

1004–PG 55

1005–PG 55

1006–PG 55

1007–PG 55

1008–PG 55

1009–PG 55

1010–PG 55

1011-PG 55

1012-PG 55

1013-PG 56

1014-PG 56

1015-PG 56

1016-PG 56

1017-PG 56

1018-PG 56

1019-PG 56

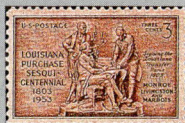

1020-PG 56

1021-PG 56

1022-PG 56

1023-PG 56

1024-PG 56

1025-PG 56

GENERAL ISSUE—SCOTT NO. 1026–1050 (1953–1955)

1026–PG 56

1027–PG 56

1028–PG 56

1029–PG 56

1030–PG 56

1031, 1054–PG 56

1031A, 1054A–PG 56

1032–PG 57

1033, 1055–PG 57

1034, 1056–PG 57

1035–1075–PG 57

1036–1058–PG 57

1037, 1059–PG 57

1038–PG 57

1039–PG 57

1040–PG 57

1041, 1075B–PG 57

1042A–PG 57

1043–PG 57

1044A–PG 57

1044–PG 57

1045–PG 57

1046–PG 57

1047–PG 57

1048–PG 57

1049–PG 57

1050–PG 57

GENERAL ISSUE—SCOTT NO. 1051–1072 (1955)

1051–PG 57   1052–PG 57   1053–PG 57   1060–PG 57

1061–PG 57   1062–PG 57   1063–PG 58   1064–PG 58

1065–PG 58   1066–PG 58   1067–PG 58

1068–PG 58   1069–PG 58   1070–PG 58

1071–PG 58   1072–PG 58

1073–PG 58

1074–PG 58

1075–PG 58

1076–PG 58

1077–PG 58

1078–PG 58

1079–PG 58

GENERAL ISSUE—SCOTT NO. 1080–1093 (1956–1957)

1080–PG 58

1081–PG 58

1082–PG 59

1083–PG 59

1084–PG 59

1085–PG 59

1086–PG 59

1087–PG 59

1088–PG 59

1089–PG 59

1090–PG 59

1091–PG 59

1092–PG 59

1093–PG 59

1094–PG 59

1095–PG 59

1096–PG 59

1097–PG 59

1098–PG 59

1099–PG 59

1100–PG 60

1104–PG 60

1105–PG 60

1106–PG 60

1107–PG 60

1108–PG 60

1109–PG 60

1110–PG 60

1111–PG 60

1112–PG 60

1113–PG 60

1114–PG 60

1115–PG 60

1116–PG 60

1117–PG 60

1118–PG 60

1119–PG 60

1120–PG 60

1121–PG 60

1122–PG 60

1123–PG 60

1124–PG 61

1125–PG 61

1126–PG 61

1127–PG 61

1128–PG 61

1129–PG 61

1130–PG 61

1131–PG 61

1132–PG 61

1133–PG 61

1134–PG 61

1135–PG 61

1136–PG 61

1137–PG 61

1138–PG 61

1139–PG 61

1140–PG 61

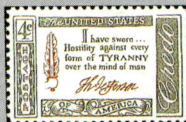

1141–PG 61

1142–PG 61

1143–PG 61

GENERAL ISSUE—SCOTT NO. 1144–1160 (1960–1961)

1144–PG 61

1145–PG 61

1146–PG 62

1147–PG 62

1148–PG 62

1149–PG 62

1150–PG 62

1151–PG 62

1152–PG 62

1153–PG 62

1154–PG 62

1155–PG 62

1156–PG 62

1157–PG 62

1158–PG 62

1159–PG 62

1160–PG 62

GENERAL ISSUE—SCOTT NO. 1161–1180 (1960–1963)

1161–PG 62   1162–PG 62   1163–PG 62   1164–PG 62

1165–PG 62   1166–PG 62   1167–PG 63   1168–PG 63   1169–PG 63

1170–PG 63   1171–PG 63   1172–PG 63   1173–PG 63

1174–PG 63   1175–PG 63   1176–PG 63   1177–PG 63

1178–PG 63   1179–PG 63   1180–PG 63

GENERAL ISSUE—SCOTT NO. 1181–1195 (1964)

1181–PG 63

1182–PG 63

1183–PG 63

1184–PG 63

1185–PG 63

1186–PG 64

1187–PG 64

1188–PG 64

1189–PG 64

1190–PG 64

1191–PG 64

1192–PG 64

1193–PG 64

1194–PG 64

1195–PG 64

1196–PG 64

1197–PG 64

1198–PG 64

1199–PG 64

1200–PG 64

1202–PG 64

1201–PG 64

1203–PG 64

1204–PG 64

1205–PG 65

1206–PG 65

1207–PG 65

1208–PG 65

1209, 1225–PG 65

1213–PG 65

1230–PG 65

1231–PG 65

1232–PG 65

1233–PG 65

1234–PG 65

1235–PG 65

1236–PG 65

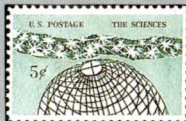

1237–PG 65

1238–PG 65

1239–PG 66

1240–PG 66

1241–PG 66

1242–PG 66

1243–PG 66

1244–PG 66

GENERAL ISSUE—SCOTT NO. 1245–1261 (1964–1965)

1245–PG 66   1246–PG 66   1247–PG 66   1248–PG 66

1249–PG 66   1250–PG 66   1251–PG 66   1252–PG 66

1253–PG 66   1254–PG 66   1255–PG 66   1256–PG 66   1257–PG 66

1258–PG 66   1259–PG 67   1260–PG 67   1261–PG 67

GENERAL ISSUE—SCOTT NO. 1262–1278 (1965)

CENTENNIAL of the SOKOLS
UNITED STATES PHYSICAL FITNESS
5¢

1262–PG 67

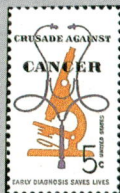

CRUSADE AGAINST CANCER
EARLY DIAGNOSIS SAVES LIVES
5¢

1263–PG 67

CHURCHILL
U.S. 5 CENTS

1264–PG 67

UNITED STATES POSTAGE 5¢
MAGNA CARTA 1215

1265–PG 67

INTERNATIONAL COOPERATION YEAR 1965
UN
UNITED STATES POSTAGE
5

1266–PG 67

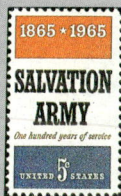

1865 ★ 1965
SALVATION ARMY
One hundred years of service
UNITED 5¢ STATES

1267–PG 67

UNITED 5 STATES

1268–PG 67

HUMANITARIAN·ENGINEER·UNITED STATES
PRESIDENT
HERBERT HOOVER
5¢

1269–PG 67

ROBERT FULTON
1765·1965
U.S. POSTAGE
5¢

1270–PG 67

UNITED STATES POSTAGE
5

1271–PG 67

U.S. POSTAGE 5¢
Stop traffic accidents
enforcement·education·engineering

1272–PG 67

JOHN COPLEY·AMERICAN ARTIST
UNITED STATES POSTAGE 5 CENTS

1273–PG 67

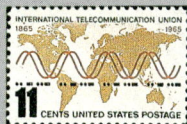

INTERNATIONAL TELECOMMUNICATION UNION
1865 — 1965
11 CENTS UNITED STATES POSTAGE

1274–PG 67

STEVENSON
U.S. 5 CENTS

1275–PG 67

5¢ U.S. POSTAGE
CHRISTMAS

1276–PG 67

THOMAS JEFFERSON
UNITED STATES

1278–PG 68

GENERAL ISSUE—SCOTT NO. 1279-1309 (1965-1966)

1279–PG 68

1280–PG 68

1281. 1297–PG 68

1282. 1303–PG 68

1283. 1304–PG 68

1283B–PG 68

1284. 1298–PG 68

1285–PG 68

1286–PG 68

1286A–PG 68

1287–PG 68

1288–PG 68

1289–PG 68

1290–PG 68

1291–PG 68

1292–PG 68

1293–PG 68

1294. 1305C–PG 68

1295–PG 68

1305–PG 68

1306–PG 68

1307–PG 68

1308–PG 68

1309–PG 69

1310–PG 69

1311–PG 69   1312–PG 69   1313–PG 69   1314–PG 69

1315–PG 69   1316–PG 69   1317–PG 69   1318–PG 69

1319–PG 69

1320–PG 69

1321–PG 69

1322–PG 69

1323–PG 69

1324–PG 69

1325–PG 69

1326–PG 69

1327–PG 69

1328–PG 70

1329–PG 70

1330–PG 70

1331–PG 70   1332–PG 70

1333–PG 70

1334–PG 70

1335–PG 70

1336–PG 70

1337–PG 70

1338, 1338A
PG 70

1338F, G–PG 70

1339–PG 70

1340–PG 70

1341–PG 70

1342–PG 70

1343–PG 70

1344–PG 70

1345–PG 70

1354–PG 71

1355–PG 71

1356–PG 71

GENERAL ISSUE—SCOTT NO. 1357–1371 (1968–1969)

1357–PG 71

1358–PG 71

1359–PG 71

1360–PG 71

1361–PG 71

1362–PG 71

1363–PG 71

1364–PG 71

1365–1368–PG 71

1369–PG 71

1370–PG 71

1371–PG 71

1372–PG 72

1373–PG 72

1374–PG 72

1375–PG 72

1376–1379–PG 72

1380–PG 72

1381–PG 72

1382–PG 72

1383–PG 72

1384–PG 72

GENERAL ISSUE—SCOTT NO. 1385–1406 (1969–1970)

1385–PG 72   1386–PG 72   1387–1390–PG 72

1391–PG 72   1392–PG 72   1393–PG 72   1393D–PG 72

1394–PG 73   1395–PG 73   1396–PG 73   1397–PG 73   1398–PG 73

1399–PG 73   1400–PG 73   1405–PG 73   1406–PG 73

1407–PG 73

1408–PG 73

1409–PG 73

1410–1413–PG 73

1414–PG 73

1415–1418–PG 73

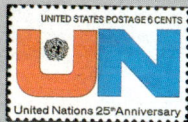

1419–PG 74

1420–PG 74

1421–PG 74

1422–PG 74

1423–PG 74

1424–PG 74

GENERAL ISSUE—SCOTT NO. 1425–1439 (1971)

1425–PG 74

WILDLIFE CONSERVATION

1426–PG 74

1427–1430–PG 74

1431–PG 74

1432–PG 74

1433–PG 74

UNITED STATES IN SPACE · · · A DECADE OF ACHIEVEMENT

1434–PG 74   1435–PG 74

1436–PG 74

1437–PG 74

1438–PG 74

1439–PG 74

128

1440–1443–PG 74

1444–PG 75

1445–PG 75

1446–PG 75

1447–PG 75

1448–1451–PG 75

1452–PG 75

1453–PG 75

1454–PG 75

1455–PG 75

1456–1459–PG 75

1460–PG 75

1461–PG 75

1462–PG 75

1463–PG 75

1464–1467–PG 75

1468–PG 75

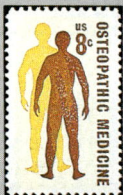

1469–PG 76

1470–PG 76

1471–PG 76

1472–PG 76

1473–PG 76

1474–PG 76

1475–PG 76

1476–PG 76

1477–PG 76

1478–PG 76

1479–PG 76

1480–1483–PG 76

1484–PG 76

1485–PG 76

1486–PG 76

1487–PG 76

1488–PG 76

1489–PG 76

1490–PG 76

1491–PG 76

1492–PG 76

1493–PG 76

1494–PG 76

1495–PG 77

1496–PG 77

1497–PG 77

1498–PG 77

1499–PG 77

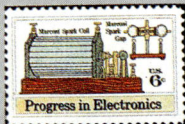

1500–PG 77

1501–PG 77

1502–PG 77

1503–PG 77

1504–PG 77

1505–PG 77

1506F–PG 77

1507–PG 77

1508–PG 77

1509, 1519–PG 77

1510–PG 77

1511–PG 77

1518–PG 77

1525–PG 77

1526–PG 77

1527–PG 77

1528–PG 78

1529–PG 78

1530–PG 78

1531–PG 78

1532–PG 78

1533–PG 78

1534–PG 78

1535–PG 78

1536–PG 78

1538–1539–PG 78
1540–1541–PG 78

1537–PG 78

1543–1546–PG 78

1542–PG 78

GENERAL ISSUE—SCOTT NO. 1547–1562 (1974–1975)

1547–PG 78

1548–PG 78

Retarded Children Can Be Helped
1549–PG 78

Christmas
1550–PG 78

Christmas 10¢ U.S.
Currier and Ives
1551–PG 78

Peace on Earth
Christmas
1552–PG 78

Benjamin West
American artist
10 cents U.S. postage
1553–PG 78

Paul Laurence Dunbar
American poet
10 cents U.S. postage
1554–PG 78

MOVIEMAKER
D.W. GRIFFITH
1555–PG 79

PIONEER ★ JUPITER
1556–PG 79

MARINER 10 ★ VENUS/MERCURY
1557–PG 79

collective bargaining
out of conflict...accord
1558–PG 79

Contributors To The Cause
Sybil Ludington   Youthful Heroine
1559–PG 79

Contributors To The Cause...
Salem Poor   Gallant Soldier
1560–PG 79

Contributors To The Cause
Haym Salomon   Financial Hero
1561–PG 79

Contributors To The Cause
Peter Francisco   Fighter Extraordinary
1562–PG 79

135

1563–PG 79

1564–PG 79

1565–PG 79

1566–PG 79

1567–PG 79

1568–PG 79

1569–PG 79

1570–PG 79

1571–PG 79

1572–PG 79

1573–PG 79

1574–PG 79

GENERAL ISSUE—SCOTT NO. 1575–1608 (1975)

1575–PG 79

1577–1578–PG 79

1576–PG 79

1581–PG 80

1582–PG 80

1584–PG 80

1585–PG 80

1579–PG 79

1580–PG 79

1590–PG 80

1592–PG 80

1593–PG 80

1594–PG 80

1595–PG 80

1596–PG 80

1597–1598–PG 80

1599–PG 80

1603–PG 80

1604–PG 80

1605–PG 80

1606–PG 80

1608–PG 80

1610–PG 80

1611–PG 80

1612–PG 80

1613–PG 80

1614–PG 80

1615–PG 80

1615C–PG 80

1629–1630–1631–PG 169

1622–PG 80

1623–PG 80

1632–PG 169

1633–1682–PG 169

1683–PG 169

1684–PG 169

1685–PG 169

1686–PG 169

1687–PG 169

1688–PG 170

1689–PG 170

1690–PG 170

1691–1692–1693–1694–PG 170

1695–PG 170

1696–PG 170

1697–PG 170

1698–PG 170

1699–PG 170

1700–PG 170

1701–PG 170

1702–1703–PG 170

GENERAL ISSUE—SCOTT NO. 1704-1718 (1977)

US Bicentennial 13c

1704-PG 170

1705-PG 170

Pueblo Art USA 13c

1706-PG 170

Pueblo Art USA 13c

1707-PG 170

Pueblo Art USA 13c

1708-PG 170

Pueblo Art USA 13c

1709-PG 170

1710-PG 171

COLORADO

1711-PG 171

USA 13c Papilio oregonius

1712-PG 171

USA 13c Euphydryas phaeton

1713-PG 171

USA 13c Colias eurydice

1714-PG 171

USA 13c Anthocaris midea

1715-PG 171

Lafayette

US Bicentennial 13c

1716-PG 171

the SEAMSTRESS

for INDEPENDENCE USA 13c

1717-PG 171

the BLACKSMITH

for INDEPENDENCE USA 13c

1718-PG 171

1719–PG 171

1720–PG 171

1721–PG 171

1722–PG 171

1723–PG 171

1724–PG 171

1725–PG 171

1726–PG 171

1727–PG 171

1728–PG 171

1729–PG 171

1730–PG 171

1731–PG 171

1732–PG 171

1733–PG 171

1734–PG 172

1735–PG 172

1737–PG 172

1738–1739–1740–1741–1742–PG 172

1744–PG 172

1745–PG 172

1746–PG 172

1747–PG 172

1748–PG 172

1749–PG 172

1750–PG 172

1751–PG 172

1752–PG 172

1753–PG 172

1754–PG 172

1755–PG 172

1756–PG 172

Canadian International Philatelic Exhibition
Toronto

This tribute features wildlife that share the Canadian-United States border.

Cette émission souvenir est consacrée à la faune vivant près
de la frontière entre les États-Unis et le Canada.

Postmaster General of the United States

1757–PG 172

1758–PG 172

1759–PG 173

1760–PG 173

1761–PG 173

1762–PG 173

1763–PG 173

1764–PG 173

1765–PG 173

143

GENERAL ISSUE—SCOTT NO. 1766–1781 (1978–1979)

1766–PG 173

1767–PG 173

1768–PG 173

1769–PG 173

1770–PG 173

1771–PG 173

1772–PG 173

1773–PG 173

1774–PG 173

1775–PG 173

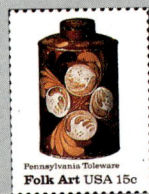
1776–PG 173

1777–PG 173

1778–PG 173

1779–PG 173

1780–PG 173

1781–PG 173

Architecture USA 15c
1782–PG 173

Endangered Flora — 15c USA
PERSISTENT TRILLIUM
1783–PG 173

Endangered Flora — 15c USA
HAWAIIAN WILD BROADBEAN
1784–PG 173

Endangered Flora — 15c USA
CONTRA COSTA WALLFLOWER
1785–PG 173

Endangered Flora — 15c USA
ANTIOCH DUNES EVENING PRIMROSE
1786–PG 173

USA 15c — Seeing For Me
1787–PG 173

Special Olympics — Skill · Sharing · Joy — USA 15c
1788–PG 174

I have not yet begun to fight — John Paul Jones — US Bicentennial 15c
1789–PG 174

Olympics 1980 Decathlon — USA 10c
1790–PG 174

USA 15c — Olympics 1980
1791–PG 174

USA 15c — Olympics 1980
1792–PG 174

Olympics 1980 — USA 15c
1794–PG 174

Olympics 1980 — USA 15c
1793–PG 174

USA Olympics 1980 15c
1795–PG 174

USA Olympics 1980 15c
1796–PG 174

USA Olympics 1980 15c
1797–PG 174

USA Olympics 1980 15c
1798–PG 174

Gerard David National Gallery — Christmas USA 15c
1799–PG 174

Christmas 15c USA
1800–PG 174

145

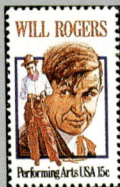

1801–PG 174   1802–PG 174   1803–PG 174   1804–PG 174

1805–1806   1807–1808   1809–1810   1811–PG 175   1813–PG 175
PG 174   PG 175   PG 175

1818–PG 175   1821–PG 175   1822   1823–PG 175   1824–PG 175
                                  PG 175

1825–PG 175

1826–PG 175

1827–PG 175

1828–PG 175

1829–PG 175

1830–PG 175

1831–PG 175

1832–PG 175

1833–PG 175

1834–PG 176

1835–PG 176

1836–PG 176

1837–PG 176

1838–PG 176

1839–PG 176

1840–PG 176

A.J.Davis 1803-1892 Lyndhurst Tarrytown NY
Architecture USA 15c

1841–PG 176

Christmas USA 15c

1842–PG 176

USA 15c
Season's Greetings

1843–PG 176

Dorothea Dix
USA 1c

1844–PG 176

Igor Stravinsky
USA 2c

1845–PG 176

Henry Clay
USA 3c

1846–PG 176

Carl Schurz
4c
USA

1847–PG 176

Pearl Buck
USA 5c

1848–PG 176

Walter Lippmann
6c
USA

1849–PG 176

Abraham Baldwin
USA 7c

1850–PG 176

Henry Knox
USA 8c

1851–PG 176

Sylvanus Thayer
USA 9c

1852–PG 176

Richard Russell
USA 10c

1853–PG 176

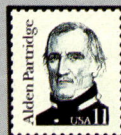

Alden Partridge
USA 11c

1854–PG 176

USA 13c
Crazy Horse

1855–PG 176

Sinclair Lewis
USA 14

1856–PG 176

Rachel Carson
USA 17c

1857–PG 177

George Mason
USA 18c

1858–PG 177

USA 19c
Sequoyah

1859–PG 177

GENERAL ISSUE—SCOTT NO. 1860-1891 (1982-1985)

1860—PG 177

1861—PG 177

1862—PG 177

1863—PG 177

1864—PG 177

1865—PG 177

1866—PG 177

1867—PG 177

1868—PG 177

1869—PG 177

Rose USA 18c
1876—PG 177

Camellia USA 18c
1877—PG 177

USA 15c Everett Dirksen
1874—PG 177

Whitney Moore Young
Black Heritage USA
1875—PG 177

Dahlia USA 18c
1878—PG 177

Lily USA 18c
1879—PG 177

1880—PG 177

1881—PG 177

1882—PG 177

USA18c
1886—PG 178

1887—PG 178

1883—PG 177

1884—PG 178

1885—PG 178

1888—PG 178

1889—PG 178

USA18c
1890—PG 178

USA18c
1891—PG 178

GENERAL ISSUE—SCOTT NO. 1892-1920 (1981-1984)

1892–PG 178

1893–PG 178

1894–PG 178

Mail Wagon 1880s
USA 9.3c
Bulk Rate
1900–PG 178

RR Caboose 1890s
Bulk Rate
1902–PG 178

Electric Auto 1917
USA 17c
1905–PG 178

Surrey 1890s
USA 18c
1906–PG 178

Fire Pumper
1860s
USA 20c
1907–PG 178

The Gift of Self
USA 18c
American Red Cross
1881–1981
1910–PG 178

SAVINGS AND LOANS
USA 18c
1911–PG 178

Professional Management
USA 18c
Joseph Wharton
1920–PG 178

1912–1916–PG 178
1917–1919–PG 178

150

GENERAL ISSUE—SCOTT NO. 1921-1933 (1981)

1921–PG 179

1922–PG 179

1923–PG 179

1924–PG 179

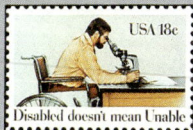
1925–PG 179

1926–PG 179

1927–PG 179

1928–PG 179

1929–PG 179

1930–PG 179

1931–PG 179

1932–PG 179

1933–PG 179

1934–PG 179

1935–PG 179

1936–PG 179

1937–PG 179

1938–PG 179

1939–PG 179

1949–PG 180

1940–PG 179

1941–PG 179

1946–1948–PG 180

1950–PG 180

1942–1945–PG 179

1951–PG 180

1952–PG 180

2003–PG 180

2004–PG 180

2005–PG 180

1953–2002–PG 180

2006–2009–PG 180

2010–PG 180

2011–PG 180

2012–PG 180

2013–PG 180

2014–PG 181

2015–PG 181

2017–PG 181

2016–PG 181

2018–PG 181

2023–PG 181

2019–2022–PG 181

2024–PG 181

2025–PG 181

2026–PG 181

2027–2030–PG 181

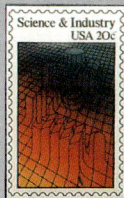

2031–PG 181

2032-2035-PG 182

2036-PG 182

2037-PG 182

2038-PG 182

2039-PG 182

2040-PG 182

2041-PG 182

2042-PG 182

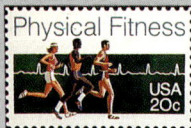

2043-PG 182

2044-PG 182

2045-PG 182

2046–PG 182

2048–2051–PG 182

2047–PG 182

2052–PG 183

2053–PG 183

2054–PG 183

2055–PG 183

2056–PG 183

2057–PG 183

2058–PG 183

2059–PG 183

2060–PG 183   2061–PG 183   2062–PG 183

2063–PG 183   2065–PG 183

2064–PG 183   2066–PG 183   2067–2070–PG 183

2071–PG 184   2072–PG 184   2073–PG 184   2074–PG 184

2075–PG 184

2080–PG 184

2076–2079–PG 184

2081–PG 184

2082–2085–PG 184

2086–PG 184

2088–PG 184

2089–PG 185

2090–PG 185

2087–PG 184

2091–PG 185

2092–PG 185

2093–PG 185

2094–PG 185

2095–PG 185

2096–PG 185

2097–PG 185

2098–PG 185

2099–PG 185

2100–PG 185

2101–PG 185

2102–PG 185

2103–PG 185

2014–PG 185

2105–PG 185

2106–PG 185

2107–PG 185

2108–PG 186

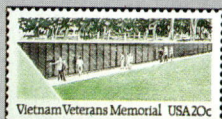
Vietnam Veterans Memorial USA 20c
2109–PG 186

JEROME KERN
Performing Arts USA
22
2110–PG 186

Domestic Mail
D
US Postage
2111–2113–PG 186

USA 22
2114–2116–PG 186

USA $10.75
2122–PG 186

School Bus 1920s
3.4 USA
2123–PG 186

Buckboard 1880s
USA
4.9
2125–PG 186

Star Route Truck
5.5 USA 1910s
2126–PG 186

USA 22 Frilled Dogwinkle

USA 22 Reticulated Helmet

USA 22 New England Neptune

USA 22 Calico Scallop

USA 22 Lightning Whelk

2117–2121–PG 186

Tricycle 1880s
6 USA
2127–PG 186

Ambulance 1860s
8.3 USA
2128–PG 187

Oil Wagon 1890s
10.1 USA
2129–PG 187

Stutz Bearcat 1933
11 USA
2130–PG 187

Stanley Steamer 1909
USA
12
2131–PG 187

Iceboat 1880s
USA
14
2134–PG 187

Dog Sled 1920s
17 USA
2135–PG 187

Bread Wagon 1880s
25 USA
2136–PG 187

Pushcart 1880s
12.5
USA
2132–PG 187

2137-PG 187

2138-2141-PG 187

2142-PG 167

2144-PG 187

2143-PG 187

2145-PG 187

2146-PG 187

2147-PG 187

2149-PG 188

2150-PG 188

2152-PG 188

2153-PG 188

2154-PG 188

2155-2158-PG 188

2159-PG 188

2160-2163–PG 188

2164–PG 188

Season's Greetings USA22

2166–PG188

CHRISTMAS

USA 22

2165–PG 188

USA22

2167–PG 188

Margaret Mitchell USA 1

2168–PG 188

Mary Lyon USA 2

2169–PG 188

Paul Dudley White MD USA 3

2170–PG 189

Father Flanagan USA 4

2171–PG 189

Hugo L. Black 5 USA

2172–PG 189

14 USA

Julia Ward Howe

2177–PG 189

Belva Ann Lockwood USA 17

2179–PG 189

USA 25

Jack London

2183–PG 189

John Harvard USA 56

2191–PG 189

Bernard Revel USA $1

2194–PG 189

Bryan $2 USA William Jennings

2195–PG 189

Bret Harte USA $5

2196–PG 189

2198-2201–PG 189

2202–PG 189

2203–PG 189

2204–PG 189

2210–PG 190

2211–PG 190

2205-2209–PG 189

2216–PG 190

GENERAL ISSUE—SCOTT NO. 2217-2223 (1986)

2217–PG 190

2218–PG 190

2219–PG 190

2220–2223–PG 190

GENERAL ISSUE—SCOTT NO. 2224-2250 (1986-1987)

2224–PG 190

2239–PG 190

2235–2238–PG 190

2240–2243–PG 190

2244–PG 191

2245–PG 191

2246–PG 191

2247–PG 191

2248–PG 191

2249–PG 191

2250–PG 191

2251–PG 191

2275–PG 191

2276–PG 191

2286–2335–PG 191

Dec 7, 1787   USA
Delaware 22
2336–PG 191

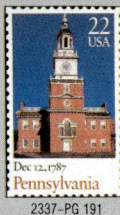
Dec 12, 1787
Pennsylvania 22
2337–PG 191

Dec 18, 1787   USA
New Jersey 22
2338–PG 191

Friendship
with Morocco
1787–1987
USA 22
2349–PG 191

William Faulkner
USA 22
2350–PG 191

Lacemaking USA 22   Lacemaking USA 22
Lacemaking USA 22   Lacemaking USA 22
2351–2354–PG 191

U.S. Constitution
We the People
1787–1987 22
2360–PG 192

CPA
Certified Public Accountants
22 USA
2361–PG 192

CHRISTMAS
22 USA
Moroni, National Gallery
2367–PG 192

USA 22 GREETINGS
2368–PG 192

Scott No.			Mint Sheet	Plate Block	Fine Unused Each	Fine Used Each

1976. COMMEMORATIVES—AMERICAN BICENTENNIAL
1976. SPIRIT OF '76

☐ 1629	13¢ Multicolored		—	—	.35	.11
☐ 1630	13¢ Multicolored		—	—	.35	.11
☐ 1631	13¢ Multicolored		—	—	.35	.11

1976. INTERPHIL '76

☐ 1632	13¢ Dark Blue, Red, Ultramarine		14.75	1.75	.35	.11

1976. STATE FLAGS

☐	13¢ All 50 States		23.00	7.50	—	—
☐	13¢ Individual States		—	—	.72	.46

☐ 1633 Delaware	1650 Louisiana	1667 West Virginia	
☐ 1634 Pennsylvania	1651 Indiana	1668 Nevada	
☐ 1635 New Jersey	1652 Mississippi	1669 Nebraska	
☐ 1636 Georgia	1653 Illinois	1670 Colorado	
☐ 1637 Connecticut	1654 Alabama	1671 North Dakota	
☐ 1638 Massachusetts	1655 Maine	1672 South Dakota	
☐ 1639 Maryland	1656 Missouri	1673 Montana	
☐ 1640 South Carolina	1657 Arkansas	1674 Washington	
☐ 1641 New Hampshire	1658 Michigan	1675 Idaho	
☐ 1642 Virginia	1659 Florida	1676 Wyoming	
☐ 1643 New York	1660 Texas	1677 Utah	
☐ 1644 North Carolina	1661 Iowa	1678 Oklahoma	
☐ 1645 Rhode Island	1662 Wisconsin	1679 New Mexico	
☐ 1646 Vermont	1663 California	1680 Arizona	
☐ 1647 Kentucky	1664 Minnesota	1681 Alaska	
☐ 1648 Tennessee	1665 Oregon	1682 Hawaii	
☐ 1649 Ohio	1666 Kansas		

1976. TELEPHONE CENTENNIAL

☐ 1683	13¢ Black, Purple, Red		14.25	1.50	.33	.10

1976. COMMERCIAL AVIATION

☐ 1684	13¢ Multicolored		14.25	3.60	.33	.10

1976. CHEMISTRY

☐ 1685	13¢ Multicolored		14.25	3.75	.33	.10

1976. BICENTENNIAL SOUVENIR SHEETS

☐ 1686	65¢ Sheet of 5		—	—	4.60	4.00
☐ 1686a	13¢ Multicolored		—	—	1.15	.91
☐ 1686b	13¢ Multicolored		—	—	1.15	.91
☐ 1686c	13¢ Multicolored		—	—	1.15	.91
☐ 1686d	13¢ Multicolored		—	—	1.15	.91
☐ 1686e	13¢ Multicolored		—	—	1.15	.91
☐ 1687	90¢ Sheet of 5		—	—	6.30	5.20
☐ 1687a	18¢ Multicolored		—	—	1.70	1.30
☐ 1687b	18¢ Multicolored		—	—	1.70	1.30
☐ 1687c	18¢ Multicolored		—	—	1.70	1.30
☐ 1687d	18¢ Multicolored		—	—	1.70	1.30

*No hinge pricing from 1941 to date is figured at (N-H ADD 15%)

Scott No.		Mint Sheet	Plate Block	Fine Unused Each	Fine Used Each
☐ 1687e	18¢ Multicolored	—	—	1.80	1.35
☐ 1688	1.20 Sheet of 5	—	—	9.25	7.50
☐ 1688a	24¢ Multicolored	—	—	2.30	1.75
☐ 1688b	24¢ Multicolored	—	—	2.30	1.75
☐ 1688c	24¢ Multicolored	—	—	2.30	1.75
☐ 1688d	24¢ Multicolored	—	—	2.30	1.75
☐ 1688e	24¢ Multicolored	—	—	2.30	1.75
☐ 1689	1.55 Sheet of 5	—	—	11.00	10.00
☐ 1689a	31¢ Multicolored	—	—	2.60	2.15
☐ 1689b	31¢ Multicolored	—	—	2.60	2.15
☐ 1689c	31¢ Multicolored	—	—	2.60	2.15
☐ 1689d	31¢ Multicolored	—	—	2.60	2.15
☐ 1689e	31¢ Multicolored	—	—	2.60	2.15

1976. BENJAMIN FRANKLIN

☐ 1690	13¢ Blue & Multicolored	13.50	1.50	.33	.11

1976. DECLARATION OF INDEPENDENCE

☐ 1691	13¢ Multicolored	—	—	.33	.12
☐ 1692	13¢ Multicolored	—	—	.33	.12
☐ 1693	13¢ Multicolored	—	—	.33	.12
☐ 1694	13¢ Multicolored	—	—	.33	.12

1976. OLYMPIC GAMES

☐ 1695	13¢ Multicolored	—	—	.57	.14
☐ 1696	13¢ Multicolored	—	—	.57	.14
☐ 1697	13¢ Multicolored	—	—	.57	.14
☐ 1698	13¢ Multicolored	—	—	.57	.14

1976. CLARA MAASS

☐ 1699	13¢ Multicolored	10.70	4.00	.34	.11

1976. ADOLPH S. OCHS

☐ 1700	13¢ Black, Green & White	8.75	1.45	.42	.11

1976. CHRISTMAS

☐ 1701	13¢ Multicolored	13.25	3.90	.26	.10
☐ 1702	13¢ Multicolored	13.25	3.65	.26	.10
☐ 1703	13¢ Multicolored	13.25	6.60	.26	.10

1977. COMMEMORATIVES

1977. WASHINGTON

☐ 1704	13¢ Multicolored	10.90	3.40	.26	.09

1977. SOUND RECORDING CENTENARY

☐ 1705	13¢ Multicolored	13.10	1.35	.26	.09

1977. PUEBLO ART

☐ 1706	13¢ Multicolored	—	—	.26	.10
☐ 1707	13¢ Multicolored	—	—	.26	.10
☐ 1708	13¢ Multicolored	—	—	.26	.10
☐ 1709	13¢ Multicolored	—	—	.26	.10

*No hinge pricing from 1941 to date is figured at (N-H ADD 15%)

Scott No.		Mint Sheet	Plate Block	Fine Unused Each	Fine Used Each
1977. TRANSATLANTIC FLIGHT					
☐ 1710	13¢ Multicolored	12.70	3.90	.28	.09
1977. COLORADO					
☐ 1711	13¢ Multicolored	12.70	3.90	.28	.09
1977. BUTTERFLIES					
☐ 1712	13¢ Multicolored	—	—	.29	.10
☐ 1713	13¢ Multicolored	—	—	.29	.10
☐ 1714	13¢ Multicolored	—	—	.29	.10
☐ 1715	13¢ Multicolored	—	—	.29	.10
1977. LAFAYETTE					
☐ 1716	13¢ Multicolored	11.00	1.60	.29	.11
1977. SKILLED HANDS					
☐ 1717	13¢ Multicolored	—	—	.36	.11
☐ 1718	13¢ Multicolored	—	—	.36	.11
☐ 1719	13¢ Multicolored	—	—	.36	.11
☐ 1720	13¢ Multicolored	—	—	.36	.11
1977. PEACE BRIDGE					
☐ 1721	13¢ Blue & White	13.00	1.55	.29	.09
1977. BATTLE OF ORISKANY					
☐ 1722	13¢ Multicolored	11.00	3.50	.28	.10
1977. ENERGY CONSERVATION AND DEVELOPMENT					
☐ 1723	13¢ Multicolored	—	—	.31	.09
☐ 1724	13¢ Multicolored	—	—	.31	.09
1977. ALTA. CALIFORNIA BICENTENNIAL					
☐ 1725	13¢ Multicolored	12.85	1.45	.32	.10
1977. ARTICLES OF CONFEDERATION					
☐ 1726	13¢ Red & Brown on Tan	12.90	1.50	.29	.10
1977. TALKING PICTURES					
☐ 1727	13¢ Multicolored	13.00	1.50	.30	.11
1977. SURRENDER AT SARATOGA					
☐ 1728	13¢ Multicolored	10.60	4.00	.30	.11
1977. CHRISTMAS					
☐ 1729	13¢ Multicolored	28.00	7.80	.29	.10
☐ 1730	13¢ Multicolored	26.00	7.80	.29	.10
1978. CARL SANDBURG					
☐ 1731	13¢ Brown, Black, White	12.80	1.60	.29	.10
1978. CAPTAIN COOK ISSUES					
☐ 1732	13¢ Dark Blue	—	1.60	.28	.09
☐ 1733	13¢ Green	—	1.60	.28	.09

*No hinge pricing from 1941 to date is figured at (N-H ADD 15%)

Scott No.		Mint Sheet	Plate Block	Fine Unused Each	Fine Used Each
1978. INDIAN HEAD PENNY					
☐ 1734	13¢ Brown & Blue Green	40.00	3.20	.34	.14
1978. NONDENOMINATED "A"					
☐ 1735	15¢ Orange	32.50	1.80	.36	.10
1978. ROSES					
☐ 1737	15¢ Multicolored	—	—	.40	.09
1980. WINDMILL—VIRGINIA					
☐ 1738	15¢ Black	—	—	.40	.09
1980. WINDMILL—RHODE ISLAND					
☐ 1739	15¢ Black	—	—	.50	.09
1980. WINDMILL—MASSACHUSETTS					
☐ 1740	15¢ Black	—	—	.50	.09
1980. WINDMILL—ILLINOIS					
☐ 1741	15¢ Black	—	—	.50	.09
1980. WINDMILL—TEXAS					
☐ 1742	15¢ Black	—	—	.50	.09
1978. HARRIET TUBMAN					
☐ 1744	13¢ Multicolored	13.50	3.90	.34	.10
1978. AMERICAN FOLK ART ISSUE					
☐ 1745	13¢ Multicolored	—	—	.39	.13
☐ 1746	13¢ Multicolored	—	—	.39	.13
☐ 1747	13¢ Multicolored	—	—	.39	.13
☐ 1748	13¢ Multicolored	—	—	.39	.13
1978. AMERICAN DANCE ISSUE					
☐ 1749	13¢ Multicolored	—	—	.37	.12
☐ 1750	13¢ Multicolored	—	—	.37	.12
☐ 1751	13¢ Multicolored	—	—	.37	.12
☐ 1752	13¢ Multicolored	—	—	.37	.12
1978. FRENCH ALLIANCE					
☐ 1753	13¢ Blue, Black & Red	10.90	1.60	.30	.09
1978. EARLY CANCER DETECTION					
☐ 1754	13¢ Brown	13.90	1.70	.27	.09
1978. JIMMIE RODGERS					
☐ 1755	13¢ Multicolored	13.90	3.90	.32	.09
1978. GEORGE M. COHAN					
☐ 1756	15¢ Multicolored	15.95	4.30	.40	.11
1978. "CAPAX" '78 SOUVENIR SHEET					
☐ 1757	13¢ Multicolored, set of 6	12.75	—	2.60	2.50
1978. PHOTOGRAPHY					
☐ 1758	15¢ Multicolored	12.50	4.70	.42	.09

*No hinge pricing from 1941 to date is figured at (N-H ADD 15%)

Scott No.		Mint Sheet	Plate Block	Fine Unused Each	Fine Used Each
1978. VIKING MISSION TO MARS					
☐ 1759	15¢ Multicolored	17.25	2.20	.42	.10
1978. AMERICAN OWL ISSUE					
☐ 1760	15¢ Multicolored	—	—	.48	.12
☐ 1761	15¢ Multicolored	—	—	.48	.12
☐ 1762	15¢ Multicolored	—	—	.48	.12
☐ 1763	15¢ Multicolored	—	—	.48	.12
1978. AMERICAN TREES ISSUE					
☐ 1764	15¢ Multicolored	—	—	.48	.12
☐ 1765	15¢ Multicolored	—	—	.48	.12
☐ 1766	15¢ Multicolored	—	—	.48	.12
☐ 1767	15¢ Multicolored	—	—	.48	.12
1978. CHRISTMAS ISSUES					
☐ 1768	15¢ Multicolored	28.75	—	.40	.10
☐ 1769	15¢ Multicolored	28.75	—	.40	.10
1979. ROBERT F. KENNEDY ISSUE					
☐ 1770	15¢ Blue	15.50	1.90	.36	.08
1979. MARTIN LUTHER KING ISSUE					
☐ 1771	15¢ Multicolored	16.50	4.60	.36	.08
1979. INTERNATIONAL YEAR OF THE CHILD					
☐ 1772	15¢ Light Brown	16.50	2.10	.36	.08
1979. JOHN STEINBECK ISSUE					
☐ 1773	15¢ Dark Blue	16.50	2.10	.36	.08
1979. ALBERT EINSTEIN ISSUE					
☐ 1774	15¢ Brown	16.50	2.10	.36	.08
1979. PENNSYLVANIA TOLEWARE ISSUE					
☐ 1775	15¢ Multicolored	—	—	.41	.08
☐ 1776	15¢ Multicolored	—	—	.41	.08
☐ 1777	15¢ Multicolored	—	—	.41	.08
☐ 1778	15¢ Multicolored	—	—	.41	.08
1979. ARCHITECTURE U.S.A. ISSUE					
☐ 1779	15¢ Light Blue & Brown	—	—	.46	.10
☐ 1780	15¢ Light Blue & Brown	—	—	.46	.10
☐ 1781	15¢ Light Blue & Brown	—	—	.46	.10
☐ 1782	15¢ Light Blue & Brown	—	—	.46	.10
1979. ENDANGERED FLORA ISSUE					
☐ 1783	15¢ Multicolored	—	—	.46	.10
☐ 1784	15¢ Multicolored	—	—	.46	.10
☐ 1785	15¢ Multicolored	—	—	.46	.10
☐ 1786	15¢ Multicolored	—	—	.46	.10
1979. SEEING FOR ME ISSUE					
☐ 1787	15¢ Multicolored	16.00	7.10	.40	.10

*No hinge pricing from 1941 to date is figured at (N-H ADD 15%)

Scott No.		Mint Sheet	Plate Block	Fine Unused Each	Fine Used Each
1979. SPECIAL OLYMPICS					
☐ 1788	15¢ Multicolored	16.00	4.00	.38	.10
1979. JOHN PAUL JONES					
☐ 1789	15¢ Multicolored	18.75	5.15	.43	.11
1979. OLYMPIC DECATHLON					
☐ 1790	10¢ Multicolored	16.00	4.90	.33	.19
1979. OLYMPIC RUNNERS					
☐ 1791	15¢ Multicolored	—	—	.46	.14
1979. OLYMPIC SWIMMERS					
☐ 1792	15¢ Multicolored	—	—	.46	.14
1979. OLYMPIC ROWERS					
☐ 1793	15¢ Multicolored	—	—	.46	.14
1979. OLYMPIC EQUESTRIAN					
☐ 1794	15¢ Multicolored	—	—	.46	.14
1979. OLYMPIC SKATER					
☐ 1795	15¢ Multicolored	—	—	.54	.12
1979. OLYMPIC SKIER					
☐ 1796	15¢ Multicolored	—	—	.54	.12
1979. OLYMPIC SKI JUMPER					
☐ 1797	15¢ Multicolored	—	—	.54	.12
1979. OLYMPIC GOALTENDER					
☐ 1798	15¢ Multicolored	—	—	.54	.12
1979. MADONNA					
☐ 1799	15¢ Multicolored	31.50	4.50	.39	.10
1979. CHRISTMAS					
☐ 1800	15¢ Multicolored	31.50	4.50	.39	.10
1979. WILL ROGERS					
☐ 1801	15¢ Multicolored	17.30	4.75	.36	.10
1979. VIETNAM VETERANS					
☐ 1802	15¢ Multicolored	16.75	4.40	.39	.10
1980. W.C. FIELDS					
☐ 1803	15¢ Multicolored	16.75	4.70	.39	.10
1980. BENJAMIN BANNEKER					
☐ 1804	15¢ Multicolored	16.75	4.70	.39	.10
1980. LETTERS PRESERVE MEMORIES					
☐ 1805	15¢ Violet & Bistre	—	—	.40	.09
1980. PRESERVE MEMORIES—P.S. WRITE SOON					
☐ 1806	15¢ Violet & Pink	—	—	.40	.09

*No hinge pricing from 1941 to date is figured at (N-H ADD 15%)

Scott No.	Mint Sheet	Plate Block	Fine Unused Each	Fine Used Each
1980. LETTERS LIFT SPIRITS				
☐ 1807 15¢ Green & Pink & Orange	—	—	.41	.09
1980. LIFT SPIRITS—P.S. WRITE SOON				
☐ 1808 15¢ Green & Yellow Green	—	—	.41	.09
1980. LETTERS SHAPE OPINIONS				
☐ 1809 15¢ Scarlet & Blue	—	—	.41	.09
1980. SHAPE OPINIONS—P.S. WRITE SOON				
☐ 1810 15¢ Scarlet & Blue	—	—	.41	.09
1980. AMERICANA SERIES				
☐ 1811 1¢ Dark Blue & Green	—	—	.11	.07
☐ 1813 3.5¢ Purple & Yellow	—	—	.12	.07
1980. NONDENOMINATED "B"				
☐ 1818 18¢ Purple	—	—	.30	.08
1980. FRANCIS PERKINS				
☐ 1821 15¢ Blue	16.40	1.75	.37	.10
1980. DOLLY MADISON				
☐ 1822 15¢ Multicolored	53.00	2.60	.37	.10
1980. EMILY BISSELL				
☐ 1823 15¢ Scarlet & Black	16.10	1.75	.37	.10
1980. HELEN KELLER—ANNE SULLIVAN				
☐ 1824 15¢ Multicolored	16.40	1.75	.37	.10
1980. VETERANS ADMINISTRATION				
☐ 1825 15¢ Carmine & Blue	—	—	.37	.10
1980. GENERAL BERNARDO de G'ALVEZ				
☐ 1826 15¢ Multicolored	—	—	.37	.10
1980. CORAL REEFS—VIRGIN ISLANDS				
☐ 1827 15¢ Multicolored	—	—	.42	.11
1980. CORAL REEFS—FLORIDA				
☐ 1828 15¢ Multicolored	—	—	.42	.11
1980. CORAL REEFS—AMERICAN SAMOA				
☐ 1829 15¢ Multicolored	—	—	.42	.11
1980. CORAL REEFS—HAWAII				
☐ 1830 15¢ Multicolored	—	—	.42	.10
1980. ORGANIZED LABOR				
☐ 1831 15¢ Multicolored	16.40	4.30	.37	.10
1980. EDITH WHARTON				
☐ 1832 15¢ Violet	16.40	4.30	.37	.10
1980. EDUCATION				
☐ 1833 15¢ Multicolored	16.40	2.60	.37	.10

*No hinge pricing from 1941 to date is figured at (N-H ADD 15%)

Scott No.		Mint Sheet	Plate Block	Fine Unused Each	Fine Used Each
1980. INDIAN ARTS					
☐ 1834	15¢ Multicolored	—	5.10	.42	.10
☐ 1835	15¢ Multicolored	—	5.10	.42	.10
☐ 1836	15¢ Multicolored	—	5.10	.42	.10
☐ 1837	15¢ Multicolored	—	5.10	.42	.10
1980. ARCHITECTURE					
☐ 1838	15¢ Black & Red	—	2.20	.46	.12
☐ 1839	15¢ Black & Red	—	2.20	.46	.12
☐ 1840	16¢ Black & Red	—	2.20	.46	.12
☐ 1841	15¢ Black & Red	—	2.20	.46	.12
1980. CHRISTMAS ISSUE					
☐ 1842	15¢ Multicolored	17.10	5.30	.39	.10
☐ 1843	15¢ Multicolored	17.10	7.40	1.00	.10
1982. DOROTHEA DIX					
☐ 1844	1¢ Black	2.00	.25	.06	.04
1983. IGOR STRAVINSKY					
☐ 1845	2¢ Brown	2.80	.27	.06	.04
1983. HENRY CLAY					
☐ 1846	3¢ Green	4.10	.30	.06	.04
1983. CARL SCHURZ					
☐ 1847	4¢ Purple	6.10	.50	.08	.04
1983. PEARL BUCK					
☐ 1848	5¢ Reddish Brown	8.20	.72	.12	.06
1985. WALTER LIPPMANN					
☐ 1849	6¢ Orange	10.00	.80	.12	.06
1985. ABRAHAM BALDWIN					
☐ 1850	7¢ Red	12.10	.82	.13	.07
1985. HENRY KNOX					
☐ 1851	8¢ Black	12.50	.95	.12	.07
1985. SYLVANUS THAYER					
☐ 1852	9¢ Green	14.50	1.30	.14	.07
1984. RICHARD RUSSELL					
☐ 1853	10¢ Blue	16.00	1.40	.16	.07
1985. ALDEN PARTRIDGE					
☐ 1854	11¢ Blue	18.00	1.60	.18	.07
1982. CRAZY HORSE					
☐ 1855	13¢ Brown	19.75	1.65	.18	.07
1985. SINCLAIR LEWIS					
☐ 1856	14¢ Green	21.00	1.70	.18	.07

*No hinge pricing from 1941 to date is figured at (N-H ADD 15%)

Scott No.		Mint Sheet	Plate Block	Fine Unused Each	Fine Used Each
1981. RACHEL CARSON					
☐ 1857	17¢ Blue Green	24.00	1.70	.22	.08
1981. GEORGE MASON					
☐ 1858	18¢ Dark Blue	27.50	1.70	.24	.10
1980. SEQUOYAH					
☐ 1859	19¢ Light Brown	30.25	1.70	.28	.10
1982. RALPH BUNCHE					
☐ 1860	20¢ Carmine	33.00	1.70	.32	.10
1983. THOMAS H. GALLAUDET					
☐ 1861	20¢ Green	33.00	1.68	.32	.10
1984. HARRY S. TRUMAN					
☐ 1862	20¢ Black & White	33.00	1.70	.32	.10
1985. JOHN J. AUDUBON					
☐ 1863	22¢ Blue	37.00	1.70	.35	.10
1984. FRANK C. LAUBACH					
☐ 1864	30¢ Dark Green	44.75	1.95	.44	.10
1981. CHARLES DREW					
☐ 1865	35¢ Gray	49.75	2.20	.50	.10
1982. ROBERT MILLIKAN					
☐ 1866	37¢ Blue	54.25	2.20	.50	.10
1985. GRENVILLE CLARK					
☐ 1867	39¢ Reddish Purple	58.00	2.50	.60	.10
1984. LILLIAN M. GILBRETH					
☐ 1868	40¢ Green	62.50	2.80	.70	.11
1985. CHESTER W. NIMITZ					
☐ 1869	50¢ Dark Brown	67.75	4.00	.83	.18
1981. EVERETT M. DIRKSEN					
☐ 1874	15¢ Dark Green	17.00	2.20	.37	.10
1981. WHITNEY M. YOUNG					
☐ 1875	15¢ Multicolored	16.75	1.80	.40	.11
1981. FLOWERS					
☐ 1876	18¢ Multicolored	—	—	.44	.12
☐ 1877	18¢ Multicolored	—	—	.44	.12
☐ 1878	18¢ Multicolored	—	—	.44	.12
☐ 1879	18¢ Multicolored	—	—	.44	.12
1981. AMERICAN WILDLIFE					
☐ 1880	18¢ Light Brown	—	—	.57	.13
☐ 1881	18¢ Light Brown	—	—	.57	.13
☐ 1882	18¢ Light Brown	—	—	.57	.13
☐ 1883	18¢ Light Brown	—	—	.57	.13

*No hinge pricing from 1941 to date is figured at (N-H ADD 15%)

Scott No.		Mint Sheet	Plate Block	Fine Unused Each	Fine Used Each
☐ 1884	18¢ Light Brown	—	—	.57	.13
☐ 1885	18¢ Light Brown	—	—	.57	.13
☐ 1886	18¢ Light Brown	—	—	.57	.13
☐ 1887	18¢ Light Brown	—	—	.57	.13
☐ 1888	18¢ Light Brown	—	—	.57	.13
☐ 1889	18¢ Light Brown	Booklet	5.50	—	—

1981. FLAG—FOR AMBER WAVES OF GRAIN
☐ 1890	18¢ Multicolored	40.00	9.80	.44	.10

1981. FLAG—FROM SEA TO SHINING SEA
☐ 1891	18¢ Multicolored	—PR.	4.10	.49	.10

1981. U.S.A.
☐ 1892	6¢ Carmine & Dark Blue	—	—	.37	.13

1981. FLAG—FOR PURPLE MOUNTAIN MAJESTIES
☐ 1893	18¢ Multicolored	—	—	.42	.11

1982. FLAG OVER SUPREME COURT
☐ 1894	20¢ Carmine & Dark blue	32.50	2.60	.36	.16

1982. MAIL WAGON
☐ 1900	9.3¢ Carmine	—	—	.21	.12

1984. RAILROAD CABOOSE
☐ 1902	11¢ Red, coil	—	—	.21	.08

1981. ELECTRIC CAR
☐ 1905	17¢ Blue	—LP.	1.85	.31	.07

1981. SURREY
☐ 1906	18¢ Brown	—LP.	1.85	.31	.07

1982. FIRE PUMPER
☐ 1907	20¢ Red Orange	—	—	.36	.18

1981. AMERICAN RED CROSS
☐ 1910	18¢ Multicolored	19.00	2.20	.44	.09

1981. SAVINGS AND LOAN
☐ 1911	18¢ Multicolored	19.00	2.20	.44	.09

1981. SPACE ACHIEVEMENT
☐ 1912	18¢ Multicolored	—	4.80	.52	.16
☐ 1913	18¢ Multicolored	—	4.80	.52	.16
☐ 1914	18¢ Multicolored	—	4.80	.52	.16
☐ 1915	18¢ Multicolored	—	4.80	.52	.16
☐ 1916	18¢ Multicolored	—	4.80	.52	.16
☐ 1917	18¢ Multicolored	—	4.80	.52	.16
☐ 1918	18¢ Multicolored	—	4.80	.52	.16
☐ 1919	18¢ Multicolored	—	4.80	.52	.16

1981. PROFESSIONAL MANAGEMENT
☐ 1920	18¢ Dark Blue & Black	19.90	2.30	.52	.11

*No hinge pricing from 1941 to date is figured at (N-H ADD 15%)

Scott No.		Mint Sheet	Plate Block	Fine Unused Each	Fine Used Each
1981. PRESERVATION OF WILDLIFE HABITATS					
☐ 1921	18¢ Multicolored	—	2.30	.51	.11
☐ 1922	18¢ Multicolored	—	2.30	.51	.11
☐ 1923	18¢ Multicolored	—	2.30	.51	.11
☐ 1924	18¢ Multicolored	—	2.30	.51	.11
1981. DISABLED PERSONS					
☐ 1925	18¢ Multicolored	20.00	2.30	.52	.11
1981. EDNA ST. VINCENT MILLAY					
☐ 1926	18¢ Multicolored	19.90	2.30	.52	.11
1981. ALCOHOLISM					
☐ 1927	18¢ Dark Blue	28.50	16.00	.46	.10
1981. ARCHITECTURE					
☐ 1928	18¢ Brown & Black	—	2.30	.51	.11
☐ 1929	18¢ Brown & Black	—	2.30	.51	.11
☐ 1930	18¢ Brown & Black	—	2.30	.51	.11
☐ 1931	18¢ Brown & Black	—	2.30	.51	.11
1981. BABE ZAHARIAS					
☐ 1932	18¢ Purple	—	2.25	.52	.11
1981. BOBBY JONES					
☐ 1933	18¢ Dark Green	—	2.25	.52	.11
1981. FREDERIC REMINGTON					
☐ 1934	18¢ Light Brown & Green	20.00	2.25	.50	.11
1981. JAMES HOBAN					
☐ 1935	18¢ Multicolored	22.50	2.85	.50	.11
1981. JAMES HOBAN					
☐ 1936	20¢ Multicolored	21.50	2.50	.50	.10
1981. YORKTOWN MAP					
☐ 1937	18¢ Multicolored	—	—	.50	.10
1981. VIRGINIA CAPES MAP					
☐ 1938	18¢ Multicolored	—	—	.50	.10
1981. CHRISTMAS—BOTTICELLI					
☐ 1939	20¢ Multicolored	44.00	2.30	.50	.10
1981. SEASONS GREETINGS					
☐ 1940	20¢ Multicolored	21.00	2.30	.50	.10
1981. JOHN HANSON					
☐ 1941	20¢ Multicolored	21.00	2.30	.50	.10
1981. DESERT PLANTS					
☐ 1942	Multicolored	—	2.45	.50	.10
☐ 1943	Multicolored	—	2.45	.50	.10

*No hinge pricing from 1941 to date is figured at (N-H ADD 15%)

Scott No.		Mint Sheet	Plate Block	Fine Unused Each	Fine Used Each
☐ 1944	Multicolored	—	2.45	.50	.10
☐ 1945	Multicolored	—	2.45	.50	.10

1981. "C" EAGLE—SINGLE
☐ 1946	20¢ Light Brown	42.50	2.60	.50	.10

1981. "C" EAGLE—COIL SINGLE
☐ 1947	20¢ Light Brown	—	—	.50	.10

1981. "C" EAGLE—BOOKLET SINGLE
☐ 1948	20¢ Light Brown	—	—	.50	.10

1981. BIGHORN SHEEP
☐ 1949	20¢ Dark Blue	—	—	.50	.10

1982. FRANKLIN ROOSEVELT
☐ 1950	20¢ Dark Blue	19.50	2.25	.50	.10

1982. "LOVE" FLOWERS
☐ 1951	20¢ Multicolored	21.00	2.25	.50	.10

1982. GEORGE WASHINGTON
☐ 1952	20¢ Multicolored	21.00	2.25	.50	.10

1982. BIRDS AND FLOWERS
☐ 1953- 2002	20¢ Multicolored	21.00	—	.50	.10

1982. THE NETHERLANDS
☐ 2003	20¢ Dark Blue & Red	21.50	2.25	.50	.10

1982. LIBRARY OF CONGRESS
☐ 2004	20¢ Rose & Dark Gray	21.50	2.25	.50	.10

1982. CONSUMER EDUCATION
☐ 2005	20¢ Light Blue & Dark Blue	—	—	.50	.10

1982. KNOXVILLE WORLD'S FAIR
☐ 2006	20¢ Multicolored	—	2.25	.50	.10
☐ 2007	20¢ Multicolored	—	2.25	.50	.10
☐ 2008	20¢ Multicolored	—	2.25	.50	.10
☐ 2009	20¢ Multicolored	—	2.25	.50	.10

1982. HORATIO ALGER
☐ 2010	20¢ Carmine & Black	21.50	2.25	.50	.10

1982. AGING TOGETHER
☐ 2011	20¢ Light Rose	21.50	2.25	.50	.10

1982. THE BARRYMORES
☐ 2012	20¢ Multicolored	20.00	2.25	.45	.10

1982. DR. MARY WALKER
☐ 2013	20¢ Multicolored	20.00	2.25	.45	.10

*No hinge pricing from 1941 to date is figured at (N-H ADD 15%)

Scott No.		Mint Sheet	Plate Block	Fine Unused Each	Fine Used Each

1982. INTERNATIONAL PEACE GARDEN
☐ 2014   20¢ Multicolored .... 20.00 | 2.25 | .45 | .10

1982. AMERICA'S LIBRARIES
☐ 2015   20¢ Orange-Red & Black .... 20.00 | 2.20 | .45 | .10

1982. JACKIE ROBINSON
☐ 2016   20¢ Multicolored .... 20.00 | 2.25 | .45 | .10

1982. TOURO SYNAGOGUE
☐ 2017   20¢ Multicolored .... 20.00 | 2.25 | .45 | .10

1982. WOLF TRAP FARM PARK
☐ 2018   20¢ Multicolored .... 20.00 | 2.25 | .45 | .10

1982. ARCHITECTURAL—WRIGHT
☐ 2019   20¢ Black and Brown .... — | — | .45 | .10

1982. ARCHITECTURE—VAN DER ROHE
☐ 2020   20¢ Black and Brown .... — | — | .45 | .10

1982. ARCHITECTURE—GROPIUS
☐ 2021   20¢ Black and Brown .... — | — | .45 | .10

1982. ARCHITECTURE—SAARINEN
☐ 2022   20¢ Black and Brown .... — | — | .45 | .10
☐ Architecture, above four attached .... 20.00 | 2.25 | .45 | .10

1982. FRANCIS OF ASSISI
☐ 2023   20¢ Multicolored .... 20.00 | 2.25 | .45 | .10

1982. PONCE DE LEON
☐ 2024   20¢ Multicolored .... 20.00 | 2.25 | .45 | .10

1982. CHRISTMAS ISSUE, CAT AND DOG
☐ 2025   13¢ Multicolored .... 13.90 | 2.20 | .45 | .10

1982. CHRISTMAS ISSUE, TIEPOLO'S "MADONNA AND CHILD"
☐ 2026   20¢ Multicolored .... 21.00 | 2.15 | .45 | .10

1982. SEASON'S GREETINGS, SLEDDING
☐ 2027   20¢ Multicolored .... 21.00 | — | .45 | .10

1982. SEASON'S GREETINGS, BUILDING SNOWMAN
☐ 2028   20¢ Multicolored .... — | — | .45 | .10

1982. SEASON'S GREETINGS, ICE SKATING
☐ 2029   20¢ Multicolored .... — | — | .45 | .10

1982. SEASON'S GREETINGS, TRIMMING TREE
☐ 2030   20¢ Multicolored .... — | — | .45 | .10
☐ Season's Greetings, above four attached .... 21.00 | 2.20 | — | —

1982. SCIENCE AND INDUSTRY
☐ 2031   20¢ Multicolored .... 21.00 | 2.20 | .45 | .10

*No hinge pricing from 1941 to date is figured at (N-H ADD 15%)

Scott No.	Mint Sheet	Plate Block	Fine Unused Each	Fine Used Each
1983. BALLOONING				
☐ 2032 20¢ Multicolored	—	—	.45	.10
1982. BALLOONING				
☐ 2033 20¢ Multicolored	—	—	.43	.10
1982. BALLOONING				
☐ 2034 20¢ Multicolored	—	—	.43	.10
1982. BALLOONING				
☐ 2035 20¢ Multicolored	—	—	.43	.10
☐ Ballooning, above four attached	17.90	2.15	—	—
1983. TREATY OF AMITY				
☐ 2036 20¢ Blue and Black	20.25	2.15	.43	.10
1983. CIVILIAN CONSERVATION CORPS				
☐ 2037 20¢ Multicolored	20.25	2.15	.43	.10
1983. JOSEPH PRIESTLEY				
☐ 2038 20¢ Rust Brown	20.25	2.15	.43	.10
1983. VOLUNTEER				
☐ 2039 20¢ Black and Red	20.25	2.15	.43	.10
1983. CONCORD				
☐ 2040 20¢ Beige	20.25	2.15	.43	.10
1983. BROOKLYN BRIDGE				
☐ 2041 20¢ Blue	20.25	2.15	.43	.10
1983. TENNESSEE VALLEY AUTHORITY				
☐ 2042 20¢ Multicolored	20.25	2.15	.43	.10
1983. PHYSICAL FITNESS				
☐ 2043 20¢ Multicolored	20.25	2.15	.43	.10
1982. SCOTT JOPLIN				
☐ 2044 20¢ Multicolored	20.25	2.15	.43	.10
1983. MEDAL OF HONOR				
☐ 2045 20¢ Multicolored	18.00	2.15	.43	.10
1983. BABE RUTH				
☐ 2046 20¢ Blue	20.25	2.15	.43	.10
1983. NATHANIEL HAWTHORNE				
☐ 2047 20¢ Multicolored	20.25	2.15	.43	.10
1983. SUMMER OLYMPICS 1984				
☐ 2048 13¢ Multicolored	—	—	.29	.10
1983. SUMMER OLYMPICS 1984				
☐ 2049 13¢ Multicolored	—	—	.29	.10
1983. SUMMER OLYMPICS 1984				
☐ 2050 13¢ Multicolored	—	—	.29	.10

*No hinge pricing from 1941 to date is figured at (N-H ADD 15%)

Scott No.		Mint Sheet	Plate Block	Fine Unused Each	Fine Used Each
1983. SUMMER OLYMPICS 1984					
☐ 2051	13¢ Multicolored	—	—	.29	.10
1983. TREATY OF PARIS					
☐ 2052	20¢ Multicolored	20.25	2.15	.41	.10
1983. CIVIL SERVICE					
☐ 2053	20¢ Multicolored	20.25	2.15	.41	.10
1983. METROPOLITAN OPERA					
☐ 2054	20¢ Yellow and Brown	20.25	2.15	.41	.10
1983. INVENTORS					
☐ 2055	20¢ Multicolored	—	—	.41	.10
1983. INVENTORS					
☐ 2056	20¢ Multicolored	—	—	.41	.10
1983. INVENTORS					
☐ 2057	20¢ Multicolored	—	—	.41	.10
1983. INVENTORS					
☐ 2058	20¢ Multicolored	—	—	.41	.10
1983. STREETCARS					
☐ 2059	20¢ Multicolored	—	—	.41	.10
1983. STREETCARS					
☐ 2060	20¢ Multicolored	—	—	.41	.10
1983. STREETCARS					
☐ 2061	20¢ Multicolored	—	—	.41	.10
1983. STREETCARS					
☐ 2062	20¢ Multicolored	—	—	.41	.10
1983. CHRISTMAS, MADONNA					
☐ 2063	20¢ Multicolored	20.25	2.15	.41	.10
1983. CHRISTMAS, SEASON'S GREETINGS					
☐ 2064	20¢ Multicolored	20.25	2.15	.41	.10
1983. MARTIN LUTHER					
☐ 2065	20¢ Multicolored	20.25	2.15	.41	.10
1984. ALASKA STATEHOOD					
☐ 2066	20¢ Multicolored	20.25	2.15	.41	.10
1984. WINTER OLYMPICS 1984					
☐ 2067	20¢ Multicolored	—	—	.41	.10
1984. WINTER OLYMPICS 1984					
☐ 2068	20¢ Multicolored	—	—	.41	.10
1984. WINTER OLYMPICS 1984					
☐ 2069	20¢ Multicolored	—	—	.41	.10

*No hinge pricing from 1941 to date is figured at (N-H ADD 15%)

Scott No.		Mint Sheet	Plate Block	Fine Unused Each	Fine Used Each
1984. WINTER OLYMPICS 1984					
☐ 2070	20¢ Multicolored	—	—	.41	.10
1984. FEDERAL DEPOSIT INSURANCE CORPORATION					
☐ 2071	20¢ Red & Yellow	17.60	1.75	.41	.10
1984. LOVE					
☐ 2072	20¢ Multicolored	17.60	1.75	.41	.10
1984. CARTER G. WOODSON					
☐ 2073	20¢ Multicolored	17.60	1.75	.41	.10
1984. SOIL AND WATER CONSERVATION					
☐ 2074	20¢ Multicolored	17.60	1.75	.41	.10
1984. CREDIT UNION					
☐ 2075	20¢ Multicolored	17.60	1.75	.41	.10
1984. ORCHIDS					
☐ 2076	20¢ Multicolored	—	—	.41	.10
1984. ORCHIDS					
☐ 2077	20¢ Multicolored	—	—	.41	.10
1984. ORCHIDS					
☐ 2078	20¢ Multicolored	—	—	.41	.10
1984. ORCHIDS					
☐ 2079	20¢ Multicolored	—	—	.41	.10
1984. HAWAII STATEHOOD					
☐ 2080	20¢ Blue & Yellow	17.60	1.75	.41	.10
1984. NATIONAL ARCHIVES					
☐ 2081	20¢ Brown & Black	17.60	1.75	.41	.10
1984. SUMMER OLYMPICS 1984					
☐ 2082	20¢ Multicolored	—	—	.41	.10
1984. SUMMER OLYMPICS 1984					
☐ 2083	20¢ Multicolored	—	—	.41	.10
1984. SUMMER OLYMPICS 1984					
☐ 2084	20¢ Multicolored	—	—	.41	.10
1984. SUMMER OLYMPICS 1984					
☐ 2085	20¢ Multicolored	—	—	.41	.10
1984. LOUISIANA WORLD'S FAIR					
☐ 2086	20¢ Multicolored	17.60	1.75	.41	.10
1984. HEALTH RESEARCH					
☐ 2087	20¢ Multicolored	17.60	1.75	.41	.10
1984. DOUGLAS FAIRBANKS					
☐ 2088	20¢ Black & White	17.60	1.75	.41	.10

*No hinge pricing from 1941 to date is figured at (N-H ADD 15%)

Scott No.		Mint Sheet	Plate Block	Fine Unused Each	Fine Used Each
1984. JIM THORPE					
☐ 2089	20¢ Black & White	17.60	1.75	.41	.10
1984. JOHN McCORMACK					
☐ 2090	20¢ Multicolored	17.60	1.75	.41	.10
1984. ST. LAWRENCE SEAWAY					
☐ 2091	20¢ Multicolored	17.60	1.75	.41	.10
1984. WATERFOWL PRESERVATION					
☐ 2092	20¢ Multicolored	17.60	1.75	.41	.10
1984. ROANOKE VOYAGES 1584					
☐ 2093	20¢ Multicolored	17.60	1.75	.41	.10
1984. HERMAN MELVILLE					
☐ 2094	20¢ Green	17.60	1.75	.41	.10
1984. HORACE MOSES					
☐ 2095	20¢ Orange & Brown	17.60	1.75	.41	.10
1984. SMOKEY THE BEAR					
☐ 2096	20¢ Multicolored	17.60	1.75	.41	.10
1984. ROBERTO CLEMENTE					
☐ 2097	20¢ Multicolored	17.60	1.75	.41	.10
1984. DOGS: BEAGLE					
☐ 2098	20¢ Multicolored	—	—	.41	.10
1984. DOGS: RETRIEVER					
☐ 2099	20¢ Multicolored	—	—	.41	.10
1984. DOGS: MALAMUTE					
☐ 2100	20¢ Multicolored	—	—	.41	.10
1984. DOGS: COONHOUND					
☐ 2101	20¢ Multicolored	—	—	.41	.10
1984. CRIME PREVENTION					
☐ 2102	20¢ Multicolored	17.60	1.75	.41	.10
1984. HISPANIC AMERICANS					
☐ 2103	20¢ Multicolored	17.60	1.75	.41	.10
1984. FAMILY UNITY					
☐ 2104	20¢ Multicolored	17.60	1.75	.41	.10
1984. ELEANOR ROOSEVELT					
☐ 2105	20¢ Blue	17.60	1.75	.41	.10
1984. NATION OF READERS					
☐ 2106	20¢ Brown & Maroon	17.60	1.75	.41	.10
1984. MADONNA AND CHILD					
☐ 2107	20¢ Multicolored	17.60	1.75	.41	.10

*No hinge pricing from 1941 to date is figured at (N-H ADD 15%)

Scott No.		Mint Sheet	Plate Block	Fine Unused Each	Fine Used Each
1984. SANTA CLAUS					
☐ 2108	20¢ Multicolored	17.60	1.75	.41	.10
1984. VIETNAM MEMORIAL					
☐ 2109	20¢ Multicolored	17.60	1.75	.41	.10
1985. JEROME KERN					
☐ 2110	22¢ Multicolored	18.25	2.00	.44	.10
1985. "D" NON-DENOMINATIONAL					
☐ 2111	22¢ Green	35.20	2.00	.44	.10
1985. "D" NON-DENOMINATIONAL COIL					
☐ 2112	22¢ Green	—	—	.44	.10
1985. "D" NON-DENOMINATIONAL BOOKLET					
☐ 2113	22¢ Green	—	—	.44	.10
1985. FLAG OVER DOME					
☐ 2114	22¢ Multicolored	35.20	2.00	.44	.10
1985. FLAG OVER DOME COIL					
☐ 2115	22¢ Multicolored	—	—	.44	.10
1985. FLAG OVER DOME BOOKLET					
☐ 2116	22¢ Multicolored	—	—	.44	.10
1985. SEASHELLS: DOGWINKLE					
☐ 2117	22¢ Brown	—	—	.44	.10
1985. SEASHELLS: HELMET					
☐ 2118	22¢ Brown	—	—	.44	.10
1985. SEASHELLS: NEPTUNE					
☐ 2119	22¢ Brown	—	—	.44	.10
1985. SEASHELLS: SCALLOP					
☐ 2120	22¢ Pink	—	—	.44	.10
1985. SEASHELLS: WHELK					
☐ 2121	22¢ Brown	—	—	.44	.10
1985. EXPRESS MAIL U.S.A.					
☐ 2122	$10.75 Multicolored	—	—	23.50	14.10
1985. SCHOOL BUS					
☐ 2123	3.4¢ Green	—	—	.11	.07
1985. BUCKBOARD					
☐ 2125	4.9¢ Dark Brown	—	—	.12	.09
1986. STAR ROUTE TRUCK					
☐ 2126	5.5¢ Carmine	.13	.09	—	—
1985. TRICYCLE 1880s					
☐ 2127	6¢ Red	—	—	.14	.05

*No hinge pricing from 1941 to date is figured at (N-H ADD 15%)

Scott No.	Mint Sheet	Plate Block	Fine Unused Each	Fine Used Each
1985. AMBULANCE				
☐ 2128 8.3¢ Green	—	—	.17	.09
1985. OIL WAGON 1890s				
☐ 2129 10.1¢ Black	—	—	.21	.06
1985. STUTZ AUTO				
☐ 2130 11¢ Green	—	—	.25	.06
1985. STANLEY STEAMER 1909				
☐ 2131 12¢ Blue	—	—	.26	.07
1985. PUSHCART 1880s				
☐ 2132 12.5¢ Black	—	—	.27	.07
1985. ICEBOAT 1880s				
☐ 2134 14¢ Blue	—	—	.31	.07
1986. DOG SLED 1920s				
☐ 2135 17¢ Blue	.33	.21	—	—
1986. BREAD WAGON 1880s				
☐ 2136 25¢ Brown	.58	.31	—	—
1985. MARY MCLEOD BETHUNE				
☐ 2137 22¢ Multicolored	18.50	2.10	.44	.10
1985. DUCKS: BROADBILL				
☐ 2138 22¢ Multicolored	—	—	.44	.10
1985. DUCKS: MALLARD				
☐ 2139 22¢ Multicolored	—	—	.44	.10
1985. DUCKS: CANVASBACK				
☐ 2140 22¢ Multicolored	—	—	.44	.10
1985. DUCKS: REDHEAD				
☐ 2141 22¢ Multicolored	—	—	.44	.10
1985. WINTER SPECIAL OLYMPICS				
☐ 2142 22¢ Multicolored	15.80	2.05	.44	.10
1985. LOVE				
☐ 2143 22¢ Multicolored	18.10	2.10	.44	.10
1985. RURAL ELECTRIFICATION ADMINISTRATION				
☐ 2144 22¢ Multicolored	18.10	2.10	.44	.10
1985. AMERIPEX SHOW				
☐ 2145 22¢ Multicolored	18.10	2.10	.44	.10
1985. ABIGAIL ADAMS				
☐ 2146 22¢ Multicolored	18.10	2.10	.44	.10
1985. BARTHOLDI, STATUE OF LIBERTY				
☐ 2147 22¢ Multicolored	18.10	2.10	.44	.10

*No hinge pricing from 1941 to date is figured at (N-H ADD 15%)

Scott No.	Mint Sheet	Plate Block	Fine Unused Each	Fine Used Each
1985. GEORGE WASHINGTON				
☐2149 18¢ Multicolored	—	—	.34	.08
1985. ENVELOPES				
☐2150 21.1¢ Multicolored	—	—	.41	.09
1985. KOREAN VETERANS				
☐2152 22¢ Red & Green	18.10	2.05	.44	.10
1985. SOCIAL SECURITY				
☐2153 22¢ Blue	18.10	2.05	.44	.10
1985. WORLD WAR I VETERANS				
☐2154 22¢ Red & Green	18.10	2.05	.44	.10
1985. HORSES: QUARTER HORSE				
☐2155 22¢ Multicolored	—	—	.44	.10
1985. HORSES: MORGAN				
☐2156 22¢ Multicolored	—	—	.44	.10
1985. HORSES: SADDLEBRED				
☐2157 22¢ Multicolored	—	—	.44	.10
1985. HORSES: APPALOOSA				
☐2158 22¢ Multicolored	—	—	.44	.10
1985. PUBLIC EDUCATION				
☐2159 22¢ Multicolored	18.10	2.05	.44	.10
1985. YOUTH YEAR: Y.M.C.A.				
☐2160 22¢ Multicolored	—	—	.44	.10
1985. YOUTH YEAR: BOY SCOUTS				
☐2161 22¢ Multicolored	—	—	.44	.10
1985. YOUTH YEAR: BIG BROTHERS				
☐2162 22¢ Multicolored	—	—	.44	.10
1985. YOUTH YEAR CAMPFIRE				
☐2163 22¢ Multicolored			.44	.10
1985. HELP END HUNGER				
☐2164 22¢ Multicolored	—	—	.44	.10
1985. MADONNA				
☐2165 22¢ Multicolored	—	—	.44	.10
1985. POINSETTIA				
☐2166 22¢ Multicolored	—	—	.44	.10
1986. ARKANSAS				
☐2167 22¢ Multicolored	—	—	.44	.10
1986. MARGARET MITCHELL				
☐2168 1¢ Brown	—	—	.03	.02
1987. MARY LYON				
☐2169 2¢ Blue	—	—	.03	.01

*No hinge pricing from 1941 to date is figured at (N-H ADD 15%)

Scott No.		Mint Sheet	Plate Block	Fine Unused Each	Fine Used Each
1986. PAUL DUDLEY WHITE M.D.					
☐ 2170	3¢ Blue	—	—	.05	.02
1986. FATHER FLANAGAN					
☐ 2171	4¢ Blue	—	—	.06	.03
1986. HUGO L. BLACK					
☐ 2172	5¢ Olive Green	—	—	.07	.03
1987. JULIA WARD HOWE					
☐ 2177	14¢ Red	—	—	.16	.06
1986. BELVA ANN LOCKWOOD					
☐ 2179	17¢ Blue Green	—	—	.19	.07
1986. JACK LONDON					
☐ 2183	25¢ Blue	—	—	.46	.11
1986. JOHN HARVARD					
☐ 2191	56¢ Brown	—	—	.60	.16
1986. BERNARD REVEL					
☐ 2194	$1.00 Green	—	—	1.05	.23
1986. WILLIAM JENNINGS BRYAN					
☐ 2195	$2.00 Violet	—	—	2.08	.51
1987. BRET HARTE					
☐ 2196	$5.00 Brown	—	—	5.25	.80
1986. STAMP COLLECTING: AMERICAN PHILATELIC ASSOC.					
☐ 2198	22¢ Multicolored	—	—	.44	.10
1986. STAMP COLLECTING: LITTLE BOY					
☐ 2199	22¢ Multicolored	—	—	.44	.10
1986. STAMP COLLECTING: MAGNIFIER					
☐ 2200	22¢ Multicolored	—	—	.44	.10
1986. STAMP COLLECTING: RUBBER STAMP					
☐ 2201	22¢ Multicolored	—	—	.46	.10
1986. LOVE					
☐ 2202	22¢ Multicolored	—	—	.41	.09
1986. SOJOURNER TRUTH					
☐ 2203	22¢ Multicolored	—	—	.41	.09
1986. TEXAS—SAN JACINTO 1836					
☐ 2204	22¢ Multicolored	—	—	.41	.09
1986. FISH: MUSKELLUNGE					
☐ 2205	22¢ Multicolored	—	—	.41	.09
1986. FISH: ATLANTIC COD					
☐ 2206	22¢ Multicolored	—	—	.41	.09
1986. FISH: LARGEMOUTH BASS					
☐ 2207	22¢ Multicolored	—	—	.41	.09

*No hinge pricing from 1941 to date is figured at (N-H ADD 15%)

Scott No.		Mint Sheet	Plate Block	Fine Unused Each	Fine Used Each
1986. FISH: BLUEFIN TUNA					
☐ 2208	22¢ Multicolored	—	—	.41	.09
1986. FISH: CATFISH					
☐ 2209	22¢ Multicolored	—	—	.41	.09
1986. PUBLIC HOSPITALS					
☐ 2210	22¢ Multicolored	—	—	.41	.09
1986. DUKE ELLINGTON					
☐ 2211	22¢ Multicolored	—	—	.41	.09
1986. AMERIPEX '86-PRESIDENTS I					
☐ 2216	22¢ Brown & Black	2.05	—	—	—
1986. AMERIPEX '86-PRESIDENTS II					
☐ 2217	22¢ Brown & Black	2.05	—	—	—
1986. AMERIPEX '86-PRESIDENTS III					
☐ 2218	22¢ Brown & Black	2.05	—	—	—
1986. AMERIPEX '86-PRESIDENTS IV					
☐ 2219	22¢ Brown & Black	2.05	—	—	—
1986. POLAR EXPLORERS: KANE					
☐ 2220	22¢ Multicolored	—	—	.41	.09
1986. POLAR EXPLORERS: GREELY					
☐ 2221	22¢ Multicolored	—	—	.41	.09
1986. POLAR EXPLORERS: STEFANSSON					
☐ 2222	22¢ Multicolored	—	—	.41	.09
1986. POLAR EXPLORERS: HENSON					
☐ 2223	22¢ Multicolored	—	—	.41	.09
1986. LIBERTY					
☐ 2224	22¢ Carmine & Blue	—	—	.41	.09
1986. NAVAJO ART					
☐ 2235	22¢ Multicolored	—	—	.41	.09
1986. NAVAJO ART					
☐ 2236	22¢ Multicolored	—	—	.41	.09
1986. NAVAJO ART					
☐ 2237	22¢ Multicolored	—	—	.41	.09
1986. NAVAJO ART					
☐ 2238	22¢ Multicolored	—	—	.41	.09
1986. T.S. ELIOT					
☐ 2239	22¢ Brown	—	—	.41	.09
1986. FOLK ART: HIGHLANDER					
☐ 2240	22¢ Multicolored	—	—	.41	.09
1986. FOLK ART: SHIP					
☐ 2241	22¢ Multicolored	—	—	.41	.09

*No hinge pricing from 1941 to date is figured at (N-H ADD 15%)

Scott No.	Mint Sheet	Plate Block	Fine Unused Each	Fine Used Each
1986. FOLK ART: NAUTICAL				
☐ 2242 22¢ Multicolored	—	—	.41	.09
1986. FOLK ART: CIGAR STORE				
☐ 2243 22¢ Multicolored	—	—	.41	.09
1986. CHRISTMAS: PEROGINO GALLERY				
☐ 2244 22¢ Multicolored	—	—	.41	.09
1986. CHRISTMAS: GREETINGS				
☐ 2245 22¢ Multicolored	—	—	.41	.09
1987. MICHIGAN STATEHOOD				
☐ 2246 22¢ Multicolored	—	—	.40	.08
1987. PAN AMERICAN GAMES				
☐ 2247 22¢ Multicolored	—	—	.40	.08
1987. LOVE				
☐ 2248 22¢ Multicolored	—	—	.40	.08
1987. JEAN BAPTISTE POINTE DU SABLE				
☐ 2249 22¢ Multicolored	—	—	.40	.08
1987. ENRICO CARUSO				
☐ 2250 22¢ Multicolored	—	—	.40	.08
1987. GIRL SCOUTS				
☐ 2251 22¢ Multicolored	—	—	.40	.08
1987. UNITED WAY UNITING COMMUNITIES				
☐ 2275 22¢ Multicolored	—	—	.40	.08
1987. AMERICAN FLAG				
☐ 2276 22¢ Multicolored	—	—	.40	.08
1987. AMERICAN WILDLIFE				
☐ 2286– 2335 22¢ Multicolored	—	—	.40ea.	.08ea.
1987. DELAWARE				
☐ 2336 22¢ Multicolored	—	—	.40	.08
1987. PENNSYLVANIA				
☐ 2337 22¢ Multicolored	—	—	.35	.06
1987. NEW JERSEY				
☐ 2338 22¢ Multicolored	—	—	.35	.06
1987. FRIENDSHIP WITH MOROCCO				
☐ 2349 22¢ Multicolored	—	—	.35	.06
1987. WILLIAM FAULKNER				
☐ 2350 22¢ Green	—	—	.35	.06
1987. LACEMAKING				
☐ 2351– 2354 22¢ Blue	—	—	.35ea.	.06ea.

*No hinge pricing from 1941 to date is figured at (N-H ADD 15%)

Scott No.			Mint Sheet	Plate Block	Fine Unused Each	Fine Used Each
1987. U.S. CONSTITUTION						
☐ 2360	22¢ Multicolored		—	—	.35ea.	.06ea.
1987. C.P.A. CERTIFIED PUBLIC ACCOUNTANTS						
☐ 2361	22¢ Multicolored		—	—	.35	.06
1987. CHRISTMAS: MARONI, NATIONAL GALLERY						
☐ 2367	22¢ Multicolored		—	—	.35	.06
1987. GREETINGS						
☐ 2368	22¢ Multicolored		—	—	.35	.06

Scott No.		Fine Unused Plate Blk	Ave. Unused Plate Blk	Fine Unused Each	Ave. Unused Each	Fine Used Each	Ave. Used Each
AIRMAIL STAMPS							
1918. FIRST ISSUE—(N-H ADD 45%)							
☐ C1	6¢ Orange	1210.00	730.00	108.00	70.00	42.00	30.00
☐ C2	16¢ Green	2460.00	1635.00	170.00	116.00	52.00	39.00
☐ C3	24¢ Carmine & Blue	1360.00	890.00	160.00	112.00	63.00	45.00
1923. SECOND ISSUE—(N-H ADD 35%)							
☐ C4	8¢ Dark Green	660.00	422.00	50.00	32.00	24.00	14.50
☐ C5	16¢ Dark Blue	3775.00	2525.00	161.00	118.00	54.00	36.00
☐ C6	24¢ Carmine	4510.00	3020.00	216.00	135.00	46.00	29.50
1926-1927. LONG MAP (N-H ADD 35%)							
☐ C7	10¢ Dark Blue	64.00	45.00	5.00	3.50	.50	.35
☐ C8	15¢ Olive Brown	78.00	54.00	6.00	4.00	3.30	2.05
☐ C9	20¢ Yellow Green	196.00	133.50	16.10	11.25	2.40	1.65
1927. LINDBERGH TRIBUTE ISSUE (N-H ADD 25%)							
☐ C10	10¢ Dark Blue	220.00	148.00	15.00	10.00	3.40	2.05
1928. BEACON (N-H ADD 20%)							
☐ C11	5¢ Carmine & Blue	72.00	48.00	8.50	6.00	.80	.55
1930. WINGED GLOBE—FLAT PRESS (N-H ADD 35%)							
☐ C12	5¢ Violet	250.00	186.00	17.00	13.00	.55	.38
1930. GRAF ZEPPELIN ISSUE (N-H ADD 20%)							
☐ C13	65¢ Green	3710.00	3100.00	415.00	310.00	400.00	285.00
☐ C14	$1.30 Brown	8560.00	6450.00	1100.00	710.00	730.00	546.00
☐ C15	$2.60 Blue	14000.00	12000.00	1710.00	1225.00	1120.00	748.00
1931-1932.							
WINGED GLOBE—ROTARY PRESS (N-H ADD 25%)							
☐ C16	5¢ Violet	166.00	118.00	7.80	5.10	.56	.36
☐ C17	8¢ Olive Bistre	67.00	43.00	3.70	2.40	.33	.32
1933. CENTURY OF PROGRESS ISSUE (N-H ADD 25%)							
☐ C18	50¢ Green	1175.00	900.00	155.00	112.00	143.00	.92

*No hinge pricing from 1941 to date is figured at (N-H ADD 15%)

Scott No.		Fine Unused Plate Blk	Ave. Unused Plate Blk	Fine Unused Each	Ave. Unused Each	Fine Used Each	Ave. Used Each
1934. DESIGN OF 1930 (N-H ADD 25%)							
☐ C19	6¢ Orange	43.00	30.00	4.10	2.90	.20	.13
1935-1937. TRANSPACIFIC ISSUE (N-H ADD 10%)							
☐ C20	25¢ Blue	46.00	34.00	2.30	1.60	2.00	1.30
☐ C21	20¢ Green	222.00	141.00	16.75	12.50	2.30	1.46
☐ C22	50¢ Carmine	226.00	141.00	17.00	12.50	6.40	5.00
1938. EAGLE (N-H ADD 20%)							
☐ C23	6¢ Blue & Carmine	14.00	9.80	.56	.40	.11	.09
1939. TRANSATLANTIC (N-H ADD 20%)							
☐ C24	30¢ Dull Blue	231.00	155.00	16.00	12.00	1.70	1.34
1941-1944. TRANSPORT PLANE (N-H ADD 20%)							
☐ C25	6¢ Carmine	1.30	.98	.22	.15	.11	.09
☐ C26	8¢ Olive Green	1.80	1.30	.24	.17	.11	.09
☐ C27	10¢ Violet	15.50	11.00	2.06	1.40	.23	.18
☐ C28	15¢ Brown Carmine	26.00	14.00	4.31	3.20	.43	.31
☐ C29	20¢ Bright Green	21.00	13.50	3.35	2.15	.40	.30
☐ C30	30¢ Blue	22.00	14.00	3.20	2.20	.41	.31
☐ C31	50¢ Orange	142.00	102.00	13.00	13.00	4.40	3.35

Scott No.		Mint Sheet	Plate Block	Fine Unused Each	Fine Used Each
1946-1947. DC-4 SKYMASTER					
☐ C32	5¢ Carmine	9.50	.63	.16	.11
☐ C33	5¢ Carmine	16.00	.65	.16	.11
1947. REGULAR ISSUE					
☐ C34	10¢ Black	27.00	1.62	.37	.11
☐ C35	15¢ Bright Blue Green	29.00	1.73	.52	.11
☐ C36	25¢ Blue	121.00	6.10	1.71	.13

Scott No.		Fine Unused Line Pair	Ave. Unused Line Pair	Fine Unused Each	Ave. Unused Each	Fine Used Each	Ave. Used Each
1948. DESIGN OF 1947							
☐ C37	5¢ Carmine	11.75	7.90	1.50	1.20	1.40	.98

Scott No.		Mint Sheet	Plate Block	Fine Unused Each	Fine Used Each
1948. NEW YORK CITY JUBILEE ISSUE					
☐ C38	5¢ Red	36.75	9.90	.17	.18
1949. DESIGN OF 1947					
☐ C39	6¢ Carmine	22.00	.86	.19	.08
1949. ALEXANDRIA BICENTENNIAL					
☐ C40	6¢ Carmine	13.40	.82	.17	.16

*No hinge pricing from 1941 to date is figured at (N-H ADD 15%)

Scott No.		Fine Unused Line Pair	Ave. Unused Line Pair	Fine Unused Each	Ave. Unused Each	Fine Used Each	Ave. Used Each
1949. DESIGN OF 1947							
☐ C41	6¢ Carmine	19.10	12.75	4.20	3.00	.13	.10

Scott No.		Mint Sheet	Plate Block	Fine Unused Each	Fine Used Each
1949. U.P.U—UNIVERSAL POSTAL UNION ISSUE					
☐ C42	10¢ Purple	24.00	2.20	.42	.42
☐ C43	15¢ Ultramarine	34.00	1.70	.52	.57
☐ C44	25¢ Carmine	48.00	10.50	.67	.70
1949. WRIGHT BROTHERS ISSUE					
☐ C45	6¢ Magenta	15.00	1.30	.26	.16
1952. HAWAII—DIAMOND HEAD					
☐ C46	80¢ Bright Red Violet	800.00	63.00	13.00	1.75
1953. 50TH ANNIVERSARY POWERED FLIGHT					
☐ C47	6¢ Carmine	7.90	.72	.23	.19
1954. EAGLE IN FLIGHT					
☐ C48	4¢ Bright Blue	15.50	3.20	.19	.14
1957. 50TH ANNIVERSARY AIR FORCE					
☐ C49	6¢ Blue	10.50	.92	.26	.13
1958. DESIGN OF 1954					
☐ C50	5¢ Red	22.00	2.30	.24	.18
1958. JETLINER SILHOUETTE					
☐ C51	7¢ Blue	24.00	1.10	.26	.10

Scott No.		Fine Unused Line Pair	Ave. Unused Line Pair	Fine Unused Each	Ave. Unused Each	Fine Used Each	Ave. Used Each
☐ C52	7¢ Blue	21.75	13.50	3.30	2.10	.14	.11

Scott No.		Mint Sheet	Plate Block	Fine Unused Each	Fine Used Each
1959. COMMEMORATIVES					
1959. ALASKA STATEHOOD					
☐ C53	7¢ Dark Blue	8.90	1.15	.23	.14
1959. BALLOON JUPITER FLIGHT					
☐ C54	7¢ Dark Blue & Red	8.90	1.15	.23	.14
1959. HAWAII STATEHOOD					
☐ C55	7¢ Rose Red	8.90	1.15	.23	.14
1959. PAN AMERICAN GAMES					
☐ C56	10¢ Red & Blue	16.75	2.30	.41	.43

*No hinge pricing from 1941 to date is figured at (N-H ADD 15%)

Scott No.		Mint Sheet	Plate Block	Fine Unused Each	Fine Used Each

1959–61. REGULAR ISSUE
☐ C57	10¢ Black & Green	126.00	13.00	2.40	1.20
☐ C58	15¢ Black & Orange	26.00	2.75	.65	.16
☐ C59	25¢ Black & Maroon	31.00	3.50	.75	.11

1960. DESIGN OF 1958
☐ C60	7¢ Carmine	21.50	.98	.22	.08

Scott No.		Fine Unused Line Pair	Ave. Unused Line Pair	Fine Unused Each	Ave. Unused Each	Fine Used Each	Ave. Used Each
☐ C61	7¢ Carmine	49.00	40.00	5.70	4.70	.35	.23

Scott No.		Mint Sheet	Plate Block	Fine Unused Each	Fine Used Each

1961. DESIGNS OF 1959–1960
☐ C62	13¢ Black & Red	28.50	3.20	.62	.17
☐ C63	15¢ Black & Orange	17.00	1.80	.42	.11

1962. JETLINER OVER CAPITOL
☐ C64	8¢ Carmine	17.50	1.10	.23	.10

Scott No.		Fine Unused Line Pair	Ave. Unused Line Pair	Fine Unused Each	Ave. Unused Each	Fine Used Each	Ave. Used Each
☐ C65	8¢ Carmine	4.20	3.40	.35	.24	.11	.08

Scott No.		Mint Sheet	Plate Block	Fine Unused Each	Fine Used Each

1963. FIRST INTERNATIONAL POSTAL CONFERENCE CENTENARY
☐ C66	15¢ Dull Red, Dark Brown & Blue	33.00	6.00	1.10	.94

1963. POSTAL CARD RATE
☐ C67	6¢ Red	21.00	3.40	.32	.18

1963. AMELIA EARHART
☐ C68	8¢ Carmine & Maroon	13.00	2.00	.37	.21

1964. DR. ROBERT H. GODDARD
☐ C69	8¢ Blue, Red, Bistre	34.00	4.10	.92	.21

1967–1969.
1967. ALASKA PURCHASE CENTENARY
☐ C70	8¢ Dark Brown	21.00	3.90	.52	.23

1967.
☐ C71	20¢ Blue, Brown, Bistre	62.10	6.60	1.34	.14

1968.
☐ C72	10¢ Carmine	27.50	1.60	.30	.09

*No hinge pricing from 1941 to date is figured at (N-H ADD 15%)

Scott No.			Fine Unused Line Pair	Ave. Unused Line Pair	Fine Unused Each	Ave. Unused Each	Fine Used Each	Ave. Used Each
☐ C73	10¢	Carmine	3.30	2.50	.44	.35	.13	.07

Scott No.			Mint Sheet	Plate Block	Fine Unused Each	Fine Used Each
1968. 50TH ANNIVERSARY AIR MAIL SERVICE						
☐ C74	10¢	Black, Blue, Red	22.00	6.30	.45	.19
1968.						
☐ C75	20¢	Red, Blue, Black	33.00	4.40	.75	.15
1969. FIRST MAN ON THE MOON						
☐ C76	10¢	Red, Blue, Brown	8.70	1.90	.29	.18
1971–1973.						
☐ C77	9¢	Red	19.50	1.25	.25	.27
☐ C78	11¢	Carmine	24.75	1.50	.29	.08
☐ C79	13¢	Carmine	29.50	1.55	.42	.10
☐ C80	17¢	Green, Blue, Red	27.00	2.22	.55	.15
☐ C81	21¢	Blue, Red, Black	23.50	2.15	.53	.15

Scott No.			Fine Unused Line Pair	Ave. Unused Line Pair	Fine Unused Each	Ave. Unused Each	Fine Used Each	Ave. Used Each
☐ C82	11¢	Carmine	1.15	.92	.32	.24	.11	.07
☐ C83	13¢	Carmine	1.00	.87	.37	.28	.11	.07

Scott No.			Mint Sheet	Plate Block	Fine Unused Each	Fine Used Each
1972. NATIONAL PARKS CENTENNIAL						
☐ C84	11¢	Multicolored	13.10	1.65	.35	.18
1972. OLYMPIC GAMES						
☐ C85	11¢	Multicolored	15.00	3.40	.37	.18
1973. PROGRESS IN ELECTRONICS						
☐ C86	11¢	Multicolored	14.10	1.80	.35	.18
1974.						
☐ C87	18¢	Red, Blue, Black	27.50	2.70	.55	.42
☐ C88	26¢	Red, Blue, Black	31.80	3.40	.77	.15
1976.						
☐ C89	25¢	Red, Blue, Black	32.50	3.50	.72	.16
☐ C90	31¢	Red, Blue, Black	38.00	4.00	.86	.14
1979.						
☐ C91	31¢	Blue, Brown, Red	76.00	5.00	1.00	.21
☐ C92	31¢	Blue, Brown, Red	76.00	5.00	1.00	.21
1979.						
☐ C93	21¢	Blue, Brown, Red	96.00	5.00	1.25	.34
☐ C94	21¢	Blue, Brown, Red	96.00	5.00	1.25	.34

*No hinge pricing from 1941 to date is figured at (N-H ADD 15%)

Scott No.			Mint Sheet	Plate Block	Fine Unused Each	Fine Used Each
1980.						
☐ C95	25¢	Multicolored	116.00	6.00	1.40	.41
☐ C96	25¢	Multicolored	116.00	6.00	1.40	.41
☐ C97	31¢	Multicolored	46.00	16.50	1.20	.42
1981.						
☐ C98	40¢	Multicolored	43.00	12.00	.97	.18
☐ C99	28¢	Multicolored	34.00	9.00	.72	.22
☐ C100	35¢	Multicolored	39.00	10.00	.80	.22
1983.						
☐ C101	28¢	Multicolored	33.00	2.60	.62	.26
☐ C102	28¢	Multicolored	33.00	2.60	.62	.26
☐ C103	28¢	Multicolored	33.00	2.60	.62	.26
☐ C104	28¢	Multicolored	33.00	2.60	.62	.26
☐ C105	40¢	Multicolored	42.00	4.00	.82	.34
☐ C106	40¢	Multicolored	42.50	3.60	.92	.36
☐ C107	40¢	Multicolored	42.50	3.60	.92	.36
☐ C108	40¢	Multicolored	42.50	3.60	.92	.36
☐ C109	35¢	Multicolored	40.00	3.30	.83	.39
☐ C110	35¢	Multicolored	40.00	3.30	.83	.39
☐ C111	35¢	Multicolored	40.00	3.30	.83	.39
☐ C112	35¢	Multicolored	40.00	3.30	.83	.39
1985.						
☐ C113	33¢	Multicolored	37.75	3.30	.63	.26
☐ C114	39¢	Multicolored	41.00	4.00	.85	.28
☐ C115	44¢	Multicolored	52.00	4.75	1.05	.30
☐ C116	44¢	Multicolored	52.00	4.75	1.05	.30

Scott No.			Fine Unused Plate Blk	Ave. Unused Plate Blk	Fine Unused Each	Ave. Unused Each	Fine Used Each	Ave. Used Each
AIRMAIL SPECIAL DELIVERY								
☐ CE1	16¢	Dark Blue	26.50	19.00	1.10	.72	.90	.65
☐ CE2	16¢	Red & Blue	14.20	10.00	.62	.44	.32	.19
SPECIAL DELIVERY STAMPS								
1885.								
☐ E1	10¢	Blue	—	—	275.00	195.00	36.00	25.00
1888.								
☐ E2	10¢	Blue	—	—	262.00	180.00	9.75	7.00
1893. (N-H ADD 80%)								
☐ E3	10¢	Orange	—	—	190.00	120.00	20.00	12.00
1894. (N-H ADD 80%)								
☐ E4	10¢	Blue	—	—	738.00	530.00	22.00	13.00
1895. (N-H ADD 80%)								
☐ E5	10¢	Blue	—	—	142.00	96.00	3.00	1.80

*No hinge pricing from 1941 to date is figured at (N-H ADD 15%)

Scott No.		Fine Unused Plate Blk	Ave. Unused Plate Blk	Fine Unused Each	Ave. Unused Each	Fine Used Each	Ave. Used Each
1902. (N-H ADD 55%)							
☐ E6	10¢ Ultramarine	—	—	105.00	72.00	3.00	1.70
1908. (N-H ADD 55%)							
☐ E7	10¢ Green	—	—	87.00	62.00	34.00	22.00
1911. (N-H ADD 40%)							
☐ E8	10¢ Ultramarine	—	—	112.00	74.00	4.30	3.30
1914. (N-H ADD 40%)							
☐ E9	10¢ Ultramarine	—	—	210.00	116.00	6.40	4.25
1916. (N-H ADD 40%)							
☐ E10	10¢ Pale Ultramarine	—	—	345.00	215.00	23.00	15.00
1917. (N-H ADD 40%)							
☐ E11	10¢ Ultramarine	—	—	20.00	14.00	.52	.36
1922–1925. (N-H ADD 30%)							
☐ E12	10¢ Deep Ultramarine	450.00	300.00	33.00	25.00	.26	.16
☐ E13	10¢ Deep Orange	280.00	186.00	28.00	19.00	1.40	.86
☐ E14	20¢ Black	55.00	41.00	4.10	3.00	2.25	1.50
1927–1951. (N-H ADD 30%)							
☐ E15	10¢ Gray Violet	7.70	5.30	1.25	.95	.11	.09
☐ E16	15¢ Orange	7.30	5.30	1.25	.95	.13	.11
☐ E17	13¢ Blue	4.70	3.40	.90	.65	.14	.09
☐ E18	17¢ Yellow	34.00	25.00	5.75	4.20	3.20	2.00
☐ E19	20¢ Black	14.00	9.50	3.00	2.00	.14	.09

Scott No.		Mint Sheet	Plate Block	Fine Unused Each	Fine Used Each
1954.					
☐ E20	20¢ Blue	37.00	4.00	.72	.11
1957.					
☐ E21	30¢ Maroon	48.50	4.50	.79	.11
1969.					
☐ E22	45¢ Red & Blue	93.50	12.00	1.80	.44
1971.					
☐ E23	60¢ Blue & Red	65.00	5.75	1.40	.14

Scott No.		Fine Unused Plate Blk	Ave. Unused Plate Blk	Fine Unused Each	Ave. Unused Each	Fine Used Each	Ave. Used Each
1911. REGISTRATION STAMPS (N-H ADD 30%)							
☐ F1	10¢ Ultramarine	1500.00	1100.00	105.00	64.00	5.50	4.00

Scott No.		Mint Sheet	Plate Block	Fine Unused Each	Fine Used Each
☐FA1	15¢ Postman	54.00	7.50	.60	.50

*No hinge pricing from 1941 to date is figured at (N-H ADD 15%)

Scott No.		Name Block 6	Name Block 4	Plain Block 4	Unused Each	Used Each

UNITED NATIONS
1951.

Scott No.		Name Block 6	Name Block 4	Plain Block 4	Unused Each	Used Each
☐1	1¢ Magenta	.82	.46	.32	.10	.06
☐2	1½¢ Blue Green	.90	.60	.37	.10	.06
☐2a	1½¢ Precancelled..................					14.00
☐3	2¢ Purple	1.20	.62	.47	.13	.09
☐4	3¢ Magenta & Blue	1.35	.87	.63	.17	.10
☐5	5¢ Blue	2.40	1.60	.90	.22	.15
☐6	10¢ Chocolate	5.50	3.00	1.45	.28	.20
☐7	15¢ Violet & Blue	5.50	3.00	1.45	.28	.20
☐8	20¢ Dark Brown	14.50	9.00	7.50	1.42	1.00
☐9	25¢ Olive Gray & Blue	14.25	7.50	6.00	1.30	.90
☐10	50¢ Indigo	120.00	77.00	63.00	12.75	1.60
☐11	$1 Red	31.00	22.00	15.00	3.30	1.50
☐1–11	First Postage Set Complete	227.00	120.00	90.00	23.00	15.00

1952.

☐12	5¢ War Memorial Bldg.	9.50	7.00	5.00	1.50	.60
☐13–14	3¢, 5¢ Fourth H.R. Day	24.00	14.00	9.00	2.50	1.15

1953.

☐15–16	3¢, 5¢ Refugees	29.00	18.00	14.50	4.50	2.00
☐17–18	3¢, 5¢ U.P.U.	38.00	25.00	22.00	6.00	2.90
☐19–20	3¢, 5¢ Technical Assist	25.00	18.00	14.00	5.00	1.50
☐21–22	3¢, 5¢ Human Rights	40.00	32.00	27.00	7.00	1.75

1954.

☐23–24	3¢, FAO (Agriculture).............	39.00	27.00	23.00	6.00	1.75
☐25–26	3¢, 8¢ OIT (Labor Org.)	53.00	37.00	30.00	8.00	2.15
☐27–28	3¢, 8¢ UN Day	64.50	51.00	43.00	10.00	4.00
☐29–30	3¢, 8¢ H.R. Day	159.00	136.00	111.00	23.00	7.10

1955.

☐31–32	3¢, 8¢ I.C.A.O.	86.00	62.00	56.00	12.00	4.50
☐33–34	3¢, 8¢ UNESCO	29.00	23.00	17.00	6.00	1.00
☐35–37	3¢, 4¢, 8¢ UN Day	77.00	60.00	52.00	12.00	2.25
☐38	3¢, 4¢, 8¢ UN Day Sheet	—	—	—	255.00	135.00
☐39–40	3¢, 8¢ Human Rights	22.00	16.00	14.00	3.10	1.75

1956.

☐41–42	3¢, 8¢ Telecommunication	22.00	15.00	13.00	2.80	2.00
☐43–44	3¢, 8¢ World Health	22.00	15.00	13.00	2.80	2.00
☐45–46	3¢, 8¢ UN Day	4.50	2.75	2.00	.40	.30
☐47–48	3¢, 8¢ Human Rights	3.50	1.90	1.00	.25	.18

Scott No.		Name Block 6	Name Block 4	Plain Block 4	Unused Each	Used Each
1957.						
☐ 49–50	3¢, 8¢ W.M.O. Meteorological	2.10	1.30	1.00	.22	.14
☐ 51–52	3¢, 8¢ U.N.E.F. 1st Printing	2.10	1.30	1.00	.22	.14
☐ 53–54	3¢, 8¢ U.N.E.F. 2nd Printing	3.60	2.60	2.10	.42	.34
☐ 55–56	3¢, 8¢ Security Council	2.60	1.50	1.15	.24	.15
☐ 57–58	3¢, 8¢ Human Rights	2.60	1.50	1.10	.24	.15
1958.						
☐ 59–60	3¢, 8¢ Atomic Energy	2.60	1.45	1.10	.24	.19
☐ 61–62	3¢, 8¢ General Assembly	2.60	1.50	1.10	.25	.19
☐ 63–64	4¢, 8¢ Regular Issues	2.60	1.40	1.05	.22	.15
☐ 65–66	4¢, 8¢ Economic Council	2.90	1.60	1.10	.29	.20
☐ 67–68	4¢, 8¢ Human Rights	2.90	1.60	1.10	.29	.20
☐ 69–70	4¢, 8¢ Flushing Meadows	3.20	1.90	1.40	.33	.21
☐ 71–72	4¢, 8¢ E.C.E.	5.50	3.60	2.80	.67	.45
☐ 73–74	4¢, 8¢ Trusteeship	4.50	3.30	2.50	.50	.32
☐ 75–76	4¢, 8¢ World Refugee Year	3.10	2.20	1.60	.40	.30
1960.						
☐ 77–78	4¢, 8¢ Palais de Chaillot	2.90	1.95	1.50	.35	.34
☐ 79–80	4¢, 8¢ Forestry Congress	2.90	1.95	1.50	.35	.34
☐ 83–84	4¢, 8¢ 15th Anniversary	2.85	1.90	1.60	.32	.38
☐ 85	4¢, 8¢ 15th Ann. Souv. Sheet	—	—	—	11.00	9.00
☐ 86–87	4¢, 8¢ International	2.90	2.25	1.60	.39	.36
1961.						
☐ 88–89	4¢, 8¢ Court of Justice	2.90	2.10	1.45	.30	.20
☐ 90–91	4¢, 7¢ Monetary Fund	2.90	2.10	1.45	.30	.20
☐ 92	30¢ Regular Issue	7.00	5.50	4.05	.95	.60
☐ 93–94	4¢, 11¢ E.C. for Latin Am.	8.50	6.10	4.60	1.25	.80
☐ 95–96	4¢, 11¢ E.C. for Africa	5.00	3.40	2.50	.60	.40
☐ 97–99	3¢, 4¢, 13¢ Children's Fund	5.50	3.80	2.70	.63	.42
1962.						
☐ 100–01	4¢, 7¢ Housing	4.90	3.10	3.00	.55	.40
☐ 102–03	4¢, 11¢ Malaria	6.60	4.30	3.80	.75	.50
☐ 104–07	1¢, 3¢, 5¢, 11¢ Reg. Issue	7.00	4.60	3.60	.73	.52
☐ 108–09	5¢, 15¢ Hammarskjold	20.00	12.75	11.00	2.10	1.20
☐ 110–11	4¢, 11¢ U.N. Congo	15.00	9.50	7.10	1.80	1.00
☐ 112–13	4¢, 11¢ Peaceful Space Use	5.00	3.40	2.60	.60	.40
1963.						
☐ 114–15	5¢, 11¢ Econ. Development	5.70	4.50	3.30	.62	.40
☐ 116–17	5¢, 11¢ Freedom—Hunger	5.70	4.50	3.30	.62	.38
☐ 118	25¢ UNTEA W. Irian	9.60	7.10	5.10	1.40	.83
☐ 119–20	5¢, 11¢, 10th Hdqrs. Anniv.	5.75	4.40	3.35	.73	.55
☐ 121–22	5¢, 11¢, 15th Anniv. H. Rights	5.75	4.40	3.35	.67	.60
1964.						
☐ 123–24	5¢, 11¢ Maritime	4.50	3.50	2.60	.67	.48
☐ 125–27	2¢, 7¢, 10¢ Reg. Issue	3.30	2.60	2.00	.62	.40

Scott No.		Name Block 6	Name Block 4	Plain Block 4	Unused Each	Used Each
☐ 128	50¢ New Regular	8.75	6.10	5.10	1.24	.80
☐ 129–30	5¢, 11¢ Trade & Develop	4.30	3.50	2.50	.70	.60
☐ 131–32	5¢, 11¢ Narcotics Control	4.70	3.60	2.80	.67	.50
☐ 133	5¢ Nuclear Tests End	1.50	1.25	.87	.26	.18
☐ 134–36	4¢, 5¢, 11¢ Education	5.10	4.00	3.10	.78	.60

1965.

☐ 137–38	5¢, 11¢ Special Fund	3.05	2.35	1.65	.35	.22
☐ 139–40	5¢, 11¢ U.N. in Cyprus	3.05	2.35	1.65	.35	.22
☐ 141–42	5¢, 11¢ I.T.U. (Satellite)	3.05	2.35	1.65	.35	.22
☐ 143–44	5¢, 15¢ Co-operation	4.60	3.30	2.60	.60	.40
☐ 145	5¢, 15¢ Min. Sheet	—	—	—	1.60	1.20
☐ 146–49	1¢, 15¢, 20¢, 25¢ Regular	33.00	23.00	19.00	3.70	3.00
☐ 150	$1 Regular Issue (1966)	24.00	18.00	13.00	2.60	2.00
☐ 151–53	4¢, 5¢, 11¢ Population Trends ..	5.00	3.70	2.70	.60	.40

1966.

☐ 154–55	5¢, 15¢ World Federation	4.60	3.60	2.80	.60	.40
☐ 156–57	5¢, 11¢ W.H.O. Building	3.60	2.80	2.10	.58	.40
☐ 158–59	5¢, 11¢ Coffee Agreement	3.60	2.80	2.10	.58	.40
☐ 160	15¢ Peacekeeping	3.10	2.60	1.90	.45	.30
☐ 161–63	4¢, 5¢, 11¢ UNICEF Anniv.	4.20	3.40	2.60	.60	.30

1967.

☐ 164–65	5¢, 11¢ Development	3.60	2.60	1.90	.45	.30
☐ 166–67	1½¢, 5¢ Regular Issue	2.20	1.25	.96	.25	.18
☐ 168–69	5¢, 11¢ Independence	3.80	3.00	2.10	.50	.40

1967.

☐ 170–74	4¢, 5¢, 8¢, 10¢, 15¢ EXPO	18.50	15.00	12.00	2.65	2.00
☐ 175–76	5¢, 15¢ Intl. Tourist Year	4.50	3.60	2.70	.62	.50
☐ 177–78	6¢, 13¢ Toward Disarm	4.50	3.60	2.70	.62	.50
☐ 179	6¢ Chagall Sheet of Six	—	—	—	1.15	.85
☐ 180	6¢ Chagall Window	1.70	.92	.72	.20	.10

1968.

☐ 181–82	6¢, 13¢, Secretariat	4.30	3.40	2.40	.50	.42
☐ 183–84	6¢, 75¢ Starcke Statue	69.00	52.00	38.00	8.10	6.00
☐ 185–86	6¢, 13¢ ONUDI	4.00	2.85	2.50	.62	.40
☐ 187	6¢ Regular Issue	1.40	1.00	.73	.18	.12
☐ 188–89	6¢, 20¢ Weather Watch	6.00	5.00	3.60	.82	.60
☐ 190–91	6¢, 13¢ Int'l. Year Human Rts. ..	8.00	6.00	4.50	1.10	.80

1969.

☐ 192–93	6¢, 13¢ UNITAR	4.10	2.90	2.40	.45	.30
☐ 194–95	6¢, 15¢ ECLA Bldg	5.10	3.80	2.80	.62	.41
☐ 196	13¢, Regular Issue	2.90	2.10	1.60	.35	.24
☐ 197–98	6¢, 13¢ Peace thru Law	3.80	3.05	2.50	.54	.32
☐ 199–00	6¢, 20¢ Labor & Devl	5.90	4.35	3.30	.76	.51
☐ 201–02	6¢, 13¢ Art Series	5.50	4.10	3.00	.69	.40
☐ 203–04	6¢, 25¢ Japan Peace Bell	6.10	5.10	4.10	.93	.62
☐ 205–06	6¢, 13¢ Mekong Basin	4.50	3.30	2.70	.60	.50

Scott No.		Name Block 6	Name Block 4	Plain Block 4	Unused Each	Used Each
☐ 207–08	6¢, 13¢ Cancer	4.20	3.30	2.65	.60	.46
☐ 209–11	6¢, 13¢, 25¢ 25th U.V. Anniv.	11.00	8.60	7.00	1.75	1.00
☐ 212	Same, Souvenir Sheet	—	—	—	2.00	1.20
☐ 213–14	6¢, 13¢ Peace, Just. Prog.	4.10	3.10	2.50	.55	.40

1971.

☐ 215	6¢ Sea Bed	1.65	1.30	.92	.20	.15
☐ 216–17	6¢, 13¢ Refugees	3.90	3.20	2.35	.56	.42
☐ 218	13¢ World Food Prog.	3.00	2.30	1.70	.38	.22
☐ 219	20¢ U.P.U. Building	4.50	3.50	2.65	.67	.50
☐ 220–21	8¢, 13¢ Anti-Discrim	4.90	4.10	2.80	.67	.50
☐ 222–23	8¢, 60¢ Regular Issue	11.50	8.10	6.60	1.45	1.02
☐ 224–25	8¢, 21¢ Intl. Schools	6.50	4.90	3.60	.86	.60

1972.

☐ 226	95¢ Regular Issue	18.50	14.00	11.00	2.50	2.10
☐ 227	8¢ Non-Proliferation	2.10	1.40	.93	.24	.18
☐ 228	15¢ World Health	4.10	2.90	1.90	.50	.31
☐ 229–30	8¢, 15¢ Environment	5.30	3.80	2.90	.60	.42
☐ 231	21¢ E.C. Europe	5.25	3.80	3.00	.60	.42
☐ 232–33	8¢, 15¢ U.N. Art Sert	6.00	4.50	3.10	.65	.43

1973.

☐ 234–35	8¢, 15¢ Disarmament	5.40	4.10	3.30	.67	.55
☐ 236–37	8¢, 15¢ Drug Abuse	5.90	4.60	3.30	.80	.62
☐ 238–39	8¢, 21¢ U.N. Volunteers	6.50	4.80	3.60	.83	.63
☐ 240–41	8¢, 15¢ Namibia	5.80	4.40	3.40	.78	.58
☐ 242–43	8¢, 21¢ Human Rights	5.50	4.20	3.00	.75	.54

1974.

☐ 244–45	10¢, 21¢ ILO Hdqr	11.00	7.60	6.00	1.25	.86
☐ 246	10¢ UPU Centenary	2.60	2.00	1.20	.30	.19
☐ 247–48	10¢, 18¢ Brazil Mural	7.50	5.60	4.50	.90	.62
☐ 249–51	2¢, 10¢, 18¢ Regular	7.10	5.50	4.10	.80	.63
☐ 252–53	10¢, 18¢ Population	6.10	4.70	3.50	.90	.54
☐ 254–55	10¢, 26¢ Law of Sea	8.25	6.50	4.80	1.20	.80

1975.

☐ 256–57	10¢, 26¢ Space Usage	14.00	9.60	8.00	2.10	1.60
☐ 258–59	10¢, 18¢ Women's Year	6.00	5.00	3.50	.78	.60
☐ 260–61	10¢, 26¢ UN 30th Anniv.	6.30	6.00	4.50	.98	.62
☐ 262	36¢ Same Souv. Sheet	—	—	—	1.25	.70
☐ 263–64	10¢, 18¢ Namibia	5.75	5.00	3.75	.72	.52
☐ 265–66	13¢, 26¢ Peacekeeping	10.00	8.00	6.00	1.15	.80

1976.

☐ 267–71	3¢, 4¢, 9¢, 30¢, 50¢ Regular	22.00	16.50	12.00	2.20	1.70
☐ 272–73	13¢, 26¢ WFUNA	13.00	9.50	6.75	1.40	.92
☐ 274–75	13¢, 31¢ UNCTAD	11.00	7.50	5.75	1.20	.64
☐ 276–77	13¢, 25¢ HABITAT	10.00	7.00	5.00	1.20	.58
☐ 278–79	13¢, 31¢ 25th Postal Anniv.	104.00	77.00	58.00	13.00	8.40
☐ 280	13¢ Food Council	2.50	2.00	1.40	.40	.28

Scott No.	Name Block 6	Name Block 4	Plain Block 4	Unused Each	Used Each
1977.					
☐ 281–82 13¢, 31¢ WIPO	11.50	8.60	6.10	1.50	1.00
☐ 283–84 13¢, 25¢ Water Conf.	10.60	7.75	5.30	1.30	1.00
☐ 285–86 13¢, 31¢ Security Council	10.70	8.10	5.90	1.30	.92
☐ 287–88 13¢, 25¢ Combat Racism	8.00	5.40	4.10	1.00	.82
☐ 289–90 13¢, 18¢ Atomic Energy	6.50	4.25	3.10	.78	.62
1978.					
☐ 291–93 1¢, 25¢, $1 Regular	23.50	18.00	14.50	3.75	3.60
☐ 294–95 13¢, 31¢ Small Pox	9.10	7.00	5.00	1.20	.74
☐ 296–97 13¢, 18¢ Namibia	6.00	4.50	3.20	.75	.52
☐ 298–99 13¢, 25¢ ICAO-Air Safety	7.50	5.10	3.60	.85	.62
☐ 300–01 13¢, 18¢ General Assembly	5.60	4.05	2.80	.75	.55
☐ 302–03 13¢, 31¢ Technical Cooperation	10.50	8.00	5.60	1.35	.82
1979.					
☐ 304–07 5¢, 14¢, 15¢, 20¢ Regular Issues	12.50	8.75	6.50	1.50	1.10
☐ 308–09 15¢, 20¢ UNDRO	7.75	6.00	4.10	.72	.50
☐ 310–11 15¢, 31¢ Intl. Year of Child	61.00	38.00	30.00	5.60	4.20
☐ 312–13 15¢, 31¢ Namibia	10.50	7.00	5.00	1.10	.64
☐ 314–15 15¢, 31¢ Court of Justice	10.45	8.00	5.60	1.30	.90
1980.					
☐ 316–17 15¢, 31¢ Economic Order	15.50	9.75	7.00	1.25	.90
☐ 318–19 15¢, 20¢, Women's Decade	7.00	5.50	4.10	.88	.67
☐ 320–21 15¢, 31¢ Peacekeeping	7.75	6.00	4.50	.92	.70
☐ 322–23 15¢, 31¢ 35th Anniversary	7.75	6.00	4.50	.92	.70
☐ 324 15¢, Same, Souvenir Sheet	—	—	—	.88	.67
☐ 325–40 15¢ World Flags	—	24.00	—	6.00	5.70
☐ 325–28 15¢ World Flags	—	7.50	—	1.85	1.42
☐ 329–32 15¢ World Flags	—	7.50	—	1.85	1.42
☐ 333–36 15¢ World Flags	—	7.50	—	1.85	1.42
☐ 337–40 15¢ World Flags	—	7.50	—	1.85	1.42
☐ 341–42 15¢, 20¢ Economic and Social Council	8.50	6.10	4.70	1.35	1.30
1981.					
☐ 343 15¢ Palestinian People	3.30	2.50	1.70	.45	.30
☐ 344–45 20¢, 35¢ Disabled Persons	9.60	6.80	5.10	1.15	.80
☐ 346–47 20¢, 31¢ Fresco	—	6.10	4.75	.92	.65
☐ 348–49 20¢, 40¢ Sources of Energy	9.90	7.75	5.60	1.20	.87
☐ 350–65 1981 World Flags	—	34.00	—	8.50	7.20
☐ 350–53 20¢ World Flags	—	7.90	—	2.15	1.70
☐ 358–61 20¢ World Flags	—	7.90	—	2.15	1.70
☐ 354–57 15¢, 20¢ World Flags	—	7.90	—	2.15	1.70
☐ 362–65 20¢ World Flags	—	7.90	—	2.15	1.70
☐ 366–67 18¢, 28¢ Volunteers Program	—	6.00	4.60	1.08	1.00
1982.					
☐ 368–70 17¢, 28¢, 40¢ Definitives	13.75	10.60	7.10	1.50	.90
☐ 371–72 20¢, 40¢ Human Environment	10.60	9.00	6.90	1.60	.92

Scott No.		Name Block 6	Name Block 4	Plain Block 4	Unused Each	Used Each
☐ 373	20¢ Space Exploration	2.40	1.75	1.30	.29	.20
☐ 374–89	World Flags	36.00	25.00	17.75	4.00	2.25
☐ 390–91	20¢, 28¢ Nature Conservation	5.70	4.20	3.50	.70	.45

1983.

☐ 392–93	20¢, 40¢ Communication	7.10	5.15	3.90	.85	.50
☐ 394–95	20¢, 37¢ Safety at Sea	7.10	5.10	3.90	.80	.52
☐ 396	20¢ World Food	2.30	1.70	1.30	.30	.20
☐ 397–98	20¢, 28¢ Trade	5.90	4.50	2.90	.65	.42
☐ 399–14	World Flags	34.00	22.00	17.00	3.70	2.20
☐ 415–16	20¢, 40¢ Human Rights	7.00	5.10	3.80	.75	.60

1984.

☐ 417–18	20¢, 40¢ Population Conference	6.90	5.10	4.00	.75	.55
☐ 419–20	20¢, 40¢ World Food Day	6.90	5.10	4.00	.75	.55
☐ 421–22	20¢, 50¢ Heritage	7.50	5.60	4.10	.90	.62
☐ 423–24	20¢, 50¢ Refugees	8.00	6.20	4.30	1.05	.70
☐ 425–50	World Flags	34.00	22.00	17.00	3.60	2.40

UNITED NATIONS
1951–1957. AIRMAILS

☐ C1	6¢ Airmail (1951)	2.40	2.00	1.50	.37	.28
☐ C2	10¢ Airmail	5.60	3.60	2.90	.57	.42
☐ C3	15¢ Airmail	27.00	20.00	17.00	4.10	2.40
☐ C4	25¢ Airmail	49.00	34.00	26.00	5.70	3.75
☐ C1–4	First Issue Airmails	72.00	49.00	38.00	7.50	5.70
☐ C5–7	4¢, 5¢, 7¢ Airmail (1957)	3.60	2.60	1.90	.50	.28

1963–1964. AIRMAILS

☐ C8–10	6¢, 8¢, 13¢ Airmail (1963)	4.00	3.10	2.50	.70	.51
☐ C11–12	15¢, 25¢ Airmail (1964)	22.00	18.70	14.80	3.70	1.10

1968–1972. AIRMAILS

☐ C13	20¢ Airmail (1968)	3.40	2.25	1.80	.50	.30
☐ C14	10¢ Airmail (1969)	1.90	1.40	1.30	.40	.25
☐ C15–18	9¢, 11¢, 17¢, 21¢ (1972)	11.00	7.50	5.60	1.25	.90

1974–1977. AIRMAILS

☐ C19–21	13¢, 18¢, 26¢ (1974)	11.00	9.00	7.00	1.50	1.10
☐ C22–23	25¢, 31¢ (1977)	14.00	11.00	7.50	2.00	1.30

		Unused Each	Used Each

UNITED NATIONS SOUVENIR CARDS

		Unused Each	Used Each
☐ 1	WHO, First Printing	3.90	—
☐ 1a	WHO, Second Printing	4.20	—
☐ 2	Art at U.N.	2.25	—
☐ 3	Disarmament	2.30	—
☐ 4	Human Rights	6.60	—
☐ 5	Universal Postal Union	6.00	—
☐ 6	World Population	21.50	—
☐ 7	Outer Space	7.75	—

Scott No.		Unused Each	Used Each
☐8	Peacekeeping	10.50	—
☐9	World Federation of U.N.	12.50	—
☐10	World Food Council	6.70	—
☐11	World Intellectual Property	4.40	—
☐12	Combat Racism	3.25	—
☐13	Namibia	3.25	—
☐14	ICAO-Air Safety	3.75	—
☐15	International Year of The Child	2.80	—
☐16	Court of Justice	2.80	—
☐17	Women's Decade	25.50	—
☐18	Economic and Social Council	5.10	—
☐19	Disabled Persons	3.40	—
☐20	Energy Sources	5.60	—

Scott No.		Name Block 6	Name Block 4	Plain Block 4	Unused Each	Used Each

UNITED NATIONS—GENEVA, SWITZERLAND
DENOMINATIONS ARE GIVEN IN SWISS CURRENCY
DESIGNS ARE SIMILAR TO U.N. NEW YORK ISSUES

1969–1970.

Scott No.		Name Block 6	Name Block 4	Plain Block 4	Unused Each	Used Each
☐1–14	5¢ to 10 franc	205.00	150.00	120.00	29.00	20.00
1971.						
☐15	30¢ Sea Bed	3.70	2.85	2.10	.45	.32
☐16	50¢ Refugees	9.50	7.50	6.00	1.55	1.20
☐17	50¢ World Food Prog.	9.50	7.50	5.50	1.25	.90
☐18	75¢ U.P.U. Building	20.00	16.00	9.00	2.15	1.60
☐19–20	30¢, 50¢ Anti-Discrim	20.00	16.10	8.75	2.15	1.75
☐21	1.10 fr. Intl. Schools	23.00	20.00	15.00	3.15	2.10
1972.						
☐22	40¢ Regular Issue	3.50	2.60	1.90	.60	.47
☐23	40¢ Non-Proliferation	13.75	10.00	7.75	2.00	1.45
☐24	80¢ World Health	18.00	13.10	9.10	2.40	1.80
☐25–26	40¢, 80¢ Environment	27.00	16.50	12.00	2.50	2.22
☐27	1.10 fr. E.C. Europe	27.00	16.50	12.50	2.50	2.22
☐28–29	40¢, 80¢ U.N. Art-Sert	27.00	16.50	12.50	2.50	2.22
1973.						
☐30–31	60¢, 1.10 fr. Disarm	25.00	17.00	12.75	3.20	2.75
☐32	60¢ Drug Abuse	9.70	6.75	5.00	1.10	.90
☐33	80¢ U.N. Volunteers	17.50	13.50	11.50	2.30	1.80
☐34	60¢ Namibia	17.50	13.50	11.50	2.30	1.80
☐35–36	40¢, 80¢ Human Rights	13.50	9.10	7.10	1.70	1.05
1974.						
☐37–38	60¢, 80¢ ILO Hdqrs.	16.00	12.00	10.50	2.00	1.60
☐39–40	30¢, 60¢ UPU Centenary	19.00	13.50	6.00	1.50	.93
☐41–42	60¢, 1 fr. Brazil Mural	25.00	17.00	12.00	2.50	1.80
☐43–44	60¢, 80¢ Population	24.00	15.00	11.00	2.40	1.82
☐45	1.30 fr. Law of Sea	24.00	13.00	8.00	2.00	1.05

Scott No.	Name Block 6	Name Block 4	Plain Block 4	Unused Each	Used Each
1975.					
☐46–47 60¢, 80¢ Space Usage	21.00	14.00	8.50	2.20	1.80
☐48–49 60¢, 90¢ Women's Year	26.00	20.00	10.50	2.90	2.10
☐50–51 60¢, 90¢ U.N. Anniv.	13.75	9.50	7.75	2.30	1.80
☐52 1.50 fr. Same, Souv. Sheet	—	—	—	2.85	1.95
☐53–54 50¢ 1.30 fr. Namibia	19.00	15.00	13.00	3.50	2.70
☐55–56 60¢, 70¢ Peacekeeping	14.50	11.00	8.50	2.20	1.70
1976.					
☐57 90¢ WFUNA	9.00	6.80	6.00	1.60	1.10
☐58 1.10 fr. UNCTAD	8.75	7.00	5.75	1.60	1.10
☐59–60 40¢ 1.50 fr. HABITAT	18.00	14.00	12.00	3.60	2.70
☐61–62 80¢, 1.10 fr. U.N. Postal Anniv.	93.00	72.00	56.00	9.70	9.00
☐63 70¢ World Food Council	6.70	5.00	4.10	1.00	.75
1977.					
☐64 80¢ WIPO	7.00	6.00	5.00	1.75	1.25
☐65–66 80¢ 1.10 fr. Water Conf.	21.00	16.00	12.00	2.70	1.90
☐67–68 80¢, 1.10 fr. Security Council	21.00	16.00	12.00	2.70	1.90
☐69–70 40¢, 1.10 fr. Combat Racism	19.00	14.00	12.00	2.40	1.95
☐71–72 80¢, 1.10 fr. Atomic Energy	21.00	16.00	12.00	3.10	2.40
☐73 35¢ Doves	3.50	2.50	1.70	.65	.48
☐74–75 80¢, 1.10 fr. Smallpox	17.00	13.00	11.00	2.50	1.90
☐76 80¢ Namibia	7.50	6.00	4.50	1.10	.80
☐77–78 70¢, 80¢ ICAO-Air Safety	15.75	12.00	9.00	2.10	1.70
☐79–80 70¢, 1.10 Fr. General Assembly	17.00	12.00	9.00	2.50	1.95
☐81 80¢ Technical Cooperation	6.50	4.70	3.90	.95	.80
1979.					
☐82–83 80¢, 1.50 UNDRO	17.00	13.00	11.00	2.50	1.90
☐84–85 80¢, 1.10 Intl. Year of The Child	46.00	32.00	24.00	5.50	1.60
☐86 1.10 fr. Namibia	12.00	9.00	6.50	1.50	1.00
☐87–88 80¢, 1.10 Court of Justice	16.00	13.00	10.00	2.50	1.80
1980.					
☐89 80¢ Economic Order..............	6.60	5.75	5.00	1.25	.90
☐90–91 40¢, 70¢ Women's Decade	10.00	7.50	6.00	1.30	.95
☐92 1.10 fr. Peacekeeping	10.00	7.50	6.00	1.30	.95
☐93–94 40¢, 70¢, 35th Anniversary	9.75	7.00	6.00	1.30	.90
☐95 40¢, 70¢ Sheet	—	—	—	2.25	.98
☐96–97 40¢, 70¢ Economic and Social Council	9.50	7.10	5.00	1.25	.80
1981.					
☐98 80¢ Palestinian People............	6.50	5.50	4.00	1.20	.80
☐99–100 40¢, 1.50 fr., Disabled Persons	12.50	9.10	7.00	2.10	1.70
☐101 80¢ Bulgarian Mural	6.50	5.50	4.00	1.20	.80
☐102 1.10 fr. Energy Sources	10.00	7.50	6.50	1.70	.90
☐103–04 40¢, 70¢ Volunteers	10.00	7.50	6.50	1.70	.90
1982.					
☐105–06 1 fr., Definitives	12.50	9.50	7.50	1.75	1.10
☐107–08 40¢, 1.20 fr., Human Environment ...	16.00	12.00	9.50	2.10	1.60

Scott No.		Fine	Ave.
UNUSED BOOKLET PANES			
☐319g	2¢ Carmine . . .	135.00	94.00
☐331a	1¢ Green	137.00	97.00
☐332a	2¢ Carmine . . .	142.00	105.00
☐1374a	1¢ Green	115.00	78.00
☐375a	2¢ Carmine . . .	105.00	78.00
☐405b	1¢ Green	60.00	40.00
☐406a	2¢ Carmine . . .	83.00	55.00
☐424d	1¢ Green	7.00	4.75
☐425e	2¢ Carmine . . .	17.00	13.00
☐462a	1¢ Green	11.00	6.50
☐463a	2¢ Carmine . . .	80.00	52.00
☐498e	1¢ Green	4.00	2.90
☐499e	2¢ Rose	4.30	3.10
☐501b	3¢ Violet I . . .	80.00	52.00
☐502b	3¢ Violet II . .	61.00	42.00
☐552a	1¢ Dark Green . . .	7.00	6.00
☐554c	2¢ Carmine	7.00	5.00
☐583a	2¢ Carmine . . .	79.00	54.00
☐632a	1¢ Green	5.00	3.10
☐1634d	2¢ Carmine . . .	3.00	2.50
☐720b	3¢ Dark Violet	39.00	27.00
☐804b	1¢ Green	3.20	2.20
☐806b	2¢ Red Carmine .	5.60	4.50
☐807a	3¢ Dark Violet . .	11.00	7.00
☐1035a	3¢ Dark Violet . .	4.50	3.00
☐1036a	4¢ Red Violet. . .	3.50	2.50
☐1213a	5¢ "ZIP"	3.00	2.50
☐1213x	5¢ Mailman	7.75	6.00
☐1213y	5¢ Zone No. . . .	12.00	9.00
☐1278a	1¢ Jeff. (8)	1.00	.75
☐1278ae	1¢ T. Gum (8) . . .	2.50	1.50
☐1278b	1¢ Green (4) . . .	.70	.45
☐1280a	2¢ Blue Gray (5) . .	1.15	.80
☐1280c	2¢ Blue Gray (6) . .	.95	.62
☐1284b	6¢ F.D.R. (8) . . .	1.60	1.10
☐1284c	6¢ F.D.R. (5) . . .	1.40	.95
☐1393a	6¢ Ike (8)	1.70	1.20
☐1393ae	6¢ T. Gum	2.10	1.35
☐1393b	6¢ Ike (5)	1.45	1.10
☐1395a	8¢ Ike (8)	2.40	1.80
☐1395b	8¢ Ike (6)	1.80	1.30
☐1395c	8¢ Ike (4)	1.70	1.20
☐1395d	8¢ Ike (7)	2.40	1.65

Scott No.		Fine	Ave.
☐1510b	10¢ Mem'l (5)	1.60	1.15
☐1510c	10¢ Mem'l (8)	2.40	1.80
☐1510d	10¢ Mem'l (6)	3.30	2.35
☐1595a	13¢ Bell (6).	2.60	1.95
☐1595b	13¢ Bell (7).	2.95	2.05
☐1595c	13¢ Bell (8).	3.55	2.55
☐1595d	13¢ Bell (5).	2.30	1.45
☐1623a	13¢ (7), 9¢ (1)	3.20	2.10
☐1623c	Same, Perf. 10	42.00	31.00
☐1736a	"A" Eagle (no denomination) .	5.40	4.05
☐1737a	15¢ Multicolored. . .	3.10	2.10
☐1742a	15¢ Multicolored. . .	3.60	2.70
☐C10a	10¢ Lindbergh . .	122.00	86.00
☐C25a	6¢ Carmine . . .	5.00	3.60
☐C39a	6¢ Small.	17.00	12.00
☐C51a	7¢ Blue	15.00	11.00
☐C60a	7¢ Carmine . . .	27.00	19.00
☐C64c	8¢ Carmine "Zip"	3.60	2.20
☐C64bx	8¢ Mailman . . .	13.00	9.50
☐C64by	8¢ Zone No. . . .	45.00	32.00
☐C72b	10¢ Carmine (8) . . .	4.10	3.10
☐C72c	10¢ Carmine (5) . . .	5.20	3.90
☐C78a	11¢ Carmine (4) . . .	2.10	1.30
☐C79a	13¢ Letter (5)	2.20	1.60

		Fine
SOUVENIR CARDS		
☐1	Truck w Gum.	86.00
	Truck w/o gum	12.00
☐2	Barcelona.	327.00
☐3	SIPEX Scenes	172.00
☐3a	SIPEX Miner	12.00
☐4	EFIMEX.	4.00
☐5	SANDIPEX	72.00
☐	Ana '69	79.00
☐	FRESNO	420.00
☐6	ASDA '69.	22.00
☐7	INTERPEX '70	53.00
☐8	COMPEX '70.	14.00
☐	ANA 1970	122.00
☐9	PHILYMPIA.	2.50
☐10	HAPEX	15.00

Scott No.		Fine		Scott No.		Fine
☐11	INTERPEX '71	2.90		☐	INTERPHIL Program with	
☐12	WESTPEX	2.90			B.E.P. Card	11.50
☐13	NAPEX '71	2.90		☐47	Science BEP	7.60
☐	ANA 1971	3.30		☐48	Science U.S.P.S.	4.10
☐14	TEXANEX	3.40		☐49	Stamp Expo '76	7.50
☐15	EXFILIMA	2.00		☐50	Colorado Statehood	3.50
☐16	ASDA '71	2.90		☐51	HAFNIA '76	3.10
☐17	ANPHILEX	1.85		☐	ANA 1976	8.10
☐18	INTERPEX '72	1.85		☐52	ITALIA '76	2.80
☐19	NOPEX	1.85		☐53	NORDPOSTA '76	2.80
☐20	BELGICA	1.85		☐54	MILCOPEX '77	2.90
☐	ANA 1972	3.00		☐55	ROMPEX '77	4.10
☐21	Olympia Phil. Munchen	1.90		☐56	AMPHILEX '77	3.30
☐22	EXFILBRA	1.90		☐	ANA 1977	4.10
☐23	Postal Forum	1.90		☐57	SAN MARCO	3.60
☐24	SEPAD '72	1.90		☐58	Puripex	3.10
☐25	ASDA '72	1.70		☐59	ASDA '77	4.10
☐26	Stamp Expo '75	2.00		☐60	ROPEX '78	3.30
☐27	INTERPEX '73	2.30		☐	Paper Money Show	5.10
☐28	IBRA	2.30		☐61	NAPOSTA '78	4.00
☐29	COMPEX '73	1.92		☐62	CENTEX '78	4.50
☐30	APEX	1.65		☐63	BRASILIANA '79	4.80
☐	ANA 1973	6.90		☐64	JAPEX '79	6.10
☐31	POLSKA	2.80			ANA '80	17.00
☐32	NAPEX '73	2.20		☐65	LONDON '80	4.50
☐33	ASDA '73	2.30		☐	Money Show '80	9.60
☐34	Stamps Expo '73	2.40		☐66	NORWEX '80	6.00
☐35	Hobby Show Chicago	2.90		☐67	NAPEX '80	10.00
☐36	MILCOPEX '72	3.00		☐	Visitor Center	8.00
☐37	INTERNABA 1974	3.10		☐68	ASDA STAMP	
☐	ANA 1974	13.00			FESTIVAL '80	13.00
☐38	STOCKHOLMIA '74	3.00		☐69	ESSEN '80	4.50
☐39	EXFILMEX '74	3.00		☐70	STAMP EXPO '81	12.00
☐40	ESPANA '75	3.00		☐	Visitor Center	7.50
☐41	NAPEX '75	8.75		☐71	WIPA '81	5.00
☐42	ARPHILA '75	2.70		☐	Paper Money	4.60
☐43	Women's Year	30.00		☐	ANA '81	11.00
☐	ANA 1975	17.00		☐72	STAMP COLLECTORS	
☐44	ASDA '75	46.00			MONTH	4.60
☐45	WERABA '76	4.10		☐73	PHILATOKYO '81	4.60
☐46	INTERPHIL '76	7.80		☐74	NORD POSKTA '81	4.20

Scott No.		Fine Unused Each	Ave. Unused Each	Fine Used Each	Ave. Used Each
POSTAGE DUE STAMPS					
1879 Perforated 12 (N-H ADD 80%)					
☐ J1	1¢ Brown	24.00	14.00	6.00	4.50
☐ J2	2¢ Brown	165.00	106.00	5.50	3.80
☐ J3	3¢ Brown	18.00	11.00	3.50	1.60
☐ J4	5¢ Brown	235.00	136.00	24.00	15.00
☐ J5	10¢ Brown	290.00	172.00	12.00	7.75
☐ J6	30¢ Brown	122.00	77.00	21.00	12.00
☐ J7	50¢ Brown	210.00	150.00	37.00	24.00
1884–1889 SAME DESIGN—PERF. 12 (N-H ADD 80%)					
☐ J15	1¢ Red Brown	31.00	22.00	3.50	2.50
☐ J16	2¢ Red Brown	39.00	28.00	3.50	2.30
☐ J17	3¢ Red Brown	392.00	265.00	105.00	68.00
☐ J18	5¢ Red Brown	196.00	126.00	10.00	7.50
☐ J19	10¢ Red Brown	165.00	108.00	7.00	4.00
☐ J20	30¢ Red Brown	102.00	66.00	25.00	17.00
☐ J21	50¢ Red Brown	980.00	700.00	121.00	76.00
1891–1893 SAME DESIGN—PERF. 12 (N-H ADD 80%)					
☐ J22	1¢ Bright Claret	10.00	7.00	.72	.55
☐ J23	2¢ Bright Claret	11.00	7.50	.68	.50
☐ J24	3¢ Bright Claret	24.00	14.00	4.10	3.10
☐ J25	5¢ Bright Claret	26.00	18.00	4.50	3.10
☐ J26	10¢ Bright Claret	53.00	35.00	11.00	7.00
☐ J27	30¢ Bright Claret	213.00	140.00	86.00	60.00
☐ J28	50¢ Bright Claret	240.00	165.00	93.00	63.00
1894 NEW SMALL DESIGN—NO WTMK.—PERF. 12 (N-H ADD 55%)					
☐ J29	1¢ Vermilion	405.00	260.00	81.00	54.00
☐ J30	2¢ Vermilion	195.00	133.00	39.00	26.00
☐ J31	1¢ Claret	19.00	13.00	5.00	3.50
☐ J32	2¢ Claret	16.00	10.00	3.00	2.50
☐ J33	3¢ Claret	65.00	38.00	21.00	14.00
☐ J34	5¢ Claret	65.00	41.00	24.00	16.00
☐ J35	10¢ Claret	65.00	38.00	15.00	11.00
☐ J36	30¢ Claret (Shades)	192.00	121.00	47.00	31.00
☐ J37	50¢ Claret (Shades)	405.00	265.00	106.00	73.00
1895 SAME NEW SMALL DESIGN—D.L. WTMK.—PERF. 12 (N-H ADD 80%)					
☐ J38	1¢ Claret	6.00	3.50	.45	.32
☐ J39	2¢ Claret	6.00	3.50	.35	.20
☐ J40	3¢ Claret	31.00	19.00	1.40	.78
☐ J41	5¢ Claret	30.00	18.00	1.20	.70
☐ J42	10¢ Claret	34.00	23.00	3.00	1.60
☐ J43	30¢ Claret	246.00	161.00	22.00	12.50
☐ J44	50¢ Claret	165.00	115.00	23.00	13.00

Scott No.		Fine Unused Each	Ave. Unused Each	Fine Used Each	Ave. Used Each
1910–1912 SMALL DESIGN—S.L. WTMK.—PERF. 12 (N-H ADD 80%)					
☐ J45	1¢ Claret	20.00	12.00	2.40	1.40
☐ J46	2¢ Claret	20.00	13.00	.30	.18
☐ J47	3¢ Claret	316.00	205.00	16.00	12.00
☐ J48	5¢ Claret	48.00	34.00	4.50	3.00
☐ J49	10¢ Claret	60.00	40.00	11.00	6.00
☐ J50	50¢ Claret	530.00	398.00	76.00	47.00
1914–1916 SAME SMALL DESIGN—S.L. WTMK. PERF. 10 (N-H ADD 80%)					
☐ J52	1¢ Carmine	38.00	25.00	9.00	6.10
☐ J53	2¢ Carmine	22.00	14.00	.30	.20
☐ J54	3¢ Carmine	34.00	205.00	11.00	8.00
☐ J55	5¢ Carmine	20.00	13.00	2.10	1.50
☐ J56	10¢ Carmine	32.00	20.00	1.50	.72
☐ J57	30¢ Carmine	121.00	78.00	16.00	11.00
☐ J58	50¢ Carmine	5050.00	3300.00	350.00	210.00
☐ J59	1¢ Rose (No Wtmk.)	860.00	640.00	150.00	105.00
☐ J60	2¢ Rose (No Wtmk.)	76.00	53.00	7.00	4.50

Scott No.		Fine Unused Plate Blk	Ave. Unused Plate Blk	Fine Unused Each	Ave. Unused Each	Fine Used Each	Ave. Used Each
1917–1926 SAME SMALL DESIGN—NO WTMK.—PERF. 11 (N-H ADD 40%)							
☐ J61	1¢ Carmine Rose	48.00	33.00	2.00	1.35	.18	.15
☐ J62	2¢ Carmine Rose	46.00	32.00	2.00	1.35	.16	.09
☐ J63	3¢ Carmine Rose	112.00	76.00	7.00	5.00	.18	.14
☐ J64	5¢ Carmine Rose	115.00	77.00	7.50	6.00	.18	.14
☐ J65	10¢ Carmine Rose	175.00	110.00	11.00	7.10	.21	.14
☐ J66	30¢ Carmine Rose	510.00	360.00	51.00	33.00	.62	.41
☐ J67	50¢ Carmine Rose	760.00	560.00	68.00	47.00	.22	.15
☐ J68	½¢ Dull Red	13.00	9.00	.90	.60	.17	.12
1930–1931 NEW DESIGN FLAT PRESS—PERF. 11 x 11 (N-H ADD 30%)							
☐ J69	½¢ Carmine	56.00	37.00	3.70	2.60	.92	.60
☐ J70	1¢ Carmine	37.00	25.00	2.80	1.90	.23	.16
☐ J71	2¢ Carmine	50.00	34.00	4.00	2.70	.25	.16
☐ J72	3¢ Carmine	242.00	175.00	16.00	12.00	1.40	.92
☐ J73	5¢ Carmine	267.00	175.00	21.00	16.00	1.80	1.21
☐ J74	10¢ Carmine	460.00	340.00	39.00	25.00	.80	.50
☐ J75	30¢ Carmine	1400.00	920.00	140.00	99.00	1.35	.80
☐ J76	50¢ Carmine	1460.00	1050.00	147.00	104.00	.37	.20
☐ J77	$1 Carmine	330.00	220.00	30.00	20.00	.17	.11
☐ J78	$5 Carmine	380.00	240.00	46.00	29.00	.22	.15

Scott No.		Fine Unused Plate Blk	Ave. Unused Plate Blk	Fine Unused Each	Ave. Unused Each	Fine Used Each	Ave. Used Each
1931–1956 SAME DESIGN—ROTARY PRESS—PERF. 11 x 10½ (N-H ADD 20%)							
☐ J79	½¢ Carmine	24.00	16.00	1.30	.83	.17	.13
☐ J80	1¢ Carmine	2.40	1.60	.19	.13	.09	.07
☐ J81	2¢ Carmine	2.40	1.60	.20	.14	.09	.07
☐ J82	3¢ Carmine	3.30	2.40	.33	.22	.09	.07
☐ J83	5¢ Carmine	4.00	2.90	.40	.31	.09	.07
☐ J84	10¢ Carmine	9.00	5.70	1.30	.92	.13	.10
☐ J85	30¢ Carmine	52.00	38.00	11.00	8.00	.13	.08
☐ J86	50¢ Carmine	63.00	44.00	13.00	9.00	.11	.08
☐ J87	$1 Red (10½x11)	320.00	199.00	46.00	33.00	.21	.17

Scott No.		Mint Sheet	Plate Block	Fine Unused Each	Fine Used Each
1959 NEW SERIES—NEW DESIGN—ROTARY PRESS—PERF. 11 x 10½ (N-H ADD 20%)					
☐ J88	½¢ Red & Black	450.00	190.00	1.80	1.40
☐ J89	1¢ Red & Black	3.30	.60	.09	.08
☐ J90	2¢ Red & Black	4.50	.62	.09	.08
☐ J91	3¢ Red & Black	6.10	.72	.09	.08
☐ J92	4¢ Red & Black	7.60	1.15	.12	.08
☐ J93	5¢ Red & Black	9.10	1.00	.14	.08
☐ J94	6¢ Red & Black	11.00	1.40	.19	.08
☐ J95	7¢ Red & Black	13.00	1.70	.20	.11
☐ J96	8¢ Red & Black	16.00	1.80	.23	.09
☐ J97	10¢ Red & Black	18.00	1.80	.26	.07
☐ J98	30¢ Red & Black	—	5.00	.67	.07
☐ J99	50¢ Red & Black	—	6.00	1.10	.07
☐ J100	$1 Red & Black	—	10.00	2.00	.07
☐ J101	$5 Red & Black	—	44.00	10.00	.16
1978 SAME DESIGN, NEW VALUES					
☐ J102	11¢ Red & Black	24.00	2.40	.31	.27
☐ J103	13¢ Red & Black	30.00	2.80	.41	.27

Scott No.		Fine

U.S. UNUSED ZIP CODE BLOCKS OF FOUR

☐1181	5¢ Battle—Wilderness	1.10
☐1182	5¢ Appomattox	1.20
☐1242	5¢ Sam Houston	.80
☐1243	5¢ Chas. M. Russell	1.30
☐1244	5¢ N.Y. World's Fair	.85
☐1247	5¢ N.J. Tercentenary	.80
☐1248	5¢ Neveda Statehood	.80
☐1249	5¢ Register & Vote	.80
☐1250	5¢ Wm. Shakespeare	.80
☐1251	5¢ Mayo Brothers	.80
☐1252	5¢ American Music	.80
☐1253	5¢ Homemakers	.80
☐1254–57	5¢ Christmas, 1964	2.70
☐1258	5¢ Verr.—Narr. Bridge	.79
☐1259	5¢ Modern Art	.79
☐1260	5¢ Radio Amateurs	.79
☐1261	5¢ Battle—N. Orleans	.79
☐1262	5¢ Physical Fitness	.79
☐1263	5¢ Cancer Crusade	.79
☐1264	5¢ Churchill Mem'l	.79
☐1265	5¢ Magna Carta	.79
☐1266	5¢ Intl. Co-op Year	.79
☐1267	5¢ Salvation Army	.79
☐1268	5¢ Dante Alighieri	.79
☐1269	5¢ Herbert Hoover	.79
☐1270	5¢ Robert Fulton	.86
☐1272	5¢ Traffic Safety	.86
☐1273	5¢ John S. Copley	.92
☐1274	11¢ Intl. Telecom. Un.	5.30
☐1276	5¢ Christmas, 1965	.84
☐1278	1¢ Thomas Jefferson	.33
☐1280	2¢ F. Lloyd Wright	.44
☐1281	3¢ Francis Parkman	.62
☐1284	6¢ F.D. Roosevelt	6.30
☐1285	8¢ Albert Einstein	1.35
☐1286	10¢ Andrew Jackson	1.30
☐1286A	12¢ Henry Ford	1.60
☐1288	15¢ O.W. Holmes	2.60
☐1289	20¢ Geo. C. Marshall	2.20
☐1290	25¢ Fred Douglass	2.50
☐1291	30¢ John Dewey	3.40
☐1292	40¢ Thomas Paine	4.60
☐1293	50¢ Lucy Stone	5.10
☐1294	$1 Eugene O'Neill	12.75
☐1306	5¢ Migr. Bird Treaty	.85
☐1307	5¢ Humane to Animals	.80

☐1308	5¢ Indiana Statehood	.77
☐1309	5¢ American Circus	.85
☐1310	5¢ 6th Intl. Phil. Exh.	.78
☐1312	5¢ Bill of rights	.78
☐1313	5¢ Polish Millennium	.78
☐1314	5¢ Natl. Park Service	.78
☐1315	5¢ Marine Reserves	.85
☐1316	5¢ Women's Clubs	.80
☐1317	5¢ Johnny Appleseed	.80
☐1318	5¢ Beautify America	.97
☐1319	5¢ Great River Road	.85
☐1320	5¢ Servicemen-Bonds	.78
☐1321	5¢ Christmas, 1966	.78
☐1322	5¢ Mary Cassatt	1.20
☐1323	5¢ National Grange	.80
☐1324	5¢ Canada Centennial	.80
☐1325	5¢ Erie Canal	.73
☐1326	5¢ Search for Peace	.73
☐1327	5¢ Henry D. Thoreau	.76
☐1328	5¢ Nebraska Statehood	.76
☐1329	5¢ Voice of America	.76
☐1330	5¢ Davy Crockett	.76
☐1331–32	5¢ Twin Space	7.50
☐1333	5¢ Urban Planning	1.15
☐1334	5¢ Finnish Independ.	1.15
☐1336	5¢ Christmas, 1967	.78
☐1337	5¢ Miss. Statehood	1.15
☐1338	6¢ American Flag	.92
☐1339	6¢ Illinois Statehood	.92
☐1341	$1 Airlift	32.00
☐1342	6¢ Support Our Youth	1.15
☐1343	6¢ Law & Order	1.15
☐1344	6¢ Register & Vote	1.15
☐1353–54	6¢ Historic Flags	3.50
☐1355	6¢ Walt Disney	1.35
☐1356	6¢ Fr. Marquette	1.10
☐1357	6¢ Daniel Boone	1.10
☐1358	6¢ Arkansas River	1.10
☐1359	6¢ Leif Erikson	1.10
☐1360	6¢ Cherokee Strip	1.10
☐1361	6¢ Trumbull Painting	1.40
☐1362	6¢ Wildlife Conserv.	1.40
☐1364	6¢ American Indian	1.40
☐1365–68	6¢ Beautify America	6.50
☐1369	6¢ American Legion	.86
☐1370	6¢ Grandma Moses	.86
☐1371	6¢ Apollo 8	1.45
☐1372	6¢ W.C. Handy	.96
☐1373	6¢ California	.96

Scott No.		Fine
☐ 1374	6¢ J.W. Powell	.96
☐ 1375	6¢ Alabama	.96
☐ 1376–79	6¢ Botanical	9.00
☐ 1380	6¢ Dartmouth Case	.90
☐ 1381	6¢ Baseball	2.40
☐ 1382	6¢ Football	1.40
☐ 1383	6¢ Eisenhower	.90
☐ 1385	6¢ Rehabilitation	.90
☐ 1386	6¢ Wm. M. Harnett	.90
☐ 1387–90	6¢ Natural History	1.35
☐ 1391	6¢ Maine Statehood	.92
☐ 1392	6¢ Buffalo	.92
☐ 1393	6¢ Eisenhower-Reg.	.85
☐ 1393D	7¢ Franklin	.90
☐ 1394	8¢ Eisenhower	.92
☐ 1396	8¢ Postal Service	1.25
☐ 1397	14¢ F. LaGuardia	1.70
☐ 1398	16¢ Ernie Pyle	2.40
☐ 1399	18¢ Dr. E. Blackwell	2.30
☐ 1400	21¢ A.P. Giannini	2.40
☐ 1405	6¢ E.L. Masters	.87
☐ 1406	6¢ Women's Suffrage	.87
☐ 1407	6¢ So. Carolina	.87
☐ 1408	6¢ Stone Mountain	.87
☐ 1409	6¢ Fort Snelling	.87
☐ 1410–13	6¢ Anti-Pollution	2.60
☐ 1414	6¢ Nativity	1.10
☐ 1414a	6¢ Precancelled	1.20
☐ 1415–18	6¢ Christmas Toys	4.60
☐ 1415–18a	6¢ Precancelled	11.00
☐ 1419	6¢ United Nations	.86
☐ 1420	6¢ Pilgrim Landing	.86
☐ 1421–22	6¢ D.A.V. & P.O.W.	1.70
☐ 1423	6¢ Sheep	.89
☐ 1424	6¢ D. MacArthur	.89
☐ 1425	6¢ Blood Donors	.89
☐ 1426	8¢ Mo. Statehood	.89
☐ 1427–30	8¢ Wildlife Cons.	1.20
☐ 1431	8¢ Antarctic Traety	.92
☐ 1432	8¢ Amer. Revolution	1.80
☐ 1433	8¢ John Sloan	.92
☐ 1434–35	8¢ Space Achievement	1.10
☐ 1436	8¢ Emily Dickinson	.92
☐ 1437	8¢ San Juan	.92
☐ 1438	8¢ Drug Addiction	.92
☐ 1439	8¢ CARE	.92
☐ 1440–43	8¢ Historic Pres.	1.16
☐ 1444	8¢ Nativity	.92
☐ 1445	8¢ Partridge	.92

Scott No.		Fine
☐ 1446	8¢ Sidney Lanier	.92
☐ 1447	8¢ Peace Corps.	.92
☐ 1448–51	2¢ Cape Hatteras	.83
☐ 1452	6¢ Wolf Trap Farm	.75
☐ 1453	8¢ Yellowstone	1.05
☐ 1454	15¢ Mt. McKinley	1.85
☐ 1455	8¢ Family Planning	.92
☐ 1456–59	8¢ Colonial Crafts.	1.12
☐ 1460	6¢ Olympic Games	1.03
☐ 1461	8¢ Olympic Games	1.12
☐ 1462	15¢ Olympic Games	2.40
☐ 1463	8¢ P.T.A.	1.03
☐ 1464	8¢ Wildlife	1.20
☐ 1468	8¢ Mail Order	1.00
☐ 1469	8¢ Osteopathic	1.00
☐ 1470	8¢ Tom Sawyer	.96
☐ 1471	8¢ Xmas-Religious	.96
☐ 1472	8¢ Xmas-Santa Claus	.96
☐ 1473	8¢ Pharmacy	.96
☐ 1474	8¢ Stamp Collectors	.96
☐ 1475	8¢ Love	.96
☐ 1476	8¢ Pamphlet Printing	.96
☐ 1477	8¢ Posting Braodside	.96
☐ 1478	8¢ Post Rider	.96
☐ 1479	8¢ Drummer	.96
☐ 1480–83	8¢ Bost. Tea Party	.96
☐ 1484	8¢ George Gershwin	.96
☐ 1485	8¢ Robinson Jeffers	.96
☐ 1486	8¢ Tanner	.96
☐ 1487	8¢ Willa Cather	.96
☐ 1488	8¢ N. Copernicus	.96
☐ 1500	6¢ Electronics	.96
☐ 1501	8¢ Electronics	.96
☐ 1502	15¢ Electronics	1.82
☐ 1504	8¢ Angus Cattle	.96
☐ 1505	10¢ Chautauqua	1.20
☐ 1506	10¢ Winter Wheat	1.20
☐ 1507	8¢ Xmas-Religious	1.15
☐ 1508	8¢ Xmas-Tree	1.10
☐ 1510	10¢ Jefferson Mem'l.	1.25
☐ 1511	10¢ Zip Code	1.25
☐ 1525	10¢ V.F.W.	1.16
☐ 1526	10¢ Robert Frost	1.16
☐ 1527	10¢ EXPO '74–Envir.	1.16
☐ 1528	10¢ Horse Racing	1.12
☐ 1529	10¢ Skylab Project	1.16
☐ 1538–41	10¢ Minerals	1.21
☐ 1542	10¢ Fort Harrod	1.16
☐ 1543–46	10¢ Cont. Congress	1.16

Scott No.		Fine
☐ 1547	10¢ Energy Conserv.	1.15
☐ 1548	10¢ Sleepy Hollow	1.15
☐ 1549	10¢ Retarded Children	1.15
☐ 1550	10¢ Xmas-Religious	1.15
☐ 1551	10¢ Xmas-Sleigh	1.20
☐ 1553	10¢ B. West.	1.20
☐ 1554	10¢ P. Dunbar	1.20
☐ 1555	10¢ D.W. Griffith	1.20
☐ 1556	10¢ Pioneer-Jupiter	1.20
☐ 1557	10¢ Mariner 10	1.20
☐ 1558	10¢ Collective Barg	1.20
☐ 1559	8¢ Sybil Ludington	1.05
☐ 1560	10¢ Salem Poor	1.25
☐ 1561	10¢ Haym Solomon	1.25
☐ 1562	18¢ Peter Francisco	2.30
☐ 1563	10¢ Lex.-Concord	1.15
☐ 1564	10¢ Bunker Hill	1.15
☐ 1565–68	10¢ Uniforms	1.20
☐ 1569–70	10¢ Apollo-Soyuz.	1.20
☐ 1571	10¢ Women's Year	1.20
☐ 1572–75	10¢ Postal Service.	1.20
☐ 1576	10¢ World Peace.	1.20
☐ 1577–78	10¢ Banking & Com.	1.20
☐ 1579	10¢ Xmas-Religious	1.20
☐ 1580	10¢ Xmas-Post Card.	1.20
☐ 1581a	1¢ Ability to Write.	.80
☐ 1582	2¢ Freedom to Speak	.80
☐ 1585	4¢ Public that Reads.	.80
☐ 1591	9¢ Freedom to Assemble	1.05
☐ 1592	10¢ Justice	1.20
☐ 1593	11¢ Freedom of Press.	1.30
☐ 1596	13¢ Eagle & Shield	1.40
☐ 1603	24¢ Old North Church	2.80
☐ 1729–31	13¢ Spirit of '76	3.60
☐ 1732	13¢ Interphil '76	1.40
☐ 1733–82	13¢ State Flags	5.00
☐ 1783	13¢ Telephone	1.40
☐ 1784	13¢ Aviation.	1.40
☐ 1785	13¢ Chemistry	1.40
☐ 1790	13¢ Ben Franklin.	1.40
☐ 1791–94	13¢ Dec. of Indep.	1.75
☐ 1795–98	13¢ Olympic Games.	2.90
☐ 1799	13¢ Clara Maass.	1.40
☐ 1700	13¢ Adolph Ochs.	1.40
☐ 1701	13¢ Nativity.	1.40
☐ 1702	13¢ Winter Pastime	1.45
☐ 1704	13¢ Wash. at Princeton	1.40
☐ 1705	13¢ Sound Recording	1.40
☐ 1706–09	13¢ Pueblo Art (6)	2.40

Scott No.		Fine
☐ 1710	13¢ Transatlantic Flight	1.45
☐ 1711	13¢ Colorado	1.45
☐ 1712	13¢ Butterflies	1.45
☐ 1716	13¢ Lafayette	1.45
☐ 1717	20¢, 13¢ Skilled Hands.	1.45
☐ 1721	13¢ Peace Bridge	1.45
☐ 1722	13¢ Herkimer.	1.45
☐ 1723	24¢, 13¢ Energy.	1.45
☐ 1725	13¢ Alta	1.45
☐ 1726	13¢ Confederation	1.45
☐ 1727	13¢ Pictures.	1.45
☐ 1728	13¢ Saratoga	1.45
☐ 1730	13¢ Mailbox.	1.45
☐ 1731	13¢ Sandburg.	1.45
☐ 1732	13¢ Capt. Cook.	1.45
☐ 1733	13¢ Capt. Cook R&S	1.45
☐ 1734	13¢ Indian Cent	1.55
☐ 1735	15¢ No Value "A" Eagle	1.65
☐ 1744	13¢ Harriet Tubman	1.40
☐ 1745–48	13¢ Quilts	1.50
☐ 1749–52	13¢ Dance	1.50
☐ 1753	13¢ French Alliance	1.50
☐ 1754	13¢ Papanicolau	1.50
☐ 1755	13¢ Jimmie Rodgers.	1.50
☐ 1756	15¢ George M. Cohan.	1.55
☐ 1757	13¢ Capex SS	2.80
☐ 1758	15¢ Photography	1.60
☐ 1759	15¢ Viking.	1.60
☐ 1760–63	15¢ Owls	1.60
☐ 1764–67	15¢ Trees	1.60
☐ 1768	15¢ Madonna.	1.60
☐ 1769	15¢ Xmas Hobby Horse.	1.60
☐ 1770	15¢ R.F. Kennedy	1.60
☐ 1771	15¢ M.L. King.	1.60
☐ 1772	15¢ Intl. Year of Child	1.60
☐ 1773	15¢ Steinbeck	1.60
☐ 1774	15¢ Einstein.	1.60
☐ 1775–78	15¢ Toleware	1.60
☐ 1779–82	15¢ Architecture	1.60
☐ 1783–86	15¢ Endangered Flora.	1.60
☐ 1788	15¢ Special Olympics	1.60
☐ 1789	15¢ John Paul Jones	2.10
☐ 1790	10¢ Olympics	1.40
☐ 1791–94	15¢ Summer Olympics	2.20
☐ 1795–98	15¢ Winter Olympics.	3.00
☐ 1799	15¢ Madonna.	1.70
☐ 100	15¢ Xmas Santa	1.70
☐ 1801	15¢ Will Rogers	1.70
☐ 1802	15¢ Vietnam Veterans.	1.70

Scott No.		Fine
☐ 1803	15¢ Fields.	1.70
☐ 1804	15¢ Banneker.	1.70
☐ 1805–10	15¢ Letter Writing	1.70
☐ 1811	15¢ Perkins.	1.70
☐ 1822	15¢ Madison	1.70
☐ 1823	15¢ Bissell.	1.70
☐ 1824	15¢ Keller/Sullivan.	1.70
☐ 1825	15¢ Vets. Admin.	1.70
☐ 1826	15¢ De Galvez	1.65
☐ 1827–30	15¢ Coral Reefs	1.65
☐ 1831	15¢ Org. Labor.	1.65
☐ 1832	15¢ Wharton	1.65
☐ 1833	15¢ Education	1.65
☐ 1834–37	15¢ Indian Masks	2.80
☐ 1838–41	15¢ Architecture	2.30
☐ 1842	15¢ Christmas Madonna . .	1.70
☐ 1849	17¢ Rachel Carson	1.70
☐ 1850	18¢ Geo. Mason	1.70
☐ 1851	19¢ Sequoyah	1.70
☐ 1859	35¢ Dr. Charles Drew	2.30
☐ 1874	15¢ Everett Dirksen	1.70
☐ 1875	15¢ Whitney Young	1.70
☐ 1876–79	18¢ Flowers.	2.10
☐ 1910	18¢ Red Cross	2.10
☐ 1911	18¢ Savings & Loan	2.10
☐ 1912–19	18¢ Space Achievement . .	2.10
☐ 1920	18¢ Management.	2.10
☐ 1921–24	18¢ Habitats	2.10
☐ 1925	18¢ Disabled	2.10
☐ 1926	18¢ Edna St. Vincent Millay .	2.10
☐ 1928–31	18¢ Architecture	2.10
☐ 1932	18¢ Babe Zaharias.	2.10
☐ 1933	18¢ Bobby Jones.	2.10
☐ 1934	18¢ Remington	2.10
☐ 1935	18¢ James Hoban	2.10
☐ 1936	20¢ James Hoban	2.10
☐ 1937–38	18¢ Yorktown, Virginia. . . .	2.10
☐ 1939	20¢ Christmas Madonna . . .	2.10
☐ 1940	20¢ Christmas Child Art. . . .	2.10
☐ 1941	20¢ John Hanson	2.10
☐ 1942–45	20¢ Desert Plants	2.10
☐ C69	8¢ Robert H. Goddard	4.10
☐ C70	8¢ Alaska Purchase	2.25
☐ C71	20¢ Columbia Jays.	7.10
☐ C72	10¢ Stars	5.50
☐ C74	10¢ 50 Years Airmail	2.60
☐ C75	20¢ U.S.A. & Jet	3.80
☐ C76	10¢ Moon Landing.	1.40
☐ C77	9¢ Delta Plane	1.20

Scott No.		Fine
☐ C78	11¢ Plane Silhouette.	1.35
☐ C79	13¢ Letter.	1.45
☐ C80	17¢ Liberty Head.	1.30
☐ C81	21¢ "USA"	2.10
☐ C84	11¢ City of Refuge.	1.30
☐ C85	11¢ Olympic Games	1.45
☐ C86	11¢ Electronics.	1.30
☐ C87	18¢ Statue of Liberty	2.10
☐ C88	26¢ Mount Rushmore	2.80
☐ C89	5¢ Plane & Globes.	2.80
☐ C90	31¢ Plane, Flag & Globes. . .	3.25
☐ C91–2	31¢ Wright Bros.	4.00
☐ C93–4	21¢ Chanute	4.50
☐ C95–6	25¢ Wiley Post	6.10
☐ C97	31¢ Olympics.	4.30
☐ C98	40¢ Mazzel.	5.00
☐ C99	28¢ Scott	3.30
☐ C100	35¢ Curtiss	4.30
☐ E22	45¢ Special Delivery.	9.00
☐ E23	60¢ Special Delivery.	6.10

U.S. UNUSED MAIL EARLY INSCRIPTION BLOCKS

Scott No.		Fine
☐ 1278	1¢ T. Jefferson	.50
☐ 1280	2¢ F.L. Wright.	.50
☐ 1281	3¢ Parkman	.80
☐ 1284	6¢ F.D. Roosevelt	7.50
☐ 1285	8¢ A. Einstein	1.80
☐ 1286	10¢ A. Jackson	1.80
☐ 1286A	12¢ Henry Ford.	2.00
☐ 1288	15¢ O.W. Holmes	3.60
☐ 1289	20¢ G.C. Marshall	3.20
☐ 1290	25¢ F. Douglass	3.60
☐ 1291	30¢ John Dewey	5.10
☐ 1292	40¢ T. Paine	5.80
☐ 1293	50¢ Lucy Stone.	7.10
☐ 1294	$1 E. O'Neill	17.75
☐ 1338	6¢ American Flag.	1.25
☐ 1340	6¢ Hemis Fair '68.	1.40
☐ 1341	$1 Airlift	39.00
☐ 1342	6¢ Support Our Youth . . .	1.31
☐ 1343	6¢ Law & Order.	1.31
☐ 1344	6¢ Register & Vote	1.31
☐ 1347–49	6¢ Historic Flags	3.55
☐ 1355	6¢ Walt Disney	1.65
☐ 1356	6¢ Fr. Marquette	1.20
☐ 1357	6¢ Daniel Boone	1.20
☐ 1358	6¢ Arkansas River	1.20
☐ 1359	6¢ Leif Erickson	1.20

Scott No.		Fine	Scott No.		Fine
☐1360	6¢ Cherokee Strip	1.40	☐1432	8¢ Bicentennial	2.30
☐1361	6¢ Trumbull Painting	1.75	☐1433	8¢ J. Sloan Painting	1.45
☐1362	6¢ Wildlife Conserv.	2.00	☐1434–35	8¢ Space Accomp.	1.45
☐1364	6¢ American Indian.	2.30	☐1436	8¢ Emily Dickinson.	1.35
☐1365–68	6¢ Beautify America	6.60	☐1437	8¢ San Juan.	1.35
☐1369	6¢ American Legion	1.25	☐1438	8¢ Drug Addiction.	1.35
☐1370	6¢ Grandma Moses	1.25	☐1439	8¢ CARE.	1.35
☐1371	6¢ Apollo 8	1.80	☐1440–43	8¢ Historic Press	1.70
☐1372	6¢ W.C. Handy	1.12	☐1444	8¢ Nativity (4).	1.10
☐1373	6¢ California.	1.12	☐1445	8¢ Partridge (4).	1.10
☐1374	6¢ J.W. Powell	1.12	☐1446	8¢ Sidney Lanier	1.40
☐1375	6¢ Alabama	1.12	☐1447	8¢ Peace Corps.	1.40
☐1376–79	6¢ Botanical	13.50	☐1448–51	2¢ Hatteras (8)	1.05
☐1380	6¢ Dartmouth Case.	1.12	☐1452	6¢ Wolf Trap Farm	1.20
☐1381	6¢ Baseball	2.85	☐1453	8¢ Yellowstone	1.35
☐1382	6¢ Football	1.65	☐1454	15¢ Mt. McKinley.	2.75
☐1383	6¢ Eisenhower	1.20	☐1455	8¢ Family Planning	1.40
☐1385	6¢ Rehabilitation	1.20	☐1456–59	8¢ Craftman	1.90
☐1386	6¢ W.M. Harnett	1.20	☐1460	6¢ Olympic Games	1.55
☐1387–90	6¢ Nat. History	1.70	☐1461	8¢ Olympic Games	1.70
☐1391	6¢ Maine.	1.12	☐1462	15¢ Olympic Games	3.10
☐1392	6¢ Buffalo	1.12	☐1463	8¢ P.T.A.	1.30
☐1393	6¢ Eisenhower	1.05	☐1464–67	8¢ Wildlife	1.50
☐1393D	7¢ B. Franklin	1.20	☐1468	8¢ Mail Order (4)	1.10
☐1394	8¢ Eisenhower	1.25	☐1469	8¢ Osteopathic	1.60
☐1396	8¢ Postal Service (4)	1.05	☐1470	8¢ Tom Sawyer	1.50
☐1397	14¢ F. LaGuardia.	2.30	☐1471	8¢ Religious	1.05
☐1398	16¢ Ernie Pyle	2.65	☐1472	8¢ Santa Claus	1.05
☐1399	18¢ Dr. E. Blackwell	3.00	☐1473	8¢ Pharmacy	1.25
☐1400	21¢ A.P. Giannini.	3.10	☐1474	8¢ Stamp Collector	1.25
☐1405	6¢ E.L. Masters	1.20	☐1475	8¢ Love	1.20
☐1406	6¢ Women's Suffrage	1.20	☐1476	8¢ Pamphlet Printing	1.35
☐1407	6¢ South Carolina	1.20	☐1477	8¢ Posting Broadside	1.35
☐1408	6¢ Stone Mountain	1.20	☐1478	8¢ Post Rider	1.35
☐1409	6¢ Fort Snelling.	1.20	☐1479	8¢ Drummer	1.35
☐1410–13	6¢ Anti-Pollution	3.30	☐1480–83	8¢ Bost. Tea Party	1.35
☐1414	6¢ Nativity	1.25	☐1488	8¢ Copernicus.	1.35
☐1414a	6¢ Precancelled.	1.30	☐1500	6¢ Electronics.	1.20
☐1415–18	6¢ Christmas Toys	6.10	☐1501	8¢ Electronics.	1.35
☐1415a–18a	6¢ Precancelled.	14.50	☐1502	15¢ Electronics.	2.30
☐1419	6¢ United Nations	1.12	☐1504	8¢ Angus Cattle.	1.30
☐1420	6¢ Pilgrim Landing	1.12	☐1505	10¢ Chautauqua	2.10
☐1421–22	6¢ D.A. & P.O.W.	2.30	☐1506	10¢ Winter Wheat	2.00
☐1423	6¢ Sheep	1.20	☐1507	8¢ Religious (4)	1.05
☐1424	6¢ Gen. MacArthur	1.20	☐1508	8¢ Xmas Tree (4).	1.05
☐1425	6¢ Blood Donors	1.20	☐1510	10¢ Jefferson Mem'l.	1.70
☐1426	8¢ Missouri (4)	1.00	☐1511	10¢ Zip Code	1.70
☐1427–30	8¢ Wildlife	1.60	☐1525	10¢ V.F.W.	1.70
☐1431	8¢ Antarctic	1.40	☐1526	10¢ Robert Frost	1.70

Scott No.		Fine
☐1528	10¢ Horse Racing (4)	1.25
☐1529	10¢ Skylab Project	1.60
☐1538–41	10¢ Minerals	1.65
☐1542	10¢ Fort Harrod	1.65
☐1543–46	10¢ Cont. Cong.	1.65
☐1547	10¢ Energy Cons.	1.65
☐1548	10¢ Sleepy Hollow	1.65
☐1549	10¢ Retarded Children	1.65
☐1550	10¢ Xmas-Religious	1.80
☐1551	10¢ Xmas-Sleigh (4)	1.30
☐1553	10¢ Benjamin West	1.65
☐1554	10¢ Paul Dunbar	1.65
☐1555	10¢ D.W. Griffith	1.65
☐1556	10¢ Pioneer-Jupiter	1.65
☐1557	10¢ Mariner 10	1.65
☐1558	10¢ Coll. Bargaining	1.65
☐1559	8¢ Sybil Ludington	1.40
☐1560	10¢ Salem Poor	1.65
☐1561	10¢ Haym Salomon	1.65
☐1562	18¢ Peter Francisco	3.60
☐1565–68	10¢ Uniforms (4)	1.30
☐1571	10¢ Women's Year	1.25
☐1572–75	10¢ Postal Service (4)	1.25
☐1576	10¢ World Peace	1.45
☐1577–78	10¢ Banking & Comm.	1.45
☐1579	10¢ Xmas-Religious	1.25
☐1580	10¢ Xmas Post Card(4)	1.25
☐1581	1¢ Ability Write	.60
☐1582	2¢ Freedom to Speak	.62
☐1584	3¢ Cast A Ballot	.72
☐1585	4¢ Public that Reads	.82
☐1591	9¢ Freedom to Assemble	1.40
☐1593	11¢ Freedom of Press	1.70
☐1596	13¢ Eagle & Shield	1.45
☐1603	24¢ Old North Church	3.80
☐1632	13¢ Interphil '76	2.10
☐1633–82	13¢ State Flags	4.10
☐1683	13¢ Telephone	2.10
☐1684	13¢ Aviation	2.10
☐1685	13¢ Chemistry	1.45
☐1690	13¢ Ben. Franklin	2.10
☐1691–94	13¢ Independence	2.40
☐1695–98	13¢ Olympic Games	2.90
☐1700	13¢ Adolph Ochs	2.05
☐1701	13¢ "Nativity" (4)	1.55
☐1702	13¢ "Winter Pastime"	2.05
☐1705	13¢ Sound Recording	2.05
☐1710	13¢ Transatlic	2.05
☐1711	13¢ Colorado	1.50

Scott No.		Fine
☐1712–15	13¢ Butterflies	1.55
☐1716	13¢ Lafayette	1.95
☐1717–20	13¢ Skilled Hands (4)	1.65
☐1721	13¢ Peace Bridge	2.05
☐1725	13¢ California	2.05
☐1726	13¢ Articles of Conf.	2.05
☐1727	13¢ Talking Pictures	2.05
☐1730	13¢ Mailbox	2.05
☐1735	15¢ Eagle Issue "A"	2.75
☐1818	18¢ Eagle Issue "B"	2.95
☐C72	10¢ Stars	6.50
☐C74	10¢ Airmail 50th Ann.	3.60
☐C75	20¢ U.S.A. Airmail	5.10
☐C76	10¢ Moon Landing	1.75
☐C77	9¢ Delta Plane	1.45
☐C78	1¢ Silhouette	2.00
☐C79	13¢ Letter	2.00
☐C80	17¢ Liberty Head	3.20
☐C81	21¢ U.S.A. Airmail	3.10
☐C84	11¢ City of Refuge	2.10
☐C85	11¢ Olympic Games	2.10
☐C86	11¢ Electronics	2.10
☐C87	18¢ Liberty	2.85
☐C88	26¢ Mt. Rushmore	4.50
☐C89	25¢ Plane & Globes	4.60
☐C90	31¢ Plane/Flag/Globes	4.80
☐E22	45¢ Arrows	12.50
☐E23	60¢ Arrows	9.75

U.S. UNUSED CENTER LINE AND ARROW BLOCKS

Scott No.		Fine Ctr Line Blk of 4	Fine Arrow Blk of 4
☐314	1¢ Imperforate	270.00	161.00
☐320	2¢ Imperforate	280.00	166.00
☐343	1¢ Imperforate	60.00	40.00
☐344	2¢ Imperforate	70.00	48.00
☐345	3¢ Imperforate	140.00	96.00
☐346	4¢ Imperforate	275.00	191.00
☐347	5¢ Imperforate	365.00	273.00
☐368	2¢ Lincoln, Imp.	235.00	187.00
☐371	2¢ Alaska-Yukon, Imperf.	320.00	240.00
☐373	2¢ Hudson-Fulton, Imperf	400.00	282.00
☐383	1¢ Imperforate	37.00	21.00
☐384	2¢ Imperforate	71.00	42.00
☐408	1¢ Imperforate	14.00	7.50

Scott No.		Fine Ctr Line Blk of 4	Fine Arrow Blk of 4
☐409	2¢ Imperforate . .	18.00	10.00
☐481	1¢ Imperforate . .	11.00	6.00
☐482	2¢ Imperforate . .	9.75	7.50
☐484	3¢ Imperforate Type II.	74.00	56.00
☐524	5¢ Green & Blk	2800.00	2600.00
☐531	1¢ Offset, Imperf.	89.00	55.00
☐532	2¢ Offset, Imperf. type IV. . . .	245.00	195.00
☐534	2¢ Offset, Imperf. Type Va. . .	104.00	71.00
☐534A	2¢ Offset, Imp. Type VI . . .	206.00	197.00
☐535	3¢ Offset, Imperf.	72.00	49.00
☐547	$2 Carm. & Blk.	2650.00	2250.00
☐573	$5 Carm. & Blk.	2400.00	1850.00
☐575	1¢ Imperforate	66.00	70.00
☐576	1½¢ Imperf..	20.00	13.00
☐577	2¢ Imperforate . .	21.00	15.00
☐611	2¢ Harding Imperf	89.00	61.00
☐620	2¢ Norse-Amer'n.	42.00	32.00
☐621	5¢ Norse-Ameri'n	136.00	112.00
☐631	1½¢ Harding, Rotary/ Imperf	30.00	17.00
☐703	2¢ Yorktown	2.50	2.00
☐832	$1 Purple & Blk .	46.00	46.00
☐833	$2 Yel./Gm./Blk	126.00	121.00
☐834	$5 Red & Blk..	585.00	515.00
☐C1	6¢ Airmail	525.00	460.00
☐C2	16¢ Airmail	760.00	740.00
☐C3	24¢ Airmail	740.00	720.00
☐C23	36¢ Airmail	3.50	3.00
☐CE2	16¢ Spec. Del. Airmail	3.00	2.50

Scott No.		Fine

1927–1940 MINT SHEETS

☐643	2¢ Vermont	310.00
☐644	2¢ Burgoyne.	440.00
☐645	2¢ Valley Forge	210.00
☐646	2¢ Molly Pitcher.	230.00
☐647	2¢ Hawaii	820.00
☐648	5¢ Hawaii	2850.00
☐649	2¢ Aeronautics	120.00
☐650	5¢ Aeronautics	770.00
☐651	2¢ George R. Clark. . . .	72.00
☐654	2¢ Edison-Flat.	200.00

Scott No.		Fine
☐655	2¢ Edison-Rotary	185.00
☐657	2¢ Sullivan.	180.00
☐680	2¢ Fallen Timbers	200.00
☐681	2¢ Ohio River Canal . . .	145.00
☐682	2¢ Mass. Bay	150.00
☐683	2¢ Carolina-Charleston. .	250.00
☐688	2¢ Braddock.	215.00
☐689	2¢ Von Steuben.	120.00
☐690	2¢ Pulaski	66.00
☐702	2¢ Red Cross	28.00
☐703	2¢ Yorktown.	33.00
☐704	½¢ Wash. Bicent'l.	22.00
☐705	1¢ Wash. Bicent'l.	29.00
☐706	1½¢ Wash. Bicent'l.	97.00
☐707	2¢ Wash. Bicent'l.	17.00
☐708	3¢ Wash. Bicent'l.	120.00
☐709	4¢ Wash. Bicent'l.	52.00
☐710	5¢ Wash. Bicent'l.	330.00
☐711	6¢ Wash. Bicent'l.	860.00
☐712	7¢ Wash. Bicent'l.	68.00
☐713	8¢ Wash. Bicent'l.	900.00
☐714	9¢ Wash. Bicent'l.	660.00
☐715	10¢ Wash. Bicent'l.	2700.00
☐716	2¢ Lake Placid	88.00
☐717	2¢ Arbor Day	38.00
☐718	3¢ Olympics	285.00
☐719	5¢ Olympics	425.00
☐724	3¢ Penn	68.00
☐725	3¢ Webster	120.00
☐726	3¢ Oglethorpe	84.00
☐727	3¢ Newburgh	29.00
☐728	1¢ Chicago	20.00
☐729	3¢ Chicago	30.00
☐732	3¢ N.R.A.	21.00
☐733	3¢ Byrd.	75.00
☐734	5¢ Kosciuszko.	146.00
☐736	3¢ Maryland	43.00
☐737	3¢ Mother's Day (R) . . .	12.50
☐738	3¢ Mother's Day (F) . . .	22.00
☐739	3¢ Wisconsin	22.00
☐740	1¢ Natl. Parks.	9.00
☐741	2¢ Natl. Parks.	12.00
☐742	3¢ Natl. Parks.	16.00
☐743	4¢ Natl. Parks.	45.00
☐744	5¢ Natl. Parks.	82.00
☐745	6¢ Natl. Parks.	130.00
☐746	7¢ Natl. Parks.	73.00
☐747	8¢ Natl. Parks.	170.00

Scott No.		Fine	Scott No.		Fine
☐748	9¢ Natl. Parks	160.00	☐862	5¢ Alcott	42.00
☐749	10¢ Natl. Parks	320.00	☐863	10¢ Clemens	210.00
☐772	3¢ Connecticut	12.00	☐864	1¢ Longfellow	12.00
☐773	3¢ San Diego	11.00	☐865	2¢ Whittier	11.00
☐774	3¢ Boulder Dam	11.00	☐866	3¢ Lowell	16.00
☐775	3¢ Michigan	10.50	☐867	5¢ Whitman	47.00
☐776	3¢ Texas	10.50	☐868	10¢ Riley	245.00
☐777	3¢ Rhode Island	11.50	☐869	1¢ Mann	10.00
☐782	3¢ Arkansas	10.50	☐870	2¢ Hopkins	9.00
☐783	3¢ Oregon	10.50	☐871	3¢ Elliot	23.00
☐784	3¢ Susan B. Anthony	15.00	☐872	5¢ Willard	54.00
☐785	1¢ Army	6.75	☐873	10¢ B.T. Washington	169.00
☐786	2¢ Army	7.75	☐874	1¢ Audubon	7.50
☐787	3¢ Army	15.00	☐875	2¢ Long	9.00
☐788	4¢ Army	46.00	☐876	3¢ Burbank	9.60
☐789	5¢ Army	63.00	☐877	5¢ Reed	34.00
☐790	1¢ Navy	7.00	☐878	10¢ Addams	150.00
☐791	2¢ Navy	7.75	☐879	1¢ Fosters	7.50
☐792	3¢ Navy	12.50	☐880	2¢ Sousa	12.00
☐793	4¢ Navy	44.00	☐881	3¢ Herbert	13.00
☐794	5¢ Navy	60.00	☐882	5¢ MacDowell	62.00
☐795	3¢ N.W. Territory	8.50	☐883	10¢ Nevin	430.00
☐796	5¢ Virginia Dare	24.50	☐884	1¢ Sturat	6.60
☐798	3¢ Constitution	9.00	☐885	2¢ Whistler	9.10
☐799	3¢ Hawaii	11.50	☐886	3¢ St. Gaudens	9.20
☐800	3¢ Alaska	11.50	☐887	5¢ French	54.00
☐801	3¢ Puerto Rico	11.50	☐888	10¢ Remington	260.00
☐802	3¢ Virgin Islands	11.50	☐889	1¢ Whitney	13.00
☐835	3¢ Ratification	15.50	☐890	2¢ Morse	12.00
☐836	3¢ Swede-Finn	12.50	☐891	3¢ McCormick	20.00
☐837	3¢ N.W. Territory	32.00	☐892	5¢ Howe	143.00
☐838	3¢ Iowa	17.00	☐893	10¢ Bell	1275.00
☐852	3¢ Golden Gate	9.50	☐894	3¢ Pony Express	27.00
☐853	3¢ N.Y. Fair	9.50	☐895	3¢ Pan American	26.00
☐854	3¢ Inauguration	28.00	☐896	3¢ Idaho	17.00
☐855	3¢ Baseball	32.00	☐897	3¢ Wyoming	16.00
☐856	3¢ Canal Zone	19.00	☐898	3¢ Coronado	14.75
☐857	3¢ Printing	9.50	☐899	1¢ Defense	8.75
☐858	3¢ Four States	9.50	☐900	2¢ Defense	12.00
☐859	1¢ Irving	7.00	☐901	3¢ Defense	15.50
☐860	2¢ Cooper	8.50	☐902	3¢ Emancipation	20.00
☐861	3¢ Emerson	12.00			

NOTE: Mint Sheets from 1941 to date are included with individual listing.

OFFICIAL STAMPS 1873 CONTINENTAL PRINTING (N-H ADD 70%)

Scott No.			Fine Unused Each	Ave. Unused Each	Fine Used Each	Ave. Used Each
☐ O1	1¢	Agricultural Department	61.00	41.00	33.00	21.00
☐ O2	2¢	. . . .	40.00	26.00	15.00	9.50
☐ O3	3¢	. . . .	33.00	22.00	4.50	3.50
☐ O4	4¢	. . . .	43.00	26.00	15.00	11.00
☐ O5	10¢	. . . .	91.00	59.00	54.00	40.00
☐ O6	12¢	. . . .	137.00	88.00	73.00	47.00
☐ O7	15¢	. . . .	89.00	54.00	51.00	32.00
☐ O8	24¢	. . . .	111.00	74.00	64.00	41.00
☐ O9	30¢	. . . .	147.00	99.00	87.00	60.00
☐ O10	1¢	Executive Department	226.00	150.00	105.00	73.00
☐ O11	2¢	. . . .	144.00	93.00	74.00	53.00
☐ O12	3¢	. . . .	178.00	118.00	66.00	44.00
☐ O13	6¢	. . . .	278.00	192.00	155.00	104.00
☐ O14	10¢	. . . .	245.00	162.00	155.00	105.00
☐ O15	1¢	Interior Department	15.00	10.00	3.00	2.00
☐ O16	2¢	. . . .	13.00	8.75	2.25	1.75
☐ O17	3¢	. . . .	21.00	14.00	2.25	1.75
☐ O18	6¢	. . . .	16.00	9.50	2.25	1.75
☐ O19	10¢	. . . .	12.00	7.75	4.25	3.10
☐ O20	12¢	. . . .	21.00	14.00	3.10	2.10
☐ O21	15¢	. . . .	37.00	23.00	8.75	6.50
☐ O22	24¢	. . . .	30.00	17.00	6.50	4.90
☐ O23	30¢	. . . .	41.00	25.00	6.50	4.90
☐ O24	90¢	. . . .	81.00	50.00	14.00	9.00
☐ O25	1¢	Justice Department	37.00	20.00	20.00	13.00
☐ O26	2¢	. . . .	56.00	35.00	22.00	15.00
☐ O27	3¢	. . . .	61.00	39.00	9.00	7.00
☐ O28	6¢	. . . .	51.00	31.00	12.00	9.00
☐ O29	10¢	. . . .	59.00	38.00	26.00	17.00
☐ O30	12¢	. . . .	44.00	27.00	14.00	11.00
☐ O31	15¢	. . . .	91.00	65.00	51.50	36.00
☐ O32	24¢	. . . .	272.00	166.00	121.00	79.00
☐ O33	30¢	. . . .	246.00	151.00	93.00	63.00
☐ O34	90¢	. . . .	367.00	222.00	182.00	123.00
☐ O35	1¢	Navy Department	30.00	20.00	12.00	8.50
☐ O36	2¢	. . . .	21.00	14.00	9.50	7.00
☐ O37	3¢	. . . .	24.00	16.00	4.50	2.40
☐ O38	6¢	. . . .	23.00	14.60	6.00	4.50
☐ O39	7¢	. . . .	149.00	99.00	66.00	41.00
☐ O40	10¢	. . . .	30.00	18.00	13.00	10.00
☐ O41	12¢	. . . .	40.00	22.00	10.50	7.50
☐ O42	15¢	. . . .	71.00	45.00	28.00	17.00
☐ O43	24¢	. . . .	74.00	48.00	33.00	20.00
☐ O44	30¢	. . . .	56.00	32.00	15.00	11.00
☐ O45	90¢	. . . .	278.00	170.00	99.00	62.00
☐ O47	1¢	Post Office Department	8.50	6.00	4.50	2.75

Scott No.			Fine Unused Each	Ave. Unused Each	Fine Used Each	Ave. Used Each
☐ O48	2¢	....	8.50	6.00	4.50	2.40
☐ O49	3¢	....	2.60	1.50	1.10	.73
☐ O50	6¢	....	7.80	5.30	2.30	1.20
☐ O51	10¢	....	34.00	23.00	21.00	11.80
☐ O52	12¢	....	17.75	12.00	5.50	3.30
☐ O53	15¢	....	20.00	13.00	8.00	5.40
☐ O54	24¢	....	27.00	17.00	10.50	6.50
☐ O55	30¢	....	26.00	16.50	8.75	6.50
☐ O56	90¢	....	41.00	25.00	13.00	8.50
☐ O57	1¢ State Department	....	37.00	23.00	12.00	8.50
☐ O58	2¢	....	82.00	60.00	31.00	19.00
☐ O59	3¢	....	29.00	19.00	9.00	6.50
☐ O60	6¢	....	28.00	18.75	9.50	6.50
☐ O61	7¢	....	59.00	36.00	18.00	11.75
☐ O62	10¢	....	36.00	23.00	14.00	8.75
☐ O63	12¢	....	73.00	48.00	30.00	18.50
☐ O64	15¢	....	57.00	38.00	19.00	12.00
☐ O65	24¢	....	145.00	91.00	90.00	57.00
☐ O66	30¢	....	135.00	87.00	61.00	40.00
☐ O67	90¢	....	305.00	180.00	121.00	82.00
☐ O68	$2	....	524.00	360.00	245.00	165.00
☐ O72	1¢ Treasury Department	....	13.00	8.50	2.40	1.80
☐ O73	2¢	....	19.00	12.00	2.30	1.45
☐ O74	3¢	....	11.00	6.50	1.60	.95
☐ O75	6¢	....	18.50	14.00	1.50	.95
☐ O76	7¢	....	38.00	23.00	12.00	6.60
☐ O77	10¢	....	37.50	23.00	5.00	3.25
☐ O78	12¢	....	38.00	23.00	3.00	1.50
☐ O79	15¢	....	39.00	24.00	4.00	2.70
☐ O80	24¢	....	162.00	101.00	58.00	36.00
☐ O81	30¢	....	54.00	39.00	4.50	3.10
☐ O82	90¢	....	62.00	40.00	4.20	3.00
☐ O83	1¢ War Department	....	53.00	35.00	4.70	3.20
☐ O84	2¢	....	56.00	35.00	5.70	4.00
☐ O85	3¢	....	48.00	31.00	1.60	.94
☐ O86	6¢	....	226.00	145.00	4.20	2.70
☐ O87	7¢	....	52.00	33.00	30.00	16.00
☐ O88	10¢	....	16.00	9.90	4.00	2.50
☐ O89	12¢	....	57.00	38.00	2.80	1.50
☐ O90	15¢	....	14.50	9.00	2.00	1.15
☐ O91	24¢	....	14.50	10.00	2.40	1.25
☐ O92	30¢	....	14.50	10.00	2.40	1.20
☐ O93	90¢	....	38.00	24.00	12.00	7.75

1879. AMERICAN PRINTING—SOFT POROUS PAPER (N-H ADD 80%)

☐ O94	1¢ Agricultural Department	....	1310.00	860.00	—	—
☐ O95	3¢	....	178.00	122.00	28.00	17.00

Scott No.		Fine Unused Each	Ave. Unused Each	Fine Used Each	Ave. Used Each
☐ O96	1¢ Interior Department	120.00	78.00	63.00	41.00
☐ O97	2¢	3.00	2.00	1.40	.80
☐ O98	3¢	2.20	1.40	1.10	.65
☐ O99	6¢	3.00	1.80	1.40	.90
☐ O100	10¢	32.00	22.00	19.00	12.50
☐ O101	12¢	59.00	36.00	32.00	20.00
☐ O102	15¢	127.00	82.00	63.00	41.00
☐ O103	24¢	1190.00	870.00	—	—
☐ O106	3¢ Justice Department	46.00	30.00	18.50	13.00
☐ O107	6¢	96.00	63.00	66.00	43.00
☐ O108	3¢ Post Office Department	11.00	6.70	2.30	1.50
☐ O109	3¢ Treasury Department	24.00	15.00	3.75	2.40
☐ O110	6¢	54.00	35.00	20.00	13.00
☐ O111	10¢	66.00	43.00	17.00	11.00
☐ O112	30¢	725.00	460.00	160.00	100.00
☐ O113	90¢	725.00	460.00	160.00	100.00
☐ O114	1¢ War Department	2.00	1.40	1.20	.90
☐ O115	2¢	3.00	2.00	1.50	1.00
☐ O116	3¢	3.00	1.70	1.10	.63
☐ O117	6¢	3.00	1.70	1.20	.69
☐ O118	10¢	15.00	11.00	8.50	5.50
☐ O119	12¢	12.50	7.50	2.10	1.50
☐ O120	30¢	42.00	28.00	29.00	15.50

1910–1911. POSTAL SAVINGS (N-H ADD 70%)

Scott No.		Fine Unused Each	Ave. Unused Each	Fine Used Each	Ave. Used Each
☐ O121	2¢ Black, D.L. Wmk	15.00	9.50	1.40	.95
☐ O122	50¢ Dark Green, D.L. Wmk	111.00	79.00	34.00	22.00
☐ O123	$1 Ultramarine, D.L. Wmk	111.00	79.00	12.00	7.75
☐ O124	1¢ Dark Violet, S.L. Wmk	4.10	2.80	1.50	.90
☐ O125	2¢ Black, S.L. Wmk	33.00	22.00	4.00	2.80
☐ O126	10¢ Carmine, S.L. Wmk	9.00	6.00	1.40	.85

Scott No.		Fine Unused Block	Ave. Unused Block	Fine Unused Each	Ave. Unused Each	Fine Used Each	Ave. Used Each
1912. PARCEL POST DUE (N-H ADD 45%)							
☐ JQ1	1¢ Dark Green	105.00	63.00	12.00	7.40	3.50	2.20
☐ JQ2	2¢ Dark Green	630.00	435.00	86.00	62.00	19.00	12.50
☐ JQ3	5¢ Dark Green	134.00	88.00	15.00	9.80	4.60	3.10
☐ JQ4	10¢ Dark Green	1560.00	1200.00	172.00	116.00	42.00	27.00
☐ JQ5	25¢ Dark Green	680.00	475.00	93.00	62.00	4.80	3.20
1912–1913. PARCEL POST STAMPS (N-H ADD 45%)							
☐ Q1	1¢ P.O. Clerk	43.00	29.00	5.50	3.30	1.25	.90
☐ Q2	2¢ City Carrier	62.00	44.00	5.50	3.80	.92	.60
☐ Q3	5¢ Railway Clerk	121.00	88.00	12.00	8.10	9.00	6.00
☐ Q4	4¢ Rural Carrier	165.00	114.00	32.00	22.00	2.60	1.75
☐ Q5	5¢ Mail Train	211.00	142.00	33.00	22.00	1.80	1.25
☐ Q6	10¢ Steamship	277.00	181.00	49.00	34.00	2.80	1.85

Scott No.		Fine Unused Block	Ave. Unused Block	Fine Unused Each	Ave. Unused Each	Fine Used Each	Ave. Used Each
☐ Q7	15¢ Mail Truck	416.00	260.00	75.00	53.00	9.75	6.00
☐ Q8	20¢ Airplane	730.00	540.00	156.00	106.00	20.00	13.00
☐ Q9	25¢ Manufacturing	405.00	275.00	81.00	55.00	6.10	4.25
☐ Q10	50¢ Dairying	1630.00	1320.00	241.00	160.00	43.00	28.00
☐ Q11	75¢ Harvesting	480.00	400.00	86.00	62.00	28.00	17.50
☐ Q12	$1 Fruit Growing	2210.00	1610.00	402.00	275.00	24.00	15.00

1925–1929. SPECIAL HANDLING STAMPS (N-H ADD 35%)

Scott No.		Fine Unused Block	Ave. Unused Block	Fine Unused Each	Ave. Unused Each	Fine Used Each	Ave. Used Each
☐ QE1	10¢ Yellow Green	19.50	12.50	2.15	1.50	1.15	.72
☐ QE2	15¢ Yellow Green	22.50	16.00	2.50	1.60	1.15	.73
☐ QE3	20¢ Yellow Green	35.50	24.00	5.00	3.10	1.90	1.25
☐ QE4	25¢ Yellow Green	235.00	166.00	28.00	17.00	8.50	5.70
☐ QE4A	25¢ Deep Green	275.00	182.00	34.00	22.00	6.50	4.62

1919–1922. U.S. OFFICES IN CHINA (N-H ADD 60%)
SHANGHAI 2¢ CHINA

Scott No.		Fine Unused Block	Ave. Unused Block	Fine Unused Each	Ave. Unused Each	Fine Used Each	Ave. Used Each
☐ K1	2¢ on 1¢	105.00	73.00	20.00	13.00	24.00	17.00
☐ K2	4¢ on 2¢	105.00	73.00	20.00	13.00	24.00	17.00
☐ K3	6¢ on 3¢	262.00	174.00	39.00	25.00	46.00	32.00
☐ K4	8¢ on 4¢	285.00	195.00	44.00	30.00	48.00	33.00
☐ K5	10¢ on 2¢	320.00	240.00	61.00	39.00	61.00	43.00
☐ K6	12¢ on 6¢	316.00	231.00	61.00	39.00	61.00	43.00
☐ K7	14¢ on 7¢	336.00	251.00	64.00	41.00	73.00	52.00
☐ K8	16¢ on 8¢ Olive Bistre	293.00	201.00	54.00	36.00	64.00	41.00
☐ K8a	16¢ on 8¢ Olive Green	296.00	201.00	54.00	37.00	64.00	42.00
☐ K9	18¢ on 9¢	291.00	191.00	55.00	36.00	64.00	42.00
☐ K10	20¢ on 10¢	291.00	191.00	55.00	36.00	64.00	42.00
☐ K11	24¢ on 12¢ Br. Car	291.00	191.00	55.00	36.00	66.00	42.00
☐ K11a	24¢ on 12¢ Cl. Br.	382.00	281.00	83.00	60.00	81.00	59.00
☐ K12	30¢ on 15¢	333.00	232.00	69.00	43.00	78.00	54.00
☐ K13	40¢ on 20¢	530.00	400.00	112.00	72.00	116.00	77.00
☐ K14	60¢ on 30¢	495.00	360.00	97.00	62.00	116.00	78.00
☐ K15	$1 on 50¢	3440.00	2210.00	660.00	420.00	510.00	320.00
☐ K16	$2 on $1	2350.00	1515.00	475.00	310.00	430.00	265.00
☐ K17	2¢ on 1¢ Loc. Sur	404.00	292.00	83.00	59.00	76.00	48.00
☐ K18	4¢ on 2¢ Loc. Sur	365.00	241.00	79.00	54.00	74.00	48.00

Scott No.		Imperforated (a) Fine	Ave.	Part Perforated (b) Fine	Ave.	Perforated (c) Fine	Ave.

1862–1971. UNITED STATES REVENUES

Scott No.		Imperforated (a) Fine	Ave.	Part Perforated (b) Fine	Ave.	Perforated (c) Fine	Ave.
☐ R1	1¢ Express	54.00	33.00	43.00	26.00	1.27	.69
☐ R2	1¢ Play Cards	785.00	510.00	377.00	240.00	96.00	62.00
☐ R3	1¢ Proprietary	550.00	320.00	106.00	73.00	.95	.62
☐ R4	1¢ Telegraph	200.00	121.00	—	—	9.20	6.00
☐ R5	2¢ Bank Ck., Blue	1.25	.67	1.40	.82	.18	.11
☐ R6	2¢ Bank Ck., Orange	—	—	93.00	64.00	.12	.08
☐ R7	2¢ Certif., Blue	11.50	6.60	—	—	31.00	19.50
☐ R8	2¢ Certif., Orange	—	—	—	—	25.00	15.75

*No hinge pricing from 1941 to date is figured at (N-H ADD 15%)

Scott No.		Imperforated (a) Fine	Ave.	Part Perforated (b) Fine	Ave.	Perforated (c) Fine	Ave.
☐ R9	2¢ Express, Blue	12.00	7.50	17.00	11.00	.43	.24
☐ R10	2¢ Express, Orange	—	—	—	—	6.25	5.00
☐ R11	2¢ Ply. Cds., Blue	—	—	117.00	72.00	3.00	1.75
☐ R12	2¢ Ply. Cds., Orange	—	—	—	—	28.00	17.00
☐ R13	2¢ Proprietary, Blue	—	—	96.00	61.00	.45	.28
☐ R14	2¢ Proprietary, Orange ...	—	—	—	—	33.00	21.50
☐ R15	2¢ U.S.I.R.	—	—	—	—	.11	.08
☐ R16	3¢ Foreign Ex.	—	—	130.00	76.00	1.95	1.14
☐ R17	3¢ Playing Cds.	—	—	—	—	96.00	59.00
☐ R18	3¢ Proprietary	—	—	132.00	81.00	1.65	.95
☐ R19	3¢ Telegraph	41.00	26.00	16.00	11.00	2.10	1.40
☐ R20	4¢ Inland Exch.	—	—	—	—	2.00	1.30
☐ R21	4¢ Playing Cards	—	—	—	—	295.00	175.00
☐ R22	4¢ Proprietary	—	—	141.00	90.00	2.15	1.20
☐ R23	5¢ Agreement	—	—	—	—	.63	.36
☐ R24	5¢ Certificate	1.60	.90	11.00	5.40	.21	.12
☐ R26	5¢ Foreign Ex.	—	—	—	—	.90	.50
☐ R27	5¢ Inland Exch.	2.80	1.70	2.90	1.70	.23	.12
☐ R28	5¢ Playing Cds.	—	—	—	—	5.40	3.30
☐ R29	5¢ Proprietary	—	—	—	—	12.00	8.00
☐ R30	6¢ Inland Exch.	—	—	—	—	1.45	.85
☐ R32	10¢ Bill of Ldg.	47.00	31.00	211.00	73.00	.93	.60
☐ R33	10¢ Certificate	79.00	58.00	76.00	54.00	.65	.45
☐ R34	10¢ Contract Bill	—	—	79.00	60.00	.65	.45
☐ R35	10¢ For Ex. Bill	—	—	—	—	3.10	2.20
☐ R36	10¢ Inland Exch.	107.00	63.00	3.15	1.95	.42	.25
☐ R37	10¢ Power of Aty.	310.00	190.00	21.00	12.00	.73	.48
☐ R38	10¢ Proprietary	—	—	—	—	16.00	11.50
☐ R39	15¢ Foreign Exch.	—	—	—	—	12.00	8.00
☐ R40	15¢ Inland Exch.	24.00	16.50	13.00	7.00	1.50	.90
☐ R41	20¢ Foreign Exch.	49.00	38.00	—	—	28.00	19.00
☐ R42	20¢ Inland Exch.	14.00	11.00	18.00	12.00	.85	.53
☐ R43	25¢ Bond	68.00	49.00	5.70	3.10	1.90	1.00
☐ R44	25¢ Certificate	7.75	6.00	6.10	3.50	.25	.13
☐ R45	25¢ Entry of Gds.	19.00	12.00	32.00	21.00	1.05	.70
☐ R46	25¢ Insurance	9.00	6.00	10.00	6.00	.75	.48
☐ R47	25¢ Life Insur.	33.00	23.00	78.00	56.00	4.70	2.15
☐ R48	25¢ Power of Atty.	5.50	3.00	17.00	9.00	.53	.34
☐ R49	25¢ Protest	23.00	12.00	131.00	99.00	5.20	3.00
☐ R50	25¢ Warehouse Rct.	38.00	25.00	132.00	99.00	21.00	14.00
☐ R51	30¢ Foreign Exch.	57.50	38.00	201.00	131.00	49.00	32.00
☐ R52	30¢ Inland Exch.	46.00	32.00	27.00	19.00	3.00	1.50
☐ R53	40¢ Inland Exch.	432.00	276.00	4.60	2.90	3.00	1.75
☐ R54	50¢ Convey, Blue	11.00	8.00	1.40	.93	.47	.33
☐ R55	50¢ Entry of Gds.	—	—	13.00	7.80	.63	.35
☐ R56	50¢ Foreign Exch.	38.00	24.00	35.00	21.00	3.60	2.10
☐ R57	50¢ Lease	22.00	14.00	42.00	27.00	4.90	2.90
☐ R58	50¢ Life Insur.	29.00	17.00	49.00	32.00	1.20	.73

*No hinge pricing from 1941 to date is figured at (N-H ADD 15%)

Scott No.		Imperforated (a)		Part Perforated (b)		Perforated (c)	
		Fine	Ave.	Fine	Ave.	Fine	Ave.
☐ R59	50¢ Mortgage	16.00	10.00	3.30	2.00	1.25	.55
☐ R60	50¢ Orig. Process	2.50	1.60	—	—	.90	.55
☐ R61	50¢ Passage Tkt.	68.00	39.00	107.00	70.00	1.25	.74
☐ R62	50¢ Prob. of Will	35.00	20.00	40.00	25.00	24.00	14.75
☐ R63	50¢ Sty. Bond, Bl.	122.00	80.00	3.70	2.20	.50	.27
☐ R64	60¢ Inland Exch.	86.00	56.00	42.00	29.00	5.50	3.20
☐ R65	70¢ Foreign Exch.	267.00	155.00	88.00	62.00	5.75	3.20
☐ R66	$1 Conveyance	12.50	8.50	270.00	150.00	2.25	1.50
☐ R67	$1 Entry of Gds.	25.00	15.00	—	—	2.00	1.00
☐ R68	$1 Foreign Exch.	56.00	33.00	—	—	1.25	.74
☐ R69	$1 Inland Exch.	15.00	10.00	220.00	126.00	.93	.50
☐ R70	$1 Lease	33.00	20.00	—	—	1.50	.85
☐ R71	$1 Life Insur.	110.00	63.00	—	—	3.80	2.40
☐ R72	$1 Manifest	58.00	40.00	—	—	24.00	15.50
☐ R73	$1 Mortgage	25.00	16.00	—	—	126.00	80.00
☐ R74	$1 Passage Tkt.	134.00	91.00	—	—	126.00	79.50
☐ R75	$1 Power of Atty.	60.00	40.00	—	—	1.80	.95
☐ R76	$1 Prob. of Will	45.00	27.00	—	—	29.00	15.00
☐ R77	$1.30 Foreign Exch.	1680.00	1210.00	—	—	38.00	22.00
☐ R78	$1.50 Inland Exch.	29.00	17.00	—	—	3.30	2.00
☐ R79	$1.60 Foreign Exch.	535.00	310.00	—	—	93.00	52.00
☐ R80	$1.90 Foreign Exch.	1645.00	1180.00	—	—	47.00	31.00
☐ R81	$2 Conveyance	122.00	56.00	596.00	345.00	2.10	1.50
☐ R82	$2 Mortgage	63.00	39.00	—	—	2.10	1.50
☐ R83	$2 Prob. of Will	1810.00	1260.00	—	—	29.00	14.00
☐ R84	$2.50 Inland Exch.	860.00	620.00	—	—	3.70	2.15
☐ R85	$3 Chart. Pty.	100.00	64.00	—	—	3.90	2.40
☐ R86	$3 Manifest	76.00	43.00	—	—	14.00	7.50
☐ R87	$3.50 Inland Exch.	781.00	523.00	—	—	28.00	16.00
☐ R88	$5 Chtr. Party	117.00	64.00	—	—	8.10	5.00
☐ R89	$5 Conveyance	43.00	27.00	—	—	5.50	3.00
☐ R90	$5 Manifest	88.00	64.00	—	—	88.00	62.00
☐ R91	$5 Mortgage	88.00	64.00	—	—	20.00	12.00
☐ R92	$5 Prob. of Will	336.00	217.00	—	—	21.00	15.00
☐ R93	$10 Chrt. Party	350.00	223.00	—	—	23.00	15.00
☐ R94	$10 Conveyance	77.00	47.00	—	—	86.00	46.00
☐ R95	$10 Mortgage	265.00	145.00	—	—	29.00	18.00
☐ R96	$10 Prob. of Will	656.00	420.00	—	—	27.00	16.00
☐ R97	$15 Mortgage	780.00	452.00	—	—	106.00	68.00
☐ R98	$20 Conveyance	54.00	35.00	—	—	35.00	21.00
☐ R99	$20 Prob. of Will	794.00	484.00	—	—	755.00	462.00
☐ R100	$25 Mortgage	544.00	362.00	—	—	93.00	57.00
☐ R101	$50 U.S.I.R.	156.00	102.00	—	—	120.00	89.00
☐ R102	$200 U.S.I.R.	1035.00	793.00	—	—	580.00	345.00

*No hinge pricing from 1941 to date is figured at (N-H ADD 15%)

Scott No.		Fine Used Each	Ave. Used Each

1871. SECOND ISSUE R103 THROUGH R131 HAVE BLUE FRAMES AND A BLACK CENTER

		Fine Used Each	Ave. Used Each
☐R103	1¢	30.00	17.00
☐R104	2¢	1.60	.95
☐R105	3¢	14.00	9.10
☐R106	4¢	47.00	32.00
☐R107	5¢	1.60	.90
☐R108	6¢	54.00	33.00
☐R109	10¢	.93	.65
☐R110	15¢	25.00	16.00
☐R111	20¢	6.00	4.50
☐R112	25¢	.95	.65
☐R113	30¢	58.00	43.00
☐R114	40¢	30.00	22.00
☐R115	50¢	1.60	.72
☐R116	60¢	63.00	41.00
☐R117	70¢	28.00	17.00
☐R118	$1	4.00	2.60
☐R119	$1.30	232.00	150.00
☐R120	$1.50	13.00	9.00
☐R121	$1.60	295.00	201.00
☐R122	$1.90	130.00	79.00
☐R123	$2	13.00	9.00
☐R124	$2.50	24.00	17.00
☐R125	$3	31.00	21.00
☐R126	$3.50	120.00	87.00
☐R127	$5	15.00	9.00
☐R128	$10	113.00	64.00
☐R129	$20	340.00	221.00
☐R130	$25	310.00	195.00
☐R131	$50	350.00	213.00

Scott No.		Fine Used Each	Ave. Used Each

1871–1872. THIRD ISSUE SAME DESIGNS AS SECOND ISSUE

☐R134	1¢ Claret & Blk. .	21.00	12.00
☐R135	2¢ Org. & Blk.	.15	.11
☐R136	4¢ Bm. & Blk. . .	31.00	19.00
☐R137	5¢ Org. & Blk.	.82	.48
☐R138	6¢ Rog. & Blk. . .	25.00	15.00
☐R139	15¢ Bm. & Blk. . .	9.10	4.60
☐R140	30¢ Org. & Blk. . .	13.00	8.00
☐R141	40¢ Bm. & Blk. . .	17.00	12.00
☐R142	60¢ Org. & Blk. . .	42.00	26.00
☐R143	70¢ Gm. & Blk. . .	32.00	21.00
☐R144	$1 Gm. & Blk. . . .	1.60	.93
☐R145	$2 Verm'n & Blk..	24.00	16.00
☐R146	$2.50 Claret & Blk. .	30.00	18.00
☐			
☐R147	$3 Gm. & Blk. . .	31.00	20.00
☐R148	$5 Verm'n & Blk..	21.00	13.00
☐R149	$10 Gm. & Blk. . .	97.00	60.00
☐R150	$20 Org. & Blk. .	370.00	252.00

1874. FOURTH ISSUE

☐R151	2¢ Org. & Blk, Gm. Paper	.12	.10

1875. ISSUE

☐R152a	2¢ Blue, Silk Paper . .	.12	.10
☐R152b	2¢ Blue, Watermarked	.12	.10
☐R152c	2¢ Blue, Rouletted	27.00	18.00

Scott No.		Fine Un-cancelled Each	Ave. Un-cancelled Each	Fine Used Each	Ave. Used Each

1898. POSTAGE AND NEWSPAPER STAMPS SURCHARGED I.R.

☐ R153	1¢ Green, Small I.R.	1.45	.85	1.15	.67
☐ R154	1¢ Green, Large I.R.	.35	.22	.30	.17
☐ R154a	1¢ Green Inverted Surch	7.75	4.60	6.00	3.80
☐ R155	2¢ Carmine, Large I.R.	.35	.17	.16	.09
☐ R155a	2¢ Carmine, Inverted Surch	1.25	.75	.98	.65
☐ R159	$5 Blue, Surch. down	178.00	106.00	141.00	107.00
☐ R160	$5 Blue, Surch. up	82.00	51.00	56.00	38.00

1898. DOCUMENTARY "BATTLESHIP" DESIGN

☐ R161	½¢ Orange	1.90	1.30	7.00	5.00
☐ R162	½¢ Dark Gray	.22	.13	.16	.11
☐ R163	1¢ Pale Blue	.11	.08	.12	.09
☐ R164	2¢ Carmine	.11	.07	.12	.09
☐ R165	3¢ Dark Blue	.65	.45	.19	.13
☐ R166	4¢ Pale Rose	.60	.32	.19	.13
☐ R167	5¢ Lilac	.50	.27	.12	.11
☐ R168	10¢ Dark Brown	.54	.30	.12	.11
☐ R169	25¢ Purple Brown	.53	.30	.16	.15
☐ R170	40¢ Blue Lilac (cut .25)	31.00	19.00	1.40	1.06
☐ R171	50¢ Slate Violet	1.65	1.05	.22	.15
☐ R172	80¢ Bistre (cut .15)	12.00	7.00	.50	.26

1898–1899. DOCUMENTARY STAMPS

☐ R173	$1 Dark Green	3.50	1.75	.60	.30
☐ R174	$3 Dark Brown (cut .18)	4.60	2.80	.40	.26
☐ R175	$5 Orange (cut .25)	—	—	1.35	.84
☐ R176	$10 Black (cut .75)	—	—	3.10	2.15
☐ R177	$30 Red (cut 25.00)	—	—	73.00	45.00
☐ R178	$50 Gray Brown (cut 1.50)	—	—	4.50	2.50
☐ R179	$100 Brown & Black (cut 12.00)	—	—	32.00	19.50
☐ R180	$500 Lake & Black (cut 180.00)	—	—	466.00	330.00
☐ R181	$100 Green & Black (cut 100.00)	—	—	356.00	255.00

1900. DOCUMENTARY STAMPS

☐ R182	$1 Carmine (cut .15)	4.50	2.80	.62	.42
☐ R183	$3 Lake (cut 8.00)	57.00	36.00	41.00	25.00

1900-1902. SURCHARGED LARGE BLACK NUMERALS

☐ R184	$1 Gray (cut .09)	2.10	1.30	.26	.18
☐ R185	$2 Gray (cut .09)	2.40	1.60	.26	.18
☐ R186	$3 Gray (cut 1.15)	21.00	13.00	11.00	7.00
☐ R187	$5 Gray (cut .40)	10.00	7.00	4.00	2.60
☐ R188	$10 Gray (cut 3.25)	44.00	29.00	10.00	6.00
☐ R189	$50 Gray (cut 80.00)	540.00	340.00	330.00	212.00
☐ R190	$1 Green (cut .35)	4.10	2.60	2.00	1.12
☐ R191	$2 Green (cut .30)	4.10	2.30	1.40	.85
☐ R192	$5 Green (cut 1.60)	25.00	15.00	12.00	8.00
☐ R193	$10 Green (cut 27.50)	215.00	140.00	150.00	91.00
☐ R194	$50 Green (cut 220.00)	955.00	610.00	675.00	435.00

Scott No.		Fine Un- cancelled Each	Ave. Un- cancelled Each	Fine Used Each	Ave. Used Each

1914. DOCUMENTARY SINGLE LINE WATERMARK

☐R195	½¢ Rose	3.80	2.40	1.85	1.25
☐R196	1¢ Rose	1.25	.67	.22	.15
☐R197	2¢ Rose	1.25	.67	.22	.15
☐R198	3¢ Rose	23.00	15.00	18.00	12.00
☐R199	4¢ Rose	5.50	3.85	.89	.65
☐R200	5¢ Rose	1.76	1.22	.35	.18
☐R201	10¢ Rose	1.65	1.00	.25	.12
☐R202	25¢ Rose	9.10	6.60	.65	.39
☐R203	40¢ Rose	7.70	5.00	.83	.52
☐R204	50¢ Rose	2.60	1.40	.50	.33
☐R205	80¢ Rose	32.00	22.00	6.30	4.00

1914. DOCUMENTARY DOUBLE LINE WATERMARK

☐R206	½¢ Rose	1.28	.83	.70	.47
☐R207	1¢ Rose	.16	.13	.12	.08
☐R208	2¢ Rose	.21	.12	.11	.07
☐R209	3¢ Rose	.86	.46	.34	.19
☐R210	4¢ Rose	1.80	1.15	.52	.30
☐R211	5¢ Rose	.85	.50	.18	.12
☐R212	10¢ Rose	.62	.45	.12	.08
☐R213	25¢ Rose	3.10	1.80	.87	.46
☐R214	40¢ Rose (cut .60)	26.00	17.00	5.60	3.30
☐R215	50¢ Rose	7.00	3.75	.29	.16
☐R216	80¢ Rose (cut 1.10)	33.00	22.00	7.30	5.00
☐R217	$1 Green (cut .06)	5.00	2.00	.26	.16
☐R218	$2 Carmine (cut .10)	12.75	7.50	.55	.29
☐R219	$2 Carmine (cut .25)	23.00	16.00	1.70	.92
☐R220	$5 Blue (cut .65)	22.00	13.00	2.10	1.30
☐R221	$10 Orange (cut 1.10)	39.00	26.00	5.50	3.50
☐R222	$30 Vermilion (cut 2.35)	103.00	76.00	12.00	7.75
☐R223	$50 Violet (cut 200.00)	835.00	560.00	600.00	412.00
☐R224	$60 Brown (cut 47.50)	—	—	111.00	69.00
☐R225	$100 Green (cut 14.50)	—	—	44.00	29.00

1917–1933. TENTH ISSUE DOCUMENTARY STAMPS—PERF. 11

☐R228	1¢ Rose	.24	.13	.15	.09
☐R229	2¢ Rose	.11	.07	.11	.07
☐R230	3¢ Rose	.55	.30	.31	.17
☐R231	4¢ Rose	.26	.16	.14	.07
☐R232	5¢ Rose	.27	.16	.14	.08
☐R233	8¢ Rose	1.80	1.24	.21	.12
☐R234	10¢ Rose	.50	.20	.13	.08
☐R235	20¢ Rose	.72	.38	.14	.08
☐R236	25¢ Rose	1.12	.60	.13	.09
☐R237	40¢ Rose	.97	.50	.15	.09
☐R238	50¢ Rose	1.29	.68	.14	.09
☐R239	80¢ Rose	3.10	2.15	.14	.08

Scott No.		Fine Un-cancelled Each	Ave. Un-cancelled Each	Fine Used Each	Ave. Used Each
☐R240	$1 Green	2.65	1.65	.12	.07
☐R241	$2 Rose	7.75	5.10	.15	.09
☐R242	$3 Violet (cut .15)	19.00	12.10	.75	.45
☐R243	$4 Brown (cut .20)	12.00	6.50	1.55	.93
☐R244	$5 Blue (cut .13)	8.50	6.00	.27	.17
☐R245	$10 Orange (cut .20)	13.50	10.00	.73	.45

1917 DOCUMENTARY STAMPS—PERF. 12

☐R246	$30 Vermilion (cut .80)	29.00	18.00	2.60	1.60
☐R247	$60 Brown (cut 1.00)	39.00	25.00	7.70	4.90
☐R248	$100 Green (cut .45)	25.00	18.00	1.50	.76
☐R249	$500 Blue (cut 9.50)	—	—	34.00	23.00
☐R250	$1000 Orange (cut 3.50)	90.00	62.00	11.00	7.50

1928–1929 DOCUMENTARY STAMPS—PERF. 10

☐R251	1¢ Carmine Rose	1.45	1.00	.53	.33
☐R252	2¢ Carmine Rose	.35	.16	.17	.12
☐R253	4¢ Carmine Rose	4.50	3.10	2.80	1.70
☐R254	5¢ Carmine Rose	.90	.55	.27	.17
☐R255	10¢ Carmine Rose	1.10	.65	.69	.48
☐R256	20¢ Carmine Rose	3.10	2.10	1.90	1.20
☐R257	$1 Green (cut 1.90)	46.00	32.00	28.00	16.00
☐R258	$2 Rose	8.50	5.50	.85	.55
☐R259	$10 Orange (cut 8.00)	43.00	31.00	14.00	9.85

1929–1930 DOCUMENTARY STAMPS—PERF. 11 x 10

☐R260	2¢ Carmine Rose	1.85	1.20	1.10	.65
☐R261	5¢ Carmine Rose	1.60	1.00	.95	.60
☐R262	10¢ Carmine Rose	6.50	4.00	3.60	2.90
☐R263	20¢ Carmine Rose	12.00	7.50	5.50	4.40

Scott No.		Fine Used Each Violet Paper (a)	Ave. Used Each	Fine Used Each Green Paper (b)	Ave. Used Each

1871–1874 PROPRIETARY (ALL USED)

☐RB1	1¢ Green & Black	3.40	2.60	5.60	4.05
☐RB2	2¢ Green & Black	5.50	3.60	9.10	7.10
☐RB3	3¢ Green & Black	8.75	6.00	32.00	18.75
☐RB4	4¢ Green & Black	6.50	4.25	12.00	8.75
☐RB5	4¢ Green & Black	114.00	72.00	102.00	71.00
☐RB6	6¢ Green & Black	32.00	20.00	86.00	62.00
☐RB7	10¢ Green & Black	157.00	100.00	36.00	24.00
☐RB8	50¢ Green & Black	695.00	510.00	880.00	655.00

Scott No.		Silk Paper (a) Fine	Ave.	Watermarked (b) Fine	Ave.	Rouletted (c) Fine	Ave.

1875–1881 PROPRIETARY STAMPS (ALL USED)

☐RB11	1¢ Green	1.85	1.05	.50	.34	33.00	22.00
☐RB12	2¢ Brown	2.05	1.30	2.00	1.20	44.00	30.00

Scott No.			Silk Paper (a) Fine	Ave.	Watermarked (b) Fine	Ave.	Rouletted (c) Fine	Ave.
☐ RB13	3¢	Orange	12.75	10.00	2.85	1.70	53.00	35.00
☐ RB14	4¢	Red Brown	4.60	3.00	3.90	2.70	—	—
☐ RB15	4¢	Red	—	—	4.40	3.10	55.00	39.00
☐ RB16	5¢	Black	88.00	58.00	76.00	52.00	631.00	422.00
☐ RB17	6¢	Violet Blue	21.00	13.00	14.00	9.50	142.00	96.00
☐ RB18	6¢	Violet	—	—	22.00	13.00	172.00	115.00
☐ RB19	10¢	Blue	—	—	186.00	111.00	—	—

Scott No.			Fine Un- cancelled Each	Ave. Un- cancelled Each	Fine Used Each	Ave. Used Each
1898 PROPRIETARY STAMPS (BATTLESHIP)						
☐ RB20	⅛¢	Yellow Green	.13	.10	.11	.08
☐ RB21	¼¢	Pale Green	.16	.10	.11	.08
☐ RB22	⅜¢	Deep Orange	.25	.17	.28	.16
☐ RB23	⅝¢	Deep Ultramarine	.26	.15	.21	.14
☐ RB24	1¢	Dark Green	.37	.20	.42	.16
☐ RB25	1¼¢	Violet	.21	.10	.20	.11
☐ RB26	1⅞¢	Dull Blue	1.45	.75	1.30	.70
☐ RB27	2¢	Violet Brown	.60	.35	.65	.35
☐ RB28	2½¢	Lake	.42	.28	.27	.15
☐ RB29	3¾¢	Olive Gray	3.90	2.50	2.60	1.75
☐ RB30	4¢	Purple	1.45	.90	1.45	.75
☐ RB31	5¢	Brown Orange	1.75	1.00	1.10	.74
1914 BLACK PROPRIETARY STAMPS—S.L. WTMK.						
☐ RB32	⅛¢	Black	.37	.23	.34	.19
☐ RB33	¼¢	Black	1.20	.73	.82	.62
☐ RB34	⅜¢	Black	.37	.23	.35	.22
☐ RB35	⅝¢	Black	2.60	1.60	2.35	1.20
☐ RB36	1¼¢	Black	1.35	.66	1.20	.65
☐ RB37	1⅞¢	Black	18.75	13.00	13.00	8.50
☐ RB38	2¼¢	Black	2.60	1.50	3.50	1.25
☐ RB39	3⅛¢	Black	51.00	35.00	33.00	22.00
☐ RB40	3¾¢	Black	14.00	8.00	9.00	6.00
☐ RB41	4¢	Black	33.00	21.00	19.00	13.00
☐ RB42	4⅜¢	Black	735.00	525.00	—	—
☐ RB43	5¢	Black	87.00	52.00	42.00	31.00
1914 BLACK PROPRIETARY STAMPS—D.L. WTMK.						
☐ RB44	⅛¢	Black	.18	.13	.14	.09
☐ RB45	¼¢	Black	.18	.13	.14	.10
☐ RB46	⅜¢	Black	.78	.60	.76	.42
☐ RB47	½¢	Black	2.70	1.65	2.10	1.27
☐ RB48	⅝¢	Black	.15	.09	.15	.10
☐ RB49	1¢	Black	4.00	2.45	1.90	1.34
☒ RB50	1¼¢	Black	.34	.21	.45	.23
☐ RB51	1½¢	Black	2.50	1.65	2.10	1.45
☐ RB52	1⅞¢	Black	.83	.52	.52	.33
☐ RB53	2¢	Black	5.10	3.40	4.20	2.80

Scott No.		Fine Un-cancelled Each	Ave. Un-cancelled Each	Fine Used Each	Ave. Used Each
☐ RB54	2½¢ Black	1.20	.75	.99	.65
☐ RB55	3¢ Black	2.80	1.95	3.10	1.90
☐ RB56	3⅛¢ Black	3.65	2.25	2.85	1.85
☐ RB57	3¾¢ Black	9.00	6.00	6.10	4.60
☐ RB58	4¢ Black	.33	.18	.25	.15
☐ RB59	4⅜¢ Black	8.00	5.90	6.10	4.25
☐ RB60	5¢ Black	1.95	1.25	1.65	.90
☐ RB61	6¢ Black	43.00	26.00	26.00	18.00
☐ RB62	8¢ Black	13.50	9.50	8.50	6.30
☐ RB63	10¢ Black	8.90	5.90	5.70	4.00
☐ RB64	20¢ Black	17.00	11.50	11.50	7.90

1919 PROPRIETARY STAMPS

☐ RB65	1¢ Dark Blue	.11	.09	.12	.08
☐ RB66	2¢ Dark Blue	.14	.10	.12	.08
☐ RB67	3¢ Dark Blue	1.05	.62	.72	.37
☐ RB68	4¢ Dark Blue	1.20	.66	.72	.37
☐ RB69	5¢ Dark Blue	1.20	.66	.72	.37
☐ RB70	8¢ Dark Blue	11.00	7.75	6.50	4.65
☐ RB71	10¢ Dark Blue	2.05	1.20	2.50	1.20
☐ RB72	20¢ Dark Blue	5.10	3.10	3.30	2.05
☐ RB73	40¢ Dark Blue	20.00	11.75	6.00	3.90

1918–1934 FUTURE DELIVERY STAMPS

☐ RC1	2¢ Carmine Rose	.15	.11	.12	.08
☐ RC2	3¢ Carmine Rose (cut 7.50)	32.00	20.00	18.00	12.00
☐ RC3	4¢ Carmine Rose	.42	.40	.12	.08
☐ RC3A	5¢ Carmine Rose	—	—	2.30	1.35
☐ RC4	10¢ Carmine Rose	.57	.39	.10	.08
☐ RC5	20¢ Carmine Rose	.78	.52	.11	.08
☐ RC6	25¢ Carmine Rose (cut .10)	3.35	2.15	.53	.32
☐ RC7	40¢ Carmine Rose (cut .10)	3.90	2.60	.53	.32
☐ RC8	50¢ Carmine Rose	1.25	.72	.30	.17
☐ RC9	80¢ Carmine Rose (cut .75)	9.70	6.60	3.60	2.20
☐ RC10	$1 Green (cut .10)	—	—	.22	.11
☐ RC11	$2 Rose (cut .08)	—	—	.25	.17
☐ RC12	$3 Violet (cut .12)	—	—	.77	.52
☐ RC13	$5 Dark Blue (cut .09)	—	—	.35	.20
☐ RC14	$10 Orange (cut .20)	—	—	.86	.55
☐ RC15	$20 Olive Bistre (cut .50)	—	—	3.80	2.50
☐ RC16	$30 Vermilion (cut .95)	—	—	4.90	3.10
☐ RC17	$50 Olive Green (cut .30)	—	—	.66	.47
☐ RC18	$60 Brown (cut .55)	—	—	2.40	1.20
☐ RC19	$100 Yellow Green (cut 5.00)	—	—	24.00	14.75
☐ RC20	$500 Blue (cut 3.00)	—	—	12.00	8.75
☐ RC21	$1000 Orange (cut 1.60)	—	7.50	7.00	4.75
☐ RC22	1¢ Carmine Rose Narrow Overprint	.13	.08	.13	.09
☐ RC23	80¢ Narrow Overprint (cut .20)	—	—	1.25	.98

Scott No.		Fine Uncancelled Each	Ave. Uncancelled Each	Fine Used Each	Ave. Used Each
☐ RC25	$1 Serif Overprint (cut .08)	1.95	1.34	.32	.20
☐ RC26	$10 Serif Overprint (cut 4.50)	—	—	4.85	3.80

1918–1929 STOCK TRANSFER STAMPS—PERF. 11 or 12

☐ RD1	1¢ Carmine Rose, Perf. 11	.42	.28	.22	.14
☐ RD2	2¢ Carmine Rose, Perf. 11	.43	.24	.13	.08
☐ RD3	4¢ Carmine Rose, Perf. 11	.19	.15	.14	.09
☐ RD4	5¢ Carmine Rose, Perf. 11	.34	.20	.13	.08
☐ RD5	10¢ Carmine Rose, Perf. 11	.18	.15	.14	.09
☐ RD6	20¢ Carmine Rose, Perf. 11	.28	.16	.13	.08
☐ RD7	25¢ Carmine Rose, Perf. 12 (cut .07)	.96	.52	.21	.13
☐ RD8	40¢ Carmine Rose, Perf. 11	1.05	.50	.14	.09
☐ RD9	50¢ Carmine Rose, Perf. 11	.32	.20	.14	.09
☐ RD10	80¢ Carmine Rose, Perf. 11 (cut .07)	1.38	.62	.26	.25
☐ RD11	$1 Green, perf. 11, Red Ovpt. (cut .40)	16.75	11.00	9.50	6.90
☐ RD12	$1 Green, Perf. 11, Black Ovpt	1.05	.55	.14	.09
☐ RD13	$2 Rose, Perf. 11	.98	.40	.13	.07
☐ RD14	$3 Violet, Perf. 11 (cut .17)	4.60	2.70	1.20	.68
☐ RD15	$4 Y. Brown, Perf. 11 (cut .07)	1.87	1.15	.13	.07
☐ RD16	$5 Blue, Perf. 11 (cut .07)	1.87	1.15	.14	.08
☐ RD17	$10 Orange, Perf. 11 (cut .07)	3.40	2.00	.36	.21
☐ RD18	$20 Bistre, Perf. 11 (cut 4.25)	19.00	13.00	.16	9.50
☐ RD19	$30 Vermilion (cut 1.05)	18.00	12.00	6.00	3.10
☐ RD20	$50 Olive Green (cut 9.75)	68.00	49.00	54.00	39.00
☐ RD21	$60 Brown (cut 4.60)	52.00	34.00	23.00	18.00
☐ RD22	$100 Green (cut 1.10)	18.00	11.00	5.00	2.90
☐ RD23	$500 Blue (cut 38.00)	—	—	115.00	63.00
☐ RD24	$1000 Orange (cut 10.00)	—	—	77.00	53.00
☐ RD25	2¢ Carmine Rose, Perf. 10	.29	.20	.11	.09
☐ RD26	4¢ Carmine Rose, Perf. 10	.29	.20	.11	.09
☐ RD27	10¢ Carmine Rose, Perf. 10	.38	.24	.10	.08
☐ RD28	20¢ Carmine Rose, Perf. 10	.38	.25	.11	.08
☐ RD29	50¢ Carmine Rose, Perf. 10	.62	.42	.19	.13
☐ RD30	$1 Green, Perf. 10	.29	.21	.11	.09
☐ RD31	$2 Rose, Perf. 10	.31	.21	.10	.08
☐ RD32	$10 Orange, Perf. 10 (cut .07)	2.60	1.60	.29	.17

1919–1928
STOCK TRANSFER STAMPS, SERIF OVERPRINT

☐ RD33	2¢ Carmine Rose, Perf. 11	1.60	.89	.76	.52
☐ RD34	10¢ Carmine Rose, Perf. 11	.45	.22	.10	.07
☐ RD35	20¢ Carmine Rose, Perf. 11	.40	.22	.11	.08
☐ RD36	50¢ Carmine Rose, Perf. 11	.92	.72	.35	.26
☐ RD37	$1 Green, Perf. 11 (cut. 11)	4.85	2.75	3.60	3.20
☐ RD38	$2 Rose, Perf. 11 (cut .12)	3.00	1.90	2.10	1.35
☐ RD39	2¢ Carmine Rose, Perf. 10	.40	.17	.14	.10
☐ RD40	10¢ Carmine Rose, Perf. 10	.35	.17	.11	.07
☐ RD41	20¢ Carmine Rose, Perf. 10	.62	.32	.10	.07

Scott No.		Fine Unused Block	Ave. Unused Block	Fine Unused Each	Ave. Unused Each	Fine Used Each	Ave. Used Each
CONFEDERATE STATES OF AMERICA (N.H. ADD 80%)							
☐1	5¢ J. Davis, Green	—	1060.00	222.00	137.00	121.00	74.00
☐2	10¢ Jefferson, Blue	—	1770.00	305.00	212.00	215.00	148.00
☐3	2¢ Jackson, Green	—	—	605.00	435.00	760.00	580.00
☐4	5¢ J. Davis, Blue	786.00	555.00	122.00	74.00	116.00	74.00
☐5	10¢ Jefferson, Rose	—	—	980.00	656.00	680.00	432.00
☐6	5¢ Davis, Lon. Print	87.00	62.00	15.00	9.00	20.00	14.00
☐7	5¢ Davis, Local Print	137.00	93.00	21.00	13.00	24.00	16.00
1863							
☐8	2¢ Jackson, Br. Red	612.00	415.00	74.00	52.00	350.00	250.00
☐9	10¢ Davis (len)	—	—	837.00	611.00	631.00	444.00
☐10	10¢ Davis (w fr. lin.)	—	—	3310.00	1985.00	1755.00	1180.00
☐11	10¢ Davis (no fr.)	84.00	64.00	14.00	8.75	19.00	13.00
☐12	10¢ Davis (fill. com)	126.00	102.00	17.00	10.00	21.00	16.00
☐13	20¢ Washington	485.00	356.00	61.00	41.50	317.00	233.00
1862							
☐14	1¢ J.C. Calhoun	1200.00	777.00	152.00	112.00	—	—

Scott No.		Fine Plate Block	Block	Fine Unused Each	Fine Used Each
1935. "FARLEY SPECIAL PRINTINGS"					
☐752	3¢ Newburgh	19.00	1.07	.21	.23
☐753	3¢ Byrd, Perf	28.00	3.25	.63	.69
☐754	3¢ Mother's Day	28.00	5.10	.91	.82
☐755	3¢ Wisconsin	29.00	5.10	.82	.83
☐756	1¢ Park	8.75	1.55	.31	.26
☐757	2¢ Park	12.00	3.05	.41	.36
☐758	3¢ Park	26.00	6.30	.73	.72
☐759	4¢ Park	35.00	11.00	1.76	1.87
☐760	5¢ Park	35.00	19.00	3.10	2.16
☐761	6¢ Park	69.00	22.00	3.30	2.11
☐762	7¢ Park	71.00	20.00	2.95	2.12
☐763	8¢ Park	71.00	20.00	2.90	2.06
☐764	9¢ Park	69.00	23.00	3.25	1.92
☐765	10¢ Park	76.00	34.00	5.60	4.60
☐766a	1¢ Chicago	—	5.10	.86	.72
☐767a	3¢ Chicago	—	6.00	.84	.66
☐768a	3¢ Byrd	—	29.00	3.77	2.22
☐769a	1¢ Park	—	16.00	1.83	1.71
☐770a	3¢ Park	—	43.00	3.12	3.60
☐771	16¢ Air Spec. Del	132.00	34.00	3.00	3.25

1935. FARLEY POSITION BLOCKS AND PAIRS

Scott No.		Center Line Block	Fine Arrow Block	Block W/Vert. Line	Pair W/Vert. Line	Block W/Horiz. Line	Fair W/Horiz. Line
☐ 752	3¢ Newburgh	51.00	81.00	20.00	9.00	13.00	4.65
☐ 753	3¢ Byrd	112.00	171.00	96.00	45.00	4.00	1.80
☐ 754	3¢ Mother's Day	12.00	16.00	4.60	2.50	4.70	2.22
☐ 755	3¢ Wisconsin	12.00	16.00	4.30	2.50	4.70	2.22
☐ 756	1¢ Park	4.75	8.00	1.85	.86	1.34	.84
☐ 757	2¢ Park	7.00	11.00	1.85	1.30	2.50	1.15
☐ 758	3¢ Park	9.10	15.00	4.10	1.65	4.10	1.60
☐ 759	4¢ Park	14.00	44.00	9.10	3.60	8.10	3.80
☐ 760	5¢ Park	21.00	54.00	16.00	6.10	13.00	5.10
☐ 761	6¢ Park	28.00	87.00	20.00	8.10	17.00	7.15
☐ 762	7¢ Park	24.00	61.00	17.00	6.00	13.00	5.10
☐ 763	8¢ Park	26.00	65.00	18.00	6.10	14.00	5.05
☐ 764	9¢ Park	27.00	70.00	20.00	7.20	17.00	6.40
☐ 765	10¢ Park	44.00	211.00	31.00	16.00	30.00	13.00
☐ 766a	1¢ Chicago	21.00	—	23.00	9.10	13.00	7.60
☐ 767a	3¢ Chicago	19.00	—	17.00	7.80	10.00	7.50
☐ 768a	3¢ Byrd	22.00	—	17.00	13.00	14.00	8.80
☐ 769a	1¢ Park	14.00	—	16.00	6.50	10.00	5.25
☐ 770a	3¢ Park	32.00	—	19.00	14.00	21.00	14.10
☐ 771	16¢ Air Spec. Del	89.00	136.00	25.00	9.10	21.00	9.00

HUNTING PERMIT STAMPS

Scott No.		Fine Plate Block	Ave. Plate Block	Fine Unused Each	Ave. Unused Each	Fine Used Each	Ave. Used Each
☐ RW1 (1934)	$1 Blue	3130.00	2410.00	216.00	145.00	52.00	36.00
☐ RW2 (1935)	$1 Rose Lake	4520.00	3815.00	280.00	187.00	108.00	64.00
☐ RW3 (1936)	$1 Brown Blk.	1960.00	1360.00	150.00	92.00	45.00	32.00
☐ RW4 (1937)	$1 Lt. Green	1280.00	1010.00	105.00	70.00	21.00	14.00
☐ RW5 (1938)	$1 Lt. Violet	1305.00	985.00	120.00	70.00	22.00	14.00
☐ RW6 (1939)	$1 Chocolate	852.00	676.00	83.00	54.00	22.00	15.00
☐ RW7 (1940)	$1 Sepia	863.00	692.00	73.00	48.00	15.00	9.60
☐ RW8 (1941)	$1 Brn. Carmine	777.00	633.00	72.00	46.00	15.00	11.00
☐ RW9 (1942)	$1 Violet Brn.	777.00	633.00	72.00	46.00	15.00	11.00
☐ RW10 (1943)	$1 Deep Rose	322.00	205.00	40.00	27.00	13.00	9.00
☐ RW11 (1944)	$1 Red Org.	305.00	191.00	37.00	25.00	9.10	7.00

Scott No.		Fine Plate Block	Ave. Plate Block	Fine Unused Each	Ave. Unused Each	Fine Used Each	Ave. Used Each
☐ RW12 (1945)	$1 Black	206.00	134.00	24.00	16.00	8.00	6.50
☐ RW13 (1946)	$1 Red Brn	220.00	146.00	23.00	17.00	7.50	5.50
☐ RW14 (1947)	$1 Black	220.00	146.00	23.00	17.00	7.50	5.50
☐ RW15 (1948)	$1 Brt. Blue	220.00	146.00	23.00	17.00	7.50	5.50
☐ RW16 (1949)	$2 Brt. Green	287.00	196.00	44.00	30.00	7.20	4.80
☐ RW17 (1950)	$2 Violet	287.00	196.00	44.00	30.00	7.20	4.80
☐ RW18 (1951)	$2 Gray Blk	287.00	196.00	44.00	30.00	7.20	4.80
☐ RW19 (1952)	$2 Ultramarine	287.00	196.00	44.00	30.00	7.20	4.80
☐ RW20 (1953)	$2 Dk. Rose Brn.	305.00	205.00	50.00	35.00	7.10	4.80
☐ RW21 (1954)	$2 Black	305.00	205.00	50.00	35.00	7.10	4.80
☐ RW22 (1955)	$2 Dk. Blue	305.00	205.00	50.00	35.00	7.10	4.80
☐ RW23 (1956)	$2 Black	305.00	205.00	50.00	35.00	7.10	4.80
☐ RW24 (1957)	$2 Emerald	305.00	205.00	50.00	35.00	7.10	4.80
☐ RW25 (1958)	$2 Black	305.00	205.00	50.00	35.00	5.30	4.00
☐ RW26 (1959)	$3 Bl./Ochre/Blk.	305.00	205.00	64.00	46.00	5.30	4.10
☐ RW27 (1960)	$3 Red Brn./Bl./Bist	305.00	205.00	64.00	46.00	5.30	4.10
☐ RW28 (1961)	$3 Bl./Bist./Brn.	330.00	220.00	81.00	52.00	5.30	4.10
☐ RW29 (1962)	$3 Bl./Brn./Blk	360.00	240.00	91.00	64.00	5.30	4.10
☐ RW30 (1963)	$3 Blk./Bl. Yel./Grn	360.00	240.00	91.00	64.00	5.30	4.10
☐ RW31 (1964)	$3 Bl./Blk./Bist	2400.00	1785.00	86.00	61.00	4.45	3.40
☐ RW32 (1965)	$3 Grn./Blk./Brn	380.00	250.00	81.00	56.00	4.45	3.40
☐ RW33 (1966)	$3 Bl./Grn./Blk.	340.00	222.00	79.00	56.00	4.45	3.40
☐ RW34 (1967)	$3 Multicolored	333.00	222.00	81.00	51.00	4.45	3.40
☐ RW35 (1968)	$3 Grn./Blk./Brn.	162.00	111.00	44.00	31.00	4.45	3.40

Scott No.		Fine Plate Block	Ave. Plate Block	Fine Unused Each	Ave. Unused Each	Fine Used Each	Ave. Used Each
☐ RW36 (1969)	$3 Multicolored	162.00	111.00	44.00	31.00	4.50	3.40
☐ RW37 (1970)	$3 Multicolored	162.00	111.00	32.00	19.00	4.50	3.40
☐ RW38 (1971)	$3 Multicolored	162.00	111.00	28.00	21.00	4.50	3.40
☐ RW39 (1972)	$5 Multicolored	121.00	81.00	21.00	13.00	4.50	3.40
☐ RW40 (1973)	$5 Multicolored	81.00	61.00	19.00	12.00	4.50	3.40
☐ RW41 (1974)	$5 Multicolored	81.00	53.00	14.00	11.00	4.50	3.40
☐ RW42 (1975)	$5 Multicolored	77.00	51.00	13.00	11.00	4.50	3.40
☐ RW43 (1976)	$5 Emerald & Blk.	71.00	46.00	13.00	11.00	460.00	4.10
☐ RW44 (1977)	$5 Multicolored	71.00	46.00	13.00	11.00	460.00	4.10
☐ RW45 (1978)	$5 Multicolored	66.00	45.00	13.00	11.00	460.00	4.10
☐ RW46 (1979)	$7.50 Multicolored	66.00	43.00	12.00	8.25	460.00	4.10
☐ RW47 (1980)	$7.50 Multicolored	62.00	41.00	12.00	7.50	4.10	3.05
☐ RW48 (1981)	$7.50 Multicolored	62.00	41.00	11.00	7.25	4.10	3.05

Scott No.		Fine Unused Each	Ave. Unused Each	Fine Used Each	Ave. Used Each

HAWAII
1851–1952. "MISSIONARIES"

			Fine Unused Each	Ave. Unused Each	Fine Used Each	Ave. Used Each
☐ 1	2¢	Blue	—	275,000.00	—	200,000.00
☐		On Cover				250,000
☐ 2	5¢	Blue	—	32,000.00		16,000.00
☐		On Cover				24,000.00
☐ 3	13¢	Blue	—	18,000.00		10,000.00
☐		On Cover				15,750.00
☐ 4	13¢	Blue	—	45,000.00	—	20,000.00
☐		On Cover				26,000.00

NOTE: Prices on the above classic stamps of Hawaii vary greatly depending on the individual specimen and circumstances of sale.

NOTE: Beware of fake cancels on Hawaiian stamps, when the value is higher used than unused.

Scott No.		Fine Unused Each	Ave. Unused Each	Fine Used Each	Ave. Used Each
1853. KING KAMEHAMEHA III					
☐5	5¢ Blue	—	510.00	—	310.00
☐6	13¢ Dark Red	—	310.00	—	300.00
☐7	5¢ on 13¢ Dark Red	—	3300.00	—	3750.00
1857.					
☐8	5¢ Blue	—	180.00	—	180.00
1861.					
☐9	5¢ Blue	—	80.00	—	80.00
1868. RE-ISSUE					
☐10	5¢ Blue	—	18.00	—	—
☐11	13¢ Rose	—	155.00	—	—
1859–1862.					
☐12	1¢ Light Blue	—	2500.00	—	2675.00
☐13	2¢ Light Blue	—	1910.00	—	1150.00
☐14	2¢ Black	—	2500.00	—	1000.00
1863.					
☐15	1¢ Black	—	160.00	—	185.00
☐16	2¢ Black	—	370.00	—	320.00
☐17	2¢ Dark Blue	—	3100.00	—	1475.00
☐18	2¢ Black	—	660.00	—	1150.00
1864–1865.					
☐19	1¢ Black	—	245.00	—	395.00
☐20	2¢ Black	—	245.00	—	390.00
☐21	5¢ Blue	—	182.00	—	185.00
☐22	5¢ Blue	—	154.00	—	160.00
1864. LAID PAPER					
☐23	1¢ Black	165.00	115.00	510.00	333.00
☐24	2¢ Black	165.00	115.00	510.00	345.00
1865. WOVE PAPER					
☐25	1¢ Blue	172.00	106.00	133.00	99.00
☐26	2¢ Blue	145.00	102.00	133.00	99.00
☐27	2¢ Rose	182.00	116.00	111.00	82.00
☐28	2¢ Rose Vert	182.00	116.00	111.00	82.00
1869. ENGRAVED					
☐29	2¢ Red	56.00	37.00	—	—

Scott No.		Fine Unused Each	Ave. Unused Each	Fine Used Each	Ave. Used Each
1864–1871.					
☐30	1¢ Purple	8.50	7.00	6.60	6.00
☐31	2¢ Vermilion	11.00	8.00	6.50	5.00
☐32	5¢ Blue	52.00	33.00	19.00	12.00
☐33	6¢ Green	20.00	14.00	7.00	5.50
☐34	18¢ Rose	91.00	58.00	18.00	11.00
1875.					
☐35	2¢ Brown	8.00	4.50	2.75	1.70
☐36	12¢ Black	44.00	28.00	22.00	14.00
☐37	1¢ Blue	5.50	4.00	6.00	3.60
☐38	2¢ Lilac Rose	90.00	54.00	33.00	19.00
☐39	5¢ Ultramarine	14.00	8.00	3.00	1.75
☐40	10¢ Black	23.00	15.00	17.00	11.00
☐41	15¢ Red Brown	42.00	26.00	25.00	16.00
1883–1886.					
☐42	1¢ Green	2.60	1.60	1.85	1.22
☐43	2¢ Rose	4.00	2.50	1.20	.72
☐44	10¢ Red Brown	19.00	13.00	11.00	6.60
☐45	10¢ Vermilion	20.00	13.00	15.00	9.50
☐46	12¢ Red Lilac	64.00	41.00	34.00	21.00
☐47	25¢ Dark Violet	86.00	55.00	45.00	28.00
☐48	50¢ Red	141.00	87.00	77.00	54.00
☐49	$1 Rose Red	205.00	131.00	88.00	60.00
☐50	2¢ Orange	162.00	101.00	—	—
☐51	2¢ Carmine	26.00	18.00	—	—
1890–1891.					
☐52	2¢ Dull Violet	4.50	2.80	1.60	1.05
☐52C	5¢ Dark Blue	111.00	76.00	85.00	56.00
1893. PROVISIONAL GOVT. RED OVERPRINT					
☐53	1¢ Purple	4.60	3.20	4.20	3.00
☐54	1¢ Blue	4.60	3.20	4.20	3.00
☐55	1¢ Green	1.85	1.25	1.80	1.50
☐56	2¢ Brown	5.40	3.30	7.00	5.20
☐57	2¢ Dull Violet	1.70	1.10	1.70	1.05
☐58	5¢ Dark Blue	11.00	5.70	12.00	7.00
☐59	5¢ Ultramarine	5.50	4.10	4.30	3.00
☐60	6¢ Green	11.00	7.10	13.00	8.00
☐61	10¢ Black	8.50	5.50	7.50	6.00
☐62	12¢ Black	9.50	5.50	11.00	6.50
☐63	12¢ Red Lilac	130.00	79.00	141.00	87.00
☐64	25¢ Dark Violet	22.00	15.00	21.00	13.00

Scott No.		Fine Unused Each	Ave. Unused Each	Fine Used Each	Ave. Used Each
BLACK OVERPRINT					
☐ 65	2¢ Vermilion	55.00	33.00	43.00	28.00
☐ 66	2¢ Rose	1.70	.95	1.80	1.30
☐ 67	10¢ Vermilion	11.00	8.00	15.00	9.50
☐ 68	10¢ Red Brown	6.50	6.00	7.00	4.50
☐ 69	12¢ Red Lilac	216.00	141.00	250.00	170.00
☐ 70	15¢ Red Brown	18.00	12.00	23.00	15.00
☐ 71	18¢ Dull Rose	24.00	14.00	26.00	16.00
☐ 72	50¢ Red	54.00	32.00	54.00	33.00
☐ 73	$1 Rose Red	108.00	69.00	106.00	68.00
☐ 74	1¢ Yellow	2.40	1.60	1.70	1.20
☐ 75	2¢ Brown	2.50	1.60	1.10	.70
☐ 76	5¢ Rose Lake	4.10	2.40	2.00	1.60
☐ 77	10¢ Yellow Green	5.30	3.70	6.00	4.50
☐ 78	12¢ Blue	12.00	6.60	9.00	7.50
☐ 79	25¢ Deep Blue	13.00	6.90	11.00	8.75
1899.					
☐ 80	1¢ Dark Green	2.10	.98	1.70	.95
☐ 81	2¢ Rose	1.70	.87	1.70	.95
☐ 82	5¢ Blue	5.00	3.20	3.40	2.10
1896. OFFICIAL STAMPS					
☐ O1	2¢ Green	30.00	18.75	21.00	13.50
☐ O2	5¢ Dark Brown	30.00	18.75	21.00	13.50
☐ O3	6¢ Deep Ultramarine	30.00	18.75	21.00	13.50
☐ O4	10¢ Rose	30.00	18.75	21.00	13.50
☐ O5	12¢ Orange	30.00	18.75	21.00	13.50
☐ O6	25¢ Gray Violet	30.00	18.75	21.00	13.50

Scott No.		Single	Block Of 4
UNITED STATES FIRST DAY COVERS UNCACHETED			
☐551	½¢ Hale	27.00	41.00
☐552	1¢ Franklin	38.00	92.00
☐553	1½¢ Harding	34.00	52.00
☐554	2¢ Washington . .	51.00	74.00
☐555	3¢ Lincoln.	51.00	74.00
☐556	4¢ Martha Washington . .	51.00	74.00
☐557	5¢ Roosevelt . .	121.00	160.00
☐558	6¢ Garfield . . .	175.00	231.00
☐559	7¢ McKinley . .	106.00	533.00
☐560	8¢ Grant.	106.00	533.00
☐561	9¢ Jefferson . .	106.00	533.00
☐562	10¢ Monroe . . .	121.00	560.00
☐563	11¢ Hayes	411.00	1080.00
☐564	12¢ Cleveland . .	127.00	710.00
☐565	14¢ Indian	303.00	1150.00
☐566	15¢ Statue of Liberty	341.00	—
☐568	25¢ Niagara Falls	422.00	1260.00
☐569	30¢ Bison.	521.00	1300.00
☐570	50¢ Arlington. . .	610.00	1330.00
☐571	$1 Lincoln Memorial . .	2780.00	5050.00
☐572	$2 U.S. Capitol . .	5610.00	—
☐573	$5 America . . .	8650.00	—
☐576	1½¢ Harding	36.00	56.00
☐581	1¢ Franklin	1605.00	—
☐582	1½¢ Harding	42.00	59.00
☐583a	2¢ Washington . .	461.00	—
☐584	3¢ Lincoln.	44.00	67.00
☐585	4¢ Martha Washington . .	44.00	67.00
☐586	5¢ Roosevelt . . .	44.00	67.00
☐587	6¢ Garfield	53.00	79.00
☐588	7¢ McKinley . . .	54.00	83.00
☐589	8¢ Grant.	61.00	86.00
☐590	9¢ Jefferson . . .	61.00	92.00
☐591	10¢ Monroe	71.00	108.00
☐597	1¢ Franklin	311.00	460.00
☐598	1½¢ Harding	41.00	63.00
☐599	2¢ Washington . .	521.00	—
☐600	3¢ Lincoln.	54.00	83.00
☐602	5¢ Roosevelt . . .	63.00	90.00
☐603	10¢ Monroe	78.00	111.00

Scott No.		Single	Block Of 4
☐604	1¢ Franklin	74.00	80.00
☐605	1½¢ Harding	49.00	71.00
☐606	2¢ Washington . .	62.00	90.00
☐610	2¢ Harding	21.00	36.00
☐611	2¢ Harding	69.00	100.00
☐612	2¢ Harding	103.00	148.00
☐614	1¢ Huguenot-Walloon	47.00	67.00
☐615	2¢ Huguenot-Walloon . . .	64.00	85.00
☐616	5¢ Huguenot-Walloon . . .	107.00	156.00
☐617	1¢ Lexington-Concord. . . .	43.00	64.00
☐618	2¢ Lexington Concord . . .	66.00	87.00
☐619	5¢ Lexington-Concord. . .	103.00	145.00
☐620	2¢ Norse-American	39.00	62.00
☐621	5¢ Norse-American	58.00	115.00
☐622	13¢ Harrison. . . .	32.00	52.00
☐623	17¢ Wilson	31.00	54.00
☐627	2¢ Sesquicentennial.	21.00	33.00
☐628	5¢ Ericsson. . . .	26.00	43.50
☐629	2¢ White Plains . .	13.00	19.00
☐630	2¢ White Plains Sheet	1200.00	—
☐631	1½ Harding	27.00	47.00
☐632	1¢ Franklin	41.00	61.00
☐633	1½¢ Harding	41.00	61.00
☐634	2¢ Washington . .	41.00	61.00
☐635	3¢ Lincoln.	41.00	61.00
☐635a	3¢ Bright Violet. .	21.00	33.00
☐636	4¢ Martha Washington . . .	41.00	61.00
☐637	5¢ Roosevelt . . .	41.00	61.00
☐638	6¢ Garfield	46.00	70.00
☐639	7¢ McKinley . . .	51.00	75.00
☐6640	8¢ Grant.	51.00	76.00
☐641	9¢ Jefferson . . .	55.00	83.00
☐642	10¢ Monroe	59.00	87.00
☐643	2¢ Vermont.	6.00	13.00
☐644	2¢ Burgoyne . . .	18.00	26.00
☐645	2¢ Valley Forge . .	8.00	14.00
☐646	2¢ Molly Pitcher .	13.00	25.00
☐647	2¢ Hawaii	14.50	32.00
☐648	5¢ Hawaii	33.00	76.00
☐649	2¢ Aero Conf. . . .	11.00	16.00

Scott No.		Single	Block Of 4
☐650	5¢ Aero Conf. . .	14.00	26.00
☐651	2¢ Clark	6.00	11.00
☐653	½¢ Hale	17.00	27.00
☐654	2¢ Electric Light .	11.00	16.00
☐655	2¢ Electric Light .	44.00	68.00
☐656	2¢ Electric Light .	59.00	—
☐657	2¢ Sullivan	5.50	11.00
☐658	1¢ Kansas	18.00	33.00
☐659	1½¢ Kansas	18.00	33.00
☐660	2¢ Kansas	18.00	33.00
☐661	3¢ Kansas	33.00	62.00
☐662	4¢ Kansas	24.00	48.00
☐663	5¢ Kansas	26.00	51.00
☐664	6¢ Kansas	41.00	74.00
☐665	7¢ Kansas	45.00	84.00
☐666	8¢ Kansas	85.00	205.00
☐667	9¢ Kansas	42.00	64.00
☐668	10¢ Kansas	45.00	68.00
☐669	1¢ Nebraska . . .	18.00	29.00
☐670	1½¢ Nebraska . . .	17.00	—
☐671	2¢ Nebraska . . .	21.00	36.00
☐672	3¢ Nebraska . . .	29.00	71.50
☐673	4¢ Nebraska . . .	33.00	76.00
☐674	5¢ Nebraska . . .	41.00	77.00
☐675	6¢ Nebraska . . .	52.00	106.00
☐676	7¢ Nebraska . . .	44.00	99.00
☐677	8¢ Nebraska . . .	55.00	112.00
☐678	9¢ Nebraska . . .	54.00	109.00
☐679	10¢ Nebraska . . .	63.00	117.00
☐6680	2¢ Fallen Timbers .	4.00	9.00
☐681	2¢ Ohio River. . . .	4.00	9.00
☐682	2¢ Massachusetts Bay Colony	4.00	9.00
☐683	2¢ Carolina-Charleston . . .	4.00	8.60
☐684	1½¢ Harding	3.60	7.70
☐685	4¢ Taft.	5.50	7.70
☐686	1½¢ Harding	4.50	6.60
☐687	4¢ Taft.	17.50	—
☐688	2¢ Braddock	5.50	16.00
☐689	2¢ Von Steuben . .	5.00	10.00
☐690	2¢ Pulaski.	4.50	5.70
☐692	11¢ Hayes	54.00	76.00
☐693	12¢ Cleveland . . .	57.00	80.00
☐694	13¢ Harrison	55.00	74.00
☐695	14¢ Indian	52.00	74.00
☐696	15¢ Liberty	66.00	89.00
☐697	17¢ Wilson	222.00	—
☐698	20¢ Golden Gate	103.00	142.00

Scott No.		Single	Block Of 4
☐699	25¢ Niagara Falls	231.00	333.00
☐700	30¢ Bison.	165.00	245.00
☐701	50¢ Arlington . . .	245.00	355.00
☐702	2¢ Red Cross. . . .	2.30	3.20
☐703	2¢ Yorktown	2.80	4.50
☐704	½¢ Olive Brown. . .	4.75	7.00
☐705	1¢ Green	6.25	7.80
☐706	1½¢ Brown	6.25	7.80
☐707	2¢ Carmine Rose .	6.25	7.80
☐708	3¢ Deep Violet . .	6.25	10.00
☐709	4¢ Light Brown. . .	6.40	11.00
☐710	5¢ Blue	6.60	11.00
☐711	6¢ Red Orange. . .	8.10	14.00
☐712	7¢ Black.	8.10	14.00
☐713	8¢ Olive Bistre . .	8.30	14.00
☐714	9¢ Pale Red . . .	10.00	15.00
☐715	10¢ Orange Yellow	14.00	18.00
☐716	2¢ Olympic Winter Games.	7.70	13.00
☐717	2¢ Arbor Day . . .	4.60	7.00
☐718	3¢ Olympic Summer Games.	6.00	9.50
☐719	5¢ Olympic Summer Games.	5.60	11.00
☐720	3¢ Washington . . .	5.50	10.00
☐721	3¢ Washington (coil)	13.00	18.00
☐722	3¢ Washington (coil)	13.00	18.00
☐723	6¢ Garfield (coil).	13.00	18.00
☐724	3¢ William Penn . .	2.10	3.40
☐725	3¢ Daniel Webster .	2.10	3.40
☐726	3¢ Gen. Oglethorpe . . .	2.10	3.40
☐727	3¢ Peace Proclama-tion.	2.10	3.40
☐728	1¢ Century of Progress.	2.10	3.40
☐729	3¢ Century of Progress.	2.10	3.40
☐730	1¢ American Philatelic Society, full sheet on cover.	110.00	11.00
☐730a	1¢ American Philatelic Society	3.00	4.50
☐731	3¢ American Philatelic Society . . .	113.00	—
☐731a	3¢ American Philatelic Society	2.20	3.30

Scott No.		Single	Block Of 4
☐732	3¢ National Recovery Administration	2.20	3.50
☐733	3¢ Byrd Antarctic	5.60	9.00
☐734	5¢ Kosciuszko	5.60	9.00
☐735	3¢ National Exhibition	40.00	—
☐735a	3¢ National Exhibition	4.60	8.00
☐736	3¢ Maryland Tercentenary	2.50	4.00
☐737	3¢ Mothers of America	2.30	4.00
☐738	3¢ Mothers of America	2.10	3.40
☐739	3¢ Wisconsin	2.30	3.80
☐740	1¢ Parks, Yosemite	3.50	4.75
☐741	2¢ Parks, Grand Canyon	3.10	4.60
☐742	3¢ Parks, Mt. Ranier	3.10	4.60
☐743	4¢ Parks, Mesa Verde	3.20	4.70
☐744	5¢ Parks, Yellowstone	3.20	4.70
☐745	6¢ Parks, Crater Lake	3.90	6.60
☐746	7¢ Parks, Acadia	4.10	9.00
☐747	8¢ Parks, Zion	4.40	17.00
☐748	9¢ Parks, Glacier Park	4.40	9.00
☐749	10¢ Parks, Smoky Mountains	9.00	16.00
☐750	3¢ American Philatelic Society, full sheet on cover	48.00	—
☐750a	3¢ American Philatelic Society	7.50	13.00
☐751	1¢ Trans-Mississippi Philatelic Expo, full sheet on cover	36.00	—
☐751a	1¢ Trans-Mississippi Philadelic Expo	6.00	8.00
☐752	3¢ Peace Commemoration	9.00	19.00
☐753	3¢ Byrd	12.00	22.00
☐754	3¢ Mothers of America	12.00	23.00
☐755	3¢ Wisconsin	12.00	23.00
☐756	1¢ Parks, Yosemite	12.00	23.00

Scott No.		Single	Block Of 4
☐757	2¢ Parks, Grand Canyon	12.00	23.00
☐758	3¢ Parks, Mount Ranier	12.00	25.00
☐759	4¢ Parks, Mesa Verde	12.00	25.00
☐760	5¢ Parks, Yellowstone	12.00	25.00
☐761	6¢ Parks, Carter Lake	15.00	27.00
☐762	7¢ Parks, Acadia	15.00	27.00
☐763	8¢ Parks, Zion	14.50	30.00
☐764	9¢ Parks, Glacier Park	14.50	29.50
☐765	10¢ Parks, Smoky Mountains	16.00	33.50
☐766a	1¢ Century of Progress	14.00	20.00
☐767a	3¢ Century of Progress	14.00	20.00
☐768a	3¢ Byrd	14.00	20.00
☐769	1¢ Parks, Yosemite	11.00	17.00
☐770a	3¢ Parks, Mount Ranier	11.00	17.00
☐771	16¢ Air Mail, special delivery	27.00	41.00

UNITED STATES FIRST DAY COVERS CACHETED

Scott No.		Single	Block Of 4
☐610	2¢ Harding	305.00	—
☐617	1¢ Lexington-Concord	120.00	—
☐618	2¢ Lexington-Concord	120.00	—
☐619	5¢ Lexington-Concord	150.00	—
☐623	17¢ Wilson	240.00	—
☐627	2¢ Sesquicentennial	62.00	—
☐628	5¢ Ericsson	175.00	—
☐629	2¢ White Plains	55.00	—
☐630	2¢ White Plains Sheet	1680.00	—
☐635a	3¢ Bright Violet	44.00	—
☐643	2¢ Vermont	52.00	129.00
☐644	2¢ Burgoyne	58.00	128.00
☐645	2¢ Valley Forge	51.00	127.00

Scott No.		Single	Block Of 4	Scott No.		Single	Block Of 4
☐646	2¢ Molly Pitcher .	92.00	—	☐722	3¢ Washington (coil)	39.00	—
☐647	2¢ Hawaii	68.00	120.00	☐723	6¢ Garfield (coil) . .	29.00	—
☐648	5¢ Hawaii	91.00	133.00	☐724	3¢ William Penn .	19.00	31.00
☐649	2¢ Aero Conf. . .	25.00	65.00	☐725	3¢ Daniel Webster	19.00	31.00
☐650	5¢ Aero Conf. . .	42.00	83.00	☐726	3¢ Gen. Oglethorpe	19.00	31.00
☐651	2¢ Clark	33.00	73.00	☐727	3¢ Peace		
☐654	2¢ Electric Light .	47.00	99.00		Proclamation .	21.00	37.00
☐655	2¢ Electric Light	121.00	270.00	☐728	1¢ Century of		
☐656	2¢ Electric Light	116.00	—		Progress. . . .	13.00	23.00
☐657	2¢ Sullivan, Auburn, N.Y.	34.00	78.00	☐729	3¢ Century of Progress. . . .	16.00	26.00
☐680	2¢ Fallen Timbers	34.00	78.00	☐730	1¢ American Philatelic		
☐681	2¢ Ohio River. . .	32.00	69.00		Society, full sheet on		
☐682	2¢ Massachusetts Bay Colony.	35.00	77.00	☐730a	cover. . . . . 1¢ American Philatelic	131.00	—
☐683	2¢ California- Charleston	35.00	77.00	☐731	Society . . . . 3¢ American Philatelic	15.00	25.00
☐684	1½¢ Harding	29.00	55.00		Society . . .	136.00	—
☐685	4¢ Taft.	29.00	55.00	☐731a	3¢ American Philatelic		
☐686	1½¢ Harding	29.00	55.00		Society	19.00	30.00
☐687	4¢ Taft.	29.00	55.00	☐732	3¢ National Recovery		
☐688	2¢ Braddock . . .	30.00	61.00		Administration	19.00	30.00
☐689	2¢ Von Steuben .	29.00	55.00	☐733	3¢ Byrd Antarctic	25.00	39.00
☐690	2¢ Pulaski.	33.00	51.00	☐734	5¢ Kosciuszko . .	21.00	32.00
☐702	2¢ Red Cross. . .	27.00	42.00	☐735	3¢ National		
☐703	2¢ Yorktown . . .	32.00	51.00		Exhibition . . .	54.00	—
☐704	1½¢ Olive Brown. .	20.00	29.00	☐735a	3¢ National		
☐705	1¢ Green	20.00	29.00		Exhibition . . .	18.00	27.00
☐706	1½¢ Brown	20.00	29.00	☐736	3¢ Maryland		
☐707	2¢ Carmine Rose	20.00	29.00		Tercentenary .	14.00	21.00
☐708	3¢ Deep Violet . .	20.00	29.00	☐737	3¢ Mothers of		
☐709	4¢ Light Brown. .	20.00	29.00		America	14.00	21.00
☐710	5¢ Blue	20.00	29.00	☐738	3¢ Mothers of		
☐711	6¢ Red Orange. .	20.00	29.00		America	16.00	24.00
☐712	7¢ Black.	20.00	29.00	☐739	2¢ Wisconsin . .	11.50	18.00
☐713	8¢ Olive Bistre . .	23.00	36.00	☐740	1¢ Parks, Yosemite	11.50	18.00
☐714	9¢ Pale Red . . .	23.00	36.00	☐741	2¢ Parks, Grand		
☐715	10¢ Orange Yellow	23.00	36.00		Canyon . . .	11.50	18.00
☐716	2¢ Olympic Winter Games.	26.00	41.00	☐742	3¢ Parks, Mt. Rainier.	11.50	18.00
☐717	2¢ Arbor Day . . .	17.00	30.00	☐743	4¢ Parks, Mesa		
☐718	3¢ Olympic Summer				Verde	11.50	18.00
	Games.	30.00	48.00	☐744	5¢ Parks,		
☐719	5¢ Olympic Summer				Yellowstone. .	14.00	21.00
	Games.	30.00	48.00	☐745	6¢ Parks, Crater		
☐720	3¢ Washington . .	30.00	48.00		Lake	14.00	21.00
☐720b	3¢ Booklet pane	141.00	—	☐746	7¢ Parks, Acadia.	14.00	21.00
☐721	3¢ Washington (coil)	39.00	—	☐747	8¢ Parks, Zion . .	14.00	21.00

Scott No.	Single	Block Of 4
☐748	9¢ Parks, Glacier Park 17.00	26.00
☐749	10¢ Parks, Smoky Mountains. . . 17.00	26.00
☐750	3¢ American Philatelic Society, full sheet on cover. 58.00	—
☐750a	3¢ American Philatelic Society 16.00	23.00
☐751	1¢ Trans-Mississippi Philatelic Expo., full sheet on cover 49.00	—
☐751a	1¢ Trans-Mississippi Philatelic Expo. 11.00	16.00
☐752	3¢ Peace Commemoration 22.00	31.00
☐753	3¢ Byrd 22.00	33.00
☐754	3¢ Mothers of America 24.00	35.00
☐755	3¢ Wisconsin Tercentenary . 24.00	35.00
☐756	1¢ Parks, Yosemite 24.00	35.00
☐757	2¢ Parks, Grand Canyon 24.00	35.00

Scott No.	Single	Block Of 4
☐758	3¢ Parks, Mount Rainier. 24.00	35.00
☐759	4¢ Parks, Mesa Verde 26.00	41.00
☐760	5¢ Parks, Yellowstone. . 26.00	41.00
☐761	6¢ Parks, Crater Lake 26.00	41.00
☐762	7¢ Parks, Acadia. 26.00	41.00
☐763	8¢ Parks, Zion . . 26.00	41.00
☐764	9¢ Parks, Glacier Park 26.00	41.00
☐765	10¢ Parks, Smoky Mountains. . . . 26.00	41.00
☐766a	1¢ Century of Progress. . . . 26.00	41.00
☐767a	3¢ Century of Progress. . . . 26.00	41.00
☐768a	3¢ Byrd 26.00	41.00
☐769a	1¢ Parks, Yosemite 26.00	41.00
☐770a	3¢ Parks, Mount Rainier. 26.00	41.00
☐771	16¢ Air Mail, special delivery 34.00	48.00

Scott No.		Single	Block	Plate Block
☐772	3¢ Connecticut Tercentenary	6.10	8.00	11.00
☐773	3¢ California Exposition	6.10	8.00	11.00
☐774	3¢ Boulder Dam	9.50	13.00	15.00
☐775	3¢ Michigan Centenary	5.50	7.50	10.00
☐776	3¢ Texas Centennial	6.10	8.50	11.00
☐777	3¢ Rhode Island Tercentenary	6.10	8.50	11.00
☐778	3¢ TIPEX	20.00	—	—
☐782	3¢ Arkansas Centennial	7.00	8.75	13.00
☐783	3¢ Oregon Territory	6.50	7.75	10.00
☐784	3¢ Susan B. Anthony	10.50	14.00	17.00
☐785	1¢ Army	4.80	6.50	8.75
☐786	2¢ Army	4.80	6.50	8.75
☐787	3¢ Army	4.80	6.50	8.75
☐788	5¢ Army	4.80	0.50	8.75
☐790	1¢ Navy	4.80	6.50	8.75
☐791	2¢ Navy	4.80	6.50	8.75
☐792	3¢ Navy	4.80	6.50	8.75
☐793	4¢ Navy	4.80	6.50	8.75
☐794	5¢ Navy	4.80	6.50	8.75
☐795	3¢ Ordinance of 1787	5.60	7.70	10.00
☐796	5¢ Virginia Dare	5.70	7.90	11.00
☐797	10¢ Souvenir Sheet	5.70	—	—

Scott No.		Single	Block	Plate Block
☐ 798	3¢ Constitution	5.60	7.90	10.50
☐ 799	3¢ Hawaii	5.60	7.90	10.50
☐ 800	3¢ Alaska	5.60	7.90	10.50
☐ 801	3¢ Puerto Rico	5.60	7.90	10.50
☐ 802	3¢ Virgin Islands	5.60	7.90	10.50
☐ 803	½¢ Franklin	2.20	3.00	4.20
☐ 804	1¢ Washington	2.20	3.00	4.20
☐ 805	1½¢ Martha Washington	2.20	3.00	4.20
☐ 806	2¢ Adams	2.20	3.00	4.20
☐ 807	3¢ Jefferson	2.20	3.00	4.20
☐ 808	4¢ Madison	2.20	3.00	4.20
☐ 809	4½¢ White House	3.30	4.90	6.90
☐ 810	5¢ Monroe	3.30	4.90	6.90
☐ 811	6¢ Adams	3.30	4.90	6.90
☐ 812	7¢ Jackson	3.30	4.90	6.90
☐ 813	8¢ VanBuren	3.30	4.90	6.90
☐ 814	9¢ Harrison	3.30	4.90	6.90
☐ 815	10¢ Tyler	4.05	6.00	7.90
☐ 816	11¢ Polk	4.05	6.00	7.90
☐ 817	12¢ Taylor	4.05	6.00	7.90
☐ 818	13¢ Fillmore	4.05	6.00	7.90
☐ 819	14¢ Pierce	4.05	6.00	7.90
☐ 820	15¢ Buchanan	4.05	6.00	7.90
☐ 821	16¢ Lincoln	4.05	6.00	7.90
☐ 822	17¢ Johnson	4.05	6.00	7.90
☐ 823	18¢ Grant	4.05	6.00	7.90
☐ 824	19¢ Hayes	4.05	6.00	7.90
☐ 825	20¢ Garfield	4.05	6.00	7.90
☐ 826	21¢ Arthur	6.20	8.70	13.00
☐ 827	22¢ Cleveland	6.20	8.70	13.00
☐ 828	24¢ Harrison	6.20	8.70	13.00
☐ 829	25¢ McKinley	6.80	9.50	13.00
☐ 830	30¢ Roosevelt	6.80	11.00	16.00
☐ 831	50¢ Taft	12.00	16.00	23.00
☐ 832	$1 Wilson	41.00	60.00	82.00
☐ 832c	$1 Wilson	22.00	31.00	41.00
☐ 833	$2 Harding	78.00	116.00	160.00
☐ 834	$5 Coolidge	122.00	201.00	305.00
☐ 835	3¢ Constitution	6.00	8.20	10.75
☐ 836	3¢ Swedes and Finns	6.00	8.20	10.75
☐ 837	3¢ Northwest Sesquicentennial	6.00	8.20	10.75
☐ 838	3¢ Iowa	6.00	8.20	10.75
☐ 852	3¢ Golden Gate Expo	6.00	8.20	10.75
☐ 853	3¢ N.Y. World's Fair	6.00	8.20	10.75
☐ 854	3¢ Washington Inauguration	6.00	8.20	10.75
☐ 855	3¢ Baseball Centennial	9.20	15.00	18.00
☐ 856	3¢ Panama Canal	5.30	7.50	9.50
☐ 857	3¢ Printing Tercentenary	5.30	7.50	9.50

	Scott No.		Single	Block	Plate Block
☐ 858	3¢	50th Statehood Anniversary	5.30	7.10	9.50
☐ 859	1¢	Washington Irving	2.05	3.00	4.30
☐ 860	2¢	James Fenimore Cooper	2.05	3.00	4.30
☐ 861	3¢	Ralph Waldo Emerson	2.05	3.00	4.30
☐ 862	5¢	Louisa May Alcott	3.40	4.70	6.10
☐ 863	10¢	Samuel L. Clemens	6.10	8.60	13.50
☐ 864	1¢	Henry W. Longfellow	2.05	3.05	4.30
☐ 865	2¢	John Greenleaf Whittier	2.05	3.05	4.30
☐ 866	3¢	James Russell Lowell	2.05	3.05	4.30
☐ 867	5¢	Walt Whitman	3.00	4.30	6.00
☐ 868	10¢	James Whitcomb Riley	5.70	8.10	13.00
☐ 869	1¢	Horace Mann	2.00	3.00	4.30
☐ 870	2¢	Mark Hopkins	2.00	3.00	4.30
☐ 871	3¢	Charles W. Eliot	2.00	3.00	4.30
☐ 872	5¢	Frances E. Willard	2.80	4.20	5.70
☐ 873	10¢	Booker T. Washington	5.60	8.00	12.50
☐ 874	1¢	John James Audubon	2.05	3.05	4.50
☐ 875	2¢	Dr. Crawford W. Long	2.05	3.05	4.50
☐ 876	3¢	Luther Burbank	2.05	3.05	4.50
☐ 877	5¢	Dr. Walter Reed	2.90	4.50	6.00
☐ 878	10¢	Jane Addams	5.70	8.50	13.00
☐ 879	1¢	Stephen Collins Foster	2.15	3.20	5.00
☐ 880	2¢	John Philip Sousa	2.15	3.20	5.00
☐ 881	3¢	Victor Herbert	2.15	3.20	5.00
☐ 882	5¢	Edward A MacDowell	2.90	4.10	6.00
☐ 883	10¢	Ethelbert Nevin	6.60	9.30	16.00
☐ 884	1¢	Gilbert Charles Stuart	2.25	3.30	5.50
☐ 885	2¢	James A. McNeill Whistler	2.25	3.30	5.50
☐ 886	3¢	Augustus Saint-Gaudens	2.25	3.30	5.50
☐ 887	5¢	Daniel Chester French	2.80	4.10	5.50
☐ 888	10¢	Frederic Remington	6.60	9.10	15.00
☐ 889	1¢	Eli Whitney	2.30	3.30	5.50
☐ 890	2¢	Samuel F.B. Morse	2.30	3.30	5.50
☐ 891	3¢	Cyrus Hall McCormick	2.30	3.30	5.50
☐ 892	5¢	Elias Howe	3.00	4.20	6.10
☐ 893	10¢	Alexander Graham Bell	9.80	16.00	26.00
☐ 894	3¢	Pony Express	3.60	4.90	7.00
☐ 895	3¢	Pan American Union	3.60	4.90	7.00
☐ 896	3¢	Idaho Statehood	3.60	4.90	7.00
☐ 897	3¢	Wyoming Statehood	3.60	4.90	7.00
☐ 898	3¢	Coronado Expedition	3.60	4.90	7.00
☐ 899	1¢	Defense	3.60	4.90	7.00
☐ 900	2¢	Defense	3.60	4.90	7.00
☐ 901	3¢	Defense	3.60	4.90	7.00
☐ 902	3¢	Thirteenth Amendment	3.60	4.90	7.00
☐ 903	3¢	Vermont Statehood	3.60	4.90	7.00
☐ 904	3¢	Kentucky Statehood	3.60	4.90	7.00
☐ 905	3¢	"Win the War"	3.60	4.90	7.00

Scott No.		Single	Block	Plate Block
☐ 906	5¢ Chinese Commemorative	4.70	6.75	10.00
☐ 907	2¢ United Nations	3.20	4.60	6.60
☐ 908	1¢ Four Freedoms	3.30	4.80	7.00
☐ 909	5¢ Poland	3.90	5.60	8.00
☐ 910	5¢ Czechoslovakia	3.75	5.60	8.25
☐ 911	5¢ Norway	3.75	5.60	8.25
☐ 912	5¢ Luxembourg	3.75	5.60	8.25
☐ 913	5¢ Netherlands	3.75	5.60	8.25
☐ 914	5¢ Belgium	3.75	5.60	8.25
☐ 915	5¢ France	3.75	5.60	8.25
☐ 916	5¢ Greece	3.75	5.60	8.25
☐ 917	5¢ Yugoslavia	3.75	5.60	8.25
☐ 918	5¢ Albany	3.75	5.60	8.25
☐ 919	5¢ Austria	3.75	5.60	8.25
☐ 920	5¢ Denmark	3.75	5.60	8.25
☐ 921	5¢ Korea	3.75	5.60	8.25
☐ 922	3¢ Railroad	5.00	7.50	11.00
☐ 923	3¢ Steamship	3.35	5.10	7.70
☐ 924	3¢ Telegraph	3.35	5.10	7.70
☐ 925	3¢ Philippines	3.35	5.10	7.70
☐ 926	3¢ Motion Picture	3.35	5.10	7.70
☐ 927	3¢ Florida	3.35	5.10	7.70
☐ 928	5¢ United Nations Conference	3.35	5.10	7.70
☐ 929	3¢ Iwo Jima	3.35	5.10	7.70
☐ 930	1¢ Roosevelt	2.85	4.05	5.35
☐ 931	2¢ Roosevelt	2.85	4.05	5.35
☐ 932	3¢ Roosevelt	2.85	4.05	5.35
☐ 933	3¢ Roosevelt	2.85	4.05	5.35
☐ 934	3¢ Army	2.85	4.05	5.35
☐ 935	3¢ Navy	2.85	4.05	5.35
☐ 936	3¢ Coast Guard	2.85	4.05	5.35
☐ 937	3¢ Alfred E. Smith	2.85	4.05	5.35
☐ 938	3¢ Texas	2.85	4.05	5.35
☐ 939	3¢ Merchant Marine	2.80	3.90	5.05
☐ 940	3¢ Honorable Discharge	2.85	3.85	5.10
☐ 941	3¢ Tennessee	2.85	3.85	5.10
☐ 942	3¢ Iowa	2.85	3.85	5.10
☐ 943	3¢ Smithsonian	2.85	3.85	5.10
☐ 944	3¢ Santa Fe	2.85	3.85	5.40
☐ 945	3¢ Thomas A. Edison	2.85	3.85	5.40
☐ 946	3¢ Joseph Pulitzer	2.85	3.85	5.40
☐ 947	3¢ Stamp Centenary	2.85	3.85	5.40
☐ 948	5¢ and 10¢ Centenary Exhibition Sheet	4.50	—	—
☐ 949	3¢ Doctors	2.60	3.50	4.50
☐ 950	3¢ Utah	2.65	3.60	4.65
☐ 951	3¢ "Constitution"	2.65	3.60	4.65
☐ 952	3¢ Everglades Park	2.65	3.60	4.65
☐ 953	3¢ Carver	2.65	3.60	4.65

Scott No.		Single	Block	Plate Block
☐ 954	3¢ California Gold	2.65	3.60	4.65
☐ 955	3¢ Mississippi Territory	2.65	3.60	4.65
☐ 956	3¢ Four Chaplains	2.65	3.60	4.65
☐ 957	3¢ Wisconsin Centennial	2.65	3.60	4.65
☐ 958	5¢ Swedish Pioneers	2.65	3.60	4.65
☐ 959	3¢ Women's Progress	2.65	3.60	4.65
☐ 960	3¢ William Allen White	2.65	3.60	4.65
☐ 961	3¢ U.S.-Canada Friendship	2.65	3.60	4.65
☐ 962	3¢ Francis Scott Key	2.65	3.60	4.65
☐ 963	3¢ Salute to Youth	2.65	3.60	4.65
☐ 964	3¢ Oregon Territory	2.65	3.60	4.65
☐ 965	3¢ Harlan Fiske Stone	2.65	3.60	4.65
☐ 966	3¢ Palomar Observatory	2.65	3.60	4.65
☐ 967	3¢ Clara Barton	2.65	3.60	4.65
☐ 968	3¢ Poultry Industry	2.65	3.60	4.65
☐ 969	3¢ Gold Star Mothers	2.65	3.60	4.65
☐ 970	3¢ Volunteer Fireman	2.65	3.60	4.65
☐ 972	3¢ Indian Centennial	2.65	3.60	4.65
☐ 973	3¢ Rough Riders	2.45	3.40	4.25
☐ 974	3¢ Juliette Low	2.45	3.40	4.25
☐ 975	3¢ Will Rogers	2.45	3.40	4.25
☐ 976	3¢ Fort Bliss	2.45	3.40	4.25
☐ 977	3¢ Moina Michael	2.45	3.40	4.25
☐ 978	3¢ Gettysburg Address	2.45	3.40	4.25
☐ 979	3¢ American Turners Society	2.45	3.40	4.25
☐ 980	3¢ Joel Chandler Harris	2.45	3.40	4.25
☐ 981	3¢ Minnesota Territory	2.45	3.40	4.25
☐ 982	3¢ Washington and Lee University	2.45	3.40	4.25
☐ 983	3¢ Puerto Rico Election	2.45	3.40	4.25
☐ 984	3¢ Annapolis, Md.	2.45	3.40	4.25
☐ 985	3¢ G.A.R.	2.45	3.40	4.25
☐ 986	3¢ Edgar Allan Poe	2.45	3.40	4.25
☐ 987	3¢ American Bankers Association	2.45	3.40	4.25
☐ 988	3¢ Samuel Gompers	2.45	3.40	4.25
☐ 990	3¢ Nat. Capital Sesqui. (Executive)	2.45	3.40	4.25
☐ 991	3¢ Nat. Capital Sesqui. (Judicial)	2.45	3.40	4.25
☐ 992	3¢ Nat. Capital Sesqui. (Legislative)	2.45	3.40	4.25
☐ 993	3¢ Railroad Engineers	2.45	3.40	4.25
☐ 994	3¢ Kansas City Centenary	2.35	3.10	4.15
☐ 995	3¢ Boy Scout	2.35	3.10	4.15
☐ 996	3¢ Indiana Ter. Sesquicentennial	2.35	3.10	4.15
☐ 997	3¢ California Statehood	2.35	3.10	4.15
☐ 998	3¢ United Confederate Veterans	2.35	3.10	4.15
☐ 999	3¢ Nevada Centennial	2.35	3.10	4.15
☐ 1000	3¢ Landing of Cadillac	2.35	3.10	4.15
☐ 1001	3¢ Colorado Statehood	2.35	3.10	4.15
☐ 1002	3¢ American Chemical Society	2.35	3.10	4.15
☐ 1003	3¢ Battle of Brooklyn	2.35	3.10	4.15

Scott No.			Single	Block	Plate Block
☐ 1004	3¢	Betsy Ross	2.35	3.10	4.15
☐ 1005	3¢	4-H Clubs	2.35	3.10	4.15
☐ 1006	3¢	B & O Railroad	2.35	3.10	4.15
☐ 1007	3¢	American Automobile Assoc.	2.35	3.10	4.15
☐ 1008	3¢	NATO	2.35	3.10	4.15
☐ 1009	3¢	Grand Coulee Dam	2.35	3.10	4.15
☐ 1010	3¢	Lafayette	2.35	3.10	4.15
☐ 1011	3¢	Mt. Rushmore Memorial	2.35	3.10	4.15
☐ 1012	3¢	Civil Engineers	2.35	3.10	4.15
☐ 1013	3¢	Service Women	2.35	3.10	4.15
☐ 1014	3¢	Gutenberg Bible	2.35	3.10	4.15
☐ 1015	3¢	Newspaper boys	2.35	3.10	4.15
☐ 1016	3¢	Red Cross	2.35	3.10	4.15
☐ 1017	3¢	National Guard	2.35	3.10	4.15
☐ 1018	3¢	Ohio Sesquicentennial	2.35	3.10	4.15
☐ 1019	3¢	Washington Territory	2.35	3.10	4.15
☐ 1020	3¢	Louisiana Purchase	2.35	3.10	4.15
☐ 1021	5¢	Opening of Japan	2.35	3.10	4.15
☐ 1022	3¢	American Bar Association	2.35	3.10	4.15
☐ 1023	3¢	Sagamore Hill	2.35	3.10	4.15
☐ 1024	3¢	Future Farmers	2.35	3.10	4.15
☐ 1025	3¢	Trucking Industry	2.35	3.10	4.15
☐ 1026	3¢	Gen. G.S. Patton, Jr.	2.35	3.10	4.15
☐ 1027	3¢	New York City	2.35	3.10	4.15
☐ 1028	3¢	Gadsden Purchase	2.35	3.10	4.15
☐ 1029	3¢	Columbia University	2.35	3.10	4.15
☐ 1030	½¢	Franklin	2.35	3.10	4.15
☐ 1031	1¢	Washington	2.35	3.10	4.15
☐ 1031a	1¼¢	Palace	2.35	3.10	4.15
☐ 1032	1½¢	Mount Vernon	2.35	3.10	4.15
☐ 1033	2¢	Jefferson	2.35	3.10	4.15
☐ 1034	2½¢	Bunker Hill	2.35	3.10	4.15
☐ 1035	3¢	Statue of Liberty	2.35	3.10	4.15
☐ 1036	4¢	Lincoln	2.35	3.10	4.15
☐ 1037	4½¢	Hermitage	2.35	3.10	4.15
☐ 1038	5¢	Monroe	2.35	3.10	4.15
☐ 1039	6¢	Roosevelt	2.35	3.10	4.15
☐ 1040	7¢	Wilson	2.35	3.10	4.15
☐ 1041	8¢	Statue of Liberty	2.35	3.10	4.15
☐ 1042	8¢	Statue of Liberty	2.35	3.10	4.15
☐ 1042a	8¢	Pershing	2.30	3.10	4.05
☐ 1043	9¢	The Alamo	2.30	3.10	4.05
☐ 1044	10¢	Independence Hall	2.30	3.10	4.05
☐ 1045	12¢	Harrison	2.30	3.10	4.05
☐ 1046	15¢	John Jay	2.30	3.10	4.05
☐ 1046a	15¢	John Jay	35.00	—	—
☐ 1047	20¢	Monticello	2.30	3.10	4.05
☐ 1048	25¢	Paul Revere	2.30	3.10	4.05

Scott No.			Single	Block	Plate Block
☐ 1049	30¢	Robert Lee	2.30	3.10	4.05
☐ 1050	40¢	John Marshall	3.05	4.60	7.75
☐ 1051	50¢	Susan Anthony	7.00	9.10	14.00
☐ 1052	$1	Patrick Henry	13.00	21.00	31.00
☐ 1053	$5	Alexander Hamilton	83.00	147.00	205.00
☐ 1054	1¢	Washington	2.10	—	—
☐ 1055	2¢	Jefferson	2.10	—	—
☐ 1056	2½¢	Bunker Hill	2.10	—	—
☐ 1057	3¢	Statue of Liberty	2.30	—	—
☐ 1058	4¢	Lincoln	2.30	—	—
☐ 1059	4½¢	The Hermitage	2.80	—	—
☐ 1059A	25¢	Paul Revere	3.10	—	—
☐ 1059Ab	25¢	Tagged	16.50	—	—
☐ 1060	3¢	Nebraska Territory	2.10	2.85	3.85
☐ 1061	3¢	Kansas Territory	2.10	2.85	3.85
☐ 1062	3¢	George Eastman	2.10	2.85	3.85
☐ 1063	3¢	Lewis & Clark	2.10	2.85	3.85
☐ 1064	3¢	Pennsylvania Academy of the Fine Arts	2.10	2.85	3.85
☐ 1065	3¢	Land Grant Colleges	2.10	2.85	3.85
☐ 1066	8¢	Rotary International	2.10	2.85	3.85
☐ 1067	3¢	Armed Forces Reserve	2.10	2.85	3.85
☐ 1068	3¢	New Hampshire	2.10	2.85	3.85
☐ 1069	3¢	Soo Locks	2.10	2.85	3.85
☐ 1070	3¢	Atoms for Peace	2.10	2.85	3.85
☐ 1071	3¢	Fort Ticonderoga	2.10	2.85	3.85
☐ 1072	3¢	Andrew W. Mellon	2.10	2.85	3.85
☐ 1073	3¢	Benjamin Franklin	2.10	2.85	3.85
☐ 1074	3¢	Booker T. Washington	2.10	2.85	3.85
☐ 1075	3¢, 8¢	FIPEX Souvenir Sheet	12.00	—	—
☐ 1076	3¢	FIPEX	1.95	2.85	3.85
☐ 1077	3¢	Wildlife (Turkey)	1.95	2.85	3.85
☐ 1078	3¢	Wildlife (Antelope)	1.95	2.85	3.85
☐ 1079	3¢	Wildlife (Salmon)	1.95	2.85	3.85
☐ 1080	3¢	Pure Food and Drug Laws	1.95	2.85	3.85
☐ 1081	3¢	Wheatland	1.95	2.75	3.85
☐ 1082	3¢	Labor Day	1.95	2.75	3.85
☐ 1083	3¢	Nassau Hall	1.95	2.75	3.85
☐ 1084	3¢	Devils Tower	1.95	2.75	3.85
☐ 1085	3¢	Children	1.95	2.75	3.85
☐ 1086	3¢	Alexander Hamilton	1.95	2.75	3.85
☐ 1087	3¢	Polio	1.95	2.75	3.85
☐ 1088	3¢	Coast & Geodetic Survey	1.95	2.75	3.85
☐ 1089	3¢	Architects	1.95	2.75	3.85
☐ 1090	3¢	Steel Industry	1.95	2.75	3.85
☐ 1091	3¢	Naval Review	1.95	2.75	3.85
☐ 1092	3¢	Oklahoma Statehood	1.95	2.75	3.85
☐ 1093	3¢	School Teachers	1.95	2.75	3.85
☐ 1094	4¢	Flag	1.90	2.70	3.60

Scott No.		Single	Block	Plate Block
☐ 1095	3¢ Shipbuilding	1.85	2.65	3.60
☐ 1096	8¢ Ramon Magsaysay	1.85	2.65	3.60
☐ 1097	3¢ Lafayette Bicentenary	1.85	2.65	3.60
☐ 1098	3¢ Wildlife (Whooping Crane)	1.85	2.65	3.60
☐ 1099	3¢ Religious Freedom	1.85	2.65	3.60
☐ 1100	3¢ Gardening Horticulture	1.85	2.65	3.60
☐ 1104	3¢ Brussels Exhibition	1.85	2.65	3.60
☐ 1105	3¢ James Monroe	1.85	2.65	3.60
☐ 1106	3¢ Minnesota Statehood	1.85	2.65	3.60
☐ 1107	3¢ International Geophysical Year	1.85	2.65	3.60
☐ 1108	3¢ Gunston Hall	1.85	2.65	3.60
☐ 1109	3¢ Mackinac Bridge	1.85	2.65	3.60
☐ 1110	4¢ Simon Bolivar	1.85	2.65	3.60
☐ 1111	8¢ Simon Bolivar	1.85	2.65	3.60
☐ 1112	4¢ Atlantic Cable	1.85	2.65	3.60
☐ 1113	1¢ Lincoln Sesquicentennial	1.85	2.65	3.60
☐ 1114	3¢ Lincoln Sesquicentennial	1.85	2.65	3.60
☐ 1115	4¢ Lincoln-Douglas Debates	1.85	2.65	3.60
☐ 1116	4¢ Lincoln Sesquicentennial	1.85	2.65	3.60
☐ 1117	4¢ Lajos Kossuth	1.85	2.65	3.60
☐ 1118	8¢ Lajos Kossuth	1.85	2.65	3.60
☐ 1119	4¢ Freedom of Press	1.85	2.65	3.60
☐ 1120	4¢ Overland Mail	1.85	2.65	3.60
☐ 1121	4¢ Noah Webster	1.85	2.65	3.60
☐ 1122	4¢ Forest Conservation	1.85	2.65	3.60
☐ 1123	4¢ Fort Duquesne	1.85	2.65	3.60
☐ 1124	4¢ Oregon Statehood	1.85	2.65	3.60
☐ 1125	4¢ San Martin	1.85	2.65	3.60
☐ 1126	8¢ San Martin	1.85	2.65	3.60
☐ 1127	4¢ NATO	1.85	2.65	3.60
☐ 1128	4¢ Arctic Explorations	1.85	2.65	3.60
☐ 1129	8¢ World Trade	1.85	2.65	3.60
☐ 1130	4¢ Silver Centennial	1.85	2.65	3.60
☐ 1131	4¢ St. Lawrence Seaway	1.85	2.65	3.60
☐ 1132	4¢ Flag	1.85	2.60	3.60
☐ 1133	4¢ Soil Conservation	1.85	2.60	3.60
☐ 1134	4¢ Petroleum Industry	1.85	2.60	3.60
☐ 1135	4¢ Dental Health	1.85	2.60	3.60
☐ 1136	4¢ Reuter	1.85	2.60	3.60
☐ 1137	8¢ Reuter	1.85	2.60	3.60
☐ 1138	4¢ Dr. Ephraim McDowell	1.85	2.60	3.60
☐ 1139	4¢ Washington "Credo"	1.85	2.60	3.60
☐ 1140	4¢ Franklin "Credo"	1.85	2.60	3.60
☐ 1141	4¢ Jefferson "Credo"	1.85	2.60	3.60
☐ 1142	4¢ Frances Scott Key "Credo"	1.85	2.60	3.60
☐ 1143	4¢ Lincoln "Credo"	1.85	2.60	3.60
☐ 1144	4¢ Patrick Henry "Credo"	1.85	2.60	3.60
☐ 1145	4¢ Boy Scouts	1.85	2.60	3.60

Scott No.			Single	Block	Plate Block
☐ 1146	4¢	Olympic Winter Games	1.85	2.60	3.60
☐ 1147	4¢	Masaryk	1.85	2.60	3.60
☐ 1148	8¢	Masaryk	1.85	2.60	3.60
☐ 1149	4¢	World Refugee Year	1.85	2.60	3.60
☐ 1150	4¢	Water Conservation	1.85	2.60	3.60
☐ 1151	4¢	SEATO	1.85	2.60	3.60
☐ 1152	4¢	American Woman	1.85	2.60	3.60
☐ 1153	4¢	50-Star Flag	1.85	2.60	3.60
☐ 1154	4¢	Pony Express Centennial	1.85	2.60	3.60
☐ 1155	4¢	Employ the Handicapped	1.85	2.60	3.60
☐ 1156	4¢	World Forestry Congress	1.85	2.60	3.60
☐ 1157	4¢	Mexican Independence	1.85	2.60	3.60
☐ 1158	4¢	U.S. Japan Treaty	1.85	2.60	3.60
☐ 1159	4¢	Paderewski	1.85	2.60	3.60
☐ 1160	8¢	Paderewski	1.85	2.60	3.60
☐ 1161	4¢	Robert A. Taft	1.85	2.60	3.60
☐ 1162	4¢	Wheels of Freedom	1.85	2.60	3.60
☐ 1163	4¢	Boys' Clubs	1.85	2.60	3.60
☐ 1164	4¢	Automated P.O.	1.85	2.60	3.60
☐ 1165	4¢	Mannerheim	1.85	2.60	3.60
☐ 1166	8¢	Mannerheim	1.85	2.60	3.60
☐ 1167	4¢	Camp Fire Girls	1.85	2.60	3.60
☐ 1168	4¢	Garibaldi	1.85	2.60	3.60
☐ 1169	8¢	Garibaldi	1.85	2.60	3.60
☐ 1170	4¢	Senator George	1.85	2.60	3.60
☐ 1171	4¢	Andrew Carnegie	1.85	2.60	3.60
☐ 1172	4¢	John Foster Dulles	1.85	2.60	3.60
☐ 1173	4¢	Echo I	1.85	2.60	3.60
☐ 1174	4¢	Gandhi	1.85	2.60	3.60
☐ 1175	8¢	Gandhi	1.85	2.60	3.60
☐ 1176	4¢	Range Conservation	1.85	2.60	3.60
☐ 1177	4¢	Horace Greeley	1.85	2.60	3.60
☐ 1178	4¢	Fort Sumter	1.85	2.60	3.60
☐ 1179	4¢	Battle of Shiloh	1.85	2.60	3.60
☐ 1180	5¢	Battle of Gettysburg	1.85	2.70	3.60
☐ 1181	5¢	Battle of Wilderness	1.85	2.70	3.60
☐ 1182	5¢	Appomattox	1.85	2.70	3.60
☐ 1183	4¢	Kansas Statehood	1.85	2.70	3.60
☐ 1184	4¢	Senator Norris	1.85	2.70	3.60
☐ 1185	4¢	Naval Aviation	1.85	2.70	3.60
☐ 1186	4¢	Workmen's Compensation	1.85	2.70	3.60
☐ 1187	4¢	Frederic Remington	1.85	2.70	3.60
☐ 1188	4¢	China Republic	1.85	2.70	3.60
☐ 1189	4¢	Naismith	1.85	2.70	3.60
☐ 1190	4¢	Nursing	1.85	2.70	3.60
☐ 1191	4¢	New Mexico Statehood	2.30	3.30	4.75
☐ 1192	4¢	Arizona Statehood	1.85	2.70	3.60
☐ 1193	4¢	Project Mercury	1.80	2.70	3.60

Scott No.			Single	Block	Plate Block
☐ 1194	4¢	Malaria Eradication	1.75	2.70	3.60
☐ 1195	4¢	Charles Evans Hughes	1.75	2.70	3.60
☐ 1196	4¢	Seattle World's Fair	1.75	2.70	3.60
☐ 1197	4¢	Louisiana Statehood	1.75	2.70	3.60
☐ 1198	4¢	Homestead Act	1.75	2.70	3.60
☐ 1199	4¢	Girl Scouts	1.75	2.70	3.60
☐ 1200	4¢	Brien McMahon	1.75	2.70	3.60
☐ 1201	4¢	Apprenticeship	1.75	2.70	3.60
☐ 1202	4¢	Sam Rayburn	1.75	2.70	3.60
☐ 1203	4¢	Dag Hammarskjold	1.75	2.70	3.60
☐ 1204	4¢	Hammarskjold "Error"	4.80	8.00	12.00
☐ 1205	4¢	Christmas	2.10	3.20	4.50
☐ 1206	4¢	Higher Education	1.45	2.60	3.70
☐ 1207	4¢	Winslow Homer	1.45	2.60	3.70
☐ 1208	4¢	Flag	1.45	2.60	3.70
☐ 1209	4¢	Jackson	1.45	2.60	3.70
☐ 1213	5¢	Washington	1.40	2.50	3.50
☐ 1225	1¢	Jackson (coil)	—	1.70	2.60
☐ 1229	5¢	Washington (coil)	—	1.70	2.60
☐ 1230	5¢	Carolina Charter	1.45	2.50	3.70
☐ 1231	5¢	Food for Peace	1.45	2.50	3.70
☐ 1232	5¢	West Virginia Statehood	1.45	2.50	3.70
☐ 1233	5¢	Emancipation Proclamation	1.45	2.50	3.70
☐ 1234	5¢	Alliance for Progress	1.45	2.50	3.70
☐ 1235	5¢	Cordell Hull	1.45	2.50	3.70
☐ 1236	5¢	Eleanor Roosevelt	1.45	2.50	3.70
☐ 1237	5¢	Science	1.45	2.50	3.70
☐ 1238	5¢	City Mail Delivery	1.45	2.50	3.70
☐ 1239	5¢	Red Cross	1.45	2.50	3.70
☐ 1240	5¢	Christmas	1.45	2.50	3.70
☐ 1241	5¢	Audubon	1.45	2.50	3.70
☐ 1242	5¢	Sam Houston	1.45	2.50	3.70
☐ 1243	5¢	Charles Russell	1.45	2.50	3.70
☐ 1244	5¢	N.Y. World's Fair	1.45	2.50	3.70
☐ 1245	5¢	John Muir	1.45	2.60	3.70
☐ 1246	5¢	John F. Kennedy	1.60	2.80	4.00
☐ 1247	5¢	New Jersey Tercentenary	1.45	2.60	3.70
☐ 1248	5¢	Nevada Statehood	1.45	2.60	3.70
☐ 1249	5¢	Register & Vote	1.45	2.60	3.70
☐ 1250	5¢	Shakespeare	1.45	2.60	3.70
☐ 1251	5¢	Drs. Mayo	1.45	2.60	3.70
☐ 1252	5¢	American Music	1.45	2.60	3.70
☐ 1253	5¢	Homemakers	1.45	2.60	3.70
☐ 1254–57	5¢	Christmas	—	4.60	7.10
☐ 1258	5¢	Verrazano-Narrows Bridge	1.35	2.40	3.40
☐ 1259	5¢	Fine Arts	1.35	2.40	3.40
☐ 1260	5¢	Amateur Radio	1.35	2.40	3.40
☐ 1261	5¢	Battle of New Orleans	1.35	2.40	3.40

Scott No.			Single	Block	Plate Block
☐ 1262	5¢	Physical Fitness	1.35	2.40	3.35
☐ 1263	5¢	Cancer Crusade	1.35	2.40	3.35
☐ 1264	5¢	Churchill	1.35	2.40	3.35
☐ 1265	5¢	Magna Carta	1.35	2.40	3.35
☐ 1266	5¢	Intl. Cooperation Year	1.35	2.40	3.35
☐ 1267	5¢	Salvation Army	1.35	2.40	3.35
☐ 1268	5¢	Dante	1.35	2.40	3.35
☐ 1269	5¢	Herbert Hoover	1.35	2.40	3.35
☐ 1270	5¢	Robert Fulton	1.35	2.40	3.35
☐ 1271	5¢	Florida Settlement	1.35	2.40	3.35
☐ 1272	5¢	Traffic Safety	1.35	2.40	3.35
☐ 1273	5¢	Copley	1.35	2.40	3.35
☐ 1274	11¢	Intl. Telecommunication Union	1.35	2.40	3.35
☐ 1275	5¢	Adlai Stevenson	1.35	2.40	3.35
☐ 1276	5¢	Christmas	1.35	2.40	3.35
☐ 1278	1¢	Jefferson	1.35	2.40	3.35
☐ 1279	1¼¢	Gallatin	—	2.20	3.05
☐ 1280	2¢	Wright	—	2.20	3.05
☐ 1281	3¢	Parkman	—	2.20	3.05
☐ 1282	4¢	Lincoln	1.35	2.40	3.35
☐ 1283	5¢	Washington	1.35	2.40	3.35
☐ 1283B	5¢	Washington	1.35	2.40	3.35
☐ 1284	6¢	Roosevelt	1.35	2.40	3.35
☐ 1285	8¢	Einstein	1.35	2.40	3.30
☐ 1286	10¢	Jackson	1.35	2.40	3.15
☐ 1286a	12¢	Ford	1.35	2.40	3.40
☐ 1287	13¢	Kennedy	1.35	2.40	3.40
☐ 1288	15¢	Holmes	1.35	2.40	3.40
☐ 1289	20¢	Marshall	1.35	2.40	3.40
☐ 1290	25¢	Douglas	1.35	2.40	3.40
☐ 1291	30¢	Dewey	2.40	3.60	4.60
☐ 1292	40¢	Paine	3.60	5.00	6.60
☐ 1293	50¢	Stone	3.80	5.60	9.00
☐ 1294	$1	O'Neill	7.00	12.00	20.00
☐ 1295	$5	Moore	63.00	99.00	134.00
☐ 1304	5¢	Washington (coil)	—	pr. 2.10	lp. 3.00
☐ 1305	6¢	Roosevelt (coil)	—	pr. 2.10	lp. 3.00
☐ 1305C	$1	O'Neill (coil)	—	pr. 10.00	lp. 14.00
☐ 1306	5¢	Migratory Bird Treaty	1.30	2.40	3.40
☐ 1307	5¢	Humane Treatment of Animals	1.35	2.40	3.40
☐ 1308	5¢	Indiana Statehood	1.35	2.40	3.40
☐ 1309	5¢	Circus	1.35	2.40	3.40
☐ 1310	5¢	SIPEX	1.35	2.40	3.40
☐ 1311	5¢	SIPEX	1.35	2.40	3.40
☐ 1312	5¢	Bill of Rights	1.35	2.40	3.40
☐ 1313	5¢	Polish Millenium	1.35	2.40	3.40
☐ 1314	5¢	National Park Service	1.35	2.40	3.40
☐ 1315	5¢	Marine Corps Reserve	1.35	2.40	3.40

Scott No.		Single	Block	Plate Block
☐ 1316	5¢ Genl. Fed. of Women's Clubs	1.35	2.40	3.40
☐ 1317	5¢ Johnny Appleseed	1.35	2.40	3.40
☐ 1318	5¢ Beautification of America	1.35	2.40	3.40
☐ 1319	5¢ Great River Road	1.35	2.40	3.40
☐ 1320	5¢ Savings Bonds	1.35	2.40	3.40
☐ 1321	5¢ Christmas	1.35	2.40	3.40
☐ 1322	5¢ Mary Cassatt	1.35	2.40	3.40
☐ 1323	5¢ National Grange	1.35	2.40	3.40
☐ 1324	5¢ Canada Centenary	1.35	2.40	3.40
☐ 1325	5¢ Erie Canal	1.35	2.40	3.40
☐ 1326	5¢ Search for Peace	1.35	2.40	3.40
☐ 1327	5¢ Thoreau	1.35	2.40	3.40
☐ 1328	5¢ Nebraska Statehood	1.35	2.40	3.40
☐ 1329	5¢ Voice of America	1.35	2.40	3.40
☐ 1330	5¢ Davy Crockett	1.35	2.40	3.40
☐ 1331–1332	Space Accomplishments	13.00 pr.	18.00	23.00
☐ 1333	5¢ Urban Planning	1.35	2.40	3.40
☐ 1334	5¢ Finland Independence	1.35	2.40	3.40
☐ 1335	5¢ Thomas Eakins	1.35	2.40	3.40
☐ 1336	5¢ Christmas	1.35	2.40	3.40
☐ 1337	5¢ Mississippi Statehood	1.35	2.40	3.40
☐ 1338	6¢ Flag	1.35	2.40	3.40
☐ 1339	6¢ Illinois Statehood	1.35	2.40	3.40
☐ 1340	6¢ Hemis Fair '68	1.35	2.40	3.40
☐ 1341	$1 Airlift	10.00	15.00	20.00
☐ 1342	6¢ Youth-Elks	1.35	2.35	3.40
☐ 1343	6¢ Law and Order	1.35	2.35	3.40
☐ 1344	6¢ Register and Vote	1.35	2.35	3.40
☐ 1345–1354	6¢ Historic Flag series of 10, all on one cover	13.00	—	—
☐ 1355	6¢ Disney	3.50	4.20	5.10
☐ 1356	6¢ Marquette	1.40	2.40	3.20
☐ 1357	6¢ Daniel Boone	1.40	2.40	3.20
☐ 1358	6¢ Arkansas River	1.40	2.40	3.20
☐ 1359	6¢ Leif Erikson	1.40	2.40	3.20
☐ 1360	6¢ Cherokee Strip	1.40	2.40	3.20
☐ 1361	6¢ John Trumbull	1.40	2.40	3.20
☐ 1362	6¢ Waterfowl Conservation	1.40	2.40	3.20
☐ 1363	6¢ Christmas	1.40	2.40	3.20
☐ 1364	6¢ American Indian	1.40	2.40	3.20
☐ 1365–1368	6¢ Beautification of America	3.10	9.70	13.00
☐ 1369	6¢ American Legion	1.35	2.40	3.20
☐ 1370	6¢ Grandma Moses	1.35	2.40	3.20
☐ 1371	6¢ Apollo 8	2.90	4.10	6.00

NOTE: From number 1372 to date, most First Day Covers have a value of 1.25 for single stamps, 2.25 for blocks of four and $3 for plate blocks of four.

JOIN US!

Application for Membership

Check one: □ Reg. □ Jr. □ Assoc. □ Life □ Club

Check one: □ Mr. □ Mrs. □ Ms. □ Club

_____

Name (please print and use first name)

_____

Street

_____

City

_____

State   Zip Code

_____

Birth Date   Occupation

ANA Bylaws require the publication of each application. If you DO NOT wish your STREET address published, please check this box. □

I herewith make application for membership in the American Numismatic Association, subject to the Bylaws of said Association. I also agree to abide by the Code of Ethics adopted by the Association.

_____

Signature of Applicant   Date

_____

Signature of Proposer (optional)   ANA No.

_____

Signature of Parent or Guardian
(Must sign for Junior applicants)

To charge to your credit card, please complete the following:

Account No. (All Digits) □ MasterCard □ Visa

☐☐☐☐☐☐☐☐☐☐☐☐☐☐☐☐☐☐

☐☐☐☐

_____
Exp. Date of Card / MasterCard Interbank No.

DUES

Regular (adult)—*U.S. only* .... $ 26*

Regular (adult)—*all other countries* 28*

Club—*any country* 30*

Junior (11-17 years old)............... 11

Associate (child or spouse of R or LM member living at member's address).. 4

Life (adult individual) 350
*Installment, $60 with application,** plus $25 per month for 12 months*

Life (club)...........................$1250

* Add $6 application fee, first year only

** Includes $10 bookkeeping fee, deducted from final payment if made within 90 days of application. Life Membership is not effective until full $350 fee is paid.

Nonmember annual subscription—*U.S. only* $28

Subscription—*all other countries* $33

Foreign applications must be accompanied by U.S. funds drawn on a U.S. bank.

Send your application to:

American Numismatic Association
P.O. Box 2366
Colorado Springs, CO 80901

MEMBERSHIP IN THE ANA COULD BE YOUR BEST INVESTMENT THIS YEAR.

As a rare coin collector or hobbyist, you continually deal with a variety of questions. How can you know that the coin you're about to purchase is not counterfeit? How can you find the detailed, current information you need to build your collection? There is no authority to help you solve all these problems. Unless you belong to the American Numismatic Association.

Coin Certification and Grading. ANA experts examine rare coins for authenticity to help safeguard against counterfeiting and misrepresentation. ANA now offers the ANACS Grading Service—third party expert opinions as to the condition of U.S. coins submitted for examination, and will issue certificates of authenticity.

Library Service. The largest circulating numismatic library in the world is maintained by the ANA. Its sole purpose is to provide you with free access to invaluable information that can't be found anywhere else.

The Numismatist. The Association's fully-illustrated magazine, considered *the* outstanding publication devoted exclusively to all phases of numismatics, is mailed free to all members.

And there are more benefits available through the ANA. Like coin insurance, special seminars, free booklets and photographic services. You can't find benefits like these anywhere else. Don't you owe it to yourself to join today?

The HOUSE OF COLLECTIBLES Series

☐ Please send me the following price guides—
☐ I would like the most current edition of the books listed below.

THE OFFICIAL PRICE GUIDES TO:

☐	199-3	**American Silver & Silver Plate** 5th Ed.	$11.95
☐	513-1	**Antique Clocks** 3rd Ed.	10.95
☐	283-3	**Antique & Modern Dolls** 3rd Ed.	10.95
☐	287-6	**Antique & Modern Firearms** 6th Ed.	11.95
☐	738-X	**Antiques & Collectibles** 8th Ed.	10.95
☐	289-2	**Antique Jewelry** 5th Ed.	11.95
☐	539-5	**Beer Cans & Collectibles** 4th Ed.	7.95
☐	521-2	**Bottles Old & New** 10th Ed.	10.95
☐	532-8	**Carnival Glass** 2nd Ed.	10.95
☐	295-7	**Collectible Cameras** 2nd Ed.	10.95
☐	548-4	**Collectibles of the '50s & '60s** 1st Ed.	9.95
☐	740-1	**Collectible Toys** 4th Ed.	10.95
☐	531-X	**Collector Cars** 7th Ed.	12.95
☐	538-7	**Collector Handguns** 4th Ed.	14.95
☐	748-7	**Collector Knives** 9th Ed.	12.95
☐	361-9	**Collector Plates** 5th Ed.	11.95
☐	296-5	**Collector Prints** 7th Ed.	12.95
☐	001-6	**Depression Glass** 2nd Ed.	9.95
☐	589-1	**Fine Art** 1st Ed.	19.95
☐	311-2	**Glassware** 3rd Ed.	10.95
☐	243-4	**Hummel Figurines & Plates** 6th Ed.	10.95
☐	523-9	**Kitchen Collectibles** 2nd Ed.	10.95
☐	291-4	**Military Collectibles** 5th Ed.	11.95
☐	525-5	**Music Collectibles** 6th Ed.	11.95
☐	313-9	**Old Books & Autographs** 7th Ed.	11.95
☐	298-1	**Oriental Collectibles** 3rd Ed.	11.95
☐	746-0	**Overstreet Comic Book** 17th Ed.	11.95
☐	522-0	**Paperbacks & Magazines** 1st Ed.	10.95
☐	297-3	**Paper Collectibles** 5th Ed.	10.95
☐	744-4	**Political Memorabilia** 1st Ed.	10.95
☐	529-8	**Pottery & Porcelain** 6th Ed.	11.95
☐	524-7	**Radio, TV & Movie Memorabilia** 3rd Ed.	11.95
☐	288-4	**Records** 7th Ed.	10.95
☐	247-7	**Royal Doulton** 5th Ed.	11.95
☐	280-9	**Science Fiction & Fantasy Collectibles** 2nd Ed.	10.95
☐	747-9	**Sewing Collectibles** 1st Ed.	8.95
☐	358-9	**Star Trek/Star Wars Collectibles** 2nd Ed.	8.95
☐	086-5	**Watches** 8th Ed.	12.95
☐	248-5	**Wicker** 3rd Ed.	10.95

THE OFFICIAL:

☐	445-3	**Collector's Journal** 1st Ed.	4.95
☐	549-2	**Directory to U.S. Flea Markets** 1st Ed.	4.95
☐	365-1	**Encyclopedia of Antiques** 1st Ed.	9.95

☐ 369-4	**Guide to Buying and Selling Antiques** 1st Ed.	$9.95
☐ 414-3	**Identification Guide to Early American Furniture** 1st Ed.	9.95
☐ 413-5	**Identification Guide to Glassware** 1st Ed.	9.95
☐ 448-8	**Identification Guide to Gunmarks** 2nd Ed.	9.95
☐ 412-7	**Identification Guide to Pottery & Porcelain** 1st Ed.	9.95
☐ 415-1	**Identification Guide to Victorian Furniture** 1st Ed.	9.95

THE OFFICIAL (SMALL SIZE) PRICE GUIDES TO:

☐ 309-0	**Antiques & Flea Markets** 4th Ed.	4.95
☐ 269-8	**Antique Jewelry** 3rd Ed.	4.95
☐ 085-7	**Baseball Cards** 8th Ed.	4.95
☐ 647-2	**Bottles** 3rd Ed.	4.95
☐ 544-1	**Cars & Trucks** 3rd Ed.	5.95
☐ 519-0	**Collectible Americana** 2nd Ed.	4.95
☐ 294-9	**Collectible Records** 3rd Ed.	4.95
☐ 306-6	**Dolls** 4th Ed.	4.95
☐ 359-7	**Football Cards** 7th Ed.	4.95
☐ 540-9	**Glassware** 3rd Ed.	4.95
☐ 526-3	**Hummels** 4th Ed.	4.95
☐ 279-5	**Military Collectibles** 3rd Ed.	4.95
☐ 745-2	**Overstreet Comic Book Companion** 1st Ed.	4.95
☐ 278-7	**Pocket Knives** 3rd Ed.	4.95
☐ 527-1	**Scouting Collectibles** 4th Ed.	4.95
☐ 494-1	**Star Trek/Star Wars Collectibles** 3rd Ed.	3.95
☐ 307-4	**Toys** 4th Ed.	4.95

THE OFFICIAL BLACKBOOK PRICE GUIDES OF:

☐ 743-6	**U.S. Coins** 26th Ed.	3.95
☐ 742-8	**U.S. Paper Money** 20th Ed.	3.95
☐ 741-X	**U.S. Postage Stamps** 10th Ed.	3.95

THE OFFICIAL INVESTORS GUIDE TO BUYING & SELLING:

☐ 534-4	**Gold, Silver & Diamonds** 2nd Ed.	12.95
☐ 535-2	**Gold Coins** 2nd Ed.	12.95
☐ 536-0	**Silver Coins** 2nd Ed.	12.95
☐ 537-9	**Silver Dollars** 2nd Ed.	12.95

THE OFFICIAL NUMISMATIC GUIDE SERIES:

☐ 254-X	**The Official Guide to Detecting Counterfeit Money** 2nd Ed.	7.95
☐ 257-4	**The Official Guide to Mint Errors** 4th Ed.	7.95

SPECIAL INTEREST SERIES:

☐ 506-9	**From Hearth to Cookstove** 3rd Ed.	17.95
☐ 530-1	**Lucky Number Lottery Guide** 1st Ed.	4.95
☐ 504-2	**On Method Acting** 8th Printing	6.95

		TOTAL

═══ **FOR IMMEDIATE DELIVERY** ═══

VISA & MASTER CARD CUSTOMERS
ORDER TOLL FREE!
1-800-638-6460

This number is for orders only; it is not tied into the customer service or business office. Customers not using charge cards must use mail for ordering since payment is required with the order—sorry, no C.O.D.'s.

OR SEND ORDERS TO

THE HOUSE OF COLLECTIBLES
201 East 50th Street
New York, New York 10022

_____ POSTAGE & HANDLING RATES _____

First Book $1.00
Each Additional Copy or Title $0.50

Total from columns on order form. Quantity_____ $_____

☐ Check or money order enclosed $_____ (include postage and handling)

☐ Please charge $_____to my: ☐ MASTERCARD ☐ VISA

Charge Card Customers Not Using Our Toll Free Number
Please Fill Out The Information Below

Account No. _____ Expiration Date_____
            (All Digits)
Signature_____

NAME (please print)_____ PHONE_____

ADDRESS_____APT. #_____

CITY_____STATE_____ZIP_____